Guide to Manuscripts and Archives in the West Virginia Collection

James W. Hess

West Virginia University Library
Morgantown
1974

Contents

Introduction

The West Virginia Collection, a subject division of the West Virginia University Library, is a repository of manuscripts, archives, maps, newspapers, photographs, and other historical materials relating to the Appalachian region. The origin of the Collection dates from 1933, when the University's Board of Governors authorized the establishment of a Division of Documents in the University Library. The State Legislature also made the Division a permissive depository for state and county records. Dr. Charles H. Ambler, head of the History Department, was primarily responsible for the creation of the Division and became its first director. Dr. Festus P. Summers was named archivist in 1935. In spite of inadequate financial and staff support, Dr. Ambler and Dr. Summers were remarkably successful in assembling significant collections of private papers and county records. They also cooperated productively with the Federal Government's Historic Records Survey. American involvement in World War II, however, brought a temporary end to the Library's historical preservation activities.

The West Virginia Collection took its present form in 1950 when Charles Shetler became curator. Over the next sixteen years, Mr. Shetler both introduced modern archival practices and conducted an extensive collecting program that dramatically expanded the Collection's holdings of all types of materials relating to the history and culture of the Appalachian region. The citizens of the state and area owe a permanent debt to Mr. Shetler for his leadership during this important period. Dr. Oscar D. Lambert, historic records specialist from 1946 until 1956, also participated significantly in this expansion of the Library's holdings. Dr. Irvin Stewart, president of the University from 1946 until 1958, and Dr. Robert F.

Munn, director of libraries from 1958 until the present, provided administrative support without which the Collection would not have existed. All of the above were active in locating and acquiring historical materials.

As West Virginia lies almost entirely within Appalachia, the West Virginia Collection includes much material relating to this periodically rediscovered region. Because West Virginia gained statehood during the Civil War, the Collection also contains many documents from that period. Historical factors have also led to a concentration on the years since the mid-nineteenth century, inasmuch as western Virginia was not densely settled and some sections were completely unsettled during most of the nineteenth century. There are, however, a few significant collections from the late eighteenth century and several from the nineteenth century prior to the separation from Virginia. Because western Virginia was a crossroad in the western spread of the United States, county records and genealogical materials contain information on many families now scattered across the country. The Collection also includes personal and organizational papers that document the intensified industrial development and exploitation of natural resources which occurred with statehood and during the early decades of the twentieth century. West Virginia was also the scene of intense conflict between capital and labor, particularly in the coal fields between 1912 and the 1930s, and the Collection reflects these sometimes bloody encounters.

Numerous books, articles, doctoral dissertations, research papers, and other studies on Appalachia or West Virginia have been produced from the resources of the Collection over the past three decades. Scholars from all over the nation have used portions of the Collection which fit into many national themes. Large parts of the Collection, however, can be properly described as unresearched material still awaiting exploration by scholars.

This volume relies heavily upon the work of those who originally processed the materials and those who prepared previous reports on manuscript holdings in the West Virginia University Library. In addition to five reports on acquisitions that appeared from 1936 to 1953, Charles Shetler in 1958 prepared *Guide to Manuscripts and Archives in the West Virginia Collection* that included holdings listed in these reports and materials acquired through June 1958. Five years later F. Gerald Ham compiled *Guide to Manuscripts and Archives in the West Virginia Collection, Number II,* that described materials added between July 1958 and October 1963. This new guide describes collections listed in the first two guides and materials added through June 1972. Although small collections of minimal significance are omitted from the new guide, they are still available at the library. Other smaller entries from early guides are combined under general headings, such as accounts and account books, Civil War, churches, and genealogy, but can still be located with the same accession numbers. Under these general headings, there are separate entries based on the volume or significance of the materials described.

The format of this volume conforms to that of the earlier two guides, except that linear measurements of shelf space have been substituted for box counts. The entries are numbered in alphabetical sequence according to the collection title. Alphabetizing in the text and index is by letter rather than word prior to the comma or period; the only exception to this rule is with family references in the index, which are placed immediately after the individuals of the same surname. Dashes are ignored.

Following the collection title, birth and death dates of individuals who are the subjects of collections are given in parentheses, followed by the type or form of the collection and the dates within which the bulk of the material falls. The size of the collection is then given in linear feet, number of items, folders, or volumes. An item can be a one-page letter, a many-paged letter, a diary, or any single record unit. Names of donors are found in the entries not in the index. Accession numbers appear at the end of the first part of the entry for the convenience of the library staff.

In the descriptions of the collections, an effort has been made to mention the nature of the material and the most important historical periods, geographical areas, events, organizations, and individuals. These are frequently distilled from detailed inventories that exist for many of the collections in the library. Oral histories and tape recordings are included as parts of collections or as individual collections; there is also a separate listing of such materials available in the library. The archives of West Virginia University are here described in a very general manner; there are more detailed listings of most record groups in the library or in the office of the University Archivist. Unless otherwise indicated, all place-names refer to West Virginia.

Of the many persons who assisted in the preparation of this *Guide,* Daniel R. Blosser played the largest role. Mr. Blosser participated in every phase of the work, from the first plans through the laborious task of indexing. Dr. Robert F. Munn, director of libraries, and Stokely B. Gribble, assistant director of libraries, contributed indispensably in allocation of staff time and conceptualization. Mrs. Pauline T. Kissler, assistant in the manuscripts section, helped to prepare not only the earlier guides but also this new volume. Mrs. Kissler's contributions to the Collection over more than two decades cannot be too warmly acknowledged. Her services in processing of materials, assistance to other staff members, and guidance to users of the Collection has been consistently outstanding. Mrs. Martha Neville, who also worked on *Guide* Number II, typed much of the manuscript for this *Guide.* Rodney Pyles, assistant curator since 1971, and Dr. George Parkinson, who became curator of the Collection in August 1972, lent indispensable assistance with galley proof and prevented many errors. The individuals mentioned above and many others who have worked with the Collection over the past forty years, deserve most of the credit for any value which this volume may have to scholars and future staff members.

J.W.H.

Guide to Manuscripts

1. **Account Books, 1795-1956. 3 ft. and 106 volumes. Gifts and loans, 1940-1969. Accession numbers are in parentheses following entries below.**

Account books and papers of the following persons and places for general stores unless otherwise indicated: A. and Manliffe Hayes, 1851-1912, and a Morgantown municipal court docket, 1873-1882 (72); the firm Winter and Haller, later Cather and Haller, at Tyrconnel Mines, 1881-1889 (82); Richard and Samuel McClure at Wheeling, 1804-1816, 1819, 1838, 1909 (119); a cabinet and coffin maker in Parkersburg, 1828-1836, 1859 (372); Isaac Caruthers in Monroe County, 1819-1840, and Erskine and Caruthers for a tavern and store at Salt Sulphur Springs, 1857-1863 (508); a tailor shop in Morgantown, 1849-1856 (535); the Mannington *Times*, 1930-1934, 1953 (609); a general store, 1873-1875 (679); a general store near Fairview, 1932-1936 (788); G. W. Orr & Son of Independence, owners and operators of the Henry D. Fortney Grain & Feed Mill, 1907-1911 (801); a store operated by Joseph Harman at Petersburg, 1881-1882 (838); a store and gristmill at Blacksville, 1850-1908 (854); the Jackson Grocery Company of Jane Lew, 1837-1956 (1019); a merchant dealing in cloth, hardware, liquors, food and other items, 1795-1798 (1029); a farmer and operator of a grist and saw mill at Jamestown, Monongalia County, 1841-1864 (1516); a New Martinsville store 1873-1882 (1529); a Glenville mortician, 1882-1936 (1702); J. S. Newmyer at Dawson Station, Fayette County, Pennsylvania, 1869-1872 (1854); a general store, inn, and tavern near Lewisburg, Greenbrier County, on the James River and Kanawha Turnpike, 1839-1840 (1904); Stephens & Minor, Brock, Pennsylvania, 1885-1892 (1908); H. C. Phillips at Pursglove, 1918-1924 (1978); Carder Lowe & Company at Shinnston, 1880-1882 (2054); and a general store, 1910-1914 (2086).

2. **Albright, Erbie Claire (d. 1964). Papers, 1915-1943. 1 ft. Gift of Erbie C. Albright estate, 1967. No. 1991.**

Correspondence, business papers, educational records of a home economics teacher and supervisor who was a graduate of West Virginia University, attended Chicago and Columbia universities, taught home economics at Morgantown High School, and was supervisor of home economics for the Monongalia County School System. The papers cover family affairs; schools in West Virginia, Pennsylvania, Michigan, and New York; West Virginia Home Economics Association; National Education Association department of home economics; World War I letters commenting on conditions at Camp Taylor, Kentucky, Richmond, Virginia, and Camp Lee; World War II material on civilian support activities.

3. **Alexander, Holmes Moss (1906-   ). Papers, 1929-1970. 1 ft. Gift of Holmes M. Alexander, 1963, 1967, 1970. Nos. 1372, 1878.**

Correspondence, literary manuscripts, photographs, and miscellaneous material of a newspaper columnist, political analyst, biographer, novelist, short story writer, and gentleman farmer.

The papers are primarily concerned with Alexander's literary and publishing activities. Other subjects include Alexander's interest in livestock raising, a proposed birth control law, and motion picture censorship in Maryland.

Correspondents include Styles Bridges, Richard A. Chase, Joseph S. Clark, Thomas J. Dodd, Dwight D. Eisenhower, Barry Goldwater, Mark O. Hatfield, Thomas C. Hennings, Marquis James, Gerald W. Johnson, Louis Johnson, Lyndon B. Johnson, John F. Kennedy, Robert F. Kennedy, Frank R. Kent, Edward Martin, H. L. Mencken, Ogden Nash, Allan Nevins, Richard L. Neuberger, Richard Nixon, William Proxmire, and Leverett Saltonstall. (RESTRICTED)

4. **Ambler, Charles H. (1876-1957). Papers, 1834-1957. 12 ft. Gift of Charles H. Ambler and Mrs. Charles H. Ambler, 1945, 1955, 1957. Nos. 122, 743, 1003, 1010.**

Personal and professional correspondence, 1914-1956, and photographs, maps, clippings, research notes, and manuscripts of published and unpublished historical and biographical studies.

There are many letters from U. S. historians in the 1920s and 1930s; a series of letters between Ambler and Robert L. Floyd, Chicago, Illinois, concerning the Floyd family; and copies of letters written from St. Petersburg, Russia, 1859-1862, by an agent of the Ross Winans' Locomotive Works of Baltimore, Maryland. Among the many typescripts are "George Rogers Clark Floyd of Logan County, West Virginia," and "Huckleberry Ranger: Lieutenant John Blue, Confederate," by Ambler, and "The Life of Henry Floyd," by Robert L. Floyd.

Other materials deal with the Civil War, education, and the statehood movement in West Virginia, and the history of counties and local areas. Writers of letters or persons mentioned include Waitman T. Willey, Samuel Woods, Lieutenant Fabricus Augustus Cather, John Brown, Wills De Hass, Alexander R. Boteler, T. J. Jackson, and James Rumsey.

5. **Ambler, H. K. Account books, 1915-1952. 3 volumes. Acquired, 1970. No. 2075.**

Account books of H. K. Ambler with the heirs of S. W. Ambler and S. M. Keys of Jefferson County. Other heirs are Letty C., Lucy J., and C. E. Ambler. There are also entries concerning the estates of H. Keys, S. W. Washington, and Jacob Zinn. There is information on management of farms and residences, business firms in the area of Charles Town, tenant and owner shares, U. S. Treasury crop allotments, and labor shortages during World War II.

6. **American Association of University Women. Morgantown Branch.** Records, 1922-1960. 2 ft. Transfer, 1961. No. 1485.

Yearbooks, clipping scrapbooks, correspondence, minutes, and financial records.

7. **American Association of University Women. West Virginia Division.** Reports, 1955-1958. 2 manuscripts, 105p. Gift of the Association, 1958. Nos. 1054, 1085.

Yearly narrative reports of the historians of the nineteen branches.

8. **American Legion, Mountaineer Post No. 127, Morgantown.** Records, 1945-1949. Transfer, 1948, 1953. Ca. 200 items. Nos. 139, 537.

Official records of the American Legion post established at West Virginia University in 1945.

9. **American Phytopathological Society.** Papers, 1941-1944. 1 ft. Gift of Julian G. Leach, 1962. No. 1586.

Correspondence of the society's president, Julian G. Leach, professor of plant pathology at West Virginia University, and papers of the society's War Emergency Committee.

10. **Appalachian Coals, Inc.** Papers, 1935-1940. 1 volume (photocopy). Original in Library of Congress, U. S. Book Exchange, 1968. No. 2030.

One volume of correspondence and photographs on the Fuel Engineering Conferences held by Appalachian Coals, Inc., Cincinnati, Ohio, 1935-1940.

11. **Appleton, John W. M. (1832-1913).** Papers, 1861-1913. 1 volume and 1 reel of microfilm (1 volume). Gift of E. A. Barnes, 1943, and loan for photoduplication by Arnold A. Barnes, 1960. Nos. 92, 1378.

Record compiled primarily from letters written by an officer in the Fifty-fourth Massachusetts Volunteers to his wife; a scrapbook containing official papers relating to Appleton's service in the Civil War and his postwar membership in the West Virginia Volunteers and National

3

Guard; family papers and newspaper clippings. There are original letters and newspaper accounts of the regiment which was among the first to enlist black soldiers.

Subjects include the attack on Fort Wagner, Charleston Harbor; the occupation of Jacksonville, Florida; and the regiment's return to Fort Warren, Boston.

12. **Armstrong, William O.** (1888-1970). Papers, 1945-1971. Ca. 20 items. Gift of Mrs. William O. Armstrong, 1971. No. 2176.

Letters, speeches, newspaper clippings, and memorabilia of William O. Armstrong, principal of Dunbar High School, Fairmont, and the first Negro to attend the graduate school at West Virginia University.

13. **Arthurdale Homestead Project.** Papers and photographs, 1930s. 1 ft. and 1 reel microfilm. Gift of Harry C. Johnson, Mrs. Michael Mayor, and Howard B. Allen, 1960, 1963. Nos. 1291, 1347, 1646.

Newspaper clippings, printed material, correspondence, and pictorial material covering the beginning and development of the resettlement project at Arthurdale. Papers include lists of applicants, methods employed in screening families for residence, and essays and other material on local and state self-help and rehabilitation projects.
Correspondents include Mrs. Franklin D. Roosevelt.

14. **Ash, Pauline Morehead,** *Collector.* Papers, (1855-1892) 1947. 1 ft. Gift of Pauline Morehead Ash, 1955. No. 776.

Genealogical material on the Clarke family and a diary of Belle Clarke; an account book of J. P. Clarke for general merchandise, farm, and labor accounts, with entries for the steamboat *General Jackson;* several account books and a map of the Wirt Oil and Mining Company operations; items relating to the West Virginia State Grange, and a ledger of William H. Hill, Cincinnati, Ohio, an agent of the Grange.

15. **Athey Family.** Correspondence, 1863-1865, 1869. 13 items. Acquired, 1963. No. 1678.

Correspondence of a Tyler County family consisting primarily of letters written from camps at New Creek, West Virginia, and Harrisonburg, Bermuda Hundred, and other points in Virginia, by two members of the Eleventh West Virginia Volunteer Infantry. There also is a letter written by a Methodist circuit rider, Loren Stewart, concerning his work around Spencer following the Civil War.

4

16. **Atkeson, Thomas Clark** (1852-1935). Papers, 1894-1934. 1 ft. Gift of Karl C. Atkeson, 1958. No. 1126.

Family history, autobiographical sketch, account books of farming operations in Putnam County, 1894-1934, and articles and pamphlets written by a state agricultural leader, founder of the state Grange, and national Grange representative in Washington. Atkeson also played a leading role in the development of the Agricultural College at Morgantown where he was a professor for many years.

17. **Attorney's Case Book.** 1 volume, 1847-1854. No. 324.

Lists of suits, with judgments and costs, probably in Lewis or Harrison County, with information on the wills of John Morrill and several members of the Mason family.

18. **Aurora, Preston County.** Land papers and typescript, 1787-1865, 1956. Gifts of Miss Oretha Susan Stemple, 1956, and E. Herbert Shaffer, 1956. Nos. 813, 906.

Land grant in Monongalia County (now Preston) to Thomas James Goff, June 25, 1787; tax receipts, 1829, 1843, for Thomas and James G. Watson; a plat of Wotring and Shaffer land; and a typescript, "The Genesis of the Aurora Community" by Martin Luther Peter.

19. **Ayers, Michael A.** Journal, 1864-1865. 2 typescripts, 34p. No. 325.

Typed copies of a Civil War diary of a sergeant major in the Eleventh West Virginia Volunteer Infantry, covering the periods April 30-June 29, 1864, and January 1-July 20, 1865.

20. **Ayres, Robert** (b. 1761). Journal, 1787-1789. 1 reel of microfilm. Gift of Fred T. Newbraugh, 1955. No. 824.

The journal of a Methodist circuit rider in eastern Pennsylvania and the Bath and Berkeley Circuits in western Virginia.

21. **Babb, John L.** Papers, 1866, 1878. 2 items. Gift of O. D. Lambert, 1955. No. 748.

Photostats of John L. Babb's teaching certificate, signed by George Harman, superintendent of Grant County schools, dated October 10, 1866; and a list of prices offered for prime skins by Pence & Clawson, New York City, January 5, 1878.

22. **Baber, Richard Plantagenet Llewellyn (1823-1885).** Papers, 1856-1962. 6 items. Gift of Mr. and Mrs. Charles George Baber, 1966. No. 1874.

Xerox copy of an article in *Biographical Encyclopedia of Ohio* on Colonel Llewellyn Baber; family information; two versions of a letter from R. P. L. Baber to A. J. Baber, Columbus, Ohio, September 14, 1856, giving family history; and a payroll receipt signed by Baber as a paymaster in the U. S. Army, 1862.

23. **Bailey, Lemuel and Samuel.** Correspondence, 1863-1903. 92 items. Gift of Mrs. Earl Jackson, 1953. No. 546.

Business and personal correspondence of Samuel and Lemuel Bailey, Lewis County, including rates of toll and tollgate keepers' receipts on the Weston-Clarksburg Turnpike; account books for a general store; a pass issued by the Department of West Virginia, Hagerstown, Maryland, July 27, 1864, and other items.

24. **Bailey, Vida,** *Collector.* Papers, 1790-1882. Ca. 50 items. Gift of Miss Vida Bailey, 1965. No. 1847.

Indentures, deeds, court papers, land grants, letters, church notices, tax and other receipts, bills, notes and other materials concerning the Bluestone River area in Summers County, especially the Josiah Meadows and Robert Lilly families. Collection includes a Church of Christ minute book kept by Thomas Lilly, 1802-1817; a land grant to Jesiah Meador signed by Governor James P. Preston, 1809; and a letter from William Sellergrit Lilly from upper Louisiana Territory telling of earth tremors, sickness, and expected Indian trouble. Places mentioned include Mercer, Raleigh, Montgomery, and Giles counties and Sinking Creek.

25. **Baker, B. J.** Records, 1865-1921. 11 reels of microfilm (53 volumes). Gift of Edward Baker, 1962. No. 1618.

Daybooks, ledgers, journals, and other mercantile records of a Petersburg general merchandise company in the South Branch Valley, and the membership and dues list of the Petersburg Council, Friends of Temperance, 1871-1878.

26. **Baker, Charles G. (1890-   ).** Papers, 1929-1936, 1945, 1952. 1 ft. Gift of Charles G. Baker, 1960. No. 1294.

Instructions to the grand jury and opinions of the judge of the Seventeenth Judicial Circuit (Monongalia County).

27. **Baker, Henry.** Papers, 1851-1957. 1 ft. Acquired, 1959. No. 1186.

Correspondence, newspaper clippings, photographs, and miscellaneous printed items of a corporal in the Fourteenth [West] Virginia Volunteer Infantry (Union) and his two daughters, Mary Baker and Nell Baker Rightmire. Subjects include Monongalia County local history; Union troop movements in the vicinity of New Creek, June 1863; and local G. A. R. affairs. The collection also includes the Register and Order Book of Post No. 5 (Morgantown), Department of West Virginia, G. A. R., 1878-1901.

28. **Baldwin, Robert D.** (1891-   ). Papers, 1928-1961. 1 ft. Gift of Robert D. Baldwin, 1962. No. 1587.

Correspondence, reports, and other papers of a professor of educational administration and coordinator of field services, West Virginia University.

Subjects include the county unit system, the election of superintendents of schools, legislative committee of the West Virginia State Education Association, the Thomas-Hall Education Bill, school taxation, and the State High School Principals Association.

Correspondents include Charles E. Hodges, Chapman Revercomb, and Melvin C. Snyder.

29. **Ball, Arthur.** Newspaper clippings, 1933-1942. 148 items. Gift of Arthur Ball, 1943, and transfer, 1954. Nos. 83, 674.

Clippings of newspaper articles written by Mr. Ball for the *Parkersburg News*, relating to Calhoun, Jackson, Kanawha, Ritchie, Wirt, and Wood County local history.

30. **Baltimore and Ohio Railroad.** Document, 1827. 1 item (typescript copy). Transfer, 1959. No. 1254.

"Petition to the President and Directors of the B. & O. Railroad Co., Setting Forth the Advantages of Constructing the Road through Kanawha County to the Ohio River, July 20, 1827."

31. **Baltimore and Ohio Railroad.** Log, 1908. 1 volume. Acquired, 1959. No. 1268.

Telegraph operator's log of the D. K. Tower near Webster, Taylor County, February 20-May 27, 1908. Aside from routine entries on train movements, the log contains many humorous anecdotes recorded by operators.

32. **Baltimore and Ohio Railroad.** Records, 1853-1864. 50 items. Gift of Louis W. Smith, 1953. No. 522.

Letter book copies of letters to various railroad officials from B. L. Jacobs, a B. & O. agent at Grafton, 1858; an envelope map showing B. & O. tracks and mileage in several states, 1853; Civil War telegrams of James Evans, provost marshal, second district of West Virginia at Grafton, 1864; and other items.

33. **Barbe, Waitman T. W.** (1864-1925). Papers, 1884-1930. 1 ft. Gift of Clara Gould Barbe and transfer, 1952, 1955, 1958. Nos. 304, 326, 496, 727, 831.

Papers of the managing editor of the Parkersburg *Daily State Journal,* 1889-1895, editor of the *West Virginia School Journal,* and member of the English faculty of West Virginia University, 1895-1925. The collection includes manuscripts of Barbe's published poetry and unpublished short stories, correspondence, notes, speeches, class lectures, illustrations for short stories drawn by John Rettig, a scrapbook of clippings of reviews and correspondence relating to Barbe's book, *Going to College,* and memorabilia.

The correspondence includes letters, in some cases accompanied by holograph verse, from Winston Churchill, Richard Harding Davis, Mary E. Wilkins Freeman, Hamlin Garland, R. W. Gilder, Edward E. Hale, William H. Hayne, Thomas Wentworth Higginson, Julia Ward Howe, William Dean Howells, Rupert Hughes, Stephen Leacock, Nicholas Vachel Lindsay, Amy Lowell, Brander Matthews, Margaret Prescott Montague, Bliss Perry, Melville D. Post, Edwin Arlington Robinson, Booth Tarkington, Charles Dudley Warner, Barrett Wendell, William Allen White, W. L. Wilson, and Owen Wister.

There is also a volume of mounted holograph letters, 1884-1895, from the following American authors, a few of whom are also included in the general collection: Edward W. Bok, George W. Cable, Kate Chopin, Danske Dandridge, Oliver W. Holmes, Clifford Lanier, Sidney Lanier, Thomas Nelson Page, Margaret J. Preston, James Whitcomb Riley, and John G. Whittier.

Most letters are brief and many are simple acknowledgements.

34. **Barbour County.** Manuscripts and articles, 1941, 1956. 3 items. Gift of C. O. Marsh, 1957. No. 959.

A manuscript, "The Old Furnace," by C. O. Marsh, which was printed in the Philippi *Barbour Democrat,* November 11, 1956, and copies of parts of various printed books dealing with furnaces and mills in Barbour County.

35. **Barbour County.** Typescript, ca. 1944. 13p. Gift of John C. Shaw, 1954. No. 649.

"Events in the History of Cove District, Barbour County, West Virginia," by John C. Shaw, covering the period ca. 1790-1944.

36. **Barns Family.** Papers, 1816-1929. Ca. 82 items. Gift of Miss Helen V. Barns, 1956, 1957, 1970, 1971. Nos. 925, 958, 970.

Papers of Thomas Rufus Barns, including his Civil War diaries while serving with Company K, Tenth Regiment, West Virginia Volunteer Infantry; Civil War ballads printed on stationery, ca. 1864; land and school records, and deeds in Monongalia, Marion, Calhoun, and Ritchie counties pertaining to Uz Barns, Mark Stratton, Francis H. Peirpont, Jr., and Bernie Hodges. There is also a diary of Bernie Hodges (Mrs. John S.) Barns, January-June 1893, concerning daily activities as a schoolteacher in Wirt County. An issue of the *Methodist Protestant Sentinel*, Fairmont, for May 12, 1860, is in the papers, as well as a letter to John S. Barns, Harrisville, July 31, 1904, from a cousin in Duluth, Minnesota. There are also views of West Virginia University, the Morgantown Country Club, and the Cheat Haven Dam and power plant, ca. 1929.

37. **Bassel, James.** Papers, 1862-1892. 66 items. Gift of Prichard Von David, n.d. No. 327.

Mainly letters written to Bassel from U. S. Army officers from various forts and camps in several western states and territories. There are no copies of Bassel's correspondence in the collection, but his career in the army to about 1870, his subsequent military service in Egypt, and his employment in China and Japan, ca. 1874-1875, as the representative of an American ship builder, are covered in the letters. There are a few letters from Thomas Handbury, a cadet at West Point in 1862; also materials on political affairs in West Virginia, including Bassel's candidacy on the People's Party ticket for governor of West Virginia in 1892, and certificates of election returns from several counties in 1892.

38. **Bassel, John (1840-1914).** Papers, 1854-1916. 36 ft. Gift of Aquilla T. Ward, 1948. Nos. 126, 1009.

Office files of a Clarksburg attorney who was counsel for the Baltimore and Ohio Railroad Company. There are few personal papers and none relating to Bassel's participation in the Constitutional Convention of 1872.

39. **Bayles, G. Harry.** Papers, 1781-1955. 1 ft. Gift of Mrs. G. Harry Bayles, 1956. No. 820.

Correspondence with the American Museum of Natural History, 1934-1952, the American Society of Civil Engineers, the Circumnavigator's Club, 1943-1954, and S. T. Wiley, the historian, at Elizabeth, Pennsylvania, 1933-1937. There is a 34-page travel account from Greece, Crete, and Egypt, 1936-1937; also other materials on Tecumseh, the Shawnee Chief; Monongalia County history; West Virginia University history; and Bayles and Vandervort genealogy.

40. **Bayles Family.** Papers, 1830-1941. 3 ft. Gift of Mrs. G. Harry Bayles, 1955. No. 779.

Correspondence and genealogical notes of John C. Bayles of Morgantown relating to the histories of the Bayles, Vandervort and other Monongalia County families. Also included are materials on the history of West Virginia University buildings and the department of buildings and grounds, compiled by Mr. Bayles; originals and copies of wills, deeds, and land surveys in Monongalia County; an account book for general merchandise, Monongalia County, 1857-1859; newspaper clippings; photographs; a Civil War manuscript poem, "The Third Virginia," and other items.

41. **Beall, C. H.** Papers, 1856-1907. 67 items. Gift of Mrs. Harry W. Paull, 1951, 1952. Nos. 257, 318, 473.

Correspondence, sheep breeding records, photographs, and other papers of a sheep grower in Brooke County.

42. **Beall, John William (1721-1814).** Class list 1779. 2 items (photocopies). Gift of Glenn D. Lough, 1965. No. 1831.

List of scholars in a short term subscription school taught by John William Beall in a cabin at the mouth of Buffalo Creek (Buffalo Station) near Fairmont in 1779. This is thought to have been the first school taught in what is now West Virginia west of the Allegheny Mountains. There is also a letter from Glenn D. Lough giving information on the class list.

43. **Bean Family.** Papers, 1833-1887. 142 items and 6 volumes. No. 484.

Papers and six manuscript volumes of Samuel and Thomas Bean and other members of the Bean settlement near Fabius, Hardy County. The volumes, 1833-1884, are accounts for the post office at Fabius, and for school taxes, blacksmithing, shoemaking, distilling, and other goods and services. There are lists of birth dates of members of the Gilmore family; scattered agricultural records; justice of the peace judgment dockets, 1848-1887; and loose business and post office records of Samuel Bean.

44. **Beckley, Alfred (1802-1888).** Papers, 1832-1856. 15 items. Gift of Charles Hodel, 1936, and Hal M. Scott, 1962. Nos. 41, 1563.

Correspondence of General Beckley, founder of the town which bears his name, and his wife, Emily Craig, and a sales agreement for land in Mercer County signed by Beckley and Edmund Lilly, July 1, 1837. Subjects include the presidential election of 1832 in Kentucky, social affairs, the cholera scourge, and Andrew Jackson's reception in Lexington, Kentucky, 1832; and Beckley family affairs.

45. **Bedinger, Henry.** Journal, 1775-1776, 1781. Typescript, 42p. Gift of Henry B. Davenport, 1931. No. 4.

Copy of two journals kept by Henry Bedinger while serving in the American Revolution in New England, New York, and Virginia. Included is a return of troops raised in Frederick County, Virginia.

46. **Bell, Raymond M.,** *Compiler.* Typescripts, 1958, 1963. 18p. Gifts of Raymond M. Bell, 1958, 1963. Nos. 1032, 1707.

"Dates of Settlement from Virginia Certificates, Washington County, Pennsylvania," 1769-1776, taken from Virginia land records; "Methodism in the Wheeling, West Virginia, District, 1785-1810."

47. **Bennett, Jonathan M. (1816-1887).** Papers, 1785-1899. 38 ft. Gift of Hunter M. Bennett, 1935. No. 32.

Correspondence and papers of a major political figure dealing largely with politics in Virginia, West Virginia, and Virginia in the Confederacy. Bennett, a lawyer, was a member of the Virginia General Assembly, 1852-1853; president of the Weston Branch of the Exchange Bank of Virginia; auditor of Virginia, 1857-1865; member of the senate of West Virginia, 1872-1876; and a member of the commission appointed to adjust the Virginia debt question in 1871.

Correspondents include James Barbour, Arthur I. Boreman, G. D. Camden, J. N. Camden, R. P. Camden, John S. Carlile, Spencer Dayton, J. H. Diss Debar, Matthew Edmiston, John W. Garrett, Nathan Goff, William L. Jackson, Joseph Johnson, Edwin Maxwell, J. H. Pendleton, Francis H. Pierpont, Beverly Randolph, John H. Reagan, William Prescott Smith, Felix Sutton, William P. Thompson, John Tyler, and P. G. Van Winkle.

48. **Bennett, Joseph and Henry.** Papers, 1849-1923. 26 items (photocopies). Loaned for copying by John E. Jacobs, 1964. No. 1731.

Letters of Henry and Joseph Bennett concerning travel by sea from New York to Chagres, Panama, overland across Panama and by ship to San Francisco in 1851. Letters from California, 1852-1853, discuss arrival of immigrants; employment conditions and wages; gambling and social life in San Francisco; investment opportunities; conditions in the gold mines; travel by steamboat to Hangtown (Placerville); churches; crime; Indians; mining profits; cost of land; ranching; blacksmith and plough shop in Santa Clara; digging a canal to take water from the American River to supply Hangtown, Coon Hollow, and Gold Hill; and Webber Run.

Two letters by Joseph Bennett from Australia in 1853 comment on mining, living conditions, profits of mining, and criminals sent from Great Britain. There is one 1849 letter to Samuel Bennett from relatives in Sheffield, England. There are several items of Jacobs family correspondence, 1880-1923, concerning family affairs, schools, economic conditions in Jackson County, and Monongalia County taxes in 1907.

49. **Bennett, Louis.** Papers, 1841-1916. 6 ft. Gift of Mrs. J. C. McKinley, 1936. No. 35.

Papers and correspondence of a Weston attorney.

50. **Bennett, Mrs. Louis.** Papers, 1900-1926. 3 ft. Gift of Mrs. Douglas B. Williams, 1962. No. 1590.

Personal correspondence, legal and financial papers, diary, and newspaper clippings of Mrs. Sallie Maxwell Bennett of Weston, wife of Louis Bennett, the Democratic gubernatorial candidate in 1908.

The collection concerns the career of her son, Louis, Jr., particularly his student days at Yale, his pioneer efforts to organize an aviation group in the state, his service in the R. A. F., and his subsequent death in World War I; Mrs. Bennett's effort to memorialize her son; family affairs; and a South American trip in the 1920s.

Correspondents include Louis Bennett, Sr. and Jr., and John W. Davis.

51. **Berkeley, Earl.** Papers, ca. 1928-1934. 2 notebooks and 300p. Transfer, 1962. No. 1551.

Notebooks and a typewritten manuscript: "Grasses of West Virginia." The work undertakes to identify and classify useful and troublesome grasses that occur wild in the state.

52. **Berkeley County.** Archives, 1788, 1793. 1 reel of microfilm. Originals in the New York Public Library. No. 837.

Land tax books.

53. **Berkeley County.** Typescripts, 1735-1861, 1923-1924. 3 items. No. 100.

A volume of typed miscellany concerning Berkeley County, 1735-1861, including information on the location of Revolutionary War soldiers' graves; Snodgrass' Tavern; excerpts from early county record books; a bibliography on Berkeley County in the colonial and revolutionary periods; lineage of Colonel George Taylor; and pioneer industries. There is a volume of correspondence of Miss Nota K. Weaver concerning family genealogies in Berkeley and Jefferson counties and a typescript genealogy of the Foreman family.

54. **Bethany College.** Autograph book, 1860, 1861, 1864. 1 reel of microfilm. Original owned by Maurice K. Gordon, 1957. No. 1004.

The autograph book of Alfred T. Pope, a student at Bethany College, containing the autographs of Alexander Campbell and sixty-three Bethany College students.

55. **Bishop, Charles Mortimer (1827-1896).** Papers, 1857-1897. 1 ft. Gift of Mrs. F. Emma Bishop, 1931. No. 8.

Papers of a Preston County farmer, merchant, and licensed exhorter of the Methodist Episcopal Church who served in the state legislature in the years 1870-1876. There are letters of H. G. Davis and William Ewin regarding land and coal properties in Preston County. Minutes of the incorporators' meeting of the Iron Valley and Pennsylvania Railroad, 1873, are included as well as scattered items relating to the Methodist Episcopal Church, Kingwood; the Northwestern Turnpike at St. George; the Grafton and Greenbrier Railroad Company; Civil War bounty claims; the Rowlesburg Lumber and Iron Company; stave making; the Wheeling Female College; political and religious speeches; and the Morgantown District Camp Meeting Association, 1877.

56. **Bittner, Van Amberg (1885-1949).** Papers, 1908-1961. 6 ft. Gift of Mrs. James R. Wohler, 1963. No. 1698.

Correspondence, legal papers, pocket diaries, photographs, printed material and clippings of Van A. Bittner, United Mine Workers international representative and organizer, member of the Steel Workers

Organizing Committee, director of the CIO Organizing Committee, and vice-chairman of the CIO Political Action Committee.

The papers pertain to Bittner's early career in the western Pennsylvania coal fields; his presidency of District No. 5, United Mine Workers, 1911-1916; and his organizational activities in southeastern Kentucky and Tennessee, Alabama, northern West Virginia, Oklahoma and Kansas, 1916-1928. Subjects include labor strife and strikes in West Virginia, 1912-1913, 1924-1928, Alabama, 1920-1921, Westmoreland County, Pennsylvania, 1911, and Oklahoma and Kansas, 1922; United Mine Workers intra-union affairs; relief for striking miners; Kansas Industrial Court; Workers Communist Party; Red International of Labor Unions; American Association for Labor Legislation; National League of People's McAdoo Clubs; labor trouble in Montana, 1920; the railway assigned coal car problem; and Bittner's activities on various state and national labor boards and committees.

There are photographs of mining towns, camps, and tent colonies, labor parades, conventions, demonstrations, and strikes; portraits of labor leaders; and pictures of the Irwin (Pennsylvania) coal field strike of 1911, the Ludlow (Colorado) Massacre of 1914, and the northern West Virginia strikes of 1924-1926.

Correspondents include Samuel Gompers, William Green, Frank J. Hayes, John L. Lewis, John Mitchell, Philip Murray, Rembrandt Peale, David Robb, T. C. Townsend, William Turnblazer, and John P. White.

57. **Blennerhassett, Harman (1765-1831).** Typescripts, 1806-1821. 10 items. No. 331.

Copies of letters and documents, most from Wood County, relating to Blennerhassett's activities. Writers of letters include Blennerhassett and James H. Neal of Parkersburg writing to or about James Wilson of Wood County. There are several petitions of Wood County citizens urging the organization of troops to protect the constitution and government from "ambitious and disorganizing Demagogues. . . ."

58. **Boardman, Daniel.** Papers 1803-1826. 14 items. Nos. 218, 231.

Letters to Daniel Boardman, New York, New York, regarding ejectment suits and the sale of his land along French and Hacker's creeks, Lewis County. Correspondents include Robert Young, a New Englander who was ejected from Boardman's land and who pled the case for his countrymen.

59. **Boggs, Ira Brooks (1890-1955).** Writings, 1927-1956. 1 reel of microfilm. Gift of the West Virginia University 4-H Club, 1957. No. 1017.

Film of columns written by Ira B. Boggs on 4-H work in West Virginia published in the *West Virginia Farm News, 4-H Suggestions,* and other club publications. Other 4-H materials are included, as well as clippings of obituaries from several state newspapers of Boggs' death.

60. **Bolton, Channing M.** Letter, 1921. 1 item (typescript copy). Gift of George S. Wallace, Jr., 1963. No. 1684.

Letter to Decatur Axtell recounting Bolton's experiences working on the construction of the Chesapeake and Ohio Railroad in Virginia and West Virginia.

61. **Bonafield, Julia A. (1863-1956).** Clippings and photograph. 1 folder. Gift of Miss Mary L. Scott, 1962. No. 1625.

Papers on the career of a Buckhannon native who served as a missionary to China and a teacher at the Girl's School, Foochow, China, 1888-1943.

62. **Boreman, Arthur I. (1823-1896).** Papers, 1836 (1850-1908). 18 ft. Gifts of Mrs. Abijah Hays, 1954, and Mrs. Earl J. Noe, n.d. Nos. 104, 639.

Personal and business papers of a lawyer, U. S. senator, circuit court judge, and the first governor of West Virginia. The bulk of the collection consists of papers relating to his judgeship and to the firm of Boreman and Bullock, Parkersburg. Letters to Boreman, 1866-1867, from Francis H. Pierpont, concern politics in West Virginia, the admission of Berkeley and Jefferson counties into the state, the Virginia debt, and Reconstruction in Virginia. There is little other material relating to the governorship or political activities.

There are manuscripts of speeches, household accounts, Civil War papers, and court case papers concerning oil well drilling and sales; railroad property inventories and operation; coal prices, shipping data, and strikes; liquid fuel transportation; steam and tow boat cargoes, navigation data, and names of boats in service on the Ohio River. There is genealogical information on P. G. Van Winkle and Ebenezer Zane, and a letter and deposition by J. H. Diss Debar.

Correspondents include J. W. Davis, D. D. T. Farnsworth, Francis H. Pierpont, D. H. Strother, J. G. Jackson, Charles J. Faulkner, and E. W. Wilson.

63. **Boughner, James Vance (1812-1882).** Papers, 1790-1888. 2 ft. Gift of Mrs. Hugh Jarvis, 1951. No. 253.

Papers of a Morgantown resident who practiced medicine and operated a pension claim office in Mt. Morris, Greene County, Pennsylvania, ca. 1847-1859, and who later conducted his claim business in Morgantown while serving with the U. S. Internal Revenue Bureau as collector for the second district of West Virginia.

The collection contains letters, accounts, and business papers of Morgantown residents, 1790-1855, including a private account book of Hugh McNeely, 1790-1800. The internal revenue returns and tax statements give the occupations of many persons in northern West Virginia, ca. 1861-1886. There are also photographs; genealogical compilations on the Statler, Morgan, and Wendell Brown families; and typescripts of Monongalia County history.

64. **Boyers, Jacob Edgar** (1832-1912). Papers, 1859-1912. 3 items. Gift of Miss Helen Boyers, 1961. No. 1477.

Papers of West Virginia's first secretary of state including his commissions in the Virginia Militia and a letter from Henry J. Samuels concerning Boyer's military command.

65. **Braddock's Field**. Clippings, September 10, 1887. 2 items. No. 333.

Newspaper clippings relating to the dedication of the monument at Braddock, Pennsylvania, at which Francis H. Pierpont made an address.

66. **Brady, Rose**. Correspondence, 1883-1885. 3 items. Gift of Mrs. Joseph Louis Barker, 1965. No. 1840.

Three letters to Rose Brady, a resident of Toledo, Illinois. There are two letters from Carrie Brady, a cousin, from Gale, Indiana, October 28, 1883, and January 9, 1884, including a report on school attendance and subjects studied. There is one letter from Joe D. Wertz in Mullinville, Kansas, March 15, 1885, who tells of starting his farm.

67. **Brand Family**. Papers, 1861-1872, 1898-1924, 1962. 52 items. Gift of the Willa Brand Estate and Frank M. Brand, 1962. Nos. 1576, 1602.

Business and official papers of Monongalia County Sheriff John M. Brand and his deputy, William N. Brand, 1861-1872; letter from E. I. Moore of Woodburn Seminary; class prophecy, June, 1898, by Friend E. Clark of West Virginia University; diaries of Willa Brand kept during a tour of Europe in 1913 and the British Isles in 1924; and genealogical notes on the family of Samuel and Elizabeth Musgrave and the McDougal family compiled by Frank M. Brand.

68. **Braxton County**. Archives, 1830-1953. 60 ft. Gift of the Braxton County Court, 1955, 1956. Nos. 789, 913.

Suit papers; record books of county officers; estate settlements; birth, marriage, and death records; election returns; deeds and volumes of deed indexes; and land and tax records. There is also a volume of World War I records of Braxton County servicemen, and several account books of the Holly River and Addison Railroad, and the Midland Railroad.

69. **Brinkman, Charles,** *Collector.* Papers, (1852-1938) 1948. 12 ft. Gifts of Charles Brinkman, 1938, 1948, and Harry M. Murray, 1958. Nos. 111, 1086.

Papers of a Grafton businessman and antiquarian, pertaining mainly to Grafton and Taylor County with scattered materials on Lewisburg and Wheeling. There are letters, account books, and other records of a Grafton general store operated by George W. Brinkman and the Mutual Building Company; typescripts by Jacob G. Matlick dealing with his Civil War service and prison experiences and with the war in and around Grafton; numerous obituaries and biographical sketches; articles on the early history of Taylor County, Wheeling, and the Baltimore and Ohio Railroad; items on Memorial Day celebrations and the location of the National Cemetery in Grafton; broadsides from Pruntytown and Grafton; and photographs of Grafton.

There are also minutes of the Grafton Rotary Club; a journal and statistical report of the Grafton Baptist Church, 1897-1906; clipping scrapbooks on Grafton and Taylor County subjects, 1868-1938; financial records; and a partial index to the scrapbooks.

70. **Brinsmade, Robert Bruce,** *Compiler.* Clippings, 1910-1911. 13 items. Transfer, 1964. No. 1753.

Clippings from the *New Dominion* (Morgantown), signed "Naturalist," arranged and corrected by Robert Bruce Brinsmade, the author. Brinsmade was an advocate of the Single Tax, an opponent of trusts and monopolies and an advocate of progressive reforms.

71. **Brooke County.** Archives, 1776-1918. 90 ft. Gift of the Brooke County Court, 1936. No. 43.

Suit papers and bound volumes of county records. A name and subject index to the loose papers and an inventory of the volumes are available in the manuscripts section. There is an account book for general merchandise sold by John Connell, 1794-1796, in Wellsburg, and other private account books, 1845-1870.

72. **Brooke County.** Records, 1787-1789, 1881-1895. 15 items. Gift of Mr. and Mrs. A. F. Young, 1957. No. 981.

An 1848 deed for land in Brooke County; an agreement between the Wellsburg and Washington Turnpike Company, and Arthur and John Henderson and J. Scott, for construction of a portion of the turnpike, 1833; records of the firms of Lewis and Hedge, and William B. Lewis and Company, Wellsburg, 1892-1894; and four unidentified account books for general merchandise, flour, feed, farming, and mill repair accounts, 1787-1789, 1880-1890.

73. **Brooke Family.** Papers, 1814-1958. 1 ft. 2 reels of microfilm and 24 items. Gift and loan of Mrs. Nan Brooke Harold, 1955, 1956, 1958. Nos. 642, 740, 810, 851, 1079, 1119.

Correspondence, photographs, clippings, biographical typescripts, and other items relating to the family of St. George Tucker Brooke (1844-1914), a professor at West Virginia University College of Law, 1878-1909. There are letters, ca. 1870, from James Harold in Ireland to his son James in New York; correspondence and student themes of Charles Frederick Tucker Brooke, a Rhodes scholar and Shakespearian authority at Yale; a family letter book, 1898-1946, compiled by Nan Brooke Harold; family and personal letters of Nan Brooke Harold; and "Family Recollections" (1865) by Thomas Brown, governor of Florida (1849-1853).

Other items include a surveyor's call book for Tucker County, 1856-1857, which includes notes on the Tucker-Randolph County boundary; a manuscript recipe book, 1814; an extract from the Civil War diary of Mrs. Charles W. Coleman recounting an excursion to the James River peninsula, 1864; and film copies of typescripts, "Autobiography of St. George Tucker Brooke, Written for His Children," and "Narrative of My Life: for My Family," by Francis T. Brooke.

74. **Brooks, William E. (1875-   ),** *Collector.* Papers, ca. 1825-1944. 1 ft. Gift of William E. Brooks, various dates. Nos. 152, 165, 249, 485.

Civil War materials collected by Dr. Brooks in writing his biographies of Grant and Lee. Included are pamphlets, scrapbooks, newspapers, photographs, and originals and copies of soldiers' letters, journals and military reports.

There are typed copies of a journal, November 3-December 2, 1863, of a civilian observer in Tennessee, who was at Grant's headquarters at the Battle of Chattanooga; letters, 1861-1864, of William Ludwig, a private in the Thirty-fourth Ohio Volunteer Infantry in Fayette, Kanawha, and Cabell counties; Confederate officers' reports on the action around Beverly in July, 1863; and a Union soldier's letter of May 9, 1863, describing the Battle of Chancellorsville.

75. **Brown, David Dare,** *Compiler.* Notebooks, ca. 1900-1957. 10 volumes. Acquired, 1962. No. 1630.

Notebooks contain correspondence, photographs, and manuscript histories of lumbering operations and old sawmills in the forest regions of central West Virginia, compiled by Brown for a projected study on lumbering in West Virginia.

76. **Brown, John (1800-1859).** Papers, 1859-1860. 67 items (photostats). Acquired, ca. 1935, 1961. Nos. 335, 336, 1475.

Court records from Charles Town, Jefferson County, relating to the trial of Brown and others for the Harpers Ferry raid; an account of the Harpers Ferry raid from the Charles Town *Independent Democrat,* October 25, 1859; Brown's petition for a writ of error which appeared in the *Daily Enquirer,* Richmond, Virginia, November 21, 1859; a letter from Brown's cousin, Luther Humphrey, dated Windham, Ohio, November 12, 1859, and Brown's reply of November 19, 1859, defending his cause.

77. **Brown, Samuel Boardman (1860-   ).** Papers, 1891-1931. 1 folder. Gift of Mrs. Elizabeth Brown Fisher, 1971. No. 2204.

Letters, diaries, and receipts of Samuel Boardman Brown, professor of geology at West Virginia University, 1892-1927. Two diaries contain geological notes made on field trips throughout West Virginia.

78. **Brown, William G. (1800-1884).** Papers, 1789 (1842-1880) 1931. Ca. 250 items. Gift of Mrs. Izetta Jewell Brown Miller, 1932. No. 15.

Deeds, surveys, plats and other papers relating to Brown's land in Preston and Monongalia counties; personal correspondence of Brown at Kingwood; and a typed copy of a letter of J. J. Phillips of Lantz, July 18, 1931, relating to the removal of Confederate remains from the Rich Mountain Battlefield.

79. **Browning, Joseph W.** Letter, 1845. 1 item. Acquired, 1961. No. 1425.

Letter from Clarksburg to Samuel Shipman, of Marietta, Ohio, requesting materials for a fair being conducted by the Ladies Sewing Society to liquidate a debt of the Presbyterian Church. Browning, a schoolmaster, comments on the unruly character of his charges and the low moral standards of Clarksburg.

80. **Bryan, William Jennings (1860-1925).** Letter, March 2, 1902. No. 337.

Letter to the president of West Virginia University, accompanying a gift of $250, the income of which was to be given as an annual prize "for the best essay in the science of government."

81. **Buffalo Academy and Seminary.** Report form, 185-. 1 item. Acquired, 1962. No. 1623.

Report form of the Buffalo Academy and Seminary, Putnam County.

82. **Bunker, Edward C. (1830-1867).** Papers, ca. (1850-1865) 1901. 1 ft. Gift of Mrs. Roger Roberts, 1962. No. 1615.

Legal papers of a Morgantown lawyer, partner of United States Senator Waitman T. Willey, prosecuting attorney of Monongalia County, state senator, and judge of the Eleventh Circuit Court. The papers include Bunker's Civil War papers, Willey's legal papers, and a few items of correspondence on land speculation and immigration in post-Civil War West Virginia.

83. **Burr-Blennerhassett Trials.** Papers, 1805-1808. 1 reel of microfilm. Originals in the National Archives, Record Group 21, United States District Court for the Southern District of Ohio, 1969. No. 2115.

Letters, military orders, affidavits, depositions and miscellaneous items relating to the proposed trial of Aaron Burr and Harman Blennerhassett, August 1, 1805, to January 21, 1808. Correspondents include James Wilkinson.

84. **Bushfield, Mrs. Louis S.** Papers, 1940-1968. 2 ft. Gift of Louis S. Bushfield, 1968. No. 2033.

Correspondence, genealogical notes and charts, magazines, newspapers, and books collected and compiled around genealogical interests in West Virginia, Pennsylvania, and Ohio.

85. **Byrnside, James M. (1814-1873).** Papers, 1869-1870. 2 items. Gift of Bertha L. Clark, 1954, 1955. Nos. 654, 705.

A ledger for a general merchandise store operated by James M. Byrnside at Peterstown, and a brief sketch of Byrnside's career as a merchant, 1833-1873.

86. **Cabell County.** Land records, 1806-1867. 1 reel of microfilm (1 volume). Original in possession of Mrs. Billie J. Dooley, 1970. No. 2136.

A listing of survey fees showing the date of survey, name of person for whom survey was made, the number of acres, and the fee charged. For the period July 1, 1810, to January 1, 1821, there are notations of the number of surveys returned and the fees sent to William and Mary College.

The second part of the volume lists land entries for the period 1806-1833, showing date, name of owner, number of acres, warrant number, and page number for recording of entry.

87. **Calabrese, Nicolo.** Tape recording, 1961. 2 reels of tape. No. 1515.

Interview with a Monongah coal miner covering his career from 1902 to 1947.

88. **Callahan, James Morton (1864-1956).** Papers, 1836-1956. 43 ft. Gifts of James M. Callahan, James M. Callahan, Jr., O. D. Lambert, Festus P. Summers, and transfers, 1948, 1954, 1956, 1957, 1960, 1961, 1962. Nos. 115, 839, 1000, 1022, 1041, 1075, 1179, 1398, 1627.

Papers of an Indiana-born professor of history, 1902-1940, and dean of the College of Arts and Sciences, 1916-1929, at West Virginia University, who wrote widely in U. S. diplomatic history and West Virginia local history.

The collection consists of correspondence, research notes, and newspaper clippings relating to Callahan's University administrative offices. There is material on his education at Johns Hopkins University and correspondence, 1869-1956, among members of the Callahan and Fulcher families in West Virginia and Indiana. There is a taped interview with Callahan, made in 1954.

Unpublished manuscripts include drafts of "History of West Virginia University"; "Presidents of West Virginia University"; "Foundations of American Northern Frontier Development"; "Foundations of American Continental Security Policy and Inter-American Relations; a Study in American Diplomacy"; "Introductions to American Expansion Policy"; "The Evolution of a Midwestern Octogenarian"; and "History of the History Department (West Virginia University)."

Correspondents include John W. Foster, Herschel V. Johnson, George H. Blakeslee, and Henry L. Stimson, F. A. Updyke, French E. Chadwick, Charles G. Fenwick, Harold Temperly, and George A. Finch.

89. **Camden.** General store records, 1917-1947. 2 ft. Gift of Jacob L. Gissy, 1954. No. 673.

Account books and business papers of a general store operated by Jacob L. Gissy in Camden.

90. **Camden, Gideon D. (1805-1891).** Papers, 1785-1958. 38 ft., 4 folders and 13 items. Acquired, 1959, 1961, 1966. Nos. 1188, 1199, 1221, 1260, 1276, 1495, 1517, 1523, 1868.

Correspondence, business and legal papers of a Harrison County lawyer, Democratic politician, member of the Virginia Convention of 1850-1851, circuit judge, and state senator.

Papers deal with Camden's legal career in land title litigation; his law partnership with John J. Allen; his extensive interests in land, timber, coal, and oil exploitation; and his political career.

Subjects include state and national politics, ca. 1830-1888; state and national elections of 1840, 1848, 1860, 1868; Tariff of 1846; Compromise of 1850; Virginia Reform Convention of 1850-1851; Whig Party; Secession crisis; New York merchants and secession; Reconstruction in West Virginia; Flick Amendment; Constitutional Convention of 1872; state capital question; senatorial contest of 1874; Democratic National Convention of 1876; the Virginia debt controversy; opening of the West Virginia oil and coal fields; railroads; immigration to West Virginia; Methodism; the slavery question; education; Meadville (Wellsburg, Virginia) Collegiate Institute; Mt. de Chantal Academy; and West Virginia University.

The collection also includes the papers of Camden's grandson, Wilson Lee Camden (1870-1956), which deal with the Camden estate and its vast coal, timber, land, railroad, and oil interests in West Virginia and Pennsylvania.

Correspondents include Jonathan M. Bennett, Jacob B. Blair, Johnson N. Camden, Alexander Campbell, John S. Carlile, Henry G. Davis, A. G. Dayton, J. H. Diss Debar, Stephen B. Elkins, Charles J. Faulkner, A. B. Fleming, John W. Garrett, David Goff, Nathan Goff, John Marshall Hagans, Granville D. Hall, Frank Hereford, Chester Hubbard, Robert M. T. Hunter, John D. Imboden, Jacob B. Jackson, Louis Johnson, John E. Kenna, John Letcher, John T. McGraw, Alexander Martin, James M. Mason, Henry M. Mathews, Lot M. Morrill, Francis H. Pierpont, Melville Davisson Post, William E. Stevenson, Peter G. Van Winkle, Thomas G. Watson, and Waitman T. Willey.

There is a calendar of the papers for the years 1785-1860.

91. **Camden, Johnson Newlon (1828-1908).** Papers, 1845-1908. 51 ft. Gifts of the estate of Johnson Newlon Camden and Roy Bird Cook, 1931, 1934, 1959. Nos. 7, 339, 1228.

Correspondence, maps, business records and other papers of a U. S. Senator, Democratic politician, and promoter of the oil industry, railroads, and coal and timber resources of West Virginia. The papers deal with Camden's purchase of land in the 1850s; his activities in oil production and refining, 1860-1875; his presidency of the Camden Consolidated Oil Company and the Baltimore United Oil Company; the affairs of the Stewart Brick Company of Parkersburg; the Virginia debt controversy; and his development of railroads, including the Ohio River Railroad, the West Virginia and Pittsburgh Railroad, and Monongahela River Railroad, 1879-1892.

Writers of letters include John D. Alderson, Jonathan M. Bennett, Gideon D. Camden, John S. Carlile, William E. Chilton, John J. Cornwell, Grover Cleveland, Henry G. Davis, Stephen B. Elkins, Charles J. Faulkner, Jr., A. B. Fleming, Frederick T. Frelinghuysen, John W. Garrett, Nathan Goff, Arthur P. Boreman, C. W. Harkness, E. S. Harkness, N. W. Harkness, Abram S. Hewitt, C. P. Huntington, John E. Kenna, James M. Mason II, John T. McGraw, John D. Rockefeller, William Rockefeller, H. H. Rogers, William P. Thompson, Clarence W. Watson, William C. Whitney, William L. Wilson, and Henry A. Wise.

92. **Camden, T. B.** Papers, 1862-1907. 1 ft. and 1 reel of microfilm. Gift of Roy Bird Cook, 1954. No. 623.

Original appraisement and account book pertaining to the estate of John S. Camden, 1862-1881. There are two ledgers of T. B. Camden, a physician, covering his medical practice in sixteen counties, listing private accounts, cost of medical care, insurance claims, and statements of Camden's income, 1865-1907. There is a scrapbook of clippings, numerous broadsides, and correspondence on professional and political activities of Camden including letters from friends regarding his dismissal as superintendent of the state hospital for the insane at Weston.

The microfilm includes entries from the diary of Thomas L. Feamster, a Confederate soldier, noting troop movements in Greenbrier County, 1861, 1864-1865, and entries from the commonplace book of Theodore Woodridge.

93. **Camels.** Typescript, 10p. Gift of A. J. Dadisman, 1951. No. 275.

A typescript, "Camel Transportation in the United States," by A. J. Dadisman, detailing the introduction of camels into the U. S., and the influence of Jefferson Davis in promoting the use of camels by the U. S. Army in the western states in the 1850s.

94. **Campbell, Alexander (1788-1866).** Papers, 1808-1809, 1862, 1864. 1 reel of microfilm (1 volume) and 2 items. Original held by the Disciples of Christ Historical Society, 1968, and transfers. Nos. 341, 2025.

"Journal of a Voyage from Ireland towards America" by the leader of the Disciples of Christ Church, beginning in England in August, 1808 and ending in New York, September 28, 1809. Also, Campbell's original will, with codicils.

95. **Campbell, Andrew Nelson (d. 1919).** Papers, 1782 (1854-1932). 6 ft. Gift of Crete Campbell, 1946, 1952, 1954. Nos. 101, 513, 653.

Business and personal papers and correspondence of a Monroe County attorney, judge, state legislator, West Virginia University regent, and Confederate Army veteran. Included are papers of the law firm of Hereford and Campbell; reports, correspondence, and other papers concerning the Deepwater Railway Company and the Tidewater Railway Company.

In the Civil War materials are rolls and lists of names of several Confederate Army units; a typed copy of Campbell's war reminiscences; correspondence concerning the organization and annual meetings of Confederate veterans organizations.

There is genealogical information on numerous Monroe County families compiled by Campbell, along with family correspondence and business records.

96. **Campbell, Archibald W.** (1839-1899). Papers, (1855-1899) 1907. Ca. 500 items. Gift of Mrs. Jessica Maurer and Mrs. Jessie C. Hill, 1932. No. 14.

Papers of the editor of the Wheeling *Intelligencer*, including clippings, correspondence, and broadsides dealing with the Civil War and political affairs. Correspondents include Jacob B. Blair, Montgomery Blair, Arthur I. Boreman, Cassius M. Clay, Schuyler Colfax, Edward Everett, Horace Greeley, Joseph Medill, Francis H. Pierpont, William H. Seward, Franz Sigel, Edwin M. Stanton, and Peter G. Van Winkle.

97. **Campbell, Charles L.,** *Compiler* (1876-   ). Typescripts, ca. 1789-1956. Ca. 50p. and 1 reel of microfilm. Originals in possession of Charles L. Campbell, 1963. No. 1314.

Typescripts compiled by a Wellsburg local historian, on the history of Holliday's Cove and the Hancock-Brooke County area. Subjects include prominent settlers, churches, schools, post office, toll roads, oil and gas wells, floods, gristmills, manufacture of gunpowder, iron and brick industries, newspapers, Indians, and the James Campbell and Alexander Morrow family genealogy.

98. **Campbell, Jacob M.** Papers, 1796 (1861-1865) 1888. 2 ft. Acquired, 1958, 1959. Nos. 1109, 1267.

Military orders, telegrams, correspondence, lists of Confederate deserters, ordnance and quartermaster returns, and a personal diary of Colonel Campbell, commander of the Fifty-fourth Pennsylvania Volunteers which operated along the line of the Baltimore and Ohio Railroad between Cumberland, Maryland, and Martinsburg, West Virginia.

Subjects include civilian-military relations; guerrilla activities of John D. Imboden, the Ringgold Raiders, and the McNeill Rangers; treatment of Confederate sympathizers; fighting in the Shenandoah Valley in the spring of 1864; and military operations in the Eastern Panhandle of West Virginia.

99. **Campbell Family.** Papers, 1795-1901. 2 reels of microfilm (4 volumes and 4 folders). Originals in possession of Mr. and Mrs. James W. Campbell, 1959, 1960. Nos. 1265, 1321.

Business and legal papers, farm records, and store accounts of James Campbell, his son, James L., and his grandson, James Wilson Campbell. The papers pertain to the management of the family plantation and country store located near Arden in Berkeley County. The collection also includes James W. Campbell's school notes on mathematics and surveying, and an account of a geological field trip through the Wood-Ritchie-Pleasants oil district in 1866.

100. **Caperton, William Gaston (1815-1852).** Family papers, 1801-1930. 1 reel of microfilm (ca. 500 items). Originals in possession of Mrs. H. A. Hereford, Sr., 1961. No. 1436.

Correspondence and miscellaneous papers of a Monroe County farmer and politician, his wife, Harriette Boswell Alexander, their daughters, Isabel and Alice Beulah, Alice's husband Frank Hereford, U. S. senator from West Virginia, and his daughter, Katherine Hereford Stoddard. There is one folder of business papers, 1820-1841, of Thomas Edgar; a few letters from Caperton's son, John, while a cadet at the Camp of Instruction, Richmond, 1861; a folder of letters concerning Isabel's trips through the American West, the British Isles, and Europe; and a folder on family genealogy.

Subjects include mid-nineteenth century life in Union, Monroe County; the excitement in Virginia following John Brown's raid; Washington, D. C., and the slavery controversy, 1860; the secession crisis in Virginia; impressment of material in Monroe County by Union troops; the effect of the war on the social and economic life of Richmond; work of the Ladies Relief Hospital in Lynchburg; and the aftermath of war in Virginia.

101. **Carbide and Carbon Chemicals Corporation.** Scrapbooks, 1907-1943. 1 reel of microfilm (5 volumes). Originals in Carbide Technical Center Library, Charleston, 1965. No. 1822.

Five scrapbooks of pictures of the Carbide and Carbon Chemicals Corporation, South Charleston.

102. **Carpenter, Charles,** *Collector.* Papers, 1813-1964. 2 ft. and 53 items. Gifts of Charles Carpenter, 1939, 1964, 1969. Nos. 57, 1773, 2106, 2119.

Manuscript and printed materials relating to the development of railroads in West Virginia, including contracts, letters, monthly situation reports, construction profiles, maps, and speeches. Railroad companies represented include Baltimore and Ohio; Charleston, Clendenin and Sutton; Coal and Coke; Greenbrier, Cheat and Elk; Hampshire Southern; Nicholas, Fayette, and Greenbrier; Roaring Creek and Belington; Western Maryland; West Virginia Midland; and West Virginia and Pittsburgh.

There are papers dealing with land transactions in Taylor County; court case papers and exhibits from Taylor and Harrison counties; a coal lease for mining and stripping; and a genealogy chart for the Morgan family. Correspondents and organizations include Charles H. and Augusta Rector; Martin Coal Company; Real Estate and Improvement Company of Baltimore City; the Ward-Bishop Addition to Bluefield; James R. Sincell; Daniel G. Payne; and Henry Warder.

There are twenty-one scrapbooks maintained by Carpenter between 1939 and 1963; subjects include descriptions of libraries and museums, rare books, newspapers, magazines, and book reviews. The collection also includes one notebook used by Carpenter while writing *History of American Schoolbooks.*

103. **Carroll, James H.** (1820-1890). Papers, 1812 (1844-1900). 2 ft. and 1 folder. Gift of Carleton C. Pierce and Carleton C. Pierce, Jr., various dates. Nos. 118, 287.

Letters, legal papers, advertising circulars, photographs, and other materials of a Kingwood attorney and postmaster. There are scattered letters relating to the War of 1812, the Mexican War, and the Civil War; post office records of Preston County dating from the 1840s; and political correspondence. Writers of letters include Nathan Goff and Benjamin F. Shaffer of Company A, Seventh West Virginia Volunteer Infantry.

104. **Casto, Russel W.** Postal records, 1950-1955. 7 volumes. Gift of Ivan Hunter, 1966. No. 1892.

Account and cash books, 1950-1955, of postmaster Russel W. Casto at Nitro.

105. **Ceredo.** Typescript, 1887. 17p. Transfer, n.d. No. 344.

A typed copy of a promotional pamphlet, "Ceredo, Advantages, Resources, and Possibilities," which was published by the Advance Printing House, Ceredo, Wayne County, 1887. Listed are shipping facilities, mineral resources, lumbering projects, social institutions, a business directory, and other data on the economic life of the area.

106. **Chadwick, French E.** (1844-1919). Letters, 1903-1914. Ca. 160 items. Acquired, 1944, and gifts of Arthur S. Dayton and Mrs. Arthur S. Dayton, 1954. Nos. 87, 695.

Correspondence between Chadwick and Albert Bushnell Hart, at Harvard University, relating to the writing and publishing of Chadwick's *Causes of the Civil War* (1906). There are also two letters from Newport, Rhode Island, to A. G. Dayton, requesting an appointment and mentioning John Bassett Moore.

107. **Chapin Family.** Papers, 1816-1892. Ca. 100 items. Gift of Mrs. Mortimer Smith, 1956. No. 828.

Letters of Phineas Chapin (1792-1857), and other family members in Kentucky, Cincinnati, Ohio, and Clarksburg. There are intimate sketches of the social life of Clarksburg in the first half of the nineteenth century; descriptions of a plantation house in Mississippi in 1860; and a few papers bearing on family business affairs, including cattle raising in Harrison County.

108. **Charleston Youth Community.** Survey of Charleston youth, 1963. 12 reels of microfilm (10 ft.). Gift of Action for Appalachian Youth, 1965. No. 1826.

Questionnaires, interviews, surveys, and summaries from a study of Charleston youth conducted by the Charleston Youth Community in 1963. (RESTRICTED)

109. **Chesapeake and Ohio Railway Company.** Records, 1867-1869. 23 items. Gift of Virginia McClung Ellis, 1955. No. 713.

Letters, reports, and newspaper clippings relating to the Virginia Central Railroad Company, later the Chesapeake and Ohio Railway Company. Most of the correspondence is between E. Fontaine, president, and John S. Cunningham of West Virginia.

110. **Chicken Farms.** Photographs, 1912-1913. 34 photographs. Gift of Gay H. Duke, 1968. No. 2014.

Pictures of Jackson County Chicken Farms, 1912-1913, compiled by Stewart A. Cody, county agent, Jackson County.

111. **Chilton, William Edwin (1858-1939).** Papers, 1917, 1928-1939. 7 ft. Gift of W. E. Chilton III, 1963. No. 1652.

Correspondence, legal papers, and speeches of a lawyer, Democratic politician, publisher of the Charleston *Gazette*, and U. S. Senator (1911-1917); and correspondence of his son, William E. Chilton, Jr., editor of the *Gazette*.

The papers cover a wide range of state and national Democratic politics during the 1930s; family affairs; the senator's business interests in West Virginia and Kentucky coal lands, and the operation and editorial policy of the Charleston *Gazette*. Other subjects include the American Protective League; Public Ownership League; the World Court; London Naval Conference; the Franklin D. Roosevelt boom, 1931-1932; prohibition; Association Against the Prohibition Amendment; bank crisis; state patronage; the money question, 1933-1938; Kanawha Coal Operators' Association; Franklin D. Roosevelt's court plan; Charleston Naval Ordnance Plant; Charleston civic affairs; WPA operations; and authorship of the Federal Reserve Act.

Correspondents include George W. Atkinson, Newton D. Baker, Alben W. Barkley, Cole L. Blease, William E. Borah, Arthur Brisbane, William G. Conley, John J. Cornwell, Josephus Daniels, John W. Davis, Charles Edison, Andrew Edmiston, James A. Farley, John N. Garner, William Green, Walter S. Hallanan, Henry D. Hatfield, Leon Henderson, Homer A. Holt, Rush D. Holt, Louis Howe, Philip C. Jessup, George W. Johnson, Louis Johnson, John Kee, John N. Kenna, H. G. Kump, Robert M. La Follette, Jr., William G. McAdoo, W. A. MacCorkle, Robert R. McCormick, Clarence W. Meadows, Dwight W. Morrow, M. M. Neely, George W. Norris, H. C. Ogden, C. W. Osenton, Robert L. Owen, Jennings Randolph, Franklin D. Roosevelt, Daniel C. Roper, Jouett Shouse, Gray Silver, C. E. Smith, Harry S Truman, Carl Vinson, Thomas J. Walsh, James E. Watson, and Burton K. Wheeler.

112. **Chitwood, Oliver Perry (1874-1971).** Papers, 1907-1969. 7 ft. Gifts of O. P. Chitwood, Donovan H. Bond, and J. William Hess, 1969, and Mrs. J. C. Appel, 1971. Nos. 992, 2073, 2219.

Correspondence, research notes, tape recording with transcript, and manuscripts of a professor of history at West Virginia University (1907-1946), professor emeritus (1946-1971), and author of several college history textbooks and biographies. Subjects include book publishing, newspaper and magazine articles, correspondence with legislators and congressmen, personal correspondence, former students, and the Democratic Convention delegate selection in 1928. Also included are materials on Chitwood's books *John Tyler: Champion of the Old South*, *The United States: A Short History*, and *Richard Henry Lee: Statesman of the Revolution*.

113. **Chrisman, Lewis H.** Papers, 1949-1964. 1 reel of microfilm (ca. 150 items). Originals in possession of West Virginia Wesleyan College, 1969. No. 2114.

Correspondence between Dr. Chrisman, professor of English at West Virginia Wesleyan College, and Dr. Edgar Wesley, professor of education at the University of Minnesota. Subjects include education, religion, politics, Dr. C. H. Ambler, West Virginia Wesleyan College, West Virginia University, and books.

114. **Churches.** Records, 1787-1965. 12 items. Gifts of James W. Carskadon, 1953, Rev. Lawrence Sherwood, 1954, Earl L. Core, 1963, A. J. Dadisman Estate, 1966, and John Corbly Chapter, D. A. R.; and acquisitions and transfers, 1961-1965. Accession numbers follow descriptions below.

Typed copy of the minute book of the Goshen (John Corbly Memorial) Baptist Church, organized about 1773 at Garards Fort, Greene County, Pennsylvania (99); letter to Sally Barns by a minister on the Redstone Circuit, Methodist Episcopal Church, written near Uniontown, Pennsylvania (246); sketch of the history of the Presbyterian Church in West Virginia with emphasis on the Fairmont Presbyterian Church (520); class roll book, 1850-1859, of the Methodist Episcopal Church, Headsville, Mineral County (581); map showing preaching points on the Greenbrier Circuit, Methodist Episcopal Church, 1787-1788, as noted in the manuscript journal of John Smith (617); session records, 1840-1889, of a Presbyterian Church at Jefferson, Pennsylvania (1484); proceedings, 1855-1876, of the West Virginia Conference of the Methodist Protestant Church (1571); a brief history and list of ministers of the Augusta Christian Church in Hampshire County, compiled by John G. Riley and Mrs. Loy E. Beery (1657); letter, 1842, from the Goshen Baptist Church of Jesus Christ, Monongalia County (1811); tape recordings, 1965, of church services at Freewill Holiness Church and Scrabble Creek Holiness Church, Gauley Bridge (1850); and work sheets from a survey of churches in Grant and Cass districts, Monongalia County, 1913-1914 (1893).

115. **Churches. Avery Methodist Protestant.** Records, 1843-1948. 8 volumes. Deposited by Ivan C. Owens, 1965. No. 1803.

Records of a church near Morgantown, including minutes, 1843-1855; register of members, baptisms, deaths, and marriages, 1919-1929; organization of the Young People's Meeting, 1935-1943; the Sunday school, 1935; and organization of the Christian Endeavor Society, 1934; minutes of the Easton-Avery Community Building, 1939-1946; minutes of the Community Center Board of Directors; and Bible Class records, 1908-1926.

116. **Churches. Baptist (Boone County).** Records, 1866-1888. 17p. (photocopy). Loaned for copying by J. Douglas Machesney, 1969. No. 2090.

Boone County Baptist Church records, including meeting book of Lowgap Baptist Church, 1866, 1888; certificates of good standing in the Old School Baptist Church, 1873, and the Baptist Church at Holly Creek, 1869; and an article of agreement concerning protection of property, Boone County, March 27, 1869.

117. **Churches. Bluestone Baptist.** Records, 1803-1856. 1 reel of microfilm (1 folder). Originals held by Miss Vida Bailey, 1960. No. 1339.

Records include minutes, 1804-1820, 1854, a manuscript hymn book, and correspondence, 1803-1809, of a Summers County church; and the minutes of the Greenbrier (Baptist) Association, 1807-1811.

118. **Churches. Clarksburg Methodist Episcopal, South.** Records, 1847, 1854-1861, 1868-1878. 1 reel of microfilm (1 volume, 148 pages, 1 item). Originals held by Clarksburg Public Library, 1964. No. 1735.

Register of the Clarksburg Station, Western Virginia Conference, Methodist Episcopal Church, South, 1847, 1854-1861, 1868-1878; minutes of Clarksburg churches, 1868-1875, 1871, 1872, 1886; an article by T. S. Wade on reasons for the lack of church records for the Civil War period; and an unfinished manuscript by Clinton F. Israel, "History of the St. Paul's Methodist Church, Clarksburg."

119. **Churches. First Christian (Connellsville).** Records, 1865-1903. 1 reel of microfilm (2 volumes). Originals in possession of the First Christian Church, Connellsville, Pennsylvania, 1960. No. 1376.

Record of ministers, members, baptisms, deaths, meetings of the church board, reports of the various church departments, and organizational history.

120. **Churches. First Presbyterian (Clarksburg).** Papers, (1798-1903) 1956. 208 items and 1 reel of microfilm. Gifts and loan of First Presbyterian Church, Clarksburg, 1956, and Mrs. Glenn V. Longacre, 1956, 1957. Nos. 853, 863, 898, 935.

Minutes of session, 1829-1870; correspondence, subscription lists, 1798-1903; typescript entitled "Fifty Years in the Wilderness," by Loyal Young, 1869; and pamphlets, photographs, and clippings.

121. **Churches. Great Bethel Baptist.** Records, 1770-1903. 1 reel microfilm (4 volumes). Originals in possession of the Great Bethel Baptist Church, Uniontown, Pennsylvania, 1961. No. 1407.

Record of monthly meetings, membership, baptisms, and the church constitution. Subjects include church discipline, policy, financial affairs, and social activities.

122. **Churches. Jones Run Baptist.** Records, ca. 1831-1959. 1 ft. Gift of Chester Harbert, 1965. No. 1849.

Six record books of a Harrison County church, containing church covenant, lists of members, and minutes. There is correspondence, receipts, reports, letters of dismission, miscellaneous papers, and a copy of "History of the Jones Run Baptist Church, Lumberport," written for the Judson Baptist Association, 1938.

123. **Churches. Kingwood Methodist.** Typescripts, ca. 1816-1896. 23p. Gift of R. Doyne Halbritter, 1957. No. 1020.

"A Brief History of Methodism in Kingwood and Vicinity from the Earliest Times to March, 1874," by W. C. Snodgrass. Also a typed "Baptismal Record," dating between 1852 and 1896, listing dates and places of birth, parents' names, and officiating ministers.

124. **Churches. Kingwood Methodist Episcopal.** Records, 1852-1937. 1 reel of microfilm (9 volumes). Originals in possession of the Kingwood Methodist Church, 1960. No. 1286.

Church record, 1852-1896, listing baptisms, marriages, probationers, members and various classes; quarterly conference records, 1899-1903, 1917-1920; church ledgers, 1910-1936; the minutes of the Women's Home Missionary Society, 1914-1937; and "A Brief History of Methodism in Kingwood and Vicinity from Our Earliest Times to March, 1874," by W. C. Snodgrass.

125. **Churches. Methodist.** Typescripts, 1844-1855, 1920. 2 items. Gift of the Reverend J. A. Earl, 1956. No. 836.

Typescript copies of the quarterly conference records, 1844-1855, of the Harrisville and West Union circuits, and a biographical sketch of Bishop Matthew Simpson Hughes.

126. **Churches. Methodist Episcopal. Grant Circuit of Winchester District.** Account book, 1871-1916. 1 reel of microfilm. Original in the possession of the Reverend Lawrence Sherwood, 1956. No. 835.

Financial account book and journal of the recording steward.

127. **Churches. Methodist Episcopal. Huntersville Circuit.** Stewards' book, 1846-1852. 1 reel of microfilm (1 volume). Original in possession of Frank A. Johnson, 1959. No. 1156.

"Stewards Book of Huntersville Circuit, Baltimore Conference of the Methodist E. Church of the United States of in [sic] America. Book Second or No. 2, 1846. Original in keeping of Recording Steward of the Huntersville Charges, Minnehaha, W.Va."

128. **Churches. Methodist Episcopal. Morgantown.** Records, 1847-1917. 1 reel of microfilm. Loan for duplication by the Wesley Methodist Church, Morgantown, 1957. Nos. 1014, 1023.

Records, including minutes of the quarterly conference and the Epworth League; lists of church members and probationers; and papers and records relating to baptisms, marriages, and pastors.

129. **Churches. Methodist Episcopal. Oakland District.** Records, 1895-1910. 294p. (photocopies). Loaned for copying by the Reverend Lawrence Sherwood, 1965. No. 1839.

Handwritten journal of the Oakland District Conference, 1895-1910. The district includes Preston and Tucker counties in West Virginia, also western Maryland and bordering areas of Pennsylvania.

130. **Churches. Methodist Episcopal, South. Western Virginia Conference.** Records, 1848-1927. 6 reels of microfilm (34 volumes). Originals in the Annie Merner Pfeiffer Library, West Virginia Wesleyan College, 1961. No. 1501.

Statistical journals, conference journals and reports, conference register, records of various missionary bodies, and financial records. There are session minutes, lists of membership, baptisms, church property, committees, and Sunday school statistics.

The collection also includes the journals and reports of the Western Virginia Conference, Methodist Protestant Church, 1855-1896.

131. **Churches. Monongalia County.** History, 1954. 1 ft. Gift of Mrs. Gideon S. Dodds, 1956. No. 818.

Material prepared by Dr. and Mrs. Gideon S. Dodds, Morgantown, including photographs of 141 church buildings, and a typescript, "A Historical Survey of the Churches of Monongalia County, West Virginia."

132. **Churches. Moorefield Presbyterian.** Records, 1825-1943. 1 reel of microfilm (4 volumes). Originals in possession of the Moorefield Presbyterian Church, 1961. No. 1518.

Session minutes, 1825-1934, the church register, 1825-1943, and a brief history of the church.

133. **Churches. North Mill Creek German Reformed.** Record book, 1771-1899. 1 reel of microfilm (1 volume). Original in possession of Grace Lutheran Church, 1960. No. 1323.

Record book of a Grant County church organized by German settlers sometime prior to 1791. These records are almost entirely in German and include records of baptisms, members, confirmations, deaths, and births. (For typescript English translations, see Historical Records Survey, Grant County, Box 33.)

134. **Churches. Romney and Springfield Presbyterian.** Typescript, 1887. 1 item (photocopy). Original in possession of Mrs. Nancy W. Allen, 1961. No. 1462.

Sketch of Romney and Springfield churches, prepared in 1887 by a committee of the Winchester Presbytery under the Reverend John A. Scott. Contains notes on the rise of Presbyterianism in the Romney area, sketches of pastors John Lye, James Black, William Henry Foote, and George Williamson Finley, and a record of church buildings. Much of the sketch is devoted to the work of Foote.

135. **Churches. St. Paul's Lutheran (Aurora).** Records, (1787-1904) 1956. Ca. 30 items. Gift of the Official Board of St. Paul's Lutheran Church, 1950, 1956. Nos. 192, 847.

Two bound manuscript volumes and loose pages of names, containing lists of communicants, baptisms, marriages, and deaths. These records were edited and published in 1957 by Karl K. Gower as *The Aurora Documents.*

136. **Churches. Somerset County, Pennsylvania.** Records, 1775-1904, 1933. 3 reels of microfilm (2 ft. typescript copies). Originals held by the Western Pennsylvania Historical Society, 1959. No. 1269.

Records of twenty-eight churches of the Evangelical Lutheran, German Reformed, Brethren, and Baptist denominations, and an unpublished master's thesis: "The Records of the Pioneer Churches of Somerset County, Pennsylvania," by Jessie M. Tomb, University of Pittsburgh, 1933. There are English translations for some of the German language records.

137. **Churches. Trinity Episcopal (Martinsburg).** Records, 1817-1921. 2 reels of microfilm (12 volumes). Originals in possession of the Trinity Episcopal Church, 1960. No. 1362.

Registers of Norborne Parish, 1832-1900; minutes of the Vestry, 1817-1921; and collection and account books, 1865-1892. The records also include the parish register, 1846-1905, of Christ Church at Bunker Hill.

138. **Churches. Trinity Episcopal (Parkersburg).** Parish registers, 1843-1930. 1 reel of microfilm (3 volumes). Originals in possession of Trinity Episcopal Church, 1960. No. 1342.

Parish registers include lists of families, baptisms, confirmations, communicants, marriages, burials, and offerings.

139. **Churches. Trinity Methodist (Martinsburg).** Records, 1856-1937. 1 reel of microfilm (2 ft.). Originals in possession of Trinity Methodist Church, 1962. No. 1605.

Church registers, 1866-1923; quarterly conference records, 1886-1927; Women's Missionary Society records, 1919-1937; financial records, invitations, programs, broadside announcements, and pamphlets.

140. **Churches. West Virginia Centennial.** Report forms and photographs, 1963. 1 ft. Gift of county chairmen of the Centennial Church History Project, 1963. No. 1667.

A county-by-county collection of report forms, photographs, and histories of churches in existence for more than a century, assembled during the state centennial year.

141. **Churches. Winchester, Virginia, Presbytery. Records, 1719-1952. 3 items. Gift of Miss Lucy M. Woodworth, 1955. No. 773.**

Two volumes of statistics of Presbyterian churches in the Winchester Presbytery, 1719-1946; and a notebook of correspondence, 1942-1952, of Robert B. Woodworth and John G. Bishop concerning the genealogy of the Poage and allied families and Woodworth's revision of *The Captives of Abb's Valley* (Staunton, Virginia, 1942).

142. **Civil War. Correspondence, 1861-1864. 1 reel of microfilm (81 items). Originals in possession of Mrs. Frances Laird Boyd, 1961. No. 1508.**

Correspondence of Miss Hattie A. Fudge, Tazewell, Virginia. A majority of the letters are written by soldiers of the Forty-fifth Virginia Regiment (Confederate) commanded by Generals John B. Floyd, W. W. Loring, and John Echols. Subjects include Floyd's military engagements, 1861; Battle of Lewisburg, 1862; skirmishes along the line of the Virginia and Tennessee Railroad; and Jubal Early's January, 1864, raid into the South Branch Valley.

143. **Civil War. Diaries, 1862-1865. 5 items and 1 reel of microfilm (1 item). Gifts of Charles H. Ambler, 1956, and Helen V. Barns, 1957; originals held by Washington and Lee University, 1964. Nos. 815, 922, 974, 1720.**

Typed copy of a Confederate soldier's diary entries for April 9-12, 1865, at Appomattox Courthouse; diaries of William M. Goudy, a corporal in Company G, First West Virginia Volunteer Infantry, 1862-1864; journal of Uz Barns, a volunteer in the Union Army from Ritchie County, who fought at Beverly, Harpers Ferry, and Deep Bottom, Virginia, and was at Richmond at the end of the war, 1862-1865; and diary of Frank Smith Reader, March 10-June 25, 1864, a private in Company I, Fifth Regiment, West Virginia Cavalry, which was earlier part of the Second Regiment, Virginia Volunteer Infantry.

144. **Civil War. Letters, 1862-1887. 11 items. Gifts of C. J. Maxwell, 1954, Mrs. Mary Outen Cole, 1954, Paul F. Price, 1961, Harry Mills, 1966, and loan for photoduplication by Mrs. C. H. Smitley, 1961. Nos. 648, 672, 1147, 1480, 1494, 1925.**

T. H. McBee to Zadoc McBee concerning Nathaniel Banks and Stonewall Jackson at Cedar Mountain, August 14, 1862; Horace Kellogg of 123rd Ohio Regiment to Rufus Maxwell concerning robberies by Confederate guerrillas in Tucker County, November 28, 1862; four letters by Harry McDonald of the Thirty-fifth Ohio Volunteer Infantry Regiment from Mississippi, Tennessee, and Alabama, 1862-1863; M. McDonald, Jr., from camp at Washington, D. C.; Sarah Jane Lough of Morgantown to Elza T. Lough of Winchester concerning Confederate troop activities in the Morgantown and Fairmont areas, May 3, 1863; Charles H. Ruggles to Benson J. Lossing concerning location of two Union Army majors captured by Mosby's guerrillas, November 26, 1864; and C. W. D. Smitley, a veteran of the Second West Virginia Cavalry, to General Franz Sigel, giving an account of his activities as a scout in western Virginia.

145. **Civil War**. Military Records Index, 1861-1865. 13 reels of microfilm. Originals in U. S. National Archives, 1964. No. 1751.

Index to service records of volunteer Union soldiers in Virginia and West Virginia, compiled from Record Group 94 in the U. S. Adjutant General's Office.

146. **Civil War**. Miscellaneous papers, 1859-1937. 129 items. Gifts and loans, 1953-1969. Accession numbers follow descriptions below.

An account of activity in Shepherdstown, 1862-1865, from the diary of a Southern sympathizer (76); manuscripts and maps relating to the war collected by E. Luther Cole (78); certificate for purchase of a Confederate bond and a note to Perry Hays regarding the sale of cotton (347); muster roll, October 31, 1864, of Company A, Thirty-sixth Virginia Infantry (438); map of the Tygart River area in Randolph and Barbour counties with notes on Beverly during the war, map of battles and installations in Pendleton, Tucker, and Randolph counties, statements concerning the death of Patrick Duff, copies of entries from the Jefferson County circuit court order book relating to the trial of John Brown, a pardon granted to J. M. Bennett by President Andrew Johnson, July 11, 1865 (572); a typescript, "Grant and Lee," by William D. Ford, letters from O. P. Chitwood and Andrew Price, and a broadside concerning the Hartford Convention, February 18, 1863 (594); certificate of discharge of Isaac W. Curry (760); records of the Sixth Virginia Infantry, 1861-1870 (871); records of Company F, Twelfth West Virginia Volunteer Infantry (915); resolution, August 10, 1866, concerning a monument to the war dead in Oak Grove Cemetery, Morgantown (989); letters of Sergeant B. F. Hughes, Company F, Third West Virginia Infantry, later Company F, Sixth West Virginia Cavalry, written from Camp David, Maryland, Camp New Creek and Camp Elkwater,

West Virginia (1021); "Constitution, Minutes, Correspondence, etc., 1883-1921, of the Society of Ex-Confederates in Hampshire County" (1052); a letter and telegrams, 1861-1864, concerning the sacking of David Goff's home, 1861, fighting around Charleston and Beverly, guerrilla activity, and substitute hiring (1304); letter on camp life in Company F, Sixtieth Virginia Regiment (Confederate) at Princeton, vouchers and accounts of James C. Collins, and Civil War cachets (1345, 1418, 1420); a provost marshal's book listing passes issued at Martinsburg (1396); records of Mason County soldiers in the Thirteenth [West] Virginia Volunteer Infantry (1541); history of the Sixth Ohio Volunteer Infantry by Col. F. C. Loveland, 1888 (1628); record book of the Eighteenth Regiment, West Virginia Militia, formerly 147th Regiment, Virginia Militia, from Palatine, Marion County, including minutes of the Mt. Harmony Literary Society, 1868-1869 (1641); customs certificate for transport of items over the Baltimore and Ohio Railroad from Berkeley County, Virginia, 1863 (1747); draft of a telegram, June 20, 1861, from General George B. McClellan at Clarksburg (1841); papers of Lt. William H. Lawrence, who commanded the Ninth Independent Company, Ohio Volunteer Sharp Shooters (2044); roster of Company E, Fifteenth Regiment, West Virginia Volunteers (2049); order, June 25, 1864, concerning a raid to the Haymond Settlement near Grafton, signed by Jno. H. Showalter (2121).

147. **Civil War.** Scrapbook, 1853 (1861-1865). Gift of Roy Bird Cook, 1956. No. 895.

A notebook of mounted originals and photocopies of letters, orders, muster rolls, clippings, photographs, maps, and telegrams relating mainly to the Civil War in southern West Virginia. Included is a typescript of a notebook of Captain W. D. Thurmond, C. S. A., including a muster roll of Thurmond's Company of Partisan Rangers; a photostat of a West Virginia battle flag showing a variant version of the state seal; original verse, "Wise's Retreat from Hawk's Nest"; muster rolls, returns, letters, and other materials relating to the Eighth, Eleventh and Thirteenth West Virginia Volunteer Infantry regiments. There is also a long letter written in 1853 by John McGee, from Sand Fork, describing agricultural practices in Lewis County.

148. **Civil War. First Regiment, West Virginia Volunteer Infantry.** Records, 1886-1899. 1 ft. Gift of Mrs. Elizabeth Karnes, 1955. No. 696.

Letters, records, and photographs concerning the First Regiment, West Virginia Volunteer Infantry, being mainly the papers of Captain A. L. Hooton, officer of ordnance and supplies. These papers deal with companies A-N, with emphasis on Company K while at camps George H. Thomas, Chickamauga Park, Georgia; Lee, Kanawha City, West Virginia; Poland, Knoxville, Tennessee; and Conrad, Columbus, Georgia, 1898-1899.

149. **Civil War. Harpers Ferry.** Records, 1863-1865. 1 reel of microfilm (3 volumes). Originals in possession of the Pennsylvania Historical Society, 1961. No. 1394.

Records of James W. Brady, provost marshal at Harpers Ferry, 1863-1865, and an order book of department headquarters at Harpers Ferry, 1863.

150. **Civil War. West Virginia.** Records, 1861-1938. 1 reel of microfilm (6 volumes). Originals in the West Virginia Department of Archives and History, 1959. No. 1194.

Military records compiled by Clifford Myers, state historian, lists West Virginia Confederate soldiers by home county and by infantry or cavalry regiment. These records also include a list of West Virginia Confederate soldiers in the Thirty-first Virginia Regiment; the record and roll of Company "G," Tenth Virginia Cavalry, Confederate; and a roster of West Virginia Union soldiers who were awarded service medals.

151. **Clark, Boyers Morgan,** *Compiler.* Records, ca. 1955. Ca. 500p. Gift of Mrs. Don Porter, 1959. No. 1234.

Genealogical record of the William Clarke, Sr., family of Upshur and Randolph counties, compiled by Boyers M. Clark. The records also include such allied lines as James Morgan, Jacob Kittle, William Kelly, and John Helmick families.

152. **Clark, Friend E.,** *Collector.* Papers, 1769-1919. 4 items. Gift of Friend E. Clark, 1936. No. 39.

Typed copies of letters from Berkeley W. Moore to Septimus Hall, written July 3-12, 1919; a copy of a letter from Colonel Charles A. Ronald, Fourth Virginia Infantry, to Governor John Letcher; and a short typed genealogy of the Davis-Cox family, 1769-1898.

153. **Clark, Mary Vinson,** *Compiler.* Manuscript, n.d. 1 reel of microfilm (1 folder). Originals in possession of Miss Mary B. Mullins, 1961. No. 1430.

Unpublished manuscript, "Mountain Ballads and Hymns," compiled by Mary C. Clark with a foreword by John W. Davis. The collection also includes a few miscellaneous ballads and notes on balladry.

154. **Clark Family.** Letters, 1885-1939. 4 ft. Gift of J. B. Clark, 1954. No. 680.

Correspondence among family members while Friend E. Clark was a student at West Virginia University and Johns Hopkins University and Frank Wells Clark was a student at West Virginia University and Harvard Law School. Some of the later letters relate to Friend E. Clark as a teacher at State College, Pennsylvania, and West Virginia University, and to the law practice of Frank Wells Clark at New Martinsville.

155. **Clarke, John P. (1825-1900). Papers, 1851-1900. 3 reels of microfilm (3 ft.). Originals in possession of Mrs. Pauline M. Ash, 1961. No. 1511.**

Correspondence, business and legal papers, surveys, account books, and a diary of a Burning Springs surveyor, oil developer, rural entrepreneur, horticulturalist, and captain of the Little Kanawha River steamer *General Jackson*.

Collection includes a brief journal of a trip from Des Moines, Iowa, to the Forks of the Platte in 1860; papers of Clarke's venture in quartz mining and milling in the Colorado Territory, 1861-1863; surveys of the Burning Springs oil region; letters from James C. Clarke, president of the Wirt Oil and Mining Company of which Clarke was superintendent; papers on the National Grange, the West Virginia Grange (Patrons of Husbandry), cooperatives, and the Ohio, Pennsylvania, and West Virginia Wool Growers Association; a diary of farming operations at Burning Springs; letters from Clarke's brother, James C., while a member of the Pennsylvania senate, 1875-1880; letterheads from Little Kanawha and Ohio Valley mercantile firms and steamboat companies; and family letters.

Other subjects include the Allegheny Valley Railroad; early history of Bethalto, Illinois; the speculative spirit and western expansion, 1860; freighting on the Great Plains during the Civil War; construction of the Chicago, Rock Island, and Pacific Railroad near Council Bluffs in 1868; and the effect of the German crisis of 1866 on American oil prices.

156. **Clarksburg Public Library, *Collector*. Miscellaneous papers, 1782-1865; 1913-1922. 1 volume and ca. 50 items (photocopies) and 1 reel of microfilm (1 volume). Originals in the Clarksburg Public Library, 1960, 1963. Nos. 1285, 1653.**

Subscription list of the Clarksburg Public Library, 1913-1922; Harrison County land papers of John Lang, 1782-1821; land office warrant of Thomas Cunningham, an 1812 veteran, for 160 acres in Illinois; letter from Melville D. Long from Point Lookout Prison, April, 1865; letter to Mrs. John J. Davis, Clarksburg, pertaining to an unexpected invasion of Baltimore by Confederates in July, 1864; and a farm diary, 1856-1861, of P. R. Page, Gloucester County, Virginia, pertaining to the operation of a grain and livestock farm in eastern Virginia.

157. **Clarkson, Roy B. (1926-   ). Typescript, 1964. 130p. Gift of Roy B. Clarkson, 1966. No. 1871.**

"Tumult on the Mountains: Lumbering in West Virginia," by Roy B. Clarkson. The manuscript of a book published in 1966.

158. **Clay County.** Archives, 1858-1900. 5 reels of microfilm (9 volumes). Originals in possession of Clay County Court, 1959. No. 1272.

Deed books, 1858-1892, and order books, 1858-1900.

159. **Claysville Borough.** Documents, 1860. 2 items. Gift of Marcus O. Bond, 1963. No. 1666.

Minutes, election results, and regulations approved by the Claysville Town Council, Wood County.

160. **Cleaver Family.** Papers, 1777-1833. 10 items. Gift of William A. Owens, 1967, 1969. No. 1945.

Land grant to William Cleaver and others for 1,000 acres on the Monongahela River, 1782; certificate for money due B. Cleaver for service in the Virginia Militia, 1783; affidavits concerning the military service of William and Benjamin Cleaver, 1774-1782; in Dunmore's War, at the Falls of the Ohio, and on General George Rogers Clark's expedition against the Indians, including the Shawnee. There is also a petition, 1777, by residents of the Tygart Valley, West Fork of the Monongahela, and Buckhannon Creek settlements requesting the formation of a new county.

161. **Clinton District Sunday School Association.** Minutes, 1894-1950. 3 volumes. Gift of the Association, 1958. No. 1080.

Minutes of a Sunday school association organized at Pisgah Church in Monongalia County, 1894.

162. **Coal Mining.** Patents, April 12, 1921. 1 item. Gift of Harold F. Stanton, 1966. No. 1898.

Letters patent issued by the U. S. Commissioner of Patents to Patrick J. Stanton, Lundale, for self-operating mine doors for locomotives.

163. **Coal Mining.** Records, 1901-1932. 2 ft. Gift of the Reverend Durward B. Brown and James Russell Brown, 1958. No. 1063.

Papers of Lloyd W. Brown, a field engineer with the West Virginia Department of Mines. The collection includes material on mine inspection, accidents, safety and other aspects of mining. There are several blueprints, maps, and drawings of various mining operations in West Virginia.

164. **Coal Mining.** Records, 1917. 8 items (photocopies). Originals held by E. B. Wray and Mrs. Sam Leslie, 1966. No. 1894.

Letters and tables showing mine workers' wages and costs in the New River and Winding Gulf Smokeless coal districts during early 1917.

165. **Coal Mining.** Scrip, ca. 1900-1951. 235 items. Gifts of A. J. Bishop, Justus C. Beury, J. M. Cassels, 1964, 1965. Nos. 1782, 1782-1, 1782-2.

Scrip used by various coal companies in West Virginia and neighboring states. For list of companies and denomination of coins see inventory sheets.

166. **Coal Mining.** Tape recordings, 1963-1964. 4 items. Recordings made by Milton Means, 1963-1964. No. 1742.

Interviews with Ralph Donham, Joseph Martin, and J. B. Riffle of Morgantown, and Cecil Urbaniak of Fairmont concerning coal mining.

167. **Coal Mining.** Tape recordings, 1967. 26 reels of tape (75 interviews). Acquired, 1967. No. 1988.

Interviews conducted by John E. Stealey III with retired coal miners in Monongalia, Randolph, Tucker, Marion, Barbour, Harrison, Preston, and Gilmer counties. There is a listing of names, dates, and locations of interviews.

168. **Coal Sample Index.** 2 typescripts. 14p. Transfer, 1951. No. 498.

Lists of coal samples from Preston and Nicholas counties showing geological horizon, property owners, location, and notebook page references.

169. **Coal Strikes.** Records, 1912-1914. 106 items (28 photostats) and 1 reel of microfilm. Gift of George S. Wallace, 1957, and copies from National Archives, 1960. Nos. 960, 1383.

Records of the coal strikes in southern West Virginia in 1912 and 1913, from the files of Colonel George S. Wallace, the acting judge advocate general, including a typed copy of a speech by Mary "Mother" Jones in several towns in 1912; records of the U. S. Senate, Record Group 46, consisting of documents from hearings before the Committee on Education and Labor, June 2-September 13, 1913.

170. **Coal Strikes.** Telegram, September 2, 1921. 1 item (photocopy). Original in the possession of Festus P. Summers, 1964. No. 1716.

Two-page telegram from the Williamson Kiwanis Club to the Prosecuting Attorney of Boone County concerning an armed group of United Mine Workers preparing to march through Logan County to Mingo County.

171. **Cochran, William.** Receipts, 1816-1838; 1862, 1925. 18 items. No. 972.

Receipts for taxes paid on real and personal property by William Cochran in Marion County and a letter from Madigan Clements of Worthington.

172. **Cockrell, Monroe F.** Correspondence, 1946-1962. 1 volume. Gift of Monroe F. Cockrell, 1962. No. 1572.

Correspondence of a Chicago antiquarian and collector with Roy Bird Cook of Charleston, pertaining to the life of Stonewall Jackson.

173. **Cole, Harry Outen (1874-1950).** Papers, 1909-1950. 2 ft. Gift of Mrs. Cole, 1954. No. 640.

Papers of a Morgantown engineer who was with the Pacific Division of the Panama Canal, 1908-1912. In addition to correspondence there are reports, speeches, newspaper clippings, U. S. documents, photographs, blueprints, and structural drawings of the Panama Canal, with some data on the proposed Nicaraguan canal.

Correspondents include Chapman Revercomb and Melvin C. Snyder. Included is a microfilm of an autobiographical sketch, "Some Episodes in the Life of Harry Outen Cole."

174. **Colgate Coal Company.** Records, 1872, 1874-1875. 74 photocopies (1 volume) and 16 items. Gifts of George E. Pyles and Harry Mitter; originals in possession of William J. Croston, 1967. Nos. 1980, 1981, 1982.

Time book, time sheets, and lists of sales, 1872-1875, of the Colgate Coal Company, near Austen, Preston County. Also included are some records of the Wesling Iron Ore Company of the same area and period.

175. **Collins, Justus (1857-1934).** Papers, 1896-1934. 24 ft. Gift of Justus C. Beury, 1965, and J. B. Wooldridge, 1964. Nos. 1784, 1824.

Correspondence, financial statements, contracts, ledger books, maps, minute books, production and shipping records, and other papers of a southern West Virginia coal operator who was also interested in timber lands, a cement company, rubber tire manufacturing, oil, and gas. Coal fields involved are Pocahontas-Flat Top, New River, Tug River, and Winding Gulf.

Subjects include Tug River and Winding Gulf Coal Operators associations and the Smokeless Coal Operators Association; marketing conditions; price fixing; profits, salaries, and taxes; Interstate Commerce Commission; mining legislation; National Recovery Administration code; U. S. Coal Commission; U. S. Fuel Administration; U. S. Railroad Administration; United Mine Workers of America; wages, workmen's compensation, "Yellow-dog" contract; Baldwin-Felts Detective Agency and mine guard system; life in mining camps; mine safety; Chesapeake and Ohio Railroad; Norfolk and Western Railroad; Virginian Railway; freight rates; and state and local politics.

Correspondents include Jairus Collins, Thomas L. Felts, Isaac T. Mann, W. P. Tams, J. J. Tierney, and managers of Collins' enterprises.

176. **Colwell, Robert C. (1884-1959).** Papers, 1917-1959. 2 ft. Transfer, 1962. No. 1546.

Correspondence, research notebooks, and departmental records of a West Virginia University physicist pertaining to his research in electronics, microwave theory, and the vibration of clamped metal plates (Chladni plates). Correspondents include S. K. Mitra.

177. **Cometti, Elizabeth, and Festus P. Summers.** Typescript, 1966. Gift of Elizabeth Cometti and Festus P. Summers, 1971. No. 2199.

Manuscript and galley proofs of *The Thirty-Fifth State*, a documentary history of West Virginia edited by Elizabeth Cometti and Festus P. Summers.

178. **Congressional Autographs.** 1899-1900. 1 volume, 73p. No. 698.

Autographs of members of the House of Representatives, the Fifty-sixth Congress, 1899, collected by Alston Gordon Dayton, the representative from West Virginia's second district.

179. **Conley, Phil M. (1887-).** Correspondence, 1912-1913. 7 items. Gift of Phil M. Conley, 1962. No. 1617.

Letters to Conley while editor of the West Virginia University *Monongalian*, giving reminiscences of West Virginia University presidents Alexander Martin, John Rhey Thompson, Eli Marsh Turner, and Daniel B. Purinton.

180. Consolidated Laundry Company. Papers, 1892, 1920-1921, 1928. 31 items. Acquired, 1964. No. 1724.

Correspondence of Phil C. Jacks, vice-president of the Consolidated Laundry Company, Charleston, concerning the sale of stock, investment advertising, and the establishment of plants in several West Virginia towns. Also included is a prospectus of the Bennett Motor Company, Huntington; a certificate from the Lewisburg Female Institute, 1892; and a typescript sketch on travel in Scotland and Greece in 1928.

181. Consolidation Coal Company. Papers, 1915-1956. 1 folder. Gift of Miss Rose Gaskill, 1959. No. 1159.

A typescript report of J. C. Gaskill, assistant consulting engineer, on accidents, fires, and explosions at the mines of the Consolidation Coal and other companies, 1886-1926, and newspaper clippings pertaining to Consolidation's operation in the Fairmont area.

182. Cook, Roy Bird (1886-1961), *Collector.* Papers, 1773 (1819-1908) 1953. 2 ft. Gift of Roy Bird Cook, 1935-1942, 1956. Nos. 81, 858.

Originals, typescripts, and photocopies of letters, clippings, newspapers, maps, photographs, and pamphlets relating mainly to the Civil War and the Tavenner family. The Civil War materials include: "Recollections of the Civil War," by E. D. Camden; "Journal of Henrietta Fitzhugh Barr, 1862-1863," a narrative with a Confederate viewpoint relating civilian affairs at Ravenswood and military events in western Virginia, "Diary Extracts, Capt. James S. Cassady, 1866," a sketch of the Kanawha Riflemen, C. S. A.; letters written by W. Cabell Tavenner in New Orleans, Louisiana, 1860-1861, to his family in Weston, showing the development of his sympathy for the Confederacy; a letter of Lieutenant W. M. McKinney, Company I, Fifteenth Regiment Indiana Volunteers, July 25, 1861, describing the battle of Rich Mountain and his travels in western Virginia; and material on Jacob W. Marshall's Guerrilla Band of the Nineteenth Virginia Cavalry.

Copyright records for western Virginia, 1822-1845, a Cook family genealogy, and notes on sources used by A. S. Withers in writing *Chronicles of Border Warfare* (Clarksburg, 1831), are in the collection, as well as surveys and other land papers for Wood and Harrison counties. Writers of letters and persons mentioned include: Henry Bedinger, J. M. Bennett, A. I. Boreman, John Brown, Frank Hereford, C. D. Hubbard, T. J. Jackson, and Enoch Rector.

183. Cook, Roy Bird (1886-1961), *Collector.* Papers, 1882-1943. 7 ft. Gift of Roy Bird Cook, 1961. No. 1528.

Correspondence, military records, clippings, account books, church records, and genealogical records collected by Roy Bird Cook primarily from the papers of Marcellus W. Zimmerman of Lewisburg.

The papers include the records of the Lewisburg Methodist Episcopal Church, 1834-1843; materials on the Old Lewisburg Academy, Lewisburg Female Institute, and the Lewisburg Seminary; marriage records, cemetery readings, and biographical sketches of area persons and families including Burnside, Beirne, Alexander, Van Bibber, Clendenin, Matthews, Reynolds, Nickell, Smith, Caldwell, Crawford, Curry, Thompson, Feamster, Creigh, Haines, Anderson, and Gilliam; papers on local history dealing with roads, taverns, schools, stage lines, old houses, newspapers, the Civil War in Lewisburg, sketches of Confederate generals, fighting in the Greenbrier area, and a manuscript, "Recollection of the Battle of Cedar Creek," by Milton Humphreys; correspondence of Thomas H. Dennis, 1899-1921, editor of the *Greenbrier Independent;* letters and military papers of Confederate General Alexander W. Reynolds, 1835-1875, pertaining to military life in the far West during the 1830s, the Seminole War, the Civil War in Tennessee, Georgia, Vicksburg, Mississippi, and West Virginia. Several of Reynolds' letters were written from Cairo and Alexandria, Egypt, where he fled following the war and served in the Army of the Khedive under the command of Confederate General W. W. Loring. Other papers include the military records of the Thirty-first Virginia Infantry Regiment, and material pertaining to the Thirteenth Virginia Infantry, Putnam County Volunteer Infantry, Berkeley County Company (organized in 1859 after the John Brown raid), Bryan's Battery, Hardy Blues, First Virginia Cavalry, Jefferson Guards, Second Virginia Infantry, Thirty-sixth Battery, Virginia Cavalry, Eighteenth West Virginia Militia, Greenbrier Light Infantry Grays, and Union and Confederate veterans organizations; and records of local business firms including Pare and Son, *Greenbrier Independent*, White Sulphur Hotel, Hopkins House, J. H. Oley Cary, and the Farmer's Bank of Virginia.

Subjects include cadet training at West Point; Confederate camps, Generals Echols, Lee, Grant, Sherman, and Early; and Presbyterianism in Greenbrier County.

184. Cook, Roy Bird (1886-1961), *Collector.* Papers, 1865-1960. 18 ft. Acquired, 1962. Nos. 1379, 1561.

Loose papers, manuscript volumes, and bound notebook volumes arranged by Dr. Cook, relating to Stonewall Jackson, the Civil War, and West Virginia local history. Correspondence and personal papers of Roy Bird Cook, 1909-1961; originals and copies of Stonewall Jackson letters and papers, 1838-1863, and members of the Jackson family, 1801-1960; correspondence and papers, 1840-1884, 1952-1955, of the Hays family, including Samuel L. and Peregrine Hays of Gilmer County; records of the Thirty-first Regiment Virginia Infantry, 1861-1877, and later correspondence, clippings, sketches, and papers about the regiment and its members.

Other Civil War and local history materials are in the papers of the following families or individuals: Camden family, Mary Belt Sprigg Camden, J. A. J. Lightburn, John McCausland, James C. MacFarland, Francis H. Pierpont, Quarrier family, and Ruffner family. Other correspondents include George W. Atkinson, J. M. Bennett, Arthur I. Boreman, John Esten Cooke, J. D. Cox, George Crook, H. G. Davis, Jubal H. Early, Charles J. Faulkner, Rutherford B. Hayes, Daniel H. Hill, C. D. Hubbard, John D. Imboden, J. J. Jackson, Albert Gallatin Jenkins, John E. Kenna, John Letcher, George McClellan, William A. MacCorkle, William McKinley, John Mosby, and Nathan B. Scott.

The notebook series of manuscripts, transcriptions, clippings, and photographic materials relate to the following topics: Stonewall Jackson, Mary Anna Morrison Jackson, Colonel George Jackson, and Thomas Jackson Arnold; the Civil War, including originals and copies of several soldiers' diaries, journals, and letters; Douglas Southall Freeman; Lewis County; Charleston and the Kanawha Valley; George Washington; Camden family; Granville Davisson Hall; and West Virginia local history.

Printed guides to these collections are available.

185. **Cooke, Philip Pendleton (1816-1850)**. Manuscript (typescript copy), ca. 1850-1864. Photocopies (1 folder). Typescript property of John D. Allen, 1959. No. 1225.

Typescript copy of Philip Pendleton Kennedy's manuscript biography of Philip Pendleton Cooke, a Martinsburg writer and poet. There is an editorial note on the authorship of the document by Professor John D. Allen who made this copy from the original manuscript in the Bevan Papers, Millwood, Virginia.

186. **Coon, Cline M.**, *Compiler.* Genealogy, 1966-1970. 2 reels of microfilm (1,016 pages). Microfilmed by the Genealogical Library of the Church of the Latter Day Saints, 1967, 1970. No. 2010.

Descendants of Philip Coon (Koon) of western Virginia by Dr. Cline M. Koon. A preliminary study, 1967, and an expanded edition, 1970.

187. **Cooper, Homer C.**, *Compiler.* Typescripts, 1959, 1963, 1969, 1970, 1971. 8 items. Gifts of Homer C. Cooper, 1959, 1969-1971. Nos. 1258, 1647, 2084.

Genealogies of the James Cooper (1780-1845), Nancy Agnes Woodell (1785), Joseph Woodell (1752-1834), and Elizabeth Woodell (d. 1820) families. Other families include Hall, Springston, Lambert, Whitman, Rodgers, McKemy, Ferrell-Farrell, Gothard, Wilson, and Patton. There is also a sketch of Joseph William Cooper, a resident of Pocahontas

County who served in the Confederate Army and a letter written from Shepherdstown, July 27, 1864, concerning army life.

188. **Cooper, Matthew M. (d. 1900).** Letters, 1934-1935. 13 items. Gift of Mrs. Walter Stuart, 1956. No. 917.

Letters to Walter Stuart, editor of the West Union *Record*, West Union, from Mrs. Beatrice H. Cooper, Sanoma, West Virginia, regarding the life of her husband, Colonel Matthew M. Cooper, a newspaper editor and politician. Mention is made of William Jennings Bryan in West Virginia and the newspaper, *The Crisis*.

189. **Core, Earl L. (1902-   ).** Papers, 1920-1969. 35 ft. Gift of Earl L. Core, 1959, 1961. Nos. 1197, 1556, 1730.

Personal and professional correspondence and office files of the chairman of the Department of Biology, West Virginia University. The papers pertain to Core's work in botanical research, as curator of the University's Herbarium, organizer of the Southern Appalachian Botanical Club, and editor of the organization's journal, *Castanea*. The papers also reflect Core's interest in religious, historical, and civic activities in Morgantown and Monongalia County.

190. **Core, Earl L., *Collector*.** Papers, ca. 1840, 1927, 1942. 3 folders. Gift of Earl L. Core, 1959. Nos. 1190, 1251, 1275.

Letters of Georgia C. Price, Blackstone, Virginia, pertaining to the nineteenth century families, local history and lore of Core and the surrounding communities in western Monongalia County; letter written ca. 1840 describing the country around Martinsburg, Ohio; and a letter from Campbell Jobes to Earl L. Core, Elm Grove, July 28, 1927.

191. **Cornwell, C. M.** Papers, 1840-1919. 1 ft. Gift of Floyd M. Cornwell, 1955. No. 803.

Papers of C. M. Cornwell, a surveyor and justice of the peace of Barbour County. Included are copies of surveys, plats, deeds, and court case papers; surveyor's notebooks and minutes of commissioners' meetings; survey calls on the re-survey of the Barbour-Taylor County line, 1894; and family correspondence.

192. **Cornwell, John Jacob (1867-1953).** Papers and records, ca. 1843 (1896-1953). 110 ft. Gift of Mrs. Eugene E. Ailes and John C. Ailes, 1957. No. 952.

Papers of the fifteenth governor of West Virginia who was a newspaper publisher in Romney, an orchardman, lawyer, and counsel for the Baltimore and Ohio Railroad. There are a few papers of W. B. Cornwell. The collection includes personal and business correspondence, 1896-1953; correspondence as governor, 1916-1922; legal papers, ca. 1843-1916; and material relating to "Cornwell Day," 1931; Baltimore and Ohio and other railroads; Romney Orchard Company, ca. 1916-1919; South Branch Development Company, ca. 1913-1926; newspaper publishing; and other subjects.

193. **Couchman, George.** Family papers, 1765-1935. Ca. 300 items. Acquired, 1959. No. 1184.

Papers of a Berkeley County farmer and his descendants include the estate papers of Nicholas Stroyer; business and legal papers of George, Henry J., Benjamin S. and Harman L. Couchman; correspondence of Adrian W. Lamon, John W. Marshall, J. Marshall Neel, the Reverend A. A. P. Neel of Shepherdstown, colportage agent of the Baltimore Conference M. E. Church South, Professor J. Wilbur Neel of Romney, and various members of the Couchman and Neel families.

The collection includes the subscription list for the Reverend C. P. Heathe, 1823; quarterly reports and manuscript minutes of the Cherry Grove Grange, No. 13, Patrons of Husbandry of West Virginia, Berkeley County, 1892, 1893; materials on Methodism in the Berkeley County area; pocket diaries; and family pictures.

194. **County Court Maps, 1895-1915.** 20 items. Transfer, 1952. No. 350.

Land plats, plans, surveys, and profiles of public roads, buildings, railroads, farms, and private residences in Brooke, Randolph, and Wetzel counties.

195. **Courtney Family.** Papers, 1804-1920. Ca. 200 items. Gift of Miss Ethel Courtney, 1962. No. 1629.

Papers of a Monongalia County farm family residing near Maidsville include the farm account books of John and John J. Courtney, 1831-1877; family Bible records and photographs; college essays of Alpheus Courtney, a West Virginia University student; manuscript ciphering book, 1817; diary of Ulysses J. Courtney, 1878-1883 (7 volumes) pertaining to lumbering, farming, and livestock operations, and community religious and social life; correspondence; steamboat bills of lading, invoices of mercantile stores; Civil War bounty receipts; a record of lumbering operations, 1878; and records of the Bethel (Methodist) Church.

Subjects include the construction of the Monongahela Valley Railroad; frontier conditions in Iowa; Morgantown Bridge Company; and Methodism within the Baltimore and West Virginia conferences.

Correspondents include Alston G. Dayton.

196. **Courtney-Lazell Family.** Papers, 1780. 16 items (some photocopies). Gift of John C. Anthony, 1966. No. 1875.

Land grants, treasury warrant records, survey maps, scale drawings, and correspondence relating to landholdings in Monongalia County, Pittsburgh coal properties, and descendants of Thomas Courtney. Grants are as early as 1780 and center in Cass District. There is a War of 1812 payroll for Captain Robert Courtney's company. Names include Thomas Lazell, Michael and William Courtney.

197. **Cover, Michael Anthony,** *Collector.* Papers, 1844-1902. 44p. (all but 2 items are photocopies). Originals in possession of Michael Cover, 1966. Nos. 1781-1, 1781-2.

Naturalization papers of Feit Spindler, Somerset County, Pennsylvania, 1844; three smallpox immunization certificates, 1804, 1811, 1830, in German; confirmation certificate of Andrew Spindler, 1868; deed between George Maust and Trustees of the St. Peter's Lutheran Church, 1870, for land in Preston County; church record of the St. Peter's Evangelical Lutheran congregation of Hazelrun, Preston County, 1861-1870, 1879-1902. The originals are two diplomas of Watson Moore from Merchant's College, Pittsburgh, 1851, 1852.

198. **Cox, Mrs. Lawrence M.** Papers, ca. 1816 (1935-1940). 1 ft. Gift of Mrs. Lenore Brown, 1959. No. 1206.

Genealogical records compiled and collected by Mrs. Cox include correspondence, Revolutionary War records of Monongalia County veterans, Bible records of various West Virginia families, and the records of the Thomas Cox, James Curtis, George Dement, John Devore, Lewis Frankenburger, Dennis Springer, Joseph Bennett, John Burrough, Ulwrick Hostetter, Samuel Hyman, James Coburn (Cobun), Daniel Vanata, David Wherry, Whitham, and Jacob Wolfe families. The collection also includes the diary of J. H. Wherry, 1859, and the papers of Comrade Lawrence M. Cox, commander of the Colonel C. W. Cramer Camp, United States Spanish-American War Veterans, Morgantown, 1937-1939.

199. **Craig, Fred E.** Papers, 1910-1945. 207 items. Gift of Fred E. Craig, 1954. No. 716.

Copies of *The Reedy News*, a Roane County newspaper, along with correspondence and papers of the editor, Fred E. Craig; data on the Prohibition party in Roane County in 1936; and clippings of obituaries from the newspaper.

200. **Cramer, C. W.** Papers, 1894-1918. 1 ft. No. 351.
Papers of a Morgantown attorney, including correspondence, broadsides, and other materials relating to politics in Monongalia County.

201. **Crawford, Stanton C.,** *Collector.* Papers, 1842-1964. 2 folders. Gift of Mrs. Stanton C. Crawford, 1968. No. 2027.
Correspondence, notes, newspaper clippings, and photographs. There is an account book for 1864-1885 kept by John A. Crawford of Holliday's Cove; a typescript carbon manuscript of *Pittsburgh as Viewed from Down River* by Crawford; and genealogical information on the Hodges-Brown-Wilson families.

202. **Crogan, Patrick J.** (1856-1949). Papers, ca. 1900-1930. 34 ft. Gift of Mrs. Bess Fawcett and Miss Mamie Fawcett, 1950. No. 201.
Correspondence and legal papers of a Preston County attorney who was counsel for the Baltimore and Ohio Railroad. There is much material on cases tried by Crogan for banks, utilities, lumber, and coal companies.

203. **Crouch, Moses H.** Papers, 1802, 1821 (1830-1899). 792 items. Gift of Paul McNeel Crouch, 1955. No. 746.
The business papers of Moses H. Crouch, a farmer and miller who lived near Huttonsville. Included are two ledgers, 1839-1889 and 1853-1870, containing records of grain sold.

204. **Crump, James M.,** *Compiler.* Typescript, ca. 1950. 1 reel of microfilm (1 item). Original in possession of James M. Crump, 1960. No. 1280.
"The Vanbibber family in Mason County," by James M. Crump, recounts the early history of Mason County, ca. 1774-1810.

205. **Cunningham, William Cephas** (1887-). Typescript, October 7, 1954. 1 item. Gift of Nellie E. Cunningham, 1954. No. 665.
A short typescript biographical sketch of Cunningham.

206. **Cupp, William E.** Papers, 1839-1948. 2 ft. Gift of Mrs. Marie Nestor, 1954. No. 656.
Business records, correspondence, newspaper clippings, photographs, and other papers of the Cupp family, including Will E. Cupp, Mary J. Cupp, and Marie Cupp Nestor, of St. George, Tucker County, West

Virginia. Included are Tucker County court fee books, 1856-1898, and personal and general store account books, 1897-1933.

207. **Currency. Confederate.** Notes, 1861-1864. 8 items (5 are photoprints). Originals in possession of H. E. Matheny, 1961. Nos. 302, 397.

Currency notes from Lewisburg, Union, Charles Town, Richmond, and Confederate States of America.

208. **Currency. United States, Confederate, State, Continental.** Notes and coin, 1772-1899. 495 items. Transfers, various dates. No. 2096.

A collection of United States, Confederate, Continental, Colonial, and State notes. The latter includes notes from Alabama, Georgia, Delaware, Virginia, Maryland, District of Columbia, South Carolina, Connecticut, Ohio, and Pennsylvania. There is also one copper U. S. one cent piece, 1841. A detailed listing is available in the library.

209. **Curry, J. N. (1863-   ).** Papers, 1894-1896, 1966. 1 folder. Gift of Mrs. Arthur R. Ward, 1969. No. 2082.

Papers of oil and gas driller and producer in Tyler County and other places. The collection consists of three diaries, January 1, 1894, through December 31, 1896; a typescript; and clippings. The diaries contain daily comment on wells drilled, including hours worked, depth of well, difficulties encountered, geologic strata, number of barrels of oil produced per hour or pressure of gas flow.

Diaries include personal affairs, wages received and paid, income from oil sold, rent on leased property, oil market quotations, local affairs in Sistersville and Tyler County, voting in elections of 1894 and 1896, fire at the Big Moses Gas Well, drilling in the United States and Mexico, salt wells in West Virginia, biographical information on W. A. Furbee, and Drake and Burning Springs wells controversy.

210. **Curry, Richard Orr (1931-   ).** Manuscript, 1961. 1 item. Gift of Richard Orr Curry, 1966. No. 1922.

Typescript of doctoral dissertation, 1961, which was later published as *A House Divided: A Study of Statehood Politics and the Copperhead Movement in West Virginia during the Civil War.*

211. **Curry, Richard Orr (1931-   ),** *Collector.* Papers, 1849-1959. 1 box. Gift of Richard Orr Curry, 1959. No. 1203.

West Virginia mountain tales by Richard Orr Curry; papers of Jacob W. Mathews, a merchant from Alvon; papers of Charles R. Mathews, judicial officer at New Helena, Nebraska; correspondence of Catherine White Hoke of Alvon, pertaining to family affairs; papers of Jacob W. Mathews including correspondence pertaining to the Confederate "Immortal Six Hundred"; Confederate veteran affairs; business papers of the firm of Hoylman and Mathews; Charles R. Mathews papers consisting of essays, business receipts, and letters pertaining to farming in Missouri, 1867, emigration from West Virginia, the Farmer's Alliance, and the New Helena Literary Society; and a brochure of the Pence Spring Oil and Gas Company (Hinton, 1903).

212. **Curtis, William B. (1821-1891).** Papers, 1830-1954. 1 reel of microfilm (5 volumes and 9 folders). Originals in possession of Charles Jerome, 1962. No. 1591.

Papers of a brigadier general of the Twelfth West Virginia Volunteer Infantry and his family from West Liberty include correspondence, business and legal papers, military and veterans' records, photographs, clippings, and account books.

Includes papers of West Liberty Post 78, Department of West Virginia G. A. R.; records and photographs of the Twelfth West Virginia Infantry Regiment; photographs, clippings and published and unpublished material pertaining to the town of West Liberty and the Normal School; local and state historical materials compiled by Maude Curtis; mercantile letterheads of Wheeling; West Liberty Presbyterian Sunday School register, 1830-1834; C. N. Short's register of funerals, 1893-1917; and a Civil War diary and account book, 1863-1865.

Subjects include Montgomery and Shotwell family history, West Liberty Academy and Bethany College.

213. **Cutright Collection.** 1887-1950. 3 ft. Gift of Miss Iva Cutright and Mrs. Allene Reed Cutright, 1950, 1954, 1955. Nos. 202, 635, 802.

The papers of genealogists in Buckhannon, consisting of correspondence, family notes, newspaper clippings, and some printed items relating to genealogy. Correspondence of Iva, Corrine, Allene, Mollie, and Pearl Cutright is included, as well as obituaries clipped from Buckhannon, Clarksburg, and Parkersburg newspapers, 1926-1939; clippings on Upshur and Harrison County history; a list of Revolutionary War soldiers and pensioners; and notes on some early settlers in the Buckhannon area, including the Carney, Westfall, and Cutright families.

214. **Dadisman, A. J. (1881-1965).** Papers, 1914-1963. 6 ft. Gift of A. J. Dadisman Estate, 1966. Nos. 879, 1873.

Papers of an agricultural economics professor at West Virginia University, including correspondence, reprints and manuscripts of articles, lecture and research notes, diaries of trips, personal ledgers, pictures, and broadsides. Subjects include Monongalia County Historical Society; wildlife; collecting trips to Canada, Alaska, Labrador, and South Africa; agriculture; genealogy of the Dadisman family; and camel transportation in the U. S. Correspondents include Charles H. Ambler, Nelle Ammons, William D. Barns, A. B. Brooks, Andrew Edmiston, Paul H. Price, Edward M. Steel, Jr., and Harry G. Wheat.

There is also a tape recording and typed transcript of an interview with Professor Dadisman conducted in 1956.

215. **Daily, John (1829-1911).** Typescript, 1861-1911. 6p. Transfer, n.d. No. 352.

A sketch of the life of John Daily, a merchant and dentist of Westernport, Maryland, and Piedmont, West Virginia, who was born at Springfield, Hampshire County. Mainly an account of Daily's Civil War service with the Eleventh Virginia Cavalry, C. S. A., and his participation in the capture of General George Crook and General Benjamin F. Kelley at Cumberland, Maryland, in February, 1865.

216. **Dana Brothers.** Papers, 1871-1889. 4 volumes and 1 reel of microfilm (2 volumes). Gift and loan of Amherst Industries, 1968. No. 2063.

Production, inventory, shipping, payroll, labor, and sales records of Dana Brothers, the partnership of George H. and S. F. Dana of Kanawha County in coal mining and general merchandise. There is also a letter book of George H. Dana created while he served as agent, 1871-1875, in England for Jos. Hall Manufacturing Company, holder of the English patent on James Leffel's turbine waterwheel.

217. **Dandridge, Danske (1858-1914).** Letters, 1869-1913. 1 ft. Gift of Miss Nina Mitchell, 1957. No. 978.

Letters to Danske Dandridge, mainly from members of her family. There are also letters from magazine editors, G. P. Putnam's Sons, William Hayes Ward, H. C. Hopkins, and Washington Gladden. Part of the correspondence relates to the Bedinger and Lawrence-Townley families.

218. **Daniel, John M.** Papers, 1891-1898. 23 items. Transfer, 1950. No. 353.

Letters, receipts, advertising circulars, and other items of a clerk of the Jefferson County Court, Charles Town.

219. **Daughters of the American Revolution, Colonel John Evans Chapter, Morgantown.** Records, 1903-1947. 3 ft. Gift of the chapter, 1948. No. 483.

Correspondence, 1903-1947; lists of names of Revolutionary War soldiers and officers, burials, location of graves, and pensions. There is a list of frontier forts in Monongalia County; data on servicemen in World Wars I and II; and genealogical information on about one hundred families.

220. **Daughters of the American Revolution, Elizabeth Ludington Hagans Chapter, Morgantown.** Records, 1892 (1903-1947). 4 ft. Gift of the chapter, 1949. No. 474.

Correspondence, reports, and other manuscripts of the Morgantown chapter of the D. A. R. relating to the history of Stewartstown, Morgantown, and Monongalia County; also genealogical materials for this area.

221. **Davis, Henry Gassaway (1823-1916).** Papers, 1865-1916. 86 ft. Gift of John T. Davis, and transfer from West Virginia University History Department, 1932, 1955. Nos. 13, 717.

Correspondence and other papers of a Democrat who served in the West Virginia Legislature, 1866-1871, and the U. S. Senate, 1871-1883. Davis was the Democratic vice-presidential nominee in 1904 and a member of several Pan-American commissions and agencies in the period 1889-1916. The collection reflects Davis' political activities and his extensive interests in lumbering, coal, and banking.

Correspondents include: John D. Alderson, George W. Atkinson, Thomas F. Bayard, August Belmont, James G. Blaine, William J. Bryan, Johnson N. Camden, Andrew Carnegie, William E. Chilton, Alston G. Dayton, Spencer Dayton, General Porfirio Diaz, Stephen B. Elkins, Charles J. Faulkner, Sr., Charles J. Faulkner, Jr., John W. Garrett, James Cardinal Gibbons, Arthur P. Gorman, Benjamin Harrison, John E. Kenna, Daniel S. Lamont, Daniel B. Lucas, James M. Mason II, William A. MacCorkle, D. W. Voorhees, Thomas J. Walsh, William C. Whitney, and William Windom.

222. **Davis, Henry Gassaway (1823-1916).** Papers, 1867-1916. 1 reel of microfilm. Transfer, 1958. No. 1028.

Two private account books, 1867-1915, and a letter book, 1898-1916, which mentions several state and national Democratic leaders including Stephen B. Elkins, and John T. McGraw. There is information on the congressional election of 1900 and the candidacy of Col. T. B. Davis. The papers also include miscellaneous clippings, newspapers, letters, and printed items relating to Davis' business affairs, the Davis Child Shelter, and the West Virginia Semi-Centennial Celebration.

223. **Davis, Innis C.** Tape recording, September 30, 1966. 1 item. No. 1919.

Tape recording of an interview with Mrs. Thomas (Innis C.) Davis in Charleston. Subjects include life in southern West Virginia during the coal strikes, 1913-1922.

224. **Davis, John J.** (1835-1916). Papers, 1800-1953. 5 ft. Gift of Mrs. Julia Davis Healy, 1960, 1967. Nos. 1366, 1385, 1946.

Correspondence, business and legal papers, essays, speeches, clippings, family photographs, and printed material of a Clarksburg lawyer, member of the Wheeling Convention of 1861, and congressman, 1873-1877.

Papers include Davis' correspondence while a law student in Lexington, Virginia, 1853-1855; letters from his aunt, Margaret Steen, 1848-1861, commenting on school teaching and society in ante-bellum Mississippi and Arkansas; letters from his fiancee, Anna Kennedy 1860-1862; letters, 1894-1916, from his brother Rezin C., a Louisville, Kentucky, lawyer and politician; correspondence between John W. Davis and Julia McDonald Davis, 1894-1900; correspondence, legal papers, accounts, and estate papers of Davis' father, John (1797-1863), a Clarksburg saddlemaker; and papers of the Clarksburg and Philippi Turnpike Company, 1850-1860.

Subjects include Woodburn Seminary; Know-Nothingism in Clarksburg, 1855; Clarksburg and Philippi Turnpike, 1850-1860; Lincoln-Douglas debates; the secession crisis in northern Virginia; the Wheeling conventions of 1861; the Reorganized Government of Virginia; West Virginia statehood; the Battle of Shiloh; Clarksburg Presbyterian Church; John S. Carlile; Reconstruction and Bourbon politics in West Virginia, 1866-1895; Kentucky and the presidential elections of 1896-1908; and the Lot Bowen Mining Company. Correspondents include George W. Atkinson, Jacob B. Blair, John W. Davis, Granville D. Hall, Henry Haymond, John J. Jacobs, Daniel B. Lucas, John W. Mason, and Francis H. Pierpont.

225. **Davis, John William** (1873-1955). Papers, 1924-1943, 1953. 32 items. Gift of Mrs. John J. D. Preston, 1969. No. 2080.

Correspondence of the 1924 Democratic presidential nominee; draft of a speech on legislative power; tickets to the Democratic National Convention in New York; and a poem concerning Davis' candidacy for president in 1924. Correspondence is between Davis and his nephew, John J. D. Preston of Charleston. Subjects mentioned include politics, World War II, Davis' law practice, and family matters.

226. **Davis, Julia McDonald (b. 1900).** Papers, 1866-1963. 2 ft. Gift of Mrs. Charles Healy, 1965. No. 1856.

Correspondence, manuscripts, class notes and other papers of an author and daughter of John W. Davis. Subjects include a biographical sketch of E. H. McDonald, Miss Davis' grandfather; reminiscences of the Civil War; memoirs of Col. A. W. McDonald; notes on the trips of John W. Davis, especially in 1924. Correspondents include John W. Davis, William L. Wilson, and Julia McDonald.

227. **Davis, William P. (1946-   ), Collector.** Papers, ca. 1920-1970. 1 ft., 1 reel of microfilm, and one tape recording. Gift and loan of William P. Davis, 1969, 1970. No. 2113.

Campaign materials of political parties and literature of controversial organizations, including newspapers, magazines, leaflets, buttons, stickers, cards and other items. There is material on the Ku Klux Klan of the 1920s, including a tape recording of Klan songs.

228. **Davis Coal and Coke Company.** Records, ca. 1898-1949, 1955. 1 ft. Gift of R. B. Wooters, 1958. Nos. 1082, 1112.

Correspondence, graphs, blueprints, maps, pictures, and other printed material relating to the coal industry in Tucker County.

229. **Davis Family.** Papers, 1809-1916. Ca. 200 items. Acquired, 1948. No. 140.

Personal and business papers of Isaac, Albert, and Silas R. Davis in Ohio and Marshall counties.

230. **Davison Family.** Papers, 1924. 8p. (photocopies). Originals in possession of Mrs. Glenn Longacre, 1960. No. 1365.

A preliminary sketch and two letters from A. H. Davison, Des Moines, Iowa, pertaining to the history of the Davison-Davisson-Davidson family.

231. **Dawson, William M. O. (1853-1916).** Papers, 1873-1960. Ca. 200 items. Gift of Donald O. Blagg, 1963. No. 1697.

Newspaper clippings and extracts, notes, biographical material, and correspondence, compiled by Donald O. Blagg for a study of the life of a Preston County editor, Republican politician, and the state's twelfth governor (1905-1909), and Blagg's unpublished manuscript on Dawson's career.

232. **Dayton, Alston G. (1857-1920).** Papers, ca. 1848-1920. 77 ft. Gifts of Arthur S. Dayton, Mrs. Arthur S. Dayton, and transfer, 1938, 1950, 1955. Nos. 52, 122, 215, 741.

Correspondence and papers of Alston G. Dayton, ca. 1875-1920, bearing on politics and the industrial development of West Virginia. Dayton was an attorney in Barbour County, in the United States House of Representatives from 1894 to 1905, and judge of the United States District Court for the northern district of West Virginia, 1905-1920. Included also are six boxes of papers, 1848-1899, of Spencer Dayton, father of Alston G. Dayton, and five boxes of papers, 1898-1910, of Fred O. Blue's law practice in Philippi.

233. **Dayton, Arthur S. (1887-1948).** Papers, 1923-1959. 2 ft. Gift of Mrs. Ruth Woods Dayton and transfer, 1959, 1964. Nos. 1216, 1723.

Correspondence of Arthur S. Dayton with American and English book dealers. There are book catalogs and clippings collected by Dayton and the West Virginia University Library.

234. **Dayton, Ruth Woods,** *Collector.* Papers (1801-1948) 1957. 1 ft. Gifts of Mrs. Ruth Woods Dayton, 1950, 1959. Nos. 206, 1066, 1216.

Correspondence, business and legal papers, college notebooks, biographical records, and photographs of Spencer Dayton (1820-1903), a Philippi lawyer, and his son, Alston G. (1857-1920), a lawyer, congressman (1895-1905), and federal judge.

Subjects include the state legislature of 1872; A. G. Dayton's college days at West Virginia University; his support of the "Big Navy" program in Congress; his tour of British Naval yards in 1903; his criticism of the poor quality of education at the university in 1913; and his judgeship and final illness.

The collection also includes "The Records of the See Family of Virginia," by T. J. J. See; history of the Jacob Warwick, Bosworth, and Sinsel families; a sketch of Harman Sinsel, member of the Wheeling Constitutional Convention, 1861-1863; papers, 1801-1837, of Adam See, a Randolph County lawyer and member of the Virginia Constitutional Convention of 1829; a household account book of Samuel and Isabella Woods, grandparents of Mrs. Arthur Dayton, in Philippi, 1849-1852; personal accounts of J. P. Thompson, 1855; and a letter by Mrs. Dayton in 1957 concerning her book, *Lewisburg Landmarks.*

Correspondents include Charles H. Ambler, H. G. Davis, David Goff, and T. J. J. See.

235. **Deakins Family.** Papers, 1778-1925. 2 ft. Gift of Guy A. Deakins, 1950, 1954. Nos. 197, 624, 629.

Materials on several generations of the Deakins family in Maryland and West Virginia. The first generation resided in Montgomery County, Maryland. From 1778 their interests are shown through deeds, agreements, surveys and plats, surveyors' field books, and court papers relative to acreage purchased in Harrison, Monongalia, Preston, Randolph, Tucker, and Upshur counties. Other papers center about Leonard M. Deakins (1747-1824) and his descendants.

Among the correspondents or persons mentioned are Salathial and Thomas James Goff; Henry, George, and William Ashby; David and Philip Menear; Thomas Parsons; Benjamin Harrison; and John Evans. There is correspondence between Francis Deakins, Montgomery County, Maryland, and Benjamin Reeder and William McCleery at Morgantown, 1790-1803. A plat of the town of Salem, ca. 1792, is included.

236. **Debar, Joseph H. Diss (1820-1905).** Letters, 1870-1871. 7 items. Gift of Festus P. Summers, 1964, and acquisition, 1962. Nos. 1577, 1711.

Letters from West Virginia's first commissioner of immigration concerning intrigues for the commissionership, the sale of lots and issuance of deeds to purchasers, and the publication and distribution of *West Virginia Handbook and Immigrants Guide* and *West Virginia Monitor and Real Estate Advertiser.*

237. **deBrahm, John Gerard William.** Report, 1773. 1 reel of microfilm (1 volume). Original in the Widener Library, Harvard University, 1962. No. 1611.

Report of John Gerard William deBrahm to Earl of Dartmouth, secretary of state for the colonies, 1773. The report covers the history, geography, names of early settlers, climate, and boundaries of East Florida and also includes several maps of the area.

238. **Demain Family.** Papers, 1878-1913. 1 ft. Gift of R. C. Eddy, 1956. No. 846.

Miscellaneous business papers of Henry, E. R., and R. H. Demain, and Huston and Demain, contractors and builders, Morgantown.

239. **Dempsey, Jack.** Typescript, n.d. 1 item (photocopy). Original in possession of William T. Bess, 1960. No. 1302.

Story of an abortive boxing match between A. P. "Pat" Canepa and Dempsey at Huntington, 1913.

240.   **Dent, Herbert Warder (b. 1880).** Papers, 1834-1937. 18 items. Gift of Mary Virginia Dent, 1945. No. 88.

Deeds of Peter T. Laishley and Samuel Arnold, Preston County, 1834 and 1837; photographs of the judges of the State Supreme Court of Appeals, 1863-1937; a map of the McGraw and Yates addition to Grafton; and Dent family genealogical data.

241.   **Dent, John.** Pension certificate, September 4, 1834. 1 item. Transfer, n.d. No. 335.

Certificate showing John Dent, Monongalia County, having served as a lieutenant in the Thirteenth Continental Virginia Regiment, and entitled to a pension commencing March 4, 1831.

242.   **Dent, Marmaduke (1801-1880).** 3 volumes, 1855-1891. Gift of Mrs. C. C. Dent, 1955. No. 733.

Daybooks relating to the practice of Dr. Dent as a physician in Monongalia County and for a general store in Granville.

243.   **Dent, Marmaduke Herbert (1849-1909).** Papers, 1870-1967. 18 items. Nos. 285, 1958. Transfer and gift of Mrs. Mary D. Grinnan, 1967. No. 285.

Diploma of Judge M. H. Dent, the first graduate of West Virginia University; letter from Dent to his son, and one letter from Mary Dent Grinnan commenting on M. H. Dent. There are newspaper clippings concerning Dent by Judge Henry Brannon, 1909, and the death of Carrie Dent Armstrong, the daughter of the judge; and pictures of the Dent family and Robert A. Armstrong.

244.   **Dent, William M. (1831-1914).** Papers, 1860, 1868. 7 items. Gift of Frank Dent, 1957. No. 976.

Correspondence, 1868, of William M. Dent and others concerning a school for girls operated by W. Giddings at Melrose, Rockingham County, Virginia; and a program for the seventh annual contest between the Columbian and the Monongalian Literary societies of the Monongalia Academy, 1860.

245.   **Dickinson, J. Q. and Co.** Papers and pictures, 1887-1957. 80 items. Originals in possession of Mrs. Turner Ratrie, 1969. No. 2112.

Correspondence, list of salt furnaces on the Kanawha River, newspaper clippings on the destruction of the Dickinson Salt Works by fire, and a historical sketch of the Kanawha Valley salt industry. There are sixty-eight pictures of the salt works at Malden.

246. **Dickson Brothers.** Journals, 1822-1854. 1 reel of microfilm (2 volumes). Originals in possession of John A. Gibson, 1962. No. 1570.

Journals of James and William Dickson, operators of a gristmill, fulling and carding mill, and a general merchandise store in Blooming Valley, Crawford County, Pennsylvania. The journals contain entries for the account of John Brown for the years 1826-1833.

247. **Dille, Thomas Ray.** Papers, ca. 1774-1939. 59 ft. Gift of the Dille family and Miss Jane Dille, 1950. Nos. 171, 191, 357.

Papers of a Morgantown attorney, genealogist, and antiquarian. There are several series of office files relating to Dille's law practice, and extensive correspondence regarding his historical and genealogical studies.

Families for which there are genealogical compilations include Dille, Ray, Stewart, McFarland, Tennant, David Evans, and John Evans. There are lists of soldiers in the Revolution, Monongalia County soldiers in the War of 1812 and the Mexican War; Monongalia County birth and death records; cemetery readings; copies of wills and indexes of will books; names in real estate and appraisement books; Monongalia Academy and Woodburn Female Seminary ledgers, 1858; and an account book of J. R. Moore, 1837.

248. **Dimmitt Family.** Papers, 1807, 1885-1890. 26p. (copies). Gift of Elizabeth Connor, 1962. No. 1569.

Papers include the will of John Dimmitt, Jefferson County, 1807; biographical sketch of Joseph S. Duckwall (1822-1892), judge of the Twenty-third Circuit Court in Berkeley Springs; and letters from Duckwall pertaining to Dimmitt family history.

249. **Dixon, Thomas W.,** *Collector.* Papers, 1869-1967. 55 items (4 reels of microfilm and 41 photocopies). Gift and loan of Thomas W. Dixon, 1965-1968. Nos. 1855, 1859, 1918, 1989, 1995, 2011, 2019.

Correspondence of William White, a surveyor from Organ Cave, Greenbrier County, 1871-1897; notice of appointment of delegates to the Congressional Convention in Charleston, 1883; cancelled checks and a daybook of Alderson Presbyterian Church and Masonic Hall, 1872-1883; papers of the Alderson Grange Cooperative Association 1879-1886; records for McVeigh Miller and others, 1893-1900; deeds, school surveys, notes, and tax receipts from Greenbrier County; inward delivery book of the Adams Express Company used at the Chesapeake and Ohio depot at Alderson, 1894-1895; account books of a store at Peterstown, businesses and Brights Mill at Alderson, 1883-1899;

account books of the West Virginia First National Bank, Alderson, 1920-1931, 1927-1944, 1930-1948; hand printed histories by Dixon of the Grange at Alderson (1878-1888) and Brights Mill; and galley proofs of *The Rise and Fall of Alderson, West Virginia*, by Dixon, 1967.

250. **Doddridge Family.** Manuscript, 1745-1857. 6 items. Gift of Mrs. J. A. Haislip and Herman Matheny, 1964. Nos. 370, 1787.

A manuscript and two typed copies, "Father of Philip Doddridge," giving information on John Doddridge (1745-1791), Philip Doddridge (1773-1832), and other family members; the will, and two typed copies, of William Parsons, Randolph County, 1828; and a letter from Cadwaller [*sic*] Doddridge, son of Philip, written from West Point, New York, commenting on the course work and complaining about the food and the routine.

251. **Donnally and Steele Kanawha Salt Works.** Records, 1813-1815. 1 volume. Gift of Roy Bird Cook, 1956. No. 894.

A daybook of the Donnally and Steele Kanawha Salt Works, listing goods bought and sold and customers' names.

252. **Double X Club of Morgantown.** Archives, 1924-1950. Ca. 200 items. Gift of the Double X Club, 1965. No. 1828.

Archives of an organization of business and professional men formed in 1924. Records include constitution, membership, officers, programs, minutes, treasurers' reports, and correspondence.

253. **Drake, Leah Bodine.** Manuscript, 1952. 1 item. Gift of Leah Bodine Drake, 1958. No. 1069.

Two-page original manuscript of the poem, "Precarious Ground," winner of the 1952 Borestone Mountain Poetry Award.

254. **Draper Collection.** Manuscripts, ca. 1730-1830. 133 reels of microfilm. Originals in the State Historical Society of Wisconsin. No. 757.

Film copies of the 486 volumes of manuscripts collected by L. C. Draper. A partial guide to these papers appears in *Descriptive List of Manuscript Collections of the State Historical Society of Wisconsin*, edited by Reuben Gold Thwaites (Madison, 1906).

255. **Dunn, Thomas L.** Ledger, 1826-1879. 1 volume. Gift of Howard M. Dunn, 1955. No. 742.

A ledger of Thomas L. Dunn of Monongalia County, containing a record of his accounts, and birth and death records of some of the early members of the Dunn family.

256. **Durrett, Braxton B. (b. 1819).** Papers, 1833-1846. 1 volume. Gift of Mrs. Bert Harter, 1952. No. 488.

Arithmetic book of Braxton B. Durrett, who lived in Spotsylvania County, Virginia, and was in Barbour County by 1850; contains rules and examples of various arithmetical processes; diary entries, October, 1841-February, 1842; and a short Durrett family record.

257. **Dyer Family.** Genealogical charts, ca. 1960. 3p. Gift of Mrs. Delbert Dyer, 1968. No. 2021.

Three genealogical charts for Roger, William, and Zebulon Dyer, covering the late 1700s and early 1800s.

258. **Earl, J. A., *Compiler.*** Typescript, ca. 1958. 4 volumes and 1 reel of microfilm (1 volume). Gift of J. A. Earl, 1958. No. 1140.

These historical sketches compiled by J. A. Earl include "The History of Methodism in West Union and Doddridge County, 1778-1958"; "The Life of Joseph H. Diss Debar"; and "A Biographical History of Schools and Education in Doddridge County, 1883"; and Louise and Edwin Jones, "A Hundred Years of Doddridge County History."

259. **Easton-Avery Farm Woman's Club.** Minutes, 1945-1959. 2 volumes. Gift of Mrs. Hattie Reiner, 1965. No. 1817.

Minutes of meetings.

260. **Eby, Cecil D., Jr.** Manuscripts, 1959, 1960. 1 ft. Gifts of Cecil D. Eby, Jr., 1960, 1961, 1965. Nos. 1412, 1584, 1827.

Manuscript and galley proofs of *The Old South Illustrated,* by Porte Crayon, edited with an introduction by Cecil D. Eby, Jr. (1959); a manuscript draft of Eby's *Porte Crayon;* manuscript of a *Virginia Yankee in the Civil War: The Diaries of David Hunter Strother* (1961); *The Life of David Hunter Strother* (1960); and photocopies of Strother's *Virginia Illustrated* and his articles in *Harper's.*

261. **E Clampus Vitus.** Papers, 1850-1966. Ca. 50p. (photocopies). Originals in possession of Boyd B. Stutler, 1968. No. 2012.

Papers relating to E Clampus Vitus, a mock-secret order founded at West Union, Doddridge County, ca. 1850, by Ephraim Bee. Most of the material is from the San Francisco, California, chapter.

262. **Edmiston, Andrew, Jr.** **(1892-1966).** Papers, 1865 (1916-1948). 1 ft. Gift of Mrs. Andrew Edmiston, 1967. No. 1994.

Correspondence, deeds, financial and military records, newspaper clippings, and photographs of a Democratic politician, member of the U. S. House of Representatives, 1933-1942, newspaper editor, and businessman from Weston, Lewis County.

Subjects include Civil War amnesty oath, land transactions, World War I and World War II, politics, Rush D. Holt, C. A. Borchert Glass Company, coal industry, U. S. War Manpower Commission, Cessna Aircraft Company, Syfo Water Company, and Thermo Electric Products.

Correspondents include David Goff, Charles E. Hodges, Charles Lively, Alfred E. Smith, Harold L. Ickes, Joe L. Smith, Jennings Randolph, Clarence W. Meadows, James A. Farley, William E. Chilton, Arthur B. Koontz, and Harley M. Kilgore.

263. **Education. West Virginia.** Scrapbooks, 1910-1960. 1 reel of microfilm (6 volumes). Originals in possession of B. B. Chapman, 1963. No. 1668.

Scrapbooks entitled: "A Documentary Case Study of Education in West Virginia, 1910-1960, Concerning Webster Springs High School, Glenville State (Normal) College, West Virginia University, and Fairmont State (Teachers) College; Including a Literary Scrapbook Typical of Those Compiled in Central West Virginia; and a 'Tale of Education courses taught in West Virginia University . . .' " collected and compiled by Berlin Basil Chapman of Oklahoma State University.

This compilation includes correspondence, faculty contracts, diplomas and teaching certificates, report cards, class lists, materials pertaining to social activities, and newspaper clippings.

264. **Education. West Virginia.** Typescript, 1952. 1 item. Gift of Earl Hudelson, 1963. No. 1683.

Typescript entitled: "The Impact of a Half Century of Professional Education. A Symposium Commemorating Fifty Years of Teacher Training in West Virginia and the Twenty-Fifth Anniversary of the College of Education of West Virginia University, Morgantown, April 25-26, 1952." Participants included Dean F. W. Stemple, chairman, H. G. Wheat, Robert Clark, Kermit A. Cook, George Colebank, Howard B. Allen, Earl Hudelson, Eston K. Feaster, and Robert D. Baldwin.

265. **Edwards, William Henry (1822-1909).** Papers, 1840-1907. 3 reels of microfilm (24 volumes, 444 items) and 1 volume (typescript copy). Originals in possession of the Department of Archives and History and Mrs. J. A. Willis, 1960, 1962. Nos. 1373, 1614, 1951.

Correspondence and papers of a lawyer, businessman, naturalist, and author of *The Butterflies of North America* (1879-1897), who resided at Coalburg. There are entomological notebooks and "Autobiographical Notes." Subjects include coal lands, scientific publications, and research on butterflies. Correspondents include Louis Agassiz, Samuel F. B. Morse, and S. H. Peabody.

266. **Edwards Family.** Papers, 1844-1951. 1 reel of microfilm. Originals held by Mrs. J. A. Willis, 1957. No. 986.

Microfilm of printed volumes relating to Colonel William Edwards, William W. Edwards, and William Henry Edwards; also copies of manuscript materials, including a diary of William Henry Edwards for 1846, and his "Journal and Preface to London Diary," 1848. Other materials relate to the family's coal interests in Kanawha County and include account books for the Coalburg-Kanawha Mining Company, 1926-1928; the Deep Hollow Coal Company, 1920-1940; and the Kanawha and Ohio Coal Company, 1864-1866.

267. **Eisenhower, Dwight D.** Typescript and tape recording, 1947. 2 items. Transfers, 1960, 1965. Nos. 1325, 1834.

Manuscript and recording of an address by General Dwight D. Eisenhower before a West Virginia University convocation on September 22, 1947.

268. **Elkins, Stephen B. (1841-1911).** Papers, 1841-1946. 8 ft. Gifts of Davis Elkins, Sr., and Davis Elkins, Jr., 1938-1952; Roy Bird Cook, 1951; Miss Virgie Harris, 1953; O. D. Lambert, 1954-1955; Hayes Memorial Library, 1954; Thomas G. Clark, 1961-1962; Mrs. K. E. Kelly, 1964. Nos. 53, 296, 548, 590, 591, 809, 1532, 1610, 1794.

Correspondence from and to a Republican U. S. Senator (1895-1911) and businessman with interests in timber, coal, and railroads. The collections include speeches, maps, deeds, contracts, reports, photographs, and newspaper clipping scrapbooks concerning political, business, and family affairs.

Subjects include interests in West Virginia, New Mexico, Texas, and California; the Hampshire and Baltimore Coal Company; the Davis Coal and Coke Company; the West Virginia Central and Pittsburgh Railway; the Morgantown and Kingwood Railroad; Berkeley Springs Hotel Company; Buckhannon Relief Oil and Gas Company; the Allegheny Improvement Company; Little Kanawha Syndicate; Wheeling Traction Company; Great Falls and Old Dominion Railroad; St. Louis and North Arkansas Railroad; Magistral Exploration Company of Mexico; Westernport Electric Railway, and other corporations.

Correspondents include A. B. White, James G. Blaine, J. N. Camden, Andrew Carnegie, T. B. Catron, Grover Cleveland, Henry G. Davis, Chauncey Depew, James A. Garfield, Cardinal James Gibbons, Ulysses S. Grant, Murat Halstead, Mark Hanna, Benjamin Harrison, Rutherford B. Hayes, William S. Herndon, R. C. Kerens, Ogden Mills, Abraham Lincoln, William McKinley, J. P. Morgan, Theodore Roosevelt, George C. Sturgiss, and William Howard Taft.

269. **Equality Oil Company.** Corporation book, 1908-1911. 1 volume. Acquired, 1961. No. 1424.

Minutes, record of wells drilled, and financial data of a Parkersburg oil company.

270. **Etna-Connellsville Coke Company.** Minute book, 1912-1932. 1 item (1 reel of microfilm). Loaned by Glenn Massey, 1968. No. 2053.

Minute book of a company with offices at Connellsville, Pennsylvania, from its date of organization.

271. **Ewin, William.** Papers, 1784-1877. 19 volumes. Gifts of O. D. Lambert, 1935, and George Phillips. Nos. 33, 106.

Several thousand pieces mounted in bound volumes. Ewin, whose home was in St. George, Tucker County, was a land speculator who owned and developed large holdings in Barbour, Preston, Randolph and Tucker counties. He was a surveyor and surveying instrument maker in Baltimore, Maryland, from about 1835 to 1850 and was a member of the West Virginia State Senate, 1879-1881.

272. **Exchange Bank of Virginia, Weston Branch.** Records, 1852-1868. 7 ft. Gift of J. W. Ross, 1935. No. 24.

Ledgers, journals, letter books, correspondence and other papers bearing on the business of the bank. Correspondents include George A. Jackson, cashier and local pension commissioner following the Civil War, and Jonathan M. Bennett, first president of the bank.

273. **Fairfax, George W.** Papers, 1808-1898. 4 reels of microfilm. Originals owned by Ralph Fairfax, 1958. Nos. 1062, 1084.

Tax receipts, promissory notes, legal papers, articles of agreement, indentures and miscellaneous correspondence of a Preston County entrepreneur and sometime law officer. The bound volumes include various Preston County court books, 1839-1866; merchandise account books, 1832-1885; and a manuscript pamphlet on a survey of the southern route from Kingwood to Morgantown, 1851. There is material also on Monongalia County.

274. **Fairfax, Ralph,** *Collector.* Records, 1844-1877. 1 reel of microfilm and 15 items. Gift of Ralph Fairfax, 1956. No. 845.

A tax book of Monongalia County, 1855, and an estate appraisement of John Fairfax for personal property "at the Glades," and "Cheat Farm," Monongalia County. Included in the appraisement list is the sale of eleven slaves. There are two lists of delinquent taxpayers; scrip from the Gladeville Furnace, 1877; a "list of the hands at Clinton (Furnace)"; and other materials.

275. **Fairfax-Warman Family.** Papers, 1811-1933. 1 ft. Acquired, 1954. No. 616.

Papers of the Fairfax and Warman families of Uniontown, Pennsylvania, Morgantown, and Kingwood. There are many letters (1811-1874) to Elizabeth Fairfax from family members and friends; papers (1840-1851) of William Warman; papers on the settlement of the John Fairfax estate; a manuscript census book of Preston County for 1830; and an account book (1857-1872) of F. B. F. Fairfax. A few advertising circulars, 1866-1931, are included, as well as clippings on Morgantown and Monongalia County, 1868-1933.

276. **Fairmont State Normal School.** Papers, June 13, 1889. 2 items. Gift of John C. Shaw, 1954. No. 657.

Typescript of an address given by John C. Shaw at graduation and a commencement program, 1889.

277. **Farmers' Advocate.** Records, 1899-1935. 7 volumes. Gift of John Skinner, 1962. No. 1559.

Subscription books, 1901-1905, 1912, 1916-1917, and account book, 1912-1935, of the Charles Town *Farmers' Advocate,* edited and published by R. C. Rissler. Records also include a farm account book, 1899-1909, of Samuel L. Rissler and Son, dealing with general farm operations in Jefferson County.

278. **Farmington.** Archives, 1896-1898. 2 items. Acquired, 1956. No. 872.

Minute book of the town council and a receipt from Lee Toothman to Joseph M. Fox, town recorder.

279. **Farnsworth, Moses.** Papers, 1821-1899. 64 items. Gift of Miss Bonny Farnsworth, 1955. Nos. 751, 771.

Correspondence, receipts, and other miscellaneous papers of Moses Farnsworth, a justice of the peace of Troy District, Gilmer County.

280. **Faulkner, Charles James (1806-1884).** Papers, 1786-1892. Ca. 400 items. Gift and loan for duplication by T. T. Perry, Jr., 1956, 1957; acquisition, 1963. Nos. 912, 934, 993, 1681.

Correspondence of a Martinsburg attorney, Virginia legislator, member of Congress, and ambassador to France during the James Buchanan administration.

Subjects include Virginia-West Virginia politics, 1827-1876; French Colonization Society; the Nat Turner insurrection; the slavery controversy; the Virginia Revolutionary debt claims; the Jackson-Calhoun schism; the nullification controversy; the election of 1840; Whig politics, 1841-1850s; the tariff of 1857; the presidential election of 1860; foreign affairs, 1868-1876; disposal of the Harpers Ferry Armory; German-American Naturalization Treaty, 1875; Belknap and the Indian Ring scandals; the speakership contest in the Forty-fourth and Forty-fifth Congress; and the election of 1876.

Other subjects include the opening of the Wheeling bridge, 1849; Strother's Hotel, Berkeley Springs; the Sixty-seventh Regiment of Virginia Militia at Martinsburg, 1846; a Thomas Haymond survey in Harrison County, 1844; the Chesapeake and Ohio Canal; Baltimore and Ohio Railroad; internal improvement schemes in Virginia and Pennsylvania; and local history of the Martinsburg and Shenandoah Valley area.

There are also business and land papers (1804-1811) of James Faulkner, Baltimore, Maryland.

Correspondents include Chester A. Arthur, George Bancroft, William W. Belknap, Orville H. Browning, Samuel S. Cox, Claudius W. Crozet, Lyman C. Draper, William M. Evarts, John W. Garrett, John W. Geary, Thomas A. Hendricks, Abram S. Hewitt, George F. Hoar, John J. Jacob, Reverdy Johnson, John Pendleton Kennedy, J. Proctor Knott, Alexander Martin, James M. Mason, Henry M. Mathews, Charles F. Mercer, John S. Mosby, John S. Pendleton, Samuel Price, Benjamin Rush, Benjamin Silliman, John Slidell, Gerrit Smith, William E. Stevenson, George W. Summers, Henry A. Wise, and Waitman T. Willey.

281. **Fayette County.** Archives, 1787-1869 (1870-1923). 19 ft. Gift of the Fayette County Court, 1939. No. 362.

Originals and copies of county and circuit court suit papers, mainly for the period after 1870.

The volumes include a minute book of the Fayetteville town council, 1873-1877; county board of education minute book, 1866-1876; a land entry book, 1831-1837; land tax books, 1849, 1855-1860; personal property books, 1855-1858, 1860-1861, 1866; registers of voters, 1866, 1867; poll books, 1872, 1890; and private account books, including a G. P. Huddleston daybook for a general store, 1850-1858; and accounts of the Gauley Tie and Lumber Company, 1887-1892.

A name, subject, and chronological card index to this collection is available in the manuscripts section.

282. **Flanagan, William J. (b. 1838).** Papers, 1826 (1857-1910) 1941. Ca. 200 items. Gift of Albert P. Flanagan, 1955. Nos. 768, 780.

Personal papers and accounts of a justice of the peace in Tucker County. The papers include deeds for land in Tucker and Randolph counties.

283. **Fleming, Aretas Brooks (1839-1923).** Papers, 1784-1924. 53 ft. Gift of A. Brooks Fleming, Jr., 1936; and transfer from West Virginia University Department of History, 1953. Nos. 40, 568.

Papers of the eighth governor of West Virginia, 1890-1893, who was an attorney in Gilmer County, prosecuting attorney of Marion County, 1863-1867, a member of the house of delegates, 1872-1875, circuit judge, 1878-1888. Fleming was closely associated with James O. Watson in the development of the coal industry and railroads in the Monongahela Valley. There are scattered papers, including several hundred sermons, of Benjamin F. Fleming (1810-1876). Among the correspondents are J. N. Camden, H. G. Davis, A. G. Dayton, S. B. Elkins, and F. H. Pierpont.

284. **Fleming, Helen M.** Papers, ca. 1812-1951. 1 ft. Gift of Mrs. Mary Lee Swiger, 1956. No. 852.

Typescripts relating to Marion County, including "In Memory of John Marshall Jacobs, a Good Churchman," "Early Days of Mining in Marion County," and "In Memory of Jessie Hickman Jamison," all written by Helen M. Fleming. There are a number of photographs of Fairmont and Marion counties, family photo albums, and seven scrapbooks of clippings of U. S. and West Virginia history, with emphasis on Marion and Monongalia counties.

285. **Fleming Family.** Papers, 1810-1943. 6 ft. Gift of Rollo Conley, 1954. Nos. 638, 644.

Business and personal papers, pamphlets, clippings, photographs and genealogies of Benjamin Fleming (1806-1891) and his son Thurston Worth (b. 1846), relating to various business enterprises carried on by the family in Fairmont. These included a large trade in manufacturing, importing and selling hats and furs, general merchandising, and fertilizer and hardwood sales.

There are many letters and advertisements from eastern mercantile houses; bills of lading showing names of steamboats on the Ohio and Monongahela rivers; current prices of furs and skins; lottery advertisements from Delaware, 1860, and Kentucky, 1866; letters from family members attending schools in Morgantown, 1863-1865; correspondence reflecting Florence Fleming's interests in the West Virginia Humane Society and the placing of homeless children; and other items relating to Fairmont.

Writers of letters or persons mentioned include W. T. Willey.

286. **Fletcher, Mrs. J. D.,** *Collector.* Papers, 1857-1954. Ca. 200 items. Gift of Mrs. J. D. Fletcher, 1958. No. 1073.

Correspondence of Martha Brand Wolfe and Charles M. Wolfe, who operated a small farm at Morgantown. The papers include some old Monongalia County land deeds of Charles I. Brand; letters from evangelists Dr. R. E. L. Jarvis and Dr. Edward D. Fellers, together with letters of Mrs. Wolfe on religion. There are also Christmas cards, local news clippings, two Brand family autograph albums, family photographs, and a newspaper clipping book, 1881-1905.

287. **Flick, William Henry Harrison (1841-1891).** Papers, 1867-1872. 1 reel of microfilm. Originals in the Duke University Library, 1960. No. 1349.

Papers of a Pendleton County lawyer and prosecuting attorney who served in the state legislature, 1868-1870, where he introduced the Flick Amendment which removed voting restrictions on those who served in the Confederacy.

Papers deal with Flick's legal practice; test oath cases; voting restrictions as a means of continuing Republican supremacy; state elections of 1868; Flick's campaign against Henry G. Davis for Congress in 1870; the West Virginia capital question; subscriptions to the Washington and Ohio Railroad; the origin of the Flick Amendment; and politics in the Second Congressional District, 1872.

Correspondents include Arthur I. Boreman, H. G. Davis, Spencer Dayton, Nathan Goff, William P. Hubbard, John J. Jacob, and William E. Stevenson.

288. **Floyd, George Rogers Clark (1810-1895).** 1843-1953. Ca. 200 items. Gift of Robert L. Floyd, 1957. No. 941.

Correspondence, clippings and other documents collected through 1953, on George Rogers Clark Floyd, secretary of state for the Territory of Wisconsin, 1845-1848, member of the West Virginia House of Delegates, 1872-1873, and longtime resident of Logan County. There is data on other members of the Floyd family.

289. **Floyd, John (1783-1837).** Miscellany, 1775-1923. Ca. 60 items. Gift of Charles H. Ambler. No. 363.

Correspondence of Charles H. Ambler relating to his studies of John Floyd; and typed copies of letters and documents concerning Floyd and John and William Preston. Correspondents include J. C. Calhoun and Henry A. Wise.

290. **Folk Singers.** Tape recording, 1961. 1 reel of tape. Transfer, 1961. No. 1506.

Recording of Dorothy Clutter Collison and Ernest Skaggs, singing traditional mountain ballads at the West Virginia State Fair, August, 1961.

291. **Folklore. Lewis County.** Manuscript, n.d. 47p. Gift of Opal Jones and Beth Curry, n.d. No. 364.

A collection of folk sayings, medicinal remedies, and words of songs collected in Lewis County by Opal Jones and Beth Curry through personal interviews with old residents.

292. **Ford, J. B.** Legal papers, ca. 1877. Ca. 50 items. Acquired, 1963. No. 1679.

Suit papers and correspondence in the case of the *Baltimore and Ohio Railroad* vs. *J. B. Ford*, general agent of the railroad at Cumberland and Wheeling.

The papers include copies of documents relative to the building of the railroad from Cumberland westward to Parkersburg and Wheeling and the activities of Ford as general agent at Cumberland and Wheeling, 1852-1874. Most of Ford's evidence deals with the role of the railroad during the Civil War and its relations with the state of West Virginia. There are copies of letters from John S. Carlile, J. W. Garrett, George B. McClellan, Francis H. Pierpont, and Edwin M. Stanton.

The correspondence is with Ford's attorney, William P. Preston of Baltimore.

293. **Ford Family.** Papers, 1829-1882. 14 items. Gift of Miss Mabel Ford, 1963. No. 1688.

Stock receipt, Taylor County Agricultural and Mechanical Society, 1870; pass, Headquarters, United States Volunteers, Grafton, August 3, 1861; passes from the toll office of Valley River Bridge, Northwestern Turnpike, 1860-1863; list of indigent school children, District 17, Taylor County; and muster fines and receipts bearing Morgantown, Fairmont, and Pruntytown imprints.

294. **Forks of Cheat Baptist Church.** Records, 1775-1830, ca. 1948. Gift of Miss Millie Hunter, 1948. Nos. 124, 365.

Typescripts, "History of the Forks of Cheat Baptist Church," and "Stewartstown," by Millie Hunter; and two typed copies of church minutes, 1775-1830, including the first constitution and lists of early members.

295. **Forman, A. H.,** *Collector.* Papers, 1936-1938. 4 volumes. Gift of A. H. Forman, 1948. No. 135.

Inventory of equipment, property, and construction in progress of the Chesapeake and Potomac Telephone Company in its West Virginia installations.

296. **Forman, L. J.** Papers, 1837-1934. 11 ft. Gift of Wilson H. Smith, 1956. Nos. 825, 834, 850.

Business papers, mainly deeds to land in Grant County, and office files of L. J. Forman, a Petersburg attorney.

297. **Fort Lewis.** Typescript, n.d. 1 item. Transfer, 1962. No. 1612.

An account of the founding of Fort Lewis on the Cowpasture River in western Virginia as related during the early 1860s to James Woodzell.

298. **Fort Van Metre.** Papers, 1780, 1966, 1969. 7 items (photocopies). Gift of Edward M. May, 1968. No. 2071.

Two maps and one description of the Fort Van Metre property; a copy of the will of Abraham Van Metre, 1780; sketch of Major Samuel McCulloch; and a picture of Shaw Hall, West Liberty College, thought to be the site of the fort.

299. **Foster, George.** Papers, 1812-1950. 2 items. Gift of Earl Hudelson, 1956. No. 816.

A typescript, "History of the George Foster Family," the family of John Foster Dulles; and a letter of transmittal and explanation from Earl Hudelson to Dr. J. M. Callahan.

300. **Fox Family.** Papers, (1762-1859) 1895. 245 items. Gifts of Miss Elizabeth M. Fox and Mrs. Carrie Fox Harmison, 1949, 1952. Nos. 150, 471, 477.

Correspondence and papers centering on William and Vause Fox in Romney and Hampshire County. There are accounts showing prices for various goods and services, including hides and leather, surveying, field labor, and weaving. There are items related to slaves, as well as material on the Literary Society of Romney; land papers; and returns and orders of the Seventy-seventh Regiment of Virginia Militia.

301. **Francisco, Lewis.** Diary, 1841-1865. 1 item. Acquired, 1950. No. 230.

Diary and commonplace book with miscellaneous entries showing place and types of employment in Parkersburg and Charleston, weather conditions, prices of clothing, board, tools, and wages.

302. **Frankenberry, Allen D.** Diaries, 1861-1870. 1 reel of microfilm (4 volumes). Originals in possession of Mrs. I. L. Van Voorhis, 1964. No. 1785.

Diaries of a member of Company K, Fifteenth Pennsylvania Volunteer Cavalry; the U. S. Signal Corps, Fourteenth Army Corps Headquarters, Department of the Cumberland, Atlanta; and the Fourth Corps in Knoxville. The diarist spent most of his time as an orderly or signalman. There is information on life in Northern camps in Tennessee, Alabama, Georgia, North Carolina, and Virginia. There is little on major battles, some on Northern troop movements and camp life. There is an account of a battle at Allatoona, Georgia, at Kenesaw Mountain, and receiving the news of Abraham Lincoln's assassination.

303. **Franklin, Alice E.,** *Collector.* Papers, 1954. 4 items. Gift of Alice E. Franklin, 1954. No. 619.

A typescript of an address, "West Virginia's Literary Heritage," read by Miss Franklin at the Morgantown Book Festival in 1954; notes on Lewis Wetzel; a bibliography of Marshall County; and a program of the festival.

304. **Freeman, Charles H.** (1854-1919). Letter book, 1908-1911. 1 volume. Gift of Mrs. Charles H. Freeman, 1960. No. 1278.

Letter book of an engineer who pioneered in the development of the Griffithsville oil fields in Lincoln County. The correspondence relates to the activities of the Big Creek Development Company, Yawkey and Freeman Company, Ltd., Yawkey and Freeman Drilling Company, Pond Creek Coal Company, and other related concerns of Freeman and

William H. Yawkey in the exploitation of oil and coal lands in the Guyandotte River and Mason County areas.

305.   **Freeman Family.** Papers, July 7, November 1, 1845. 2 items. Gift of Miss Carrie Freeman, 1951. No. 248.

A contract between Fayette Freeman and others for a subscription school to be opened in Lewis County, and four pages of accounts of Stephen Freeman showing prices of clothing, hardware, and household articles.

306.   **French, William Henderson.** Typescript, 1961. 1 item. Gift of James H. Martin, 1962. No. 1581.

Address by James H. Martin, September 16, 1961, at the dedication of the Colonel William Henderson French (1812-1872) marker, Mercer County. French was from a noted pioneer family and served in the Confederate Army.

307.   **Frissell, John (1810-1882).** Ca. 1858-1888. 1 volume and ca. 50 items. Gift of J. Ben Robinson, 1957. No. 932.

A scrapbook and folders of clippings, advertisements, letters, manuscripts of speeches, and notes on medical practice, compiled by Dr. John Frissell, a physician at the Wheeling Hospital and medical superintendent of military prisoners and soldiers in Wheeling during the Civil War. The scrapbook is a folio volume, "Register of the Sick and Wounded, U. S. A. General Hospital." There is also information on the Medical Society of the City of Wheeling, the West Virginia Medical Society, medical conventions in West Virginia, and Wheeling local history.

308.   **Fry, Henry H.** Letters, 1862-1864. 41 items. Gift of Glenn Massey, 1962. No. 1552.

Civil War letters from a Union soldier in the Army of the Potomac, to his wife in Greene County, Pennsylvania. Fry was in the Peninsula Campaign, 1862, and later stationed at various islands off the South Carolina coast. He was killed in 1864 near Bermuda Hundred, Virginia. The letters reveal little about military movements, but do comment on camp life and fraternization between Union and Confederate soldiers.

309.   **Frye, Thomas B.** Papers, 1875-1903. Ca. 200 items. Acquired, 1965. No. 1805.

Letters, receipts, and business papers of a resident of Keyser who was an agent for Hartford Fire Insurance Company and the Phoenix Insurance Company of Hartford. Frye was later a traveling agent for Green and Laing, Hardware and Cutlery, Wheeling, and others, and a dealer in general merchandise.

310.   **Furness, Horace Howard.** Letters, 1887, 1901. 2
       items. Gift of Robert F. Munn, 1964. No. 1772.

Two letters from Furness to Francis N. Thorpe regarding an honor
extended to Furness by Columbia University and a lack of communications from J. B. McMaster.

311.   **Gall, David W. (1851-1939).** Papers, 1884-1935. 1 ft.
       Gift of Miss Mamie Gall, 1960. No. 1360.

Account books, letter copy book, scrapbooks, and newspaper clippings
of the founder and editor of the Philippi *Jeffersonian-Plaindealer*, lawyer, and Democratic state senator.

Subjects include the early history of Philippi, the wartime death of
Gall's sons in 1915 and 1917, financial affairs of the newspaper, and
Gall's column "Washington Special" written from the nation's Capitol
and published in several West Virginia newspapers.

312.   **Gallaher, DeWitt Clinton (1845-1926).** Papers,
       1869-1870. 5 items (2 reels of microfilm and 3
       photostats). Gift and loan of Mrs. Montague Blun-
       don, 1964, 1965. Nos. 1790, 1853.

Diary of DeWitt Clinton Gallaher, August 7, 1869, to August 4, 1870,
covering travel of a Virginian to New York, studies in Berlin, and European travel. There are descriptions of Niagara Falls, Albany, Saratoga,
and Fort Ticonderoga in New York, and European sites. The collection
includes a notebook used for study of German, 1869, and photostats of
newspaper clippings concerning Gallaher and Company E, First Virginia
Cavalry, Confederate.

313.   **Ganoe, Lloyd B., *Collector*.** Papers, ca. 1836-1925. 1
       ft. Gift of Lloyd B. Ganoe, 1959. No. 1229.

Correspondence, business and legal papers, family photographs, clippings, and account books of Zebulon Musgrave; his son Eli, a Fairmont
merchant and mortician; Daniel Turney, a clergyman; and his son, William L., a Fairmont merchant and druggist. There is also a post office
record book, 1894-1897, kept by Eli Musgrave.

Aside from family and business affairs and estate settlements, subjects include Missouri frontier life and society in 1836; strife at Lecompton, Kansas Territory, in 1857; local history of the Fairmont area;
Fairmont Normal School; and the Monongahela Gas and Coal Company
of West Virginia.

314.   **Garrison, Alpheus.** Papers, 1804-1888. 1 ft. Gift of
       Earl L. Core, 1959. No. 1182.

Business, legal, and Civil War papers of Captain Alpheus Garrison, Company E, Seventeenth Regiment, West Virginia Infantry, who was later

sheriff of Monongalia County and postmaster at Pedlar Run. The collection contains county and post office receipts.

315. **Garrison, M. J., and Company.** Records, 1858-1922. 18 volumes and 42 items. Gift of Mrs. W. E. Campbell, 1955. Nos. 697, 712, 734.

Business records of the firm of M. J. Garrison and Company, Wadestown, in the operation of a general store and the buying and selling of livestock and wool. There are other papers relating to the Wadestown Telephone Company; lumber buying and selling; leasing of oil and gas lands and drilling, with names of oil companies operating in the area.

316. **Gatewood, A. C. L.** Papers, 1801-1816, 1855-1919. 1 reel of microfilm. Originals in possession of Harry L. Sheets, 1961. No. 1519.

Correspondence, diary, and farm account book of a Confederate officer and Pocahontas County cattleman and farmer.

The correspondence deals primarily with Gatewood's activities as adjutant general and chief of staff of the West Virginia Division, United Confederate Veterans. The Civil War diary, March 11-December 15, 1865, covers action of Company F, Eleventh Virginia Cavalry, "Laurel Brigade," Rosser Cavalry Division, from Staunton to Appomattox. The farm account book, 1866-1869, also contains an account of Gatewood's Civil War experiences including fighting in western Virginia and Jones' northwestern Virginia raid of 1863. The account book, 1801-1805, 1816, pertains to the John Rodgers estate. There are a few papers of Gatewood's father, Samuel V. Gatewood.

Other subjects include farming and stock raising in Pocahontas County, the Warm Springs of North Carolina, William and Mary College, Virginia Military Institute, Ann Smith Academy, Greenbrier Male Academy, Civil War in the Bath County, Virginia area, and the cattle trade in the Kanawha Valley.

317. **Gatewood, William B. (1835-1908).** Papers, 1861-1909. 1 ft. Gift of Mrs. Lorene Gatewood, 1968. No. 2061.

Correspondence, memo books, legal and business papers of a farmer and deputy sheriff residing in the Cabin Creek District near Coalburg, Kanawha County. Subjects include farm prices, land, coal, politics, and the Paint Creek Railroad.

318. **Gauley Mountain Coal Company.** Papers, 1908-1951. 9 items. Gift of Gauley Mountain Coal Company, 1966. No. 1921.

Letter from William N. Page concerning dangers in coal mining; abstracts of land titles granted to Robert Morris in 1795; World War II production statistics for Gauley Mountain Coal Company; contract between the United Mine Workers of America, the Gauley Mountain Coal Company, and Charleston General Hospital concerning hospitalization of miners and their families; the life of Robert Hamilton Morris, director of the American Institute of Mining Engineers, 1946; and Pocahontas coal seams.

319. **Genealogies.** Notebooks, 1940-1957. 60 notebooks. Gift of Mrs. Eloise Bosson, 1957. No. 928.

Looseleaf notebooks of genealogies of West Virginia families and records of cemetery readings and early marriages in Randolph, Harrison, Lewis, Barbour, and Upshur counties, collected and compiled by Miss Minnie McWhorter in Weston.

Family names included are: Alderson, Alkire, Anderson, Atkinson, Bailey, Ball, Barnes, Barnet, Bartlett, Bassel, Bennedum, Bennett, Blake, Bonnett, Boughman, Brake, Burr, Bush, Carber, Carpenter, Carroll, Casto, Champe, Cheuvront, Chrislip, Cookman, Coplin, Corder, Couch, Cummins, Cunningham, Curry, Custis, Cutright, Davidson, Davis, Donnally, Douglass, Dyer, Eagan, Eastwood, Fairbank, Farnsworth, Fell, Flesher, Gaston, Gates, Girty, Goff, Goodloe, Hacker, Hagerman, Hall, Hamilton, Hamrick, Hardman, Hart, Hatcher, Haymond, Hiner, Hinzeman, Holt, Hughes, Hurst, Hutton, Jackson, Jewell, Kester, Knight, Laidley, Lawson, Lee, Lightburn, Lincoln, Lorentz, Loudin, Lowther, McLane, McWhorter, Mahan, Makowicz, Mann, Marple, Martin, Mathews, Maxwell, Moore, Morgan, Morrison, Neely, Nichols, Norris, Nutter, Peterson, Phillips, Poff, Pringle, Quarrier, Queen, Raines, Reger, Riddel, Ritter, Ruffner, Shoulders, Sims, Sleeth, Smith, Stalnaker, Starcher, Stitler, Stout, Strader, Straley, Stump, Swisher, Talbott, Tenney, Teter, Thomas, Thornhill, Tucker, Van Horn, Waggoner, Ward, Washington, Weimer, West, Westfall, White, Whittlesey, Williams, Wilson, Winans, Woodford.

320. **Genealogies.** Records, 1796-1944. 74 items. Gift of Mrs. J. A. Forbes, 1966. No. 1920.

Family histories, correspondence, wills, marriage licenses and bonds, statements, petitions, and newspaper clippings pertaining to the McCoy, Hiner, Seybert, and Vint families. Also included are two 4 percent registered Confederate bonds issued in 1864.

321. **Genealogies.** Records, 1944-1963. 1 reel of microfilm (198p.). Loan for duplication by Bush Swisher, 1963. No. 1788.

Genealogical information on Bear-Baer and allied families in Pennsylvania and West Virginia, compiled by Earle E. Baer. There is information on Swisher-Bush, Smith-Townsend-Jackson families and the Boreman, Cook, Edwards, Jackson, Keller, Kurtz-Kurz, Newman, Pursglove, Sellers, Smith, Spencer, Stalnaker-Steinaker, Watson, and Young-Jung families.

322. **Genealogies.** Records, 1962. Ca. 200 items. Gift of Miss Helen A. Wesp, 1962. No. 1613.

Genealogical records of Alexander Scott, the Scott families of Virginia, Ohio, Pennsylvania, and Indiana and the allied families of Morgan Barker, Barrickman, Bouslog, Caddis, Carpenter, Carr, Chesney, Chipps, Claypoole, Clayton, Cunningham, Daugherty, Davis, Dent, Dragoo, Drummond, Ewing, Fortney, Goodnight, Hamilton, Harrison, Hess, Lindsey, McClelland, McFarland, Marchand, Martin, Menefee, Neely, Pindall, Price, Shively, Strothers, and Wilson. These records also include copies of letters and other documents relating to the early history of western Virginia.

323. **Genealogies.** Typescripts, 1934-1935. 7 items (photocopies). Originals in possession of E. E. Myers, 1961. No. 1415.

Copyrighted genealogical compilations by Howard B. Grant include "The Engle Family of Barbour County, West Virginia"; "Joseph Corder of Barbour County, Virginia"; "William Benson of Barbour County, Virginia"; "Henry Harper of Randolph County, Virginia"; "Old Families of Barbour County, Virginia"; "William Corder of Barbour County, Virginia"; and "Marriage Bonds of Barbour County, Virginia, 1843."

324. **Genealogies.** Typescripts and records, 1771-1971. Ca. 420 items (some photocopies). Gifts and loans, various dates. Accession numbers are in parentheses after names.

Genealogical information and records on the following families: Ankrom (308), Arnett (96), Arthur (1227), Baker (2009), Ball (2213), Bane (720, 1971), Barr (2183), Baxter (1762), Bayles (186), Breakiron (186), Carter (1728), Casto (1099), Coburn (1992), Conaway (308), Conn (1483), Cuppy (1039), Dameron (1025), Damron (1025), Davis (186, 1114, 1214), Dew (308), Drake (720), DuBois (897), Dunn (600), Dyer (1114), Evans (2184), Everly (45), Fawcett (1048), Feathers (1114), Fisher (1400), Fleming (308), Garden (897), Gould (1799), Gregg (2183), Griffith (1074), Hanna (897), Hawker (186), Hawley (495, 1114), Houston (1031), Inghram (308), Ingram (720), Jackson (2001), Jenkins (1227), Johnson (1728), Keadle (1670), Keister (1114), Lowther (1279), Lynch (1533), McCoy (2213), Marple (1099), Mason (1037), Masters (2184), Meriweather (1074), Minor (720, 1266), Moore (1136), Morris (308, 2197), Nestor (793), Nicholas (1037), Peck (1114), Pierpoint (600, 1992), Pierpont (1992), Poffenbarger (1299),

Prather (2213), Price (1728), Propst (1114), Reed (186), Reynolds (2197), Ripley (2183), Ruffner (308), Reger (1099), Romine (1963), Russell (2213), Schaub (1413), Scott (555), Seibert (1869), Shobe (1413), Soper (2213), Sweeney (897), Talbot (2212), Tannehill (2213), Thistle (2213), Thornburn (897), Trembly (1114), Van Meter (897), Vandervort (186), Wagle (116), Walker (440), Watson (600), Weaver (1463), Wells (2184, 2213), Westfall (2118), Whitman (1139).

325. **Genealogies. Kanawha County.** Typescript, ca. 1955. 77p. Gift of Mrs. R. E. Humphries and Mrs. Aubrey W. Love, 1957. No. 933.

Bound typescript of family Bible records compiled for the John Young Chapter, National Society, Daughters of the American Revolution, Charleston, by Mrs. W. S. Johnson, Evelyn Tormen Ballard, and Mrs. R. E. Humphries. Includes the family names of Allen, Anderson, Ashley, Bowling, Bower, Durry, Franklin, Glover, Johnson, Kincaid, Mathews, Overholt, Pennell, Rader, Savage, Settle, Stephenson, Ten Eyck, Thornberry, and Young.

326. **Genealogies. Monongalia County.** Records, ca. 1945. Gift of Mrs. Rachel Cox, 1945, and transfer, n.d. Nos. 97, 323.

A guide to local history and genealogy, compiled by L. D. Arnett. Includes an index to the family Bible records compiled by Rachel Cox. There are also lists of census publications on West Virginia, names of Monongalia County cemeteries, and lists of family records, marriages, wills, Revolutionary soldiers, and genealogical books and collections. Also, typed genealogies, mainly of Monongalia County families, as recorded in family Bibles. Family names traced include Baker, Beall, Burris, Chipps, Clark, Colebank, Crow, Dean, Evans, Fleming, Gapin, Garlow, Haldeman, Hall, Henry, Hickman, Hill, Hyman, Jenkins, Kelley, Lynch, Miller, Mitchell, Moore, Morrison, Musgrave, O'Neal, Pethtel, Pindall, Price, Ross, Rush, Scott, Smith, Shelby, Shriver, Steele, and VanCamp.

327. **General Store. Fairmont.** Records, 1854-1907. 21 volumes. Gift of Miss Mary Fleming, 1951. No. 314.

Records of the general store of B. A. "Moose" Fleming, Fairmont, relating costs and prices for construction materials, groceries, labor, drayage, clothing and fuel; includes miscellaneous medicinal recipes.

328. **General Store. Gilmer County.** Records, 1903-1924. 1 ft. Acquired, 1968. No. 2048.

Invoices, postal records, and receipts from a general store at Coxs Mills, Lucerne.

329. **General Store. Knob Fork.** Records, 1897-1919. 2 volumes. Gift of Mr. and Mrs. Glenn Jolliffe, 1956. No. 811.

A daybook of goods ordered, 1901-1904; and a ledger containing various accounts, 1897-1919, of A. Jolliffe and Son, Knob Fork.

330. **Glasscock, William E. (1862-1925).** Papers, 1906-1925. 12 ft. Gift of William E. Glasscock, Jr., 1931, and loan by Paul W. Haddock, 1961. Nos. 6, 1447.

Correspondence, speeches, newspaper clippings, and other papers of the thirteenth governor of West Virginia, 1909-1913. Subjects include political, social, and economic affairs, 1904-1913; the presidential election of 1904 and 1912; the Paint Creek and Cabin Creek coal strikes, 1912-1913; and Glasscock's role as collector of internal revenue for West Virginia.

Correspondents include George W. Atkinson, Albert J. Beveridge, William E. Edwards, Davis Elkins, Stephen B. Elkins, Henry Ford, William Green, Henry D. Hatfield, Hiram W. Johnson, James S. Lakin, Virgil A. Lewis, Isaac T. Mann, Robert R. McCormick, John T. McGraw, George W. Perkins, Gifford Pinchot, Ira E. Robinson, Theodore Roosevelt, Nathan B. Scott, Mark Sullivan, Howard Sutherland, William H. Taft, and I. C. White.

There are also papers relating to the Morgantown *Republican,* a campaign newspaper established by Glasscock to support his gubernatorial candidacy and the Taft ticket in 1908.

331. **Glassworkers.** Oral histories, 1965, 1966. 2 reels of tape and 1 typescript. Gift of West Virginia University History Department and Elizabeth Cometti, 1965, 1966. No. 1836.

Interviews conducted by students of Dr. Elizabeth Cometti with Oscar DuBois, a retired glassworker of Morgantown, and Edward W. Shay, a Morgantown glassworker. There is information on glassworking techniques and wages. Shay was an organizer for the American Flint Glassworkers' Union and comments on union conflicts, immigration restriction, William Blizzard, the Ku Klux Klan, Mary "Mother" Jones, Governors E. F. Morgan and H. D. Hatfield, and yellow dog mines.

332. **Glenn Family.** Genealogy, 1661-1950. 1 typescript. Gift of Mrs. Lee Sanders, 1956. No. 849.

A history of the Glenn family from New Amsterdam to western Virginia, entitled "Scotia, the Glenn-Sanders House, or History of the Glenn Family."

333.   **Goff, David.** Papers, 1826-1904. 2 ft. Gifts of Francis P. Fisher, 1954; Mrs. W. G. Smith, 1957; Mrs. C. W. Harding, 1957; Mrs. Ada Bosworth Harding, 1958; and Mrs. Ruth Woods Dayton, 1962. Nos. 627, 975, 983, 1027, 1557.

Papers of a Beverly attorney and land promoter in Randolph, Harrison, and Tucker counties. Goff was prosecuting attorney, 1835, and superintendent of schools of Randolph County, 1853, a member of the Virginia Assembly, and a state senator from Randolph County, 1875-1877. The papers, mainly letters to Goff, deal with land transactions; the sale of slaves; politics; the Civil War; the founding of the Clarksburg *Conservative;* bridge building of Lemuel and Eli Chenoweth; a proposed turnpike from Beverly to Fairmont; proposed railroads from Pittsburgh to Pocahontas County and from Parkersburg to Tygart Valley River; Canaan Valley railroad; the Washington and Ohio Railroad; mail routes; Goff family history; and the West Virginia Constitutional Convention of 1872; Sons of Temperance; and West Virginia politics, 1871.

Correspondents include: J. M. Bennett, A. I. Boreman, G. D. Camden, John S. Carlile, J. H. Diss Debar, Spencer Dayton, Charles J. Faulkner, William MacCorkle, John J. Jacob, Henry M. Matthews, Samuel Price, and P. G. Van Winkle.

334.   **Goff, Guy D.** Papers, 1911-1931. 2 ft. Gift of Mrs. Anita Baker Goff, 1933, and transfer, 1954. Nos. 17, 622.

Typed copies of letters written by Goff from France, 1918-1920, as a member of General John J. Pershing's legal staff; typed copies of speeches, 1920-1931; a scrapbook of clippings on labor violence in Milwaukee, Wisconsin, 1911-1912; and a scrapbook of clippings on the appointment of Goff as United States district attorney for the eastern district of Wisconsin, 1912.

335.   **Goff, Nathan, Jr.** (1843-1920). Papers, ca. 1866-1899. 17 ft. Gifts of Mrs. Guy D. Goff and Mrs. Carroll Reece, 1950; the Rutherford B. Hayes Library, 1957; and Leonard Davis, 1967, 1969. Nos. 213, 953, 1940.

Correspondence, letter books, pamphlets, newspapers, and papers on cases tried before Goff as a United States circuit judge, 1892-1911. Goff also served as secretary of the navy, 1881; in Congress, 1883-1889, 1913-1919, and in the West Virginia Legislature, 1867-1868.

336. **Gore, Howard M. (1877-1947).** Papers, 1908-1947. 19 ft. Gifts of Claude and Truman Gore, 1950. Nos. 193, 198.

Papers of the seventeenth governor, 1925-1929, of West Virginia. The main series begins during World War I when Gore was assistant food administrator in West Virginia. Other papers concern his career in Washington, 1921-1925, as a specialist in livestock marketing in the Department of Agriculture, assistant secretary of agriculture, and secretary, 1924-1925. Other series relate to the period of his governorship; producers' co-ops; the Farm Bureau; the West Virginia Public Service Commission; the Weston and Union livestock sales companies; cattle production; and politics.

337. **Grant County.** Justice dockets, 1865-1923. 13 volumes. Acquisition, 1961, and gift of Edward Baker, 1962. Nos. 358, 1619.

Justice dockets of the Milroy District, 1865-1923, and one case book of Henry Feaster, justice of the peace, Grant Township, 1870-1873.

338. **Gray, Fred W.** Papers, 1922-1940. Ca. 200 items. Gift of Earl L. Core, 1962. No. 1573.

Correspondence and notes of a Philippi botanist, who worked in the field of cryptograms, particularly the study of lichens and cladoniae.

339. **Great Kanawha Coal, Oil & Metallurgic Company.** Papers, 1866-1894. 16 items. Gift of Col. Harvey E. Sheppard, 1969. No. 2117.

Correspondence and legal papers concerning land in Kanawha County on Cabin and Slaughter creeks, coal and railroad possibilities, interest rates, livestock breeding and costs, and the organization of the Great Kanawha Coal, Oil & Metallurgic Company.

340. **Green, Thomas (1798-1881).** Diary, 1826-1827. 1 volume (photocopy). Original in the Virginia Historical Society, 1963. No. 1651.

"Journal—during a Tour through the States of Ohio and Kentucky commenced—Saturday the 29 July 1826," by Thomas Green of Richmond. This journal concludes on April 1, 1827, at Chillicothe. Green's western trip was for the purpose of pursuing land matters, but the journal contains notes on the social, political, and economic life of the old West. Green visited Front Royal, Harrisonburg, Warm Springs, Kanawha Falls, and the Salines of Virginia, crossed the river at Gallipolis, passed through the principal towns and cities of southern Ohio including Cincinnati and Columbus, toured much of western and central

Kentucky, visited the Shakers at South Union and Pleasant Hill, watched the canal construction at Louisville, and visited Transylvania University in Lexington.

341. **Greenbrier Valley Industrial Exposition Association.** Ledgers, 1885-1888. 2 items (1 reel of microfilm). Loan for photoduplication by Thomas W. Dixon, 1966. No. 1910.

Ledgers listing show exhibits, exhibitors, and prizes, with some description of the items shown.

342. **Gregory, Mahala Chapman Mace.** Manuscript, 1940. 1 volume. Gift of Berlin B. Chapman, 1967. No. 1948.

A bound "copybook" of songs written from memory by Mahala Gregory, age 80. Contains poems, hymns, hand-drawn illustrations, and a short biography of Mrs. Gregory.

343. **Guseman, Jacob (1786-1878).** Records, 1836-1866, 1930. 8 volumes. Gift of Lawrence Burns, 1959. No. 1196.

Ledgers and daybooks of Jacob Guseman, a Preston County entrepreneur who operated a general merchandise store, a fulling mill, sawmill, gristmill, and other manufactories at Muddy Creek.

344. **Hacker Family.** Manuscript, 1880. 1 reel of microfilm (1 volume, 698p.). Original owned by William D. Hacker, Jr., 1958. No. 1059.

Microfilm, copy of a bound manuscript, "Sketches and Incidents in the Lives and Characters of my Ancestors, Historical and Biographical," by William Hacker.

345. **Hadsell, Richard M.,** *Collector.* Papers, 1880-1935. 2 reels of microfilm. Originals in Record Group 40 (Records of the U. S. Department of Commerce) and Record Group 174 (Records of the U. S. Department of Labor), National Archives, 1969. No. 2122.

Correspondence, reports, petitions, agreements, newspaper clippings and magazine articles relating to the soft coal industry and labor conditions, generally in southern West Virginia. Subjects covered include the eight-hour day; strikes; consolidation of coal operations; freight rates; government contracts for coal; Paint and Cabin creeks, 1912-1913; working conditions in the Polack Cigar Factory, Wheeling, 1914; investigation of the Gay Coal and Coke Company, Logan County, 1917;

investigation of the Wheeling Can Company, 1918; labor conditions in West Virginia, 1917; publicity releases of Winding Gulf Operators Association, 1923-1925; eviction of miners; labor conditions in Logan County, 1923.

Correspondents include D. T. Evans, Carl Hayden, W. E. Borah, M. M. Neely, Van A. Bittner, J. P. White, F. J. Hayes, Mary "Mother" Jones, Thomas Haggerty, Woodrow Wilson, and J. J. Cornwell.

346. **Hagans, Harrison (1796-1867).** Papers, 1818-1895. 11 ft. Gift of J. P. Barnes, 1932. No. 12.

Papers of the Hagans family of Preston County, including Harrison, Elisha, George M., Henry C., John Marshall, Zer, and others. There are letters and accounts and other papers, 1818-1867, and account books and other business records, 1818-1895, relating to various business enterprises conducted by the family. A chain of general merchandise stores was established, with outlets in Petersburg, Somerfield, and Bryants, Pennsylvania; Oakland, Maryland; and at Brandonville, Kingwood, Greenville, and Palatine, West Virginia. Harrison Hagans was postmaster, 1822-1841, at Brandonville; and president of the Greenville Mining and Manufacturing Company which produced iron in Preston County in the 1830s. Other papers reveal Hagans' interests in the development of roads in the county, along with schools; churches; the Preston Telegraph Company; a fulling mill, 1827; and a linseed oil mill, 1842. Hagans developed, patented, and sold in three states, ca. 1845, a washing and wringing machine, and also completed working models of a mowing machine and a threshing machine. Included in the collection is a volume of minutes of the quarterly conference of the Methodist Episcopal Church, 1834-1859.

347. **Halbritter, R. Doyne,** *Collector.* 15 items (1 reel of microfilm). Gift and loan for photoduplication by R. Doyne Halbritter, 1958, 1960. Nos. 1036, 1070, 1295.

Typescript copies from records of the Kingwood Methodist Church; articles on the Judy, Cuppy, Cuppett, and Guseman families; a copy of John Fairfax's will, 1843; minutes of a meeting of the board of education, Reno School District, Preston County, 1880; a letter from Senator J. P. Dolliver; letter from John Scott to James H. Carroll, Richmond, February 20, 1840, concerning a bill to permit construction of a road from German Settlement through Kingwood to Morgantown; and an account book, 1862-1871, of Samson W. Smalley, a carpenter and contractor from Oakland, Maryland.

348. **Hall, Arthur A.** Typescripts and tape recording, 1956. 3 items. Acquired, 1956. No. 878.

Tape recording and two typescripts of an interview with Arthur A. Hall, professor emeritus of electrical engineering, West Virginia University, and Morgantown city manager in 1922. Subjects covered include West Virginia University history, development of public utilities in Morgantown, and other local history.

349. **Hall, Granville Davisson (1837-1934).** Papers, 1861-1928. 1 ft. Gift of Mrs. Granville Davisson Hall, 1936, 1941. Nos. 42, 77.

Correspondence of Granville Davisson Hall, reporter for the Wheeling *Intelligencer* during the Wheeling conventions, 1861-1863; secretary of state of West Virginia, 1865-1873; and author of a number of works of fiction and historical studies about West Virginia. Included are many typescript copies of articles by Hall, and newspaper clippings regarding the publication of his books, politics, and history.

The letters mainly concern the formation, early statehood period, and Civil War activities in West Virginia. The correspondents include: William E. Borah, A. W. Campbell, John S. Carlile, Roy B. Cook, William M. O. Dawson, Charles J. Faulkner, A. B. Fleming, Nathan Goff, Henry Haymond, C. D. Hubbard, Dana L. Hubbard, William P. Hubbard, Flora Farnsworth Leonard, R. S. Northcott, Anna Pierpont Siviter, W. E. Stevenson, Joseph P. Tumulty, and W. T. Willey.

350. **Hall, Septimus (1847-1926).** Papers, 1871-1919. 1 folder. Gift of Miss Ethel Gorrell, 1962. Nos. 561, 1634.

Correspondence of a state legislator and member of the Constitutional Convention of 1872. Subjects include state politics, 1882-1886, and the Virginia Debt Commission, 1913-1916. Correspondents include Johnson N. Camden and William E. Chilton.

The papers also include an autograph album with the signatures of the members of the state legislature, 1881-1882; a biographical sketch of the blind poet, John S. Hall (1845-1923), and a collection of his poetry; a letter regarding Hall's commission as a notary public in Wetzel County; invoices from the West Virginia Penitentiary and Sweeneys & Co., Wheeling, steam engine manufacturers; and a typed copy of the Democratic state platform for 1912.

351. **Hall, Warren E. (1891-1969).** Papers, 1916-1969. 1 ft. Gift of Mrs. Elinor M. Hall, 1970. No. 2131.

Correspondence, newspaper clippings, sermons, radio addresses and a photograph of Warren E. Hall, a Presbyterian minister in Flint and Wyandotte, Michigan, and Morgantown. The collection consists mostly of sermons; correspondence covers the early years, 1916-1926. The radio addresses were made in Michigan and Morgantown.

352. **Hall, William.** Papers, 1850-1853, 1861. 3 items. Gift of Miss Edna Jenkins, 1957. No. 1001.

The account book of William Hall at Egypt, 1850-1853, with entries for wages paid to loggers, boarding accounts, sales of farm produce and general merchandise, and other items.

353. **Hallanan, Walter Simms (1890-1962).** Papers, 1919-1961. 5 ft. Gift of Miss Elizabeth V. Hallanan, 1963. No. 1659.

Correspondence, newspaper clippings, photographs, and printed material of the Republican national committeeman, state political leader, and president of the Plymouth Oil Company.

Subjects include Republican national conventions, 1928-1960; state and local politics, 1919-1961; National Petroleum Council; Plymouth and related oil companies; Republican rejection of the League of Nations; and Hallanan's role as temporary chairman of the 1952 Republican National Convention.

Correspondents include Michael L. Benedum, John W. Bricker, John J. Cornwell, John W. Davis, Thomas E. Dewey, Dwight D. Eisenhower, Leonard W. Hall, Warren G. Harding, Henry D. Hatfield, Will H. Hays, Herbert Hoover, Herbert Hoover, Jr., Arthur Krock, Alfred M. Landon, Louis Johnson, William E. Jenner, Henry R. Luce, Theodore R. McKeldin, William C. Marland, Richard Nixon, Chapman Revercomb, Harold E. Stassen, Harold E. Talbot, Earl Warren, and Sinclair Weeks.

354. **Hamilton Family.** Typescript, n.d. 9p. Gift of Bryan Hamilton. No. 371.

A typescript, "Hamilton Family History and Life on the Frontier," by Bryan Hamilton, covering the period ca. 1747-1862.

355. **Hammond Fire Brick Company.** Papers, 1900-1931. 7 ft. Gifts of A. D. Mastrogiuseppe, Jr., and others, 1969, 1971. Nos. 2083, 2166.

Correspondence and business records of the Hammond Fire Brick Company of Hammond, Marion County, West Virginia. There are shipping records, 1907-1913; freight bills, 1906-1909, 1921-1923; bills and orders, 1900-1931; one payroll book showing deductions for store, coal, etc.; one unrelated account book for a store at Lancaster; and several cancelled checks drawn on the Hammond Fire Brick Company.

356. **Hampshire County.** Archives, 1736-1949. 107 ft. Gift of the Hampshire County Court, 1937, 1951. Nos. 51, 282.

Court case papers, and miscellaneous papers from various county offices, 1736-1949; volumes of record books, 1820-1948; and account books of banks, churches, general stores, insurance firms, physicians, estate settlements, and gristmills. A partial index of plaintiffs, defendants, and subjects in the case papers, and a checklist of the bound volumes are available in the manuscripts section.

357. **Hampshire County.** Deeds, 1796-1886. 10 photostats. Originals owned by Mrs. Joe P. Kuykendall, 1957. No. 936.

Copies of deeds for land in Hampshire County, granted mainly to William Inskeep.

358. **Hamrick Family.** Papers, 1891-1948. 45 items. Gift of Gordon T. Hamrick, 1971. No. 2190.

Deeds, leases, teaching certificates, and other documents relating to the Hamrick family of Webster County, West Virginia.

359. **Hansford, Felix G.** Papers, 1790-1876. 1 ft. Acquired, 1958, 1959, 1961. Nos. 1089, 1192, 1464.

Correspondence, business, legal, and land papers of a Kanawha County justice of the peace, entrepreneur, president of the Giles, Fayette and Kanawha Turnpike Company. Also included is a manuscript map of the Kanawha River from Clifton to Point Pleasant.

Subjects include the George Boxley slave plot, 1816; cholera scourge in Louisville, 1833; Washington Temperance Society; James River and Kanawha Turnpike Company; the building and operation of the Giles, Fayette and Kanawha Turnpike; Whig politics in the 1840s; Missouri and the westward movement, 1841; the Kansas struggle, 1858; Albert Gallatin's western lands; southern reaction to John Brown's raid, 1859; church activities in the Kanawha Valley; salt industry in the Kanawha Valley; Hansford's gristmill, sawmill, and boat building activities, and family affairs.

Correspondents include Alfred Beckley, Claudius Crozet, Edward Herndon, Thomas E. Jackson, J. M. Maury, and George W. Summers.

360. **Hanson, Thomas.** Journal, April 8-August, 1774. 1 reel of microfilm. Original in the Library of Congress, 1958. No. 1033.

Journal of a surveying party including Hanson, John Floyd, James Nocks, Roderick McCray, and Mordecai Batson. The Journal describes the route taken from Fincastle County, Virginia, to the Ohio River and Kentucky, with mention of Gauley Mountain, Coal and New rivers, and other western Virginia geographical locations. Included is a list of persons for whom the surveys were made.

361. **Hansrote, Hazel Groves,** *Compiler.* Typescripts, 1958, 1959. 8 items. Gift of Mrs. Hazel Groves Hansrote, 1958, 1959. Nos. 1045, 1113, 1181, 1207, 1263.

Genealogical records of the Finley (Findley, Findlay), Andrew Johnson, Lincoln, Sencindiver, and Sheakley families; correspondence; a sketch of Andrew Johnson Patterson, grandson of President Andrew Johnson; and records pertaining to President Andrew Johnson and Patterson family history; and a compilation entitled "18th and 19th Century People . . . , Relating to Early Virginia, (West) Virginia, and Kentucky Families."

362. **Hanway, Samuel.** Papers, 1782-ca. 1818. 11 items. No. 570.

Manuscript surveys and plats of land in Monongalia and Preston counties by Samuel Hanway, county surveyor. There are papers showing acreage and owners; an early plat of Morgantown showing streets, lots and numbers; plat of courses of the Monongalia and Preston County boundary; maps of Monongalia and Preston counties, including a map of eleven tracts of land on Prichard and Whiteday Creek, Monongalia County, which notes the Morgantown-Clarksburg Road, Cratzer's Tavern, and the Van Swearing(en) Walnut Tavern and Mill.

363. **Hardman, Sam W.,** *Compiler.* Typescript, 1928. 1 item. Transfer, 1959. No. 1255.

"History of Big and Little Skin Creek Community (Vandalia), Lewis County, West Virginia," compiled by Sam W. Hardman. The typescript also includes "Names of Pioneer Settlers Prior to 1860," by W. H. Peterson.

364. **Hardy and Hampshire Counties.** Records, ca. 1750-1922. 1 reel of microfilm (1 volume). Originals in possession of Mrs. R. S. Kuykendall, 1959. No. 1171.

Copies of Fairfax grants and surveys made or copied by James William Kuykendall, county surveyor; record of the town lots in Moorefield; extracts from Hardy and Hampshire County records; cemetery readings; muster roll of the McNeill Rangers, 1861-1865; prospectus for Kuykendall family history, and local history items.

The volume contains detailed records for Cunningham, Harness, Kuykendall, Parsons, and Van Meter families. Other records pertain to the Casey, Fisher, Hite, Hopkins, McMechan, McNeill, Marshall, Moore, Pancake, Renick, Seymour, Sherrard, Welton, and Yocum families.

365. **Hardy County.** Minute book, 1786-1791. 3 items. Transfer, 1953. No. 233.

Copies of the first minute book of the Hardy County Court.

366. **Hardy County.** Papers, 1788-1941. 1 ft. Gift of Mrs. Charles E. Williams, Sr., 1964. No. 1745.

A travel journal, ca. 1857; a diary, 1941; survey records, 1894-1896; account books, 1788-1811/1891-1894; Branson family correspondence, 1839-1845; county and parish tax levies, 1800; a book of geographic terms and facts, 1836; and a Branson family record book.

People mentioned include Captain Eddie Rickenbacker. Places mentioned include: Cincinnati, Ohio, and Romney, Evansville, Clarksburg, Parkersburg, Coolville, Athens, Branch Mountain, Moorefield, Front Run Valley, Camp Branch Run, Sapling Lick Ridge, Hanging Rock Ridge, Little Ridge, Cacapon River, Kim's Run, and Lost River.

367. **Hardy County.** Typescripts, ca. 1949. 3 items. 178p. Gifts of Alvin Edward Moore and Ralph E. Fisher, 1958. Nos. 1072, 1144.

"Frontier Cross-Section: A History of Hardy County and Moorefield, West Virginia"; "Later History of Moorefield and Hardy County," by Alvin Edward Moore; and history and inventory list of newspapers published in Hardy County, compiled by Ralph E. Fisher.

368. **Hardy County. Cemetery Readings.** Typescripts, 1968. 12p. Gift of James Funkhouser, 1968. No. 2045.

Typescripts of Hardy County cemetery readings, compiled by James Funkhouser. Listings are for the Kimsey's Run Brethren Church, Harper, Chrisman, Inskeep, Miller, and Strawderman cemeteries, and an unnamed cemetery near Lost City. In addition there are readings from the Wilkins, Sager, and Dispanet family cemeteries.

369. **Harmer, Harvey W. (1865-1961).** Papers, 1842-1961. 2 ft. and 2 tape recordings. Gift of the heirs of Harvey W. Harmer, 1957, 1963. Nos. 930, 1686.

Correspondence, speeches, essays, clippings, and account books of a Clarksburg lawyer, Republican state senator, and Harrison County local historian.

Subjects include local history of Clarksburg and Shinnston; the Progressive Movement, women's suffrage, and prohibition in West Virginia; West Virginia Wesleyan College; West Virginia Historical Society; Methodism in Harrison County and the state; Methodist missions in Korea, China, India, the Philippines, and the United States; gristmills and covered bridges in West Virginia; America First Day, 1922; Edward Grandison Smith; Parkersburg Branch of the Baltimore and Ohio Railroad; family and personal history; history of the Mason-Dixon Line; the (Clarksburg) 50-Year Club; Nutter Fort Methodist Church; and the Harrison County Fair. Also, tape recordings of an interview relating to Mr. Harmer's career as an attorney in Clarksburg.

370. **Harmison, Charles.** Land papers, 1866-1914. 19 items. Gift of Mrs. Joe P. Kuykendall, 1957. No. 948.

Photostats of land papers, including deeds, abstracts, agreements, and surveys, for land in Hampshire and Harrison counties; and Harrison County, Missouri, 1755-1913.

371. **Harned, Joseph E.** (1870-1931). Manuscripts, n.d. 1 ft. Gift of Earl L. Core, 1961. No. 1543.

Correspondence of an Oakland, Maryland, pharmacist and original manuscript of his *Wild Flowers of the Alleghenies* (1931).

372. **Harold, Nan Brooke,** *Collector.* Papers, 1859-1958. 1 ft. Gift of Mrs. Nan Brooke Harold, 1949, 1950, 1960. Nos. 160, 161, 162, 163, 1288, 1307, 1329.

Letters, 1891, of St. George Tucker Brooke regarding the cadet corps at West Virginia University; clippings and newspapers regarding the Civil War, West Virginia University history, James Rumsey, and Virginia and West Virginia local history.

Also a diary, 1906; a recorded interview, 1958; and postcards, 1906-1928, of Mrs. Harold, daughter of Professor St. George Tucker Brooke of the West Virginia University law faculty. The collection pertains to university life and social activities in Morgantown, ca. 1906-1910, as seen through the eyes of a co-ed; family affairs; and the activities of her brother, Charles Frederick Tucker Brooke, a Rhodes scholar and Shakesperian authority.

373. **Harper, Charles P.** Letters, July 2, 6, 1926. 2 items. Gift of Charles P. Harper, 1949. No. 154.

Letters from the state auditor and treasurer regarding a point of law relating to state funds.

374. **Harpers Ferry.** Typescript, June 23, 1821. 9p. No. 374.

A sketch of the town and its geographical setting, copied from a manuscript owned by Mrs. E. Bruce Allen, Moorefield. Included are short notes on the history of the site of the town, description of the rivers, public buildings, school, circulating library, tavern, religious denominations, and nationalities represented among the 1351 inhabitants.

375. **Harpers Ferry Seminary.** Records, April 28, 1819. 1 photostat. No. 373.

A list of pupils in the school, and the lesson arrangement for April 28, 1819.

376. **Harris, Thomas M.** (1813-1906). Papers, 1861-1892. 53 items. Gift of Mrs. John T. Harris, 1942. No. 80.

Letters, commissions, reports, a photograph, and clippings relating to General Harris' services with the Tenth West Virginia Infantry. There are a few items concerning the trial of Mary E. Surratt and others, and letters regarding Harris' book *The Assassination of Abraham Lincoln* (Boston, 1892).

377. **Harrison, Benjamin** (1833-1901). Letters, 1886-1900. 40 items. Gift of A. T. Volwiler, 1949. No. 157.

Typed copies of forty letters written by Benjamin Harrison to Stephen B. Elkins.

378. **Harrison, Jordan.** Account book, 1814-1817, and 2 typescripts. Gift of R. Noel Pedicord, 1939. No. 63.

An account book from Skimino, York County, Virginia, which mentions several members of the Bates, Cole, Harrison, More, and Smith families. The journal lists expenses incurred in moving from York County to Mount Pleasant, Ohio, in 1817. There is a typed index to names in the journal, and a typed narrative on the Harrison and Bates families.

379. **Harrison, Samuel.** Ledger, 1822-1831. 1 volume. Acquired, 1953. No. 550.

Samuel Harrison's ledger for an inn and a cooperage business, apparently in Virginia.

380. **Harrison, Thomas W.** Papers, 1799 (1834-1907). 28 items. Gift of S. R. Harrison, Jr., 1956. No. 827.

Business and personal papers of a Clarksburg resident and a letter from R. Claiborne to George Jackson, dated July 1, 1799, concerning a broad spectrum of national issues.

381. **Harrison and Doddridge Counties.** Papers, 1778-1955. 1 ft. Gift of Mrs. Glenn V. Longacre, 1957. Nos. 1015, 1018.

Newspaper clippings, mainly from Doddridge and Harrison counties, concerning marriages, deaths, and family history; weather and flood data; and letters of World War I servicemen and nurses, and other persons. There is a series of published letters of L. P. Willis who was a teacher in the Philippine Islands and Japan for twenty years. Also included are papers of the Hickman family of Harrison County, and a photostat copy of a letter of a committee of the State Medical Society inviting participation in the study of the medical botany of the state, 1868.

382. **Harrison County.** Land records, 1786-1789, ca. 1800-1913. 3 items and 1 reel of microfilm (1 volume). Gift of Sam M. Semple; microfilmed originals in possession of Mrs. Louis D. Cinci, 1954, 1961. Nos. 633, 1521.

A land grant, March 21, 1786, from Patrick Henry to Thomas Proctor of Philadelphia, Pennsylvania, for three thousand acres along the Hughes River; a manuscript plat of the land; and a volume of field notes taken in laying out the town of Montgomery [Harrison County?] by Abraham Nelson, Jr., for Colonel Thomas Proctor, 1788-1789. Microfilmed material includes abstracts of Harrison County titles by Attorney George W. Bland.

383. **Harrison County.** Tax book, 1831-1832. 1 volume, 322p. No. 241.

An alphabetical list of taxpayers showing the amount of assessment and amount paid on poor tax, horses, land, and slaves.

384. **Harrison County Labor Federation.** Archives, 1958-1969. 9 ft., 1 reel of microfilm. Gift and loan of Harrison County Labor Federation, AFL-CIO, 1969. No. 2089.

Archives of the Harrison County Labor Federation including correspondence, pictures, pamphlets, periodicals, and minutes of meetings. There is material pertaining to all member unions in the county and to the Committee on Political Education (COPE). Microfilm contains the minutes of the Federation's executive board meetings from 1962 to 1968 and the minutes of COPE meetings from 1958 to 1969.

385. **Hartzell, B. F. (1880-1957).** Correspondence, Jan. 25, 1953; April 29, 1957. 2 letters. Gift of Dr. Earl L. Core, 1968. No. 2040.

Two letters giving information about B. F. Hartzell, a resident of Shepherdstown and a noted botanist.

386. **Hatfield, Coleman.** Typescript, 1968. 190p. (photocopies). Gift of Coleman Hatfield, 1969. No. 2120.
Copy of a manuscript, "Tales of the Feuding Hatfields," by Coleman Hatfield. Much of the material pertains to humorous anecdotes and family stories passed down through the various generations of Hatfields. (RESTRICTED)

387. **Hatfield, Henry Drury (1875-1962).** Papers and correspondence, 1913-1958. 9 ft. Gift of the estate of H. D. Hatfield, 1963, and Miss Karolyn Karr, 1967. Nos. 1661, 1955.
Correspondence, farm records, legal and financial records, speeches, medical files, photographs, newspaper clippings, and a biographical sketch of Henry D. Hatfield, Governor, 1913-1917, U. S. Senator, 1929-1935, and who was also chief surgeon and founder of Huntington Memorial Hospital.

Subjects include West Virginia and national politics, 1928-1933, 1944-1957; National Republican conventions of 1912, 1928, 1944, 1948, and 1952; criticism of the New Deal and the Fair Deal; the NRA; the Virginia-West Virginia debt controversy; the West Virginia Anti-Communist League; Army-McCarthy controversy; United Mine Workers medical welfare cases; Mary "Mother" Jones; the Kessler-Hatfield Hospital and Training School; Hatfield's farming interests; and Sycamore Coal, Guyan Eagle Coal, Tidewater Coal and Coke, and other coal companies in which Hatfield had an interest.

Correspondents include William Blizzard, John W. Bricker, William E. Chilton, Jr., William G. Conley, Thomas E. Dewey, Everett M. Dirksen, Benjamin F. Fairless, Walter F. George, Walter S. Hallanan, Harvey W. Harmer, Cecil B. Highland, Herbert Hoover, Harley M. Kilgore, John L. Lewis, Robert R. McCormick, William C. Marland, Joseph W. Martin, Jr., Clarence W. Meadows, Matthew M. Neely, H. C. Ogden, Okey L. Patteson, Carroll Reece, Chapman Revercomb, Robert A. Taft, and Kenneth Wherry.

388. **Haymond, Luther (1809-1909).** Diary and surveyor's book, 1830-1833, 1849. 2 items, 33p., 22p. Gifts of Mrs. Sally Ailes, 1955, and Mrs. Logan Carroll, 1965. Nos. 772, 1797.
Diary of observations by Luther Haymond (1809-1909), a surveyor, while traveling by horse from Harrison County to Baltimore, Maryland. There are descriptions of Baltimore, Romney, Charles Town, and other places. The surveyor's book shows the first five-mile section of the Weston and Fairmont Road. Haymond was engineer for the Weston and Fairmont Turnpike Co., 1849.

389.	**Haymond, William** (1771-1848). Typescript, 1893. 1 item. 22p. Transfer, 1963. No. 1695.

"Family Record of William Haymond, Father of Rebeckah Haymond, who married Thomas Watson, May 13th, Anno Domini, 1813," includes typescript copies of the family Bible record and letters of Haymond, a pioneer resident of the Palatine tract in Marion County, to his nephew, Luther Haymond, 1842 (eight letters). The letters are personal recollections of frontier life in the Monongahela, Tygart, Ohio, and Kanawha valleys, covering the period ca. 1780-1793. Subjects include the settlement of Morgantown, Clarksburg, Williamstown, the Palatine tract, Coburn's Fort; land surveys in Harrison County; trapping and hunting; road surveying; and Indian warfare.

390.	**Haymond Family.** Papers, 1783 (1825-1867). 52 items. Gift of Mrs. Frank M. Atterholt, 1955. No. 724.

Correspondence and papers received by Thomas Haymond, the surveyor, and Luther Haymond, postmaster, at Clarksburg, concerning land in Harrison County.

391.	**Haymond-Fleming Law Firm.** Papers, 1760-1936. 1 ft. No. 544.

Correspondence of A. F. Haymond and A. Brooks Fleming, Fairmont attorneys. Writers of letters include J. M. Bennett, G. D. Camden, J. Carlile, Henry Mathews, and F. H. Pierpont mentioning politics, separation from Virginia, the Arthurdale community development, and routine legal business. Included are land and legal papers, 1760-1797, from Hampshire, Monongalia, and Ohio counties, mentioning Patrick Henry and Henry Lee. Also in the collection are estate papers and marriage records; stock certificates of early West Virginia public utility and industrial firms; and miscellaneous personal papers of A. Brooks Fleming.

392.	**Hayner Distilling Co.** Letter and circular, December 12, 1900. 2 items. No. 375.

Letter and circular from Dayton, Ohio, quoting prices for whiskey, wine, brandy, gin, and rum.

393.	**Hays, R. L.,** *Collector.* Papers, 1825-1890. 7 items. Gift of R. L. Hays, 1933. No. 16.

Notes of William Queen and William Norris; a letter of H. N. Ogden, with a printed circular, to Peregrine Hays, October 27, 1890, regarding instruction in English being given by Ogden at West Virginia University.

394.	**Heck, Colonel Jonathan M.** Typescript, n.d. 3p. Gift of Mrs. Paul R. Cockshutt, 1971. No. 2206.

A biographical sketch of Jonathan M. Heck, a native of Morgantown, a lieutenant colonel in the Confederate Army who commanded the Twenty-fifth Virginia Infantry at the Battle of Rich Mountain in Randolph County in 1861. Also included is a description of Heck's Second Empire house located in Raleigh, North Carolina.

395. **Heebink, Gerald (1895-1956).** Papers, ca. 1927-1956. 13 ft. Transfers, 1958, 1961. Nos. 1142, 1470.

The papers of an extension dairyman in the West Virginia University College of Agriculture pertaining to Heebink's work with artificial breeders' cooperatives; the Dairy Herd Improvement Association; and the dairy cattle organizations in West Virginia and the United States. Other material includes annual reports, speeches, notebooks, and articles.

396. **Helvetia.** Typescript, 1960. 18p. (photocopy). Original in possession of Edwin A. Smith, 1960. No. 1346.

Unpublished manuscript, "Helvetia, the Swiss Land of West Virginia," by Edwin A. Smith, is the history of a Randolph County community established in 1869 by a group of Swiss immigrants.

397. **Hendershot, R. H.** Shipping bills, ca. 1850-1854. 1 volume. Gift of Nanon L. Hendershot, 1940. No. 71.

Volume of shipping bills showing names of steamboats, masters, cargoes, and destinations of boats departing from Powhatan Point [Ohio?]. Pittsburgh, Wheeling, and Marietta, Ohio, were the usual destinations.

398. **Henderson, John.** Manuscript, 1961. 1 item (photocopy). Original in possession of Earl L. Core, 1961. No. 1539.

Sketch, written by Bessie Ammons, of a Disciples of Christ minister who served several communities in the western part of Monongalia County in the 1860s.

399. **Henderson, Noah.** Papers, 1859-1909. 116 items. Gift of Ralph Fordyce, 1955. No. 787.

Personal papers of Noah Henderson of Monongalia County, consisting mainly of incoming correspondence, a few deeds, tax receipts, bills, surveys, plats, and oil and gas leases. Included are eight letters written to Henderson by Alpheus Garrison, a Union soldier during the Civil War.

400. **Henderson-Tomlinson Families.** Papers, (1798-1859) 1936. 1 reel of microfilm (1 unbound typescript volume). Typescripts in possession of Mrs. Josephine Phillips, 1961. No. 1426.

Journals and papers of the Henderson-Tomlinson family, copied by Ronald Good, Historical Research Project, National Youth Administration, 1936, from the originals in possession of Jock B. Henderson of Williamstown.

There papers pertain to frontier life in the Parkersburg-Marietta area and include a journal on the settlement of Alexander Henderson's land on the Little Kanawha, 1798-1803; his plantation accounts; letters on the Burr conspiracy; an account of a duel between Henderson and Stephen R. Wilson, 1803; letters of and materials on Archibald Henderson, United States Marine Corps Commandant, Washington, D. C.; papers and a sketch of a pioneer, Isaac Williams; a newsclipping on Margaret Blennerhassett, 1859; the Tomlinson family record; and A. B. Tomlinson's account of the Indian mounds and frontier settlement at Grave Creek.

Correspondents include Michael Cresap. There is a name index to the collection.

401. **Hendricks.** Business records, 1897-1944. 25 ft. Gift of W. A. O'Dell, 1954. No. 659.

Correspondence, business papers, and account books of several companies in the town of Hendricks. Included are records of J. E. Poling and Company; Hendricks Lumber Company; Piedmont Grocery Company; C. W. Harvey & Company; J. C. Orrick and Son Company; and the Baer Grocery Company of Cumberland, Maryland.

402. **Henry, Michael.** Document, September, 1790. 1 item. No. 376.

Sworn complaint by Michael Henry of Monongalia County against John Pierpont for unlawfully holding a slave belonging to Henry.

403. **Henshaw Family.** Correspondence, 1786, 1809-1891. 62 items. Acquired, 1955. No. 730.

Letters to the Henshaw family at Mill Creek, Berkeley County, by relatives.

404. **Herd Books.** Records, 1916-1923. 2 volumes. Gift of J. R. Caldwell, 1951. No. 298.

Record of cattle bred, diagrams showing color markings, buyers, and prices.

405. **Hereford, Frank (1825-1891).** Correspondence, 1866-1901. 2 reels of microfilm (2 folders). Originals in possession of Mrs. H. A. Hereford, Sr., 1960. Nos. 1367, 1386.

Correspondence of a lawyer, Democratic congressman, 1871-1877, and U. S. senator, 1877-1881, from West Virginia. Subjects include West Virginia politics; the "Salary Grab" Act of 1873; the political activities of Johnson N. Camden and H. G. Davis; and Hereford's attempt to secure a position on the Utah Commission, 1886. Correspondents include Johnson N. Camden, Charles J. Faulkner, John E. Kenna, J. W. McCreery, and Daniel W. Voorhees.

406. **Hess, James R.,** *Collector.* Legal documents and receipt, 1760-1800. 4 items. Gift of James R. Hess, 1966. No. 1931.

Documents include a naturalization certificate issued in 1760; a warrant of indebtedness, 1770; and a warrant sworn against Samuel May by his wife, 1771. The receipt is for insurance with the Mutual Assurance Society, Richmond, Virginia, in 1800.

407. **Hess Dustless Mining Machine Co.** Certificate, July 3, 1912. 1 item. Gift of Mrs. Susie Rudd, 1966. No. 1890.

Certificate of Incorporation of the Hess Dustless Mining Machine Company, July 3, 1912, in the town of Ansted, Fayette County.

408. **Hill, Jacob I.** Papers, 1858-1874. 21 items. No. 377.

A contract signed by Hill to teach Latin, Greek, and mathematics in the Huttonsville Academy in 1858; an amnesty oath and other papers signed by Hill, a captain in the Confederate Army; a certificate of election as superintendent of schools in Randolph County, 1873; and other papers.

409. **Hill, Joseph H. (b. ca. 1850).** 1 typescript, 1939. 6p. Gift of James L. Creasy, 1939. No. 61.

Reminiscences of Joseph H. Hill, including the Civil War period in Nicholas County.

410. **Hill, Sanford.** Typescript, 1954. 12p. (photostat). Original owned by the Industrial Information Institute, Inc., 1958. No. 1076.

Typescript entitled "Sanford and His Almanacs" tells the story of a man who was handicapped throughout his life but was a dry goods store owner, a surveyor, a civil engineer, and a weather prognosticator for several almanacs.

411. **Hinkle, Leafy,** *Collector.* Papers, 1882-1934. 6 items. Gift of Mrs. Leafy Hinkle, 1954. No. 689.

Population data for nine West Virginia cities in 1930, 1932, and 1934; receipt for a coffin, 1882; and clippings on the deaths of the Reverend Benjamin Stout, Bridgeport, and Dr. M. S. Holt, Weston.

412. **Hirst, Daniel (b. 1809).** Notebooks, 1825-1846. 8 items. Gift of Donald Lee Cunard, 1966. No. 1866.

Seven notebooks and booklets, one folder of miscellaneous material, notes and class materials of Daniel Hirst, who taught school in Loudoun County, Virginia, around 1826 and later. There are exercises and definitions on practical mathematics, surveying, algebra, geometry, simple accounting and English grammar.

413. **Hoblitzell, John D., Jr. (1912-1962).** Papers, 1956-1962. 3 ft. Gift of Mrs. John D. Hoblitzell, Jr., 1962. No. 1580.

Correspondence, speeches, and newspaper clippings of a state Republican chairman, U. S. senator, and member of the 1960 Republican National Convention platform committee.

Subjects include state and national Republican politics, 1956-1961; the 1958 Congressional election; the 1960 presidential campaign; the State Chamber of Commerce; State Economic Development Agency; Ohio Valley Improvement Association; and West Virginia University.

Correspondents include Sherman Adams, Stephen Ailes, Meade Alcorn, W. W. Barron, Harry Byrd, Robert Byrd, Erwin D. Canham, Clifford P. Case, John Sherman Cooper, Carl T. Curtis, Everett M. Dirksen, Henry Dworshak, Dwight D. Eisenhower, Allen J. Ellender, Hiram L. Fong, Barry Goldwater, Leonard W. Hall, Walter S. Hallanan, Ken Hechler, Bourke Hickenlooper, Hubert H. Humphrey, Lyndon B. Johnson, Elizabeth Kee, Thomas H. Kuchel, Henry Cabot Lodge, Edward Martin, Jack Miller, Arch A. Moore, Thruston B. Morton, Karl Mundt, Harold Neely, Richard M. Nixon, Jennings Randolph, Carroll Reece, Chapman Revercomb, A. Willis Robertson, Richard B. Russell, Leverett Saltonstall, Fred A. Seaton, John M. Slack, John Sparkman, Strom Thurmond, Cecil H. Underwood, and Alexander Wiley.

414. **Hoffman, John E. (d. 1863).** Papers, 1862-1863. Ca. 200 items. Gift of Mrs. Hardin R. Harmer, 1961. No. 1520.

Correspondence, military papers, and a diary of a Morgantown lieutenant in Company C, Third West Virginia Cavalry, Army of the Potomac. Hoffman saw action at Cedar Mountain, Second Bull Run,

Chancellorsville, and Gettysburg and was killed in action on November 24, 1863. Correspondence is primarily from his father, John H., a Morgantown lawyer, his family, and his lady friends, and pertains to life in Morgantown during the Civil War. The diary covers the period, January 1-November 24, 1863.

415. **Hoffman, John Stringer (1821-1877).** Papers, ca. 1856-1883. 1 ft. Gift of Robert S. Wilson, 1963. No. 1703.

Legal correspondence and papers of a Clarksburg lawyer who specialized in land title litigation and served as associate judge of the Supreme Court of Appeals of West Virginia, 1862-1876.

Papers pertain to lands in the central counties of West Virginia. Subjects include: the James Swan lands; European immigration to West Virginia following the Civil War; New York Southern Land Company; Philadelphia International Land Association; state economic development during Reconstruction; and timberlands on Shaver's Mountain.

Correspondents include J. M. Bennett, John S. Carlile, William Henry Edwards, David Goff, and Cyrus Hall.

One volume is a record of the settlement of the estate of Judge John S. Hoffman, November 18, 1877-January 1, 1892 (eleventh and last settlement), by G. D. Camden and J. R. Boggess.

416. **Holme, Frank (1868-1904).** Papers, ca. 1894-1941. Ca. 200 items. Acquired, 1959. Nos. 1167, 1178.

Papers of Frank Holme, illustrator for the Pittsburgh *Press*, Chicago *Times*, and San Francisco *Chronicle* during the 1890s; founder of the Palette and Chisel Club, the School of Illustration in Chicago, and the Bandar Log Press. Includes correspondence, newspaper clippings, original etchings, a wash painting, photographs, and printed materials.

Subjects include the School of Illustration; the Bandar Log Press; The Frank Holme Memorial Group; the life of Holme and his wife, Ida Van Dyke; and an exhibition of drawings by John T. McCutcheon, Frank Holme, and William Schmedtgen at the Chicago Art Institute in 1897.

Correspondents include Vause Marshall and George Ade.

417. **Holt, Helen.** Papers, 1938-1959. 8 ft. Gift of Helen Holt (Mrs. Rush D. Holt), 1965. No. 1858.

Correspondence and papers of a delegate to the West Virginia Legislature, 1955-1956; West Virginia secretary of state, 1957-1959; and assistant commissioner of public institutions, 1959-1960. Subjects include school appropriation; acts of the legislature; lists of Republican officials; positions taken by Mrs. Holt on political issues; reading improvement program in industry; aid for the blind and mentally ill; review of the business and occupation tax; salaries of state road commission engineers; Summersville Dam Project; Korean veterans' bonus bonds; vocational rehabilitation; property assessment; workmen's compensation; handicapped children; Interstate Highway 77; prisoners' aid movement; Weston State Hospital; Meadow River Flood Control Project; West Virginia Training School at St. Marys; capital punishment; and juvenile delinquency. Included are form letters, news releases, newspaper clippings, and speeches.

Correspondents include J. G. Bradley, William Langer, Irvin Stewart, and Cecil Underwood. (RESTRICTED)

418. **Holt, Homer Adams (b. 1898).** Papers, 1937-1944. 2 ft. Gift of Homer A. Holt, 1961. No. 1450.

Correspondence, messages, and state papers of West Virginia's twentieth governor, 1937-1941, and manuscript drafts of *West Virginia: A Guide to the Mountain State,* 1941.

Subjects include the controversy over the review policies and contents of the West Virginia *Guide;* dispute with the Surplus Commodities Corporation over the distribution of food to striking miners in the southern coal fields, 1939; the H. G. Kump-M. M. Neely primary contest, 1942; support for Rush D. Holt's isolationist policies; the gubernatorial race, 1940; the contest between the Steel Workers' Organizing Committee and the Weirton Steel Employees' Security League, 1937; Holt's opposition to the "Little Hatch Bill"; the establishment of a merit council in the Department of Public Assistance, 1939-1940; and Holt's presidential address before the West Virginia Bar Association, 1944.

Correspondents include John J. Cornwell, John W. Davis, Rush D. Holt, George W. Johnson, Paul V. McNutt, Matthew M. Neely, Milo Perkins, Lee Pressman, Jennings Randolph, Chapman Revercomb, Franklin D. Roosevelt, and William H. Vanderbilt.

419. **Holt, Rush Dew (1905-1955).** Papers, 1851-1955. 184 ft. Gift of Mrs. Rush D. Holt, 1956, 1963. Nos. 867, 873, 1701.

Correspondence and papers of Rush Dew Holt, Lewis County, as a sports writer, teacher, West Virginia state legislator at various dates from 1931 to 1949, and U. S. senator from West Virginia, 1935-1941. Material includes clippings, scrapbooks, photographs, speeches, phonograph recordings, writings, press releases, political cartoons, and printed matter. Also included are personal papers of Dr. M. S. Holt (1850-1939), father of Senator Holt, and Ralph K. Chase (1900-1947), brother-in-law of the senator.

Subjects include: state and national politics, 1920-1954; U. S. Senator Matthew M. Neely; the public utilities industry and investigations of the industry by the West Virginia House of Delegates; the Wheeler-Rayburn Holding Company Act; taxation and the cost of government; the National Recovery Administration; Huey P. Long; organized labor (including the United Mine Workers of America, the Congress of Industrial Organizations, the American Federation of Labor, the Progressive Miners of America, John L. Lewis, and Van A. Bittner); the Works Progress Administration; Harry L. Hopkins; Walter Thurmond; the Guffey Coal Act; the National Bituminous Coal Commission; the National Labor Relations Board; public education; the Supreme Court reorganization bill; the anti-lynching bill; social security and government relief; political patronage and graft; reciprocal trade agreements; the Roosevelt Administration's foreign policy; and the America First Committee. Correspondents include Michael L. Benedum, Van A. Bittner, Hugo L. Black, Harry F. Byrd, William G. Conley, Roy Bird Cook, Charles E. Coughlin, John B. Easton, Andrew Edmiston, James A. Farley, Hamilton Fish, John N. Garner, William Green, Walter S. Hallanan, Sigfrid Hauck, Homer A. Holt, Matthew S. Holt, Sr., Harry L. Hopkins, Harold Ickes, Anna Jarvis, Hiram Johnson, John Kee, Robert G. Kelly, H. G. Kump, Robert M. LaFollette, Jr., William Lemke, John L. Lewis, Huey P. Long, Sam Mallison, Clarence W. Meadows, H. L. Mencken, Matthew M. Neely, Gerald P. Nye, George N. Peek, Claude Pepper, Jennings Randolph, John E. Rankin, James Roosevelt, Upton Sinclair, Gerald L. K. Smith, Walter R. Thurmond, Hector B. Trujillo, Harry S Truman, John R. Turner, Burton K. Wheeler, Walter White, and Aubrey Williams.

There are processing notes for the correspondence during the years 1928-1942 which give a fuller description of the collection.

The papers of M. S. Holt, Sr., concern the newspaper business, horse breeding, local, state, and national politics, the Socialist Party of West Virginia, and the practice of medicine. There are medical account books, an account book for the Weston *Republican*, ca. 1879-1880, and two daybooks for the Weston *Republican*, 1881-1893.

The papers of Ralph K. Chase include legal and personal correspondence, law school notebooks, and materials relating to the U. S. Maritime Commission; papers of Andrew E. Holt, brother of Rush D. Holt, and papers relating to the Weston Cash Grocery and other family matters.

Also included are seventeen tape recordings of speeches by Senator Holt and other current affairs and political campaigns. (RESTRICTED)

420. **Holt Family.** Papers, 1887-1926. 43 items. Gift of Harry Keyes, 1954. No. 628.

Papers of Samuel T. H. Holt, and other members of the Holt family of Philippi. There are deeds centering in Randolph, Barbour, and Tucker counties; correspondence; a medical prescription; and a clipping on Whitescarver Hall, Broaddus Institute, Philippi. Mention is made of the Wheeling Development Company.

421. **Holt-Keyes Families.** Papers, 1878-1944. 2 ft. Gift of Harry Keyes, 1954. No. 631.

Business and personal correspondence of several members of the Holt and Keyes families of Barbour County, including Ben. M., Charles,

Samuel T. H., and Stephen Holt, and W. G. and Bertha Holt Keyes. The collection includes records of firms operated by these families, mainly the Keyes Lumber Company, the Holt Ice Company, and Holt's Mill; genealogical material on the Holt family; records relating to foundries, coal, coke, building supplies, general merchandise, farm and construction work, mine post sales, and the Elk Creek Oil and Gas Company.

422. **Hominy Falls Mine Disaster.** Tape recordings, May 8, 1968. 5 reels. Loaned for reproduction by Jim Comstock, 1968. No. 2047.

Interviews conducted with six survivors of the Hominy Falls mine disaster, Nicholas County, West Virginia, which occurred on May 18, 1968. Interviews were conducted at the Sacred Heart Hospital on May 18, 1968. (RESTRICTED)

423. **Hope Manufacturing and Coal Company.** Records, 1876-1906. 9 reels of microfilm (28 volumes). Transfer, 1961. No. 1535.

Daybooks and ledgers of a company store operated by the Hope Manufacturing and Coal Company in Mason City. The Hope Company was also an early producer of salt in the Mason County area.

424. **Hopkins, Andrew Delmar (1857-1948).** Papers, 1787, 1826 (1873-1943). 2 ft. Transfer, 1949, and gift of Raymond W. Sooy, 1956. Nos. 143, 904.

Correspondence, reports, clippings, project notes, and other materials of Dr. Andrew D. Hopkins who was vice-director of the West Virginia Agricultural Experiment Station, professor of entomology at West Virginia University, 1890-1902, forest entomologist with the U. S. Department of Agriculture, 1902-1923, and a researcher in bioclimatics with the USDA at Kanawha Farms, Wood County, 1923-1933.

425. **Hornor, Louise, Family.** Papers, ca. 1783-1956. 2 reels of microfilm (2 volumes and 11 folders). Originals in possession of Miss Louise Hornor, 1959. No. 1161.

The collection includes records of the Joshua Allen, Bartlett, William Ferguson, J. C. Garrett, Gore, Green, Joseph Mayse, Richards, Robinson, Joshua Smith, and other Harrison County families; an obituary clipping book; the minute book of the Hepzibah Baptist Church, 1861-1888; and two letters from Governor Howard M. Gore to Mrs. C. L. Hornor, 1926.

426. **Hotel.** Register, 1885-1888. 1 item. Gift of Ray Jenkins, 1954. No. 678.

Register for the Talbott House at St. George, W. B. Jenkins & Brother, proprietors.

427. **Hough, Clara.** Diary, 1876-1877. 2 items. Gift of John Koval, 1949. No. 158.

Diary of Miss Clara Hough, Morgantown, for the year 1877; and notes, 1876, on a letterhead of West Virginia University, bearing the name of Miss Mamie Hough.

428. **Howard, Adolphus P.** Papers, 1850-1938. 1 ft. Gifts of Adam J. Gibas and H. H. Howard, 1952. Nos. 511, 515, 517.

Family and business papers of John F. Howard, his son, Adolphus P., and other members of the Howard family. The business correspondence includes information on A. P. Howard's interests and enterprises; farming; livestock; fruit and produce, Wellsville, Ohio; a printing firm in Columbus, Ohio; the J. W. & A. P. Howard Company, a tannery in Corry, Pennsylvania; banking in Pittsburgh, Pennsylvania; and a farm at Congo, West Virginia. Some of the 1850 correspondence is to A. G. DeSellem, Port Homer, Ohio, regarding the American Missionary Association and antislavery activities.

429. **Howe, William.** Order book, 1795. 1 volume. Gift of W. H. Sawyers, 1932. No. 11.

A regimental order book of troops under the command of General Sir William Howe, at Newcastle and Whitely, England, July, 1795.

430. **Hubbard Family.** Papers, 1794-1914. 1 ft. Gift of Chester R. Hubbard, 1955, 1960. Nos. 755, 805, 1316.

Papers, mainly correspondence, of the Hubbard family of New Haven and Litchfield, Connecticut, and Wheeling. There are several hundred letters which document the growth of the family and its business enterprises in Wheeling. Correspondents include Chester D. Hubbard, General John Hubbard, Stephen B. Elkins, John W. Mason, and W. T. Willey.

There are manuscripts of addresses and an essay on languages by C. D. Hubbard; photographs of public buildings in McDowell County and the tollgate on the National Road at Leatherwood Lane, Wheeling; and a grant, July 3, 1794, from Levi Hollingsworth to Robert Morris for 20,000 acres in Ohio County. Included also are a number of letters written in Wheeling which comment on the statehood movement and Civil War activities in that city; and a typescript, "Reminiscences of His Schoolboy Days," by Joseph Bell (1819-1908), which describes early nineteenth century Wheeling.

431. **Hughes, Alfred.** Stock certificates, 1852-1865. 4 items. No. 841.

Stock certificates for the Manufacturers & Farmers Bank of Wheeling, 1852; the Goose Creek Oil Company of Wheeling, 1865; and the Hugh McCulloch Oil & Mining Company, 1865; also a receipt from the Wheeling Water Works, 1862.

432. **Hunt, Nancy (1820-1891).** Letter, July 26, 1737. 1 item. Gift of Charles A. Goddard, 1937. No. 89.

A letter, July 26, 1737, from W. Beverley, one of the commissioners for Lord Fairfax on the survey of the Rappahannock and Potomac rivers to William Fairfax, and Fairfax's reply, discussing the report on the survey and its maps.

433. **Hunter, Bernard E.,** *Collector.* Papers, ca. 1922-1959. 1 ft. Gift of Bernard E. Hunter, 1959. Nos. 1165, 1208.

Correspondence, notes, clippings, and articles on the town of Bath (Berkeley Springs), West Virginia Foundation for Crippled Children, the State Health Department, and the genealogy of the Allen-Kesecker, Buzzard, Joseph Cox, Ensminger, John Grove, Gano, Gore, High, Wheat, and Zeilor families.

434. **Huntington State Hospital.** Papers, 1863-1897. Ca. 30 items. Transfer, 1970. No. 2149.

Correspondence and documents pertaining to the West Virginia Asylum for the Incurables, now Huntington State Hospital, mainly concerning the location of a suitable site by the office of the secretary of state. Correspondents include John W. Davis and W. A. MacCorkle.

435. **Hutter, Gottlieb, and Sons.** Account books, 1858-1934. 1 ft. Gift of Alfred Hutter, 1962. No. 1588.

Account books of tinsmiths from Moorefield, Hardy County.

436. **Ice, W. T., Jr.** Journal, 1908-1932. 1 volume. Gift of Charles Carpenter, 1961. No. 1419.

Business journal of a Philippi attorney.

437. **Ice's Ferry.** Typescripts, ca. 1700-1920. 30p. Gifts of John C. Bayles, 1949; and transfer, 1953. Nos. 379, 553.

An account of the Ice family and of Ice's Ferry in Monongalia County, with comments on frontier and pioneer life in western Virginia, apparently written by Virginia H. Conaway of Marion County. Also a typescript, "Historical Notes on Ice's Ferry," by John L. Johnston written in 1920, which locates and describes early settlements; roads; forts; Indian trails, villages and tribes; industries; the land office; and men and families prominent in the development of the areas near Ice's Ferry and in Monongalia County. Mention is made of the proposed construction of a dam and recreation area on the Cheat River.

438.   **Iden, Mrs. Gay,** *Collector.* Papers, 1897, 1910, 1941. 6 items. Gift of Ralph Bennett, 1970. No. 2155.

Correspondence, pictures, and charts collected by Mrs. Gay (Bennett) Iden, including two letters written by J. T. McFarlane, from aboard the U.S.S. *Bear* on an expedition to the South Pole in 1941; one hand-drawn chart showing the rate schedule of the Monongahela and Ohio Packet Company, ca. 1910; one photo showing a group of West Virginia University co-eds in 1897; one photo of an M. & O. Packet boat; and a picture postcard showing boats on the Monongahela around 1910.

439.   **Indians.** Document, 1776. 1 item. Transfer, 1953. No. 578.

Information against David Ross, charging him with committing acts to incite Indian attacks in Pittsylvania County, Virginia.

440.   **Indians.** Typescripts, 1925, 1928. 8 items, 13p. Gifts of John L. Johnston, ca. 1925, and F. A. Chapman, ca. 1929. Nos. 1, 2.

Sketches of the Great and Little Warrior trails and the McCullough Trail, and an illustrated description, made by F. A. Chapman, Wellsburg, of a mill found near Johnstown, Pennsylvania, which was used in Indian harvest ceremonies.

441.   **Ingalls, James Monroe (1837-1927).** Service records, 1865-1898. 1 reel of microfilm. Gift of Prof. H. W. Gould, 1966. No. 1903.

Selected documents from the service record of Col. James Monroe Ingalls, U. S. Army, who was professor of military science and tactics and professor of mathematics at West Virginia University, 1877-1878. The collection includes correspondence and memoranda, 1878-1884, concerning the retention of Ingalls at WVU or the assignment of another qualified officer, comments on the inadequacy of the law governing the apportionment of officers to land-grant colleges, and a catalog of the professional works and papers of Ingalls.

Correspondents include William W. Belknap, James R. Thompson, George W. McCrary, Rutherford B. Hayes, Waitman T. Willey, and George C. Sturgiss.

442. **Iron Furnaces.** Typescripts, 1954, 1959. 6p. Gift of Philip H. Trout, 1959. No. 1250.

Notes on the early iron furnaces in the Allegheny-Botetourt-Roanoke County area of Virginia; a brief history of the John Tayloe family, early pioneers in the iron industry; and photographs of the Tayloe iron furnace at Cloverdale, Botetourt County.

443. **Irons, J. C.** Letter, June 28, 1898. 1 item. Transfer. No. 381.

To William Campbell, Charles Town, regarding arrangements for the next Democratic convention.

444. **Ison, W. O.** Letters, 1873-1880. Ca. 200 items. Gift of H. M. Hickerson, 1940. No. 73.

Letters written to Professor W. O. Ison, Morgantown, mainly from members of his immediate family.

445. **Jackson, George (1757-1831).** Letter, February 22, 1803. 1 item. Gift of Boyd B. Stutler, 1964. No. 1748.

Letter from a Clarksburg attorney, justice of the peace, delegate to the Virginia General Assembly, 1785-1791, 1794, and U. S. congressman, 1795-1797, 1799-1803, "To the Freeholders of the Northwestern Congressional District of Virginia." Jackson expresses his intention not to run for reelection and comments on the political situation and the issues of the day.

446. **Jackson, Thomas Jonathan (1824-1863).** Papers, 1845-1862, 1951. 123 items. Loans and gifts of D. H. Hill Arnold, 1936; Mrs. Marie Pifer, 1954; station WLW, Cincinnati, Ohio, 1951, and acquisition, 1962. Nos. 47, 264, 636, 1597.

Three original letters, 1855, 1856, and 1858; 188 photostats of letters written by Jackson from various places in the United States, Mexico, and at sea, to his sister and niece; and a script of a radio broadcast, "Stonewall Jackson," over station WLW on August 21, 1951.

447. **Jackson, William A. (1865-1957).** Papers, 1892-1930. 2 reels of microfilm. Gift of William A. Jackson, 1954. No. 660.

Papers and records of W. W. Smith, J. G. Jackson, and W. A. Jackson, and of various businesses established by these men in Jane Lew. There are many papers of the firm of Jackson and Burnside, cattle dealers, relating to the shipping and sale of livestock to commission merchants in New Jersey, Baltimore, Maryland, and Pittsburgh, Pennsylvania. Also included are accounts and correspondence of the West Virginia Christian Endeavor Society and papers commenting on Democratic politics, ca. 1916; the American Aberdeen-Angus Breeders Association; the board of education at Jane Lew; sale of lumber; South Penn Oil Company, Fink; the Parkersburg-Buckhannon Oil and Gas Company; and the Jane Lew High School Athletic Association.

448. **Jackson County.** Records, 1848-1858. 2 volumes. Gift of C. A. Hill, 1954. No. 662.

Execution book, 1848-1850, and county court fee book, 1850-1858.

449. **Jackson County.** Cemetery Readings, ca. 1966-1971. 25p. Gift of Rev. C. Shirley Donnelly, 1971. No. 2217.

Cemetery readings from Jackson County, ca. 1800-1966, including the Barnett Cemetery at Rock Castle; the Foster Chapel Cemetery; the Levi Moore Cemetery; the Given Cemetery; the Fairview Cemetery; the Mt. Moriah Church Cemetery; and the Pleasant Hill Cemetery.

450. **Jacob, F. H. and Samuel.** Papers, 1824-1921. Ca. 200 items. Gift of Robert Jacob, 1955. No. 792.

Personal and business papers of Samuel Jacob, and F. H. Jacob of Wellsburg. There are a few items relating to the Wellsburg Manufacturing Company, ca. 1870, and six unidentified cash and account books, 1832-1849, 1871-1911.

451. **Jacob, John Jeremiah (1829-1893).** Papers, 1866-1878. Ca. 200 items. Gift of Mrs. Nannie Jacob Baird, 1933. No. 22

Correspondence, petitions, certificates, reports, and other official and private papers of the fourth governor of West Virginia, 1871-1877, who was an attorney in Hampshire County, a legislator, 1869, and judge of the first West Virginia Judicial Circuit.

Correspondents include Stephen B. Elkins, John J. Davis, and J. Marshall Hagans.

452. **Jacobs, Thomas P.** Papers, 1890, 1918. 2 items. Loan from Paul L. Morgan, 1964. No. 1739.

A certificate of membership in the West Virginia Historical and Antiquarian Society issued to T. P. Jacobs of New Martinsville on February 4, 1890, and a typescript letter from J. M. Mason, University of Virginia, August 9, 1918, to T. P. Jacobs concerning the printing and circulation of a five-page typescript letter on the Virginia debt controversy.

453. James River and Kanawha Company. Certificate, March 4, 1840. 1 item. Gift of J. N. Alderson, 1952. No. 493.

A certificate of three shares of stock issued to Joseph Alderson.

454. Jamestown Exposition. Document, March 13, 1907. 5p. Acquired, 1964. No. 1729.

Contract between George A. Vincent and Virgil A. Lewis concerning items owned by Vincent used in the West Virginia exhibit at the Jamestown Exposition.

455. Jarvis, Anna (1864-1948). Papers, 1858-1958. 2 ft. (1 reel of microfilm). Loan of Lawrence Burns, 1959, and gift of Mrs. Rose Basigio, 1961. Nos. 1175, 1439.

Correspondence, speeches, business and legal papers, newspaper clippings, and photographs of the founder of Mother's Day. The collection includes papers of Anna's father, Grandville E. Jarvis; the notes and typescript drafts of "Recollections of Ann M. Jarvis, 1833-1905," by Anna Jarvis; and the papers of the Fairmont songwriter, William Lynett.

Subjects include Miss Jarvis' efforts to institute Mother's Day on a state by state basis, and her later protest against the commercialization of the day of remembrance; Jarvis coal and farm lands in Taylor County; real estate holdings in Philadelphia; Quaker City Cab Company; and Miss Jarvis' activities in the library department of a Philadelphia insurance company.

Correspondents include Mrs. W. R. Hearst, Spessard L. Holland, John T. McGraw, John W. Mason, Matthew M. Neely, and Jennings Randolph.

456. Jefferds, Joseph C., *Collector.* Papers, 1896-1965. 3 ft. Gift of Joseph C. Jefferds, 1967. No. 1983.

Correspondence, sketches, records, charts, broadsides, newspapers, pamphlets, books, and one West Virginia University cadet uniform of 1898. There are typescript carbon copies of county court records from Bath County, Virginia, and Greenbrier and Pocahontas counties, West Virginia; list of scholars attending Lewisburg Academy 1883-1885; and genealogical material on Arbuckle, Beard, Bell, Boone, Bright, Burger, Burr, Cooley, Cunningham-Gudgell, Dickinson, Feamster, Gillilan, Gilmore, Griffith, Handley, Haptonstall, Hunter, Kincaid, Lisle, Lyle-Montgomery, Mann-McClintic, Mathews, Mauzy, McCue, McMillion, McNeel, Poage, Price, Quarrier, Rader, Renick, Revercomb, Shrewsbury, Steele, Walkup, Warwick, and Young-Kemper families.

Correspondents include T. E. Hodges.

457. **Jefferson County.** Archives, 1802-1913. 63 ft. Gift of the Jefferson County Court, 1937, 1941. No. 382.

Court case papers, 1802-1913, and county record books, 1830-1905; included are records for retail merchandising, 1884-1894, in Jefferson County. A partial name and subject index to the case papers and a checklist of the bound volumes are available in the manuscripts section.

458. **Jenkins, Samuel R. (b. 1870).** Diaries and pictures, 1890-1934. 1 ft. Gift of Charles Carpenter, 1964. No. 1761.

Eighteen diaries, 1890-1934, of Samuel R. Jenkins, a civil engineer from Grafton. There is considerable detail during the period 1890-1892 when Jenkins was a student at West Virginia University. He did surveys and supervised construction work in various parts of West Virginia, Pennsylvania, and New Jersey, read widely, and commented on works of Henry George, John W. Draper, and John Fiske. There are pictures of Jenkins and of an engineering job done by him for the American Bridge Company at Ambridge, Pennsylvania, in 1902. There is also a student laboratory manual containing direction for a course of experiments in chemistry.

459. **Jenkins Family.** Papers, 1832-1951. 2 ft. Gift of John E. Jenkins, 1955. No. 790.

Miscellaneous family papers of John E. Jenkins, Albright, relating to Preston County. Included are correspondence and genealogies of Preston County families and papers dealing with education and churches in the county. Bound volumes include a minute book, "Regimental Courts of Enquiry," for the One Hundred Fourth Regiment, Virginia Militia, later the Twenty-fourth Regiment, West Virginia Militia, 1836-1866; and a minute book of the Brandonville and Terra Alta Telephone Company, 1903-1923.

460. **Johns Hopkins University Alumni Association. West Virginia Branch.** Minutes and correspondence, 1913-1958. 1 ft. Gift of Mrs. A. M. Reese, 1966. No. 1876.

Records of an association of Johns Hopkins alumni at West Virginia University, including two minute books, 1913-1924 and 1925-1958. Members include J. M. Callahan, O. P. Chitwood, Friend E. Clark, and A. M. Reese.

461. **Johnson, Adam W.** Letter, October 23, 1861. 1 item. Gift of William M. Selvey, Jr., 1951. No. 286.

Letter of a Confederate soldier in the Wise Legion in the Greenbrier Valley, commenting on food, field conditions, and the need for writing paper.

462. **Johnson, David Dale** (1875-1954). Papers, 1891-1954. 3 ft. Gift of Mrs. David Dale Johnson, 1959. No. 1236.

The papers of a member of the English faculty of West Virginia University, 1902-1946, include his notes and essays written while a student at Marietta College; lecture notes, outlines, and bibliographies used in his English courses; addresses given at various clubs and civic organizations; religious talks; departmental reports; and notes and papers dealing with his estate. There is a detailed index to the papers prepared by Professor Johnson.

463. **Johnson, Frank A.,** *Collector.* Papers, 1786-1886. 3 items. Gift of Frank A. Johnson, 1959. No. 1170.

Account book of Matthew Wallace, a Mill Point physician, containing notes, a list of medical books, and the medical account of George B. Moffett; sentiment book of Anna McNeel Wallace, 1883-1886; and typescript copies of a sermon and journals, 1786-1788, of John Smith, a Methodist circuit rider, pertaining to his labors on the Greenbrier, Redstone, and Holston circuits.

464. **Johnson, George W.** (1837-1902). Papers, 1860-1960. 5 ft. Gift of Mrs. Jessie F. Steenbergen, 1963. No. 1655.

Diaries, correspondence, notes, receipts, and newspaper clippings of a lumberman and stockman from Morgantown. Subjects include Johnson's agricultural activities, his extensive timber dealings in Monongalia County, and the rafting of logs to Pittsburgh and intermediate points on the Monongahela River.

465. **Johnson, Mary McKendree,** *Collector.* Papers, 1913 (1932-1958). 6 ft. Acquired, 1958. Nos. 1100, 1132.

Correspondence, notes, and clippings of a genealogist and local historian from Parkersburg. The collection contains data on nearly three hundred Virginia-West Virginia families, lists of Revolutionary War pensioners, copies of county and parish records, news clippings pertaining to the history of Parkersburg and Wood County and early settlers in western Virginia; one folder of John J. Jackson papers, 1837-1884; and a microfilm copy of a newspaper series, "Your Famous Forefathers," compiled by Mrs. Johnson and Mrs. Mary Henderson Turner, which appeared in the Romney *Hampshire Review,* 1953-1954.

466. **Johnson Family.** Papers, 1783-1939. Ca. 30 items. Gift of Miss Annie Dent Davis, n.d. No. 148.

Letters, notes, and copies of land and legal papers of Edgar Johnson Davis, relating to the Abraham Johnson family in the eastern Panhandle. Included are letters and clippings of Annie Dent Davis, and a mimeographed study, *Abraham Johnson and Descendants*, by Miss Davis.

467. **Johnston, Jesse.** Diary, 1861-1864. 1 reel of microfilm (1 volume). Original in possession of the Pennsylvania Historical Society, 1961. No. 1395.

The original manuscript and a typed copy of Johnston's Civil War diary. Serving with Company L, Second Regiment, West Virginia Volunteer Cavalry, Johnston fought at Princeton, Lewisburg, Sinking Creek, and Wytheville. Captured and subsequently exchanged, he served in Washington until mustered out of service.

468. **Jones, Clement Ross (1871-1939).** Papers, ca. 1750 (1890-1958). 7 ft. Gift of Mrs. C. Ross Jones, 1943, 1959, 1960, 1961. Nos. 84, 1173, 1312, 1490.

Papers of a genealogist and former dean of the College of Engineering, West Virginia University, 1911-1932, include family correspondence, academic records, business and legal papers, newspaper clippings, photographs, and genealogical studies and correspondence.

Subjects include Jones' social, fraternal, and professional activities; family affairs; university affairs; the reorganization of the College of Engineering, 1931-1932; the Athens Lumber Company, 1921-1932; the fiftieth anniversary of the American Society of Mechanical Engineers, 1930; photographs concerning West Virginia University in World War I; and letters and clippings of Thomas B. Wilgus of Greene County, Pennsylvania, later of Monongalia County, relating mainly to political affairs in Monongalia County.

Genealogical studies and correspondence pertain to the Butcher, Calvert, Creel, Davis, DeHaven, Dils, Foley, Foote, Ford, Gough, Gambrill, Hardin, Iglehart, Jones, Kincheloe, King, Lewis, Logan, McQuilkin, Melrose, Monroe, Neal, Peadro, Pennybacker, Phelps, Shelby, Simpson, Spencer, Tavenner, Vaulx, Warder, Waters, Wickliffe, Woodyard, and allied Ohio Valley and western Virginia families.

Correspondents include Howard M. Gore, Matthew M. Neely, and John R. Turner.

469. **Jones, Mary "Mother."** Letter, 1920. 1 item. Gift of Mrs. Fred Mooney, 1965. No. 1823.

Letter from Mary "Mother" Jones to T. V. Powderly, Department of Labor, Washington, D. C. "Mother" Jones introduces Fred Mooney, secretary-treasurer of the United Mine Workers, District No. 17, asks Powderly to get him a passport, and says she doesn't know when she will leave for Mexico.

470. **Judy, Elvin Lycurgus** (1870-1954). Papers, 1756-1949. 1 ft. Gift of Mrs. E. L. Judy, 1954. No. 634.

The papers of a Petersburg attorney and author of *History of Grant and Hardy Counties, West Virginia* (Charleston, 1951). These papers, mainly the sources used in the writing of the county history, consist of copies and originals of correspondence, land records, census and military records, and genealogical information for the eastern Panhandle counties, Monongalia County, and the border counties of Virginia and Maryland.

471. **Kanawha County.** Archives, 1779-1933. 152 ft. Gift of the Kanawha County Court, 1938, and Roy Bird Cook, 1939. Nos. 58, 145.

Court case papers, 1779-1933, and county record books, 1806-1927. The bound volumes include private account and minute books of the Coal River and Kanawha Mining and Manufacturing Company, 1851-1858; the Winifrede Mining and Manufacturing Company, 1850-1858; the steamboat *Crockett*, 1836; a sawmill, 1879; and general merchandise and salt accounts, 1822-1823, 1864-1865. A name and subject index to the case papers and a checklist of the bound volumes are in the manuscript section.

472. **Kanawha County Court.** Records, 1806-1861. 26 items (photocopies and 1 reel of microfilm). Transfers from the Kanawha County Court House, 1967, 1968, and Department of Archives and History, 1970. Nos. 1961, 2151.

Deeds, wills, and partition agreements, and records of an 1845 case, *Reynolds* v. *McFarland*, known as the "Salt Case."

473. **Kanawha County Relief Administration.** Records, 1933-1934. Ca. 1,000p. Gift of John T. Morgan, 1969. No. 2077.

Three volumes of typescript material containing correspondence, minutes of meetings, photographs, maps, charts, tables, blueprints, and reports.

474. **Kellogg, Joseph M.,** *Compiler.* Notebooks, ca. 1945-1958. 1 reel of microfilm (8 volumes). Originals in possession of Mrs. Bert Harter, 1962. No. 1626.

Genealogical records, compiled by Professor Joseph M. Kellogg, Lawrence, Kansas, of the Henkel, McCann, Johnson, Mitchell, and Teter families. The records include copies of many nineteenth century documents. Allied families mentioned are Apple, Eschmann, Grisemer, Hammer, Harper, Hite, Pearies, Peterson, Ruleman, Scholl, See (Zeh), Simmons, Skidmore, and Westfall-Kortrecht. Most of these families settled in the South Branch Valley and the counties of Harrison, Lewis, Randolph, Barbour, Braxton, and Gilmer. One volume contains the history and various records of the German settlers of the Tulpehocken District of Berks County, Pennsylvania, and miscellaneous records of several Shenandoah Valley and western Virginia counties.

475.   **Kelly, Henry R.**, *Collector.* Scrapbooks, 1854-1955. 1 volume and 1 reel of microfilm (1 volume). Acquired, 1959. No. 1205.

Scrapbook of a Parkersburg postal clerk, Edwin P. Kelly, containing receipts from the estate of W. R. Kelly; historical clippings pertaining to Wood County and World War II; and the scrapbook, 1854-1921, of A. L. Collins containing statements from numerous Parkersburg mercantile houses, criminal reward notices, and a few legal papers.

476.   **Kelly, Robert G.** Papers, 1929, 1932-1941. Ca. 300 items. Gift of Robert G. Kelly, 1967. No. 1959.

Correspondence, telegrams, newspaper clippings, reports, and speeches of a Democratic Party official; correspondence and minutes of Democratic State Executive Committee meetings. Subjects include West Virginia gubernatorial campaign of 1932, political patronage, federal relief programs in West Virginia, Rush Holt's senatorial campaign of 1934, the Holt-Kelly feud, and the miner's strike of 1939.

Correspondents include Robert G. Kelly, Herman Guy Kump, M. M. Neely, Joe L. Smith, Homer A. Holt, Gory Hogg, James R. Moreland, Charles R. Wilson, Charles E. Hodges, James A. Farley, and Aubrey Williams.

477.   **Kendall, Norman F.**, *Compiler.* Scrapbook, 1962. 1 volume. Transfer, 1962. No. 507.

Genealogical and local history compilation entitled, "No. 6 History of Mannington District, Marion County, West Virginia."

478.   **Kennedy, John Pendleton (1795-1870).** Papers, 1820-1898, ca. 1953. 2 reels of microfilm and 3 items (photocopies). Originals in possession of the Peabody Institute Library, Baltimore, Maryland, 1959, 1960; and Library of Congress, 1970. Nos. 1220, 1301, 2168.

Papers of a Baltimore essayist and novelist include a checklist of the Kennedy collection in the Peabody Institute Library; an alphabetical checklist of Kennedy's incoming correspondence; and selected materials pertaining to the Berkeley Springs-Martinsburg-Winchester area, visits to Richmond, Salt Sulphur, and White Sulphur Springs, and a journey to Philadelphia, New York, Pittsburgh, Cincinnati, and Louisville in 1850, from Kennedy's journal, 1848-1862; letters of John P. Kennedy to his wife, 1828-1855; and his diary, 1829-1832.

There are also selected letters and portions of a diary copied from originals in the Library of Congress, describing visits to Berkeley Springs and White Sulphur Springs, 1848-1857.

479. **Keyser.** Financial statement, 1928-1929. 41p. No. 385.

A mimeographed list of receipts and disbursements.

480. **Kilgore, Harley Martin (1893-1956).** Papers, 1937-1956. 24 ft. Gifts of Senator and Mrs. Harley Martin Kilgore, 1952, 1957, 1958, 1961. Nos. 491, 967, 1068, 1108.

The papers of a U. S. senator from West Virginia who at the time of his death was a member of the Senate Appropriations Committee and the ranking Democratic member of the Senate Judiciary Committee. The papers include bills introduced by Kilgore, with related correspondence, 1941-1952; a general correspondence file, 1937-1956, arranged alphabetically by folder subject headings; legislation, 1954-1956, arranged by folder subject headings; Senate Subcommittee on War Mobilization, 1942-1949; Truman Committee, 1943-1949; Committee on Military Affairs, 1941-1942; Senate Appropriations, 1955-1956; National Science Foundation, 1942-1955; Judiciary Committee, 1943-1956; correspondence relating to West Virginia, 1940-1956, arranged by subject; and miscellaneous pictorial materials relating to World War II, the Civil War, U. S. politics, and West Virginia.

Additional subjects include Kilgore's work as a juvenile judge in Beckley; the Joseph Rosier-Clarence L. Martin contested senatorship, 1941; activities of John L. Lewis, 1939-1950; disabled veterans; California politics, 1949-1954; displaced German Jews; Civil Aeronautics Administration; B'nai B'rith; U.S.S. *West Virginia;* Charleston (West Virginia) *Labor's Daily;* and the text of a discussion of the Lincoln papers in the Library of Congress made by Senator Kilgore and David C. Mearns.

Correspondents include Bernard Baruch, Charles F. Brannan, Alben W. Barkley, Harry F. Byrd, Solon J. Buck, Price Daniel, Everett M. Dirksen, Guy M. Gillette, Theodore F. Green, W. Averell Harriman, Thomas Hennings, George Jessell, Lyndon B. Johnson, Estes Kefauver, Franklin D. Roosevelt, Adlai E. Stevenson, Stuart Symington, Harry S Truman, and Millard E. Tydings.

481. **Kingwood.** Petition, 1840. 1 item (photocopy). Original in the Virginia State Library, 1961. No. 1460.

Petition requesting the Virginia legislature to authorize the establishment of permanent streets in Kingwood. For the accompanying plat of the town see the map file.

482. **Koontz, Arthur B.** (1885-1963). Papers, 1907-1964. 164 items. Gift of Mrs. Arthur B. Koontz, 1966. No. 1912.

Pictures, correspondence, telegrams, and memorabilia of a corporation lawyer, banker, businessman, Democratic candidate for governor in 1920 and the U. S. Senate in 1934, a Democratic National Committeeman, 1940-1958, a member of West Virginia University's Board of Governors, and holder of the Order of Vandalia for service to West Virginia University. Subjects include the Democratic National Committee, the Democratic Convention and campaign of 1956, and Koontz's bequests to colleges and universities.

483. **Kramer, William.** Account book, 1860-1895. 1 volume. No. 133.

An account book of Dr. S. E. B. Kramer, a physician in Smithtown; included are dates of residents' births and deaths, and other data relative to Smithtown and vicinity.

484. **Krebs, Charles E.** (1870-1954). Papers, 1912-(1935) 1939. 1 reel of microfilm (3 volumes). Loan from C. G. Krebs, 1964. No. 1792.

Scrapbooks, mainly of newspaper clippings, maintained by a mining engineer, geologist, and businessman from Charleston. The scrapbooks contain clippings, announcements, and a few letters relating to Krebs' business, Charleston civic affairs, and professional engineering organizations. Topics include the oil boom at Blue Creek in 1912; oil field development in Kanawha and Clay counties; oil and coal shipments on the C. & O.; coal, oil, gas, and coke production figures; report on the coal strike of 1922; surveys of West Virginia's coal, oil, and gas resources; machinery used in coal production; disputed land claims of the Colonial Timber and Coal Corporation, 1923; the New River Coal field; drainage areas and water power in West Virginia; Hinton Dam; Pennsylvania bituminous districts; rate hearings of the United Fuel Gas Company; early coal and gas operations in West Virginia; Norfolk and Western Railway affairs; silicosis cases resulting from the Hawks Nest tunnel construction, 1933; and bituminous coal prices in West Virginia and the U. S., 1906-1925.

485. **Ku Klux Klan, Monongalia County.** Manuscripts, ca. 1868. 4p. Gift of Mrs. Nan Brooke Harold. No. 386.

Four manuscript sheets of notes, apparently extracted from a bound volume, containing the constitution, oaths, members' names, and other data on the Blacksville Klan.

486. **Kump, Herman Guy (1877-1962).** Papers, 1907-1957. 39 ft. Gift of Cyrus S. Kump, 1962. No. 1609.

Correspondence, legal papers, speeches, clippings, photographs, and printed material of a Randolph County prosecuting attorney, mayor of Elkins, judge of the Twenty-second Judicial Circuit, Democratic politician, and state governor, 1933-1937.

Subjects include John T. McGraw's senate contest, 1911; Canadian Reciprocity Agreement, 1911; woman suffrage; State Prohibition Amendment, 1911-1912; *Virginia* v. *West Virginia;* Joseph Brown lynch case; New Deal operations and agencies in the state; Kump's legal practice; Red House Resettlement Project; Five-Year Plan for West Virginia; state and national elections, and state politics, 1908-1936.

Correspondents include T. Coleman Andrews, Newton D. Baker, Alben W. Barkley, Harry F. Byrd, Richard E. Byrd, John J. Cornwell, John J. Davis, John W. Davis, James A. Farley, John Nance Garner, William E. Glasscock, Henry D. Hatfield, J. Edgar Hoover, Harold L. Ickes, Douglas MacArthur, John T. McGraw, Franklin D. Roosevelt, John F. Sly, Howard Sutherland, and Clarence Wayland Watson.

487. **Kuykendall, James William.** Papers, 1765-1926. 4 ft. Gift of Mrs. R. S. Kuykendall, 1960. No. 1180.

Papers of a land surveyor from Hardy County include family and business correspondence, 1888-1926; letters from George Benson Kuykendall on family genealogy, 1911-1914; Kuykendall's correspondence as a member of the county board of education, 1908-1915; account books, diaries, surveying notes, Sunday school class book, 1876-1923; and plats, surveys, and deeds of land in the Hardy-Grant County area.

488. **Kuykendall, Mrs. Joe P.,** *Collector.* Records, 1749-1864. 3 items (photocopies). Originals in possession of Mrs. Joe P. Kuykendall, 1959. No. 1174.

A Thomas Fairfax deed, 1749; stock certificate of the South Branch Bridge Company, 1858; and a Confederate 4 percent registered bond, 1864.

489. **Ladies of the Maccabees, Progressive Hive No. 8. Morgantown.** Papers, 1907-1946. Ca. 60 items. Gifts of the estate of Daisie Fleming Reeves, 1963, 1967. No. 1687.

Correspondence, reports, and history of Progressive Hive No. 8, Ladies Auxiliary of the fraternal order, Knights of the Maccabees. There are additional papers concerning the Woman's Benefit Association which was originally named the Ladies of the Maccabees.

490. **Ladwig, Mrs. Otto Worthington (b. 1882).** Papers, 1899-1943. Ca. 80 items. Gift of Miss Cornelia Ladwig, 1965. No. 1812.

Papers of Mrs. O. W. Ladwig of Clarksburg and Wilsonburg, Harrison County, president of the Clarksburg Women's Club, 1931-1932, consisting of letters and materials addressed to Mrs. Ladwig. Subjects include the West Virginia Federation of Women's Clubs, the National Council of Women of the U. S., Inc., the George Washington Bicentennial Committee, the *Clubwoman*, Federated Garden Clubs of West Virginia, the General Federation of Women's Clubs, Chicago Exposition of 1933, the World Court, and the International Disarmament Conference, 1932.

491. **Laishley, Peter T.** Papers, 1809-1915. 1 ft. and 1 reel of microfilm. Loan, 1954; originals gift of Mrs. G. Harry Bayles, 1955. No. 670.

Correspondence, business papers, and an account book of Peter T. Laishley, a Methodist minister, physician, and merchant in Monongalia County. There are papers on the settlement of the estate of Richard Laishley in England; marriages performed by Laishley; Laishley family birth and marriage notes; accounts for services as a minister and physician, 1833-1839; and other items on church and local history.

492. **Lakin, James S. (b. 1864).** Correspondence, 1912-1933. 117 items. Gift of Joseph C. Gluck, 1964. No. 1748.

Correspondence of a member and president, 1921-1929, of the State Board of Control, which directed the financial operations of all state institutions from 1909 to 1933. Most of the letters are between Lakin and Dr. Henry D. Hatfield; subjects include medical and hospital affairs, the Greater Huntington Hospital Association, the Kessler-Hatfield Hospital in Huntington, and applications for political office. There are occasional references to politics and business conditions. There are a few letters between Lakin and John W. Davis when Davis was U. S. Solicitor General, 1913-1916, and U. S. Ambassador to Great Britain, 1920.

493. **Lambert, Frederick B.,** *Collector and Compiler.* Papers, ca. 1809-1959. 47 reels of microfilm (459 volumes). Originals in possession of Frederick B. Lambert, 1959, 1960. Nos. 1244, 1270, 1281.

Clipping scrapbooks; original manuscripts and typescript copies of census, school, vital statistics, and court records; obituary notices and cemetery readings; personal recollections and biographical sketches; and genealogical and historical notes pertaining to the Guyandotte Valley (Cabell, Wayne, and Logan counties) and the surrounding Ohio Valley area.

Included are records of the Barboursville schools, 1819-1869; minute book of the Barboursville Common Council, 1905-1911; records of numerous Baptist, Methodist, Presbyterian, and Congregational churches; and a few census and court records for Kanawha, Putnam, Mason, Lincoln, and Boone counties, West Virginia, and Lawrence and Gallia counties, Ohio.

Subjects include Indians, early settlers, Ansell Ferry Company, Guyandotte Navigation Company, Guyandotte Turnpike Company, James River and Kanawha Turnpike, Covington and Ohio, Chesapeake and Ohio, and local railways, toll bridges, stage lines, and other subjects pertaining to river and overland transportation; early industrial development, gristmills, salt works, and oil and coal fields; social customs, taverns, sports, newspapers, famous murders and hangings; slavery, the "underground railroad" and the free Negro; immigration, history of Huntington, Ceredo, Kenova, Martha, Love, Bloomingdale, Milton, Salt Rock, Guyandotte, and other area towns and villages; educational development, Marshall Academy and College, Morris Harvey College, Mercer Academy, and free public schools; floods; Civil War, Confederate companies, and the Guyandotte Massacre; and the Hatfield-McCoy feud. There is a detailed index to the collection.

494.   **Lambert, Oscar Doane (1888-1959).** Papers, 1770-1929, 1944-1959. 4 ft. Gift of O. D. Lambert, 1953, and transfer, 1958, 1961. Nos. 552, 1047, 1505.

Correspondence of a history professor, historian, and manuscript collector for the West Virginia Collection, pertaining to his professional activities. There is a typescript, "Autobiography of Oscar D. Lambert," and a recorded interview with Lambert concerning his academic career. There are copies of maps and photographs relating to land in the Northern Neck of Virginia, Joist Hite, Jesse Hughes, Henry G. Davis, Alexander L. Wade, and Lord Fairfax; a photostat of a Benjamin Franklin letter, February 27, 1770; and clippings on World War I and II and national politics.

495.   **Land Grants and Papers, 1749-1870.** 40 items (8 photocopies). Gifts of James M. Callahan, 1903; J. W. Ross, 1934; Irvin Stewart, 1956; Carl Lantz, 1958; Josephine Phillips, 1961; E. B. McCue, 1934; Blake Snider, 1948; Grace Field Gibson, 1953; Mrs. Joseph

C. Gluck, 1953; H. A. Alt, 1954; transfers; and loans for duplication by Ward Wood, Mrs. Joe P. Kuykendall, and Paul L. Morgan, 1967. Nos. 128, 245, 315, 349, 387, 388, 391, 392, 393, 423, 525, 533, 584, 686,·908, 961, 1468, 1542, 1796, 1953, 1967.

Documents pertaining to land in Virginia, West Virginia, Pennsylvania, and Ohio, including treasury warrants, surveys, agreements, deeds, and grants signed by Governors Patrick Henry, James Monroe, John Tyler, and Joseph Johnson.

496. **Lantz, William and R. S.** Papers, 1880-1892. Ca. 30 items. Gift of Carl Lantz, 1958. No. 1038.

Papers of two Blacksville postmasters containing mail reports, letters on post office affairs and politics, petitions for mail route, and printed materials relating to politics and agriculture.

497. **Larew, Peter.** Papers, 1790-1892. 1 reel of microfilm (4 folders). Originals in possession of Robert LaRue, 1962. No. 1603.

Papers of a pioneer Monroe County family including a manuscript ciphering book, 1790, a diary of a journey to southwestern Ohio, 1810, a manuscript militia manual and company roster, and various business, church, and legal papers of county militia captain, Peter Larew. The papers of his son, John M., include a general merchandise account book, the estate papers, and various business and legal documents. The collection also contains a series of letters, 1876-1892, from John Larew's sons in California commenting upon schoolteaching, agriculture, and travel in the Far West.

498. **Largent, Mary,** *Collector.* Papers, 1883, 1916. 6 items. Gift of Mary Largent, 1955. No. 767.

Copies of poems written by Hu Maxwell; a sketch of the history of leather and its use among the early settlers in America, by E. C. Ambrose; and a Paw Paw High School annual for 1916 containing a brief history of the town of Paw Paw.

499. **Latham, George Robert** (1832-1917). Papers, 1869-1917. 58 items. Gift of Julia Latham, 1939. No. 66.

Correspondence, manuscripts of speeches, and other papers relating to Latham's service with the Second Regiment, West Virginia Volunteer Infantry, during the Civil War, and as United States consul at Melbourne, Australia, 1867-1870. The West Virginia statehood movement is discussed in some of the manuscripts.

500. **Latham, Jean Lee (b. 1902).** Typescripts, ca. 1947-1955. 528p. Gift of Miss Jean Lee Latham, 1959. No. 1232.

Typescript copies of *This Dear Bought Land,* a story of the Jamestown settlement; *Trail Blazer of the Seas,* the story of Matthew Fontaine Maury; and a serialization, *Carry On, Mr. Bowditch,* written by Jean Lee Latham.

501. **Layman, Mildred Hassler.** Papers, ca. 1750-1952. 3 ft. Gift of Mrs. John F. Laughlin, Jr., 1959. No. 1177.

Papers and correspondence of the William Haymond Chapter, D. A. R., Fairmont, including genealogical correspondence, clippings and notebooks, and family genealogical records and notes. One reel of microfilm contains the typescript notes and manuscripts of Edgar Wakefield Hassler pertaining to John Connolly and western Pennsylvania during the period of the French and Indian War and the War of Independence.

502. **Lear, Tobias.** Letter, July 25, 1815. 1 item. Gift of Mrs. Logan Carroll, 1965.

Letter from Tobias Lear, Accountant's Office, Department of War, Washington, to John L. Gillmeyer, Morgan Town, Virginia, July 25, 1815, concerning enlistment and muster of recruits.

503. **Lecky, Howard L.** Typescripts, 1971. 49p. Loan for duplication by Rena B. Jefferson, 1971. No. 2198.

Copies of articles published in a Waynesburg, Pennsylvania, newspaper, a continuation of Lecky's *Tenmile Country and Its Pioneer Families.*

504. **Lederer, Anna.** Transcript, ca. 1940. 1 reel of microfilm (2 volumes). Originals in possession of James M. Crump, 1959. No. 1243.

"The Boot Shaped Bend," by Anna Lederer, is an unpublished history of the Ohio Valley country about Pomeroy, Ohio, and Hartford and New Haven, West Virginia. There is a separate index.

505. **Lee, Howard Burton (b. 1879).** Papers, 1912-1964. 94 items. Gift of Howard B. Lee, 1970. No. 2139.

Correspondence and photographs used by Lee in the writing of his book, *Bloodletting In Appalachia,* 1969, concerning the coal fields of West Virginia and the attempts by workers to unionize. The photographs show individuals, coal camps, mine guards, and scenes from the Paint Creek-Cabin Creek area in 1912-1913, Matewan, and Monongalia County during the 1925-1929 period.

Correspondents include Gordon C. Felts, Coleman A. Hatfield, Henry D. Hatfield, Chapman Revercomb, and Walter R. Thurmond.

506. **Lee, Richard Henry (1732-1794).** Correspondence, 1773-1790. 8 items (photocopies). Originals in the Henry E. Huntington Library, San Marino, California, 1966. No. 1932.

Copies of letters, 1773-1790, by Richard Henry Lee. (RESTRICTED)

507. **Lee, Robert E. (1807-1870).** Papers, 1861-1867. 9 items (8 photocopies). Gift of N. T. Downs, 1957, and acquisition, 1961. Nos. 394, 971, 1513.

Letters from Lee to General Winfield Scott and Lieutenant Roger Jones, April 20, 1861; Mrs. Sarah A. Lawton, January 8, 1863; a committee of Washington College, August 24, 1865, regarding his election to the presidency of that institution; Reverdy Johnson, January 27, 1866, and July 7, 1866; David S. G. Cabell, February 25, 1867; and Dion C. Pharr, May 18, 1867, concerning a request for information on Washington College. In addition there is an original order, signed by Lee, to Major David Goff at Beverly, concerning arms intended for Colonel George A. Porterfield at Grafton.

508. **Leeper, Harry T.,** *Collector.* Papers, 1779-1898. 1 ft. Gift of Harry T. Leeper, 1951. Nos. 251, 348.

Correspondence and miscellaneous papers of the Bowman, Leeper, and Veach families; manuscripts, compiled by Thomas M. Leeper, concerning Nathaniel Cochran, including his Indian capture and imprisonment; the Confederate raid into Marion County in 1863; history of the town of Monongah and the Monongah High School; history of the Leeper family; the flood of 1888 in Marion County; and a narrative of a rafting journey from Worthington to McKeesport, Pennsylvania, in 1882. There are also a few teachers' daily registers, 1881-1891, some of which show marriage and death records of pupils, and other materials on Marion County.

509. **Leonian, Nell Lanham (b. 1892).** Typescripts, 1967. 43p. Gift of Mrs. Leon H. Leonian, 1967. No. 2000.

Sketches, 1892-1967, by a Morgantown resident of her early life, some family history on the Baileys, Lanhams, and Peppers; teaching experiences in southern West Virginia; and life at West Virginia University as a student and a teacher.

510. **Levassor, Eugene.** Papers, 1796-1894. 2 ft. Acquired, 1960. No. 1363.

Correspondence, business and legal papers, maps and printed materials of a French émigré, land speculator, and merchant from Cincinnati and Parkersburg. Subjects include Levassor's extensive landholdings in Kanawha, Lincoln, Jackson, Wood, Wirt, and Monongalia counties, and activities of his land agents; James Swann lands; the coming of the Northwestern Virginia Railroad to Parkersburg; the Panic of 1857 in that city; oil fever in the Wood County area, 1859-1866; and the activities of J. H. Diss Debar, West Virginia's first commissioner of immigration.

Correspondents include J. H. Diss Debar, James M. Laidley, Charles Lisez, and Alexander Quarrier.

511. **Lewis, Virgil Anson (1848-1913).** Papers, 1895-1912. 2 ft. Gift of Virginia and Lucie Lewis, 1961. No. 1507.

Published and unpublished manuscripts, correspondence, and speeches of the first state historian and archivist and a former state superintendent of schools. Subjects include the exploration, Indian wars, and settlement of western Virginia; the Tory Insurrection in the Valley of Lost River, 1781; the West Virginia new state movement; Masonry in West Virginia; Andrew S. Rowan; the reminiscences of B. M. Skinner, commander of the Ninth West Virginia Volunteer Infantry Regiment, 1861-1864; and various West Virginia authors.

Correspondents include George W. Atkinson, Waitman Barbe, Danske Dandridge, William M. O. Dawson, Granville D. Hall, Hu Maxwell, Mrs. Alexander McVeigh Miller, and Melville D. Post.

512. **Lewis County.** Archives, 1775-1933. 103 ft. Gift of the Lewis County Court, 1939. No. 62.

Court cases, 1775-1933, and county record volumes and private account books, 1817-1932. The private accounts include records of a harness maker, millers, druggists, printers, and general merchants.

A checklist of the bound volumes is available, as well as a chronological, subject, and name index to the suit papers.

513. **Lewis Family.** Papers, 1825-1936. 8 ft. Gift of Mrs. William Peters, 1953. No. 551.

Personal and business papers of the Lewis family, mainly of John D. (1800-1882), Charles C., Sr. (b. 1839), and Jr. (b. 1865), of Kanawha County. For the period 1825-1875 there are papers of various members of the Ruffner, Dickinson, and Wilson families of West Virginia, Virginia, Ohio, Kansas, Missouri, and other states.

The business papers relate to farming operations, the purchase and sale of slaves, salt manufacturing and trade, the Old Sweet Springs Company, coal, iron, oil, lumbering, railroads, and real estate in Kanawha, Clay, Boone, Fayette, and Nicholas counties. There are newspaper clippings, speeches, and other papers reflecting the Lewis' interests in the Democratic Party in the period 1914-1920. Settlement papers and correspondence regarding the estates of John D. Lewis, and Joel, Daniel, and Andrew Ruffner are in the collection. The personal papers include diaries, scrapbooks, photographs, and letters. Travel accounts in the United States, South America, and Europe are given in the correspondence, as well as comments on schools in West Virginia and Virginia; the building of a church in Kanawha County in 1834; missionary work in Colombia, South America, 1874-1875; Civil War and postwar conditions in Virginia, Pennsylvania, Ohio, Kentucky, and Missouri; conditions at Camp Chase, in the Civil War; and material relating to World War I.

514. **Lightburn, Joseph Andrew Jackson (1824-1901).** Papers, 1861-1865. 5 items. Gifts of Mrs. Grace W. Lightburn and Mrs. Jason Bailey, 1955, and the State Department of Archives and History, 1935. Nos. 34, 750.

Originals and photocopies of two commissions of General Lightburn, signed by F. H. Pierpont and Abraham Lincoln; a military map of the area around Atlanta, Georgia; materials on the celebration honoring Lightburn at Weston in 1865; and a copy of a letter written by Lightburn mentioning the siege of Vicksburg and battle losses.

515. **Lightburn, Joseph B.** Papers, 1958-1959. 19 items. Gift of Joseph B. Lightburn, 1959. No. 1224.

Correspondence and writings of the mayor of Jane Lew and one-time Republican nominee for Congress pertain to fluoridation, United Nations, foreign aid, income tax, socialism, the Revised Standard Version of the Bible, and Lightburn's conservative interpretation of Americanism.

516. **Lightburn Family.** Papers, 1836-1935. 266 items. Gift of Mrs. Luther G. Lightburn, 1951. No. 292.

Letters, legal and land papers, tax receipts, and other papers of Benjamin, John F. C. L., Benjamin F. M. V. and J. A. J. Lightburn in Lewis County. Included are a pocket account book of the Lightburn Mill, 1836-1855; 32 items bearing on General J. A. J. Lightburn's Civil War activities, including correspondence, orders, and reports; correspondence between J. A. J. Lightburn and Soule & Co., relative to pension claims; agricultural implement advertisements, 1890; notebooks of sermon outlines written by General Lightburn who was ordained a Baptist minister in 1867; and newspaper clippings bearing on the Lightburn family.

517. **Lilly, Armistead Abraham (1878-1956).** Typescripts, 1928, 1936, 1949, 1956. 4 items. Gift of R. G. Lilly, 1957. No. 1095.

Three typescript speeches of A. A. Lilly, including the welcome address delivered at the Lilly reunion, 1949; Lincoln Day dinner speech delivered at Sutton, 1936; a speech delivered before the Republican convention in Charleston, presenting Senator Guy D. Goff for nomination as a candidate for president of the United States; and a memorial of the Kanawha County circuit court on the death of A. A. Lilly in 1956.

518. **Lindsay, Rella,** *Collector.* Papers, 1791-1908. 7 items. Gift and loan of Mrs. Rella Lindsay, 1969. No. 2091.

A Bible record of the Lambert, Lynch, and other families from Harrison and Ritchie counties; two checks drawn on the Ritchie County Bank; a picture of Civil War soldiers in a central West Virginia town, possibly West Union; a postcard of Pikes Peak as seen in 1900; and a postcard entitled "Sailor Jean and his Trolleyette," 1903.

519. **Livingston, Adam.** Manuscript, ca. 1770. 1 item. Gift of the American Catholic Historical Society, 1950. No. 209.

A mimeographed copy of a manuscript, "Livingston's Conversion, History of Adam Livingston, Middle Way, Since Called 'Clip,' Jefferson County, Virginia," being an account of the conversion of Adam Livingston to the Catholic Church in Middleway. The original is in the library of Georgetown College.

520. **Logan.** Papers, ca. 1900-1924. 9 items (photocopies). Originals in possession of Jim Browning, 1958. No. 1150.

Papers include an account by a lifelong resident of the founding of the town of Logan and an essay on West Virginia autumns.

521. **Logan County.** Census, 1850. 1 typescript, 43p. Gift of the Logan County Court, n.d. No. 396.

Typed copy of the federal population schedule.

522. **Longacre, Mrs. Glenn V.,** *Collector.* Papers, 1814-1915. 27 items. Gift of Mrs. Glenn V. Longacre, 1955. No. 736.

Photostats of deeds, surveys, plats, and grants, the latter signed by Thomas M. Randolph, David Campbell, and William Smith, governors of Virginia, in 1820, 1838, and 1847, for land in Harrison and Doddridge counties; a school attendance sheet for 1865; and a report to the board of education of the number of school-age children in District No. 4 of Doddridge County in 1869. Also included are a number of photographs taken around Webster Springs showing the hotel, a subscription school, and public school classes, ca. 1900, along with two photographs of lumbering activities near Holly River. There is also a typescript, "An Adventure of Two Years in Webster Springs High School, 1915-1917," by Maud M. Hull; and a short history of the Webster Hardwood Lumber Company at Dixie.

523. **Loomis, Mahlon (1826-1886).** Typescript. 1 item. Gift of Guy E. Groves, 1968. No. 2037.
An account entitled "Chronological History of Dr. Mahlon Loomis— Inventor of the Radio."

524. **Lowther, William (1742-1814).** Typescript, ca. 1959. 1 item. Gift of Harold M. King, 1959. No. 1193.
Biographical record of the life of William Lowther, a Revolutionary War veteran and western Virginia pioneer.

525. **Lumber Corporations. Tucker County.** Minutes, 1884-1910. 3 volumes. Gift of W. A. Bradley, 1959. No. 1163.
Minute books of the J. L. Rumbarger Lumber Company, 1884-1910, the Condon-Lane Boom and Lumber Company, 1892-1910, and the Dry Fork Lumber Company, 1904-1910. These three companies had their central office in Philadelphia and were under the financial control of R. F. Whitmer. The collection also includes typescripts pertaining to the Dry Fork Lumber Company, William Whitmer & Sons, Parsons Pulp and Paper Company, J. L. Rumbarger Lumber Company, Condon-Lane Boom and Lumber Company, and the Holstein Lumber Company.

526. **Lynch, George N.** Papers, 1835-1898. 28 items. Gift of Mrs. John Newcommer, 1960. No. 1340.
Deeds and other legal papers of a farmer from Jefferson County. The collection also includes several legal documents, 1874-1877, pertaining to Dr. Nicholas Marmion of Harpers Ferry.

527. **Lynch, John R.** Papers, 1856 (1908-1924). 11 items. Gift of Mrs. Myra Lynch Mick, 1955. No. 764.
Papers of a resident of Glenville include a notebook containing measurements of lumber, a memo book of logs sold, a tally book of rafts floated down the Little Kanawha River, a stock certificate in the Gilmer County Fair Association, and West Virginia Department of Agriculture statistics for 1920.

528. **Lynchburg Coal & Coke Company.** Records, 1934-1940. 4 volumes. Gift of G. Ralph Spindler, 1956. No. 862.

Mine office daily reports, 1938-1940, and statistics on bituminous coal production, 1934-1935.

529. **McBee, Sanford (b. 1877).** Typescript, 1962. 6p. (photocopy). Loan for duplication by Michael Cover, 1964. No. 1771.

Typescript entitled "A Detailed Report of the Jones Raid in the Civil War of 1861" by Sanford McBee.

530. **McBee, Z. T.** Correspondence, 1856-1896. 108 items. Gift of T. Fleming Price, 1934. No. 25.

Letters sent to Z. T. McBee and members of his immediate family at Clinton Furnace, Monongalia County, mainly from Jackson Steele in Kansas, concerning crops, business conditions, and prices.

531. **McCalla, John M.** Papers, 1793-1870. Ca. 200 items. Acquired, 1959. No. 1209.

Papers of a Lexington, Kentucky, attorney and editor of the Lexington *Kentucky Gazette*, include payrolls of jurors and witnesses, Circuit Court, District of Kentucky, Frankfort, 1830-1838; correspondence, briefs, and other papers in the case of *William Clark* v. *U. S.*, 1852-1870; newspaper clippings from Lexington and other newspapers pertaining to national and Kentucky politics in the Jacksonian era; and a few pamphlets.

532. **McCamic, Charles (1874-1956).** Papers, 1919-1956. 32 ft. Gift of Mrs. Charles McCamic, 1957. No. 939.

The office files of Charles McCamic of the law firm of McCamic and Clarke, Wheeling. McCamic was president of the Interstate Bridge Company; president and director of the Northeast Mississippi Oil Company; director of the Sehon-Stevenson Company; president and director of the American Bridge, Tunnel and Turnpike Company; and a member of the West Virginia House of Delegates in 1905. The files contain correspondence, case papers, and business reports of clients; also papers of the companies with which McCamic was associated. The papers of the War Effort Committee of the West Virginia Bar Association, including correspondence from servicemen in World War II, are also in the collection.

533. **McChesney, James Z.** Papers, 1853-1959. 235p. Loan for duplication by Boyd Stutler, 1968. No. 2051.

Typescript copies of correspondence, diary entries, biographical sketches of Confederate veterans, manuscripts recounting battles, rosters of Confederate cavalry and infantry companies, and newspaper clippings of Pvt. James Z. McChesney of the Confederate States Army. Subjects include Confederate military activities, military activity in Shenandoah Valley, McCausland's march on Chambersburg, Pennsylvania, and information on various units and battles.

534. **McClaugherty, John.** Papers, 1841-1872. 18 items. Transfer, 1960. No. 1334.

Correspondence and receipts of a farmer and slave owner from Princeton, Mercer County, pertaining to family affairs and estate settlements, and a letter written from Camp Pryor giving an account of the Battle of First Bull Run.

535. **McCleery, William (1741-1821).** Papers, (1770-1857) 1945. 373 items bound in 2 volumes. Gift of Mrs. Margaret Brown Stoetzer, 1947, 1949. No. 146.

The papers of Colonel William McCleery of Morgantown, a Revolutionary War veteran, attorney, county clerk, prosecuting attorney, representative from Monongalia County to the Federal Constitutional Convention, founder of the Presbyterian Church in Morgantown, and landholder and purchasing agent. The papers include correspondence, typescripts, land records, and some printed materials. Much of the correspondence is between McCleery and his agent, Benjamin Oden of Upper Marlboro, Maryland, regarding a debt owed McCleery by General Henry Lee. Later letters to Matthew Gay concern the purchase, operation, and sale of the Monongalia Iron Works, and landholdings in Ohio and Indiana. The typescripts include sketches of McCleery, Isabelle Stockton McCleery, John Minor, and James Swan.

Correspondents include William Shinn and James and John Swan. Other letters are by or mention Aaron Burr, William Haymond, Thomas Jefferson, Zacquill Morgan, and John Rutherford.

536. **McColloch Family.** Papers, 1784-1861. 9 items (photocopies). Loan for duplication by Samuel W. McColloch, 1968. No. 2038.

Land grants, military commissions, bill of sale, and agreements concerning the interests of the McColloch and Jacob families.

537. **McCormick, John B.** Diary, (1859-1860) 1868. 1 item. Acquired, 1950. No. 232.

Diary of a Methodist Protestant Church itinerant minister in northwestern Virginia. The volume contains daily entries from September 24, 1859, through February 6, 1860. Also listed are the churches in his charge to 1868, including Laurel Lick, Harmony, Bethel, Harrisville circuit, Fairview, Sanko, and Middlebourne. Entries from January 23 to February, 1860, are made in Washington County, Pennsylvania.

McCormick was received into the Western Virginia Conference September 2, 1858, and was assigned in turn to the Greenbrier, Pocahontas, Lewis, Harrisville, and Tyler circuits.

538. **McCoy Family.** Papers, 1761-1903. 1 ft. Gift of William McCoy, 1953. No. 558.

Business correspondence and papers, including land grants and deeds, 1761-1881, surveys, wills, and account books of William McCoy, Sr. and Jr., of Pendleton County. There are papers on the administration of estates; management of property in Mercer, Pendleton, and Randolph counties, and in Augusta and Highland counties, Virginia, for absentee owners; and on farm operations. There is material on the Central Bank of Virginia at Staunton; the Moorefield and North Branch Turnpike Company; and on military units in the eastern parts of West Virginia during the Civil War, including letters, orders, and requisitions.

539. **McCulty, Roy L.** Papers, 1918-1961. Ca. 200 items. Gift of Mrs. Roy McCulty, 1970. No. 2129.

Papers of a Roane County businessman who served in the West Virginia House of Delegates from 1943 to 1956 and in the state senate from 1957 to 1961. The collection includes letters, photographs, a scrapbook, clippings pertaining to McCulty's career, and two notebooks containing digests of bills introduced during the 1960 session of the state legislature.

540. **McElroy, Charles S.** Papers, 1903-1946. 15 items. Gift of Miss Margaret E. Stewart, 1968. No. 2055.

Correspondence, deeds, stock certificates, and miscellaneous material of a Fairview businessman. Included is a typescript copy of the bylaws for the Retail Merchants Protective Association of Amos.

541. **McFee, William (b. 1881) and Beatrice.** Papers, 1942 (1952-1953), 1964. 18 items. Gift of Tasker H. Williams, 1964, 1965. No. 1770.

Letters, postcards, and pictures belonging to William and Beatrice McFee. Correspondents include Van Wyck Brooks, James T. Babb, Cass Canfield, Hester and Cedric Crowell, and Edmund Wilson.

542. **McGinnis, William Hereford (1855-1930).** Papers, 1834-1954. 22 ft. Gift of W. W. Goldsmith, 1956. No. 855.

The personal business papers of a Beckley lawyer who was prosecuting attorney of Raleigh County, 1892-1896, a senator in 1902, judge of the Supreme Court of Appeals, 1922-1924, chairman for a number of years of the executive committee of the Democratic Party in Raleigh County, and delegate to the national convention in 1920. There are case papers, correspondence and other records of the Hatcher-McGinnis Law Firm, 1834-1930; family photographs; and materials relating to the Methodist Church and World War I.

543. **McGraw, John Thomas (1856-1920).** Papers, (1842-1927) 1948. 4 ft. Acquired, 1944, 1948. No. 86.

Papers of an attorney in Grafton who served as an attorney for the Baltimore and Ohio Railroad and was prosecuting attorney of Taylor County, assistant to Governor J. B. Jackson, collector of internal revenue for West Virginia, and a member of the Democratic National Committee. There are case papers and letters pertaining to McGraw's law practice; records relating to the purchase, sale, and development of timber, coal, and oil lands; and records of his directorships in the Grafton and Greenbrier Railroad, and the Iron Valley and Morgantown Railroad companies. The papers reflect many aspects of activities of the Democratic Party in West Virginia, ca. 1880-1899. There is a scrapbook of Rose McGraw relating largely to Mount de Chantal Academy at Wheeling.

Correspondents include J. N. Camden, John J. Cornwell, H. G. Davis, Alston G. Dayton, C. J. Faulkner, A. B. Fleming, John B. Floyd, Alvaro F. Gibbens, Septimus Hall, J. J. Jackson, John J. Jacob, Virgil A. Lewis, Earl W. Oglebay, William A. Ohley, George C. Sturgiss, A. B. White, I. C. White, W. P. Willey, and William L. Wilson.

544. **McGrew, H. George.** Papers, 1865-1885. Ca. 250 items. Gift of Mrs. Roger Roberts, 1962. No. 1622.

Correspondence, sermons and religious writings, and accounts of a graduate of Wesleyan University and Harvard Law School, Methodist missionary to India (ca. 1876-1885), and son of Representative James Clark McGrew of Kingwood.

Subjects include West Virginia politics; social activities in Kingwood; conditions in the Indian mission field; nautical improvements tested at the Brooklyn Navy Yard, 1879; Northwestern University; and the Republican National Convention of 1880.

545. **McIlroy Family.** Papers, ca. 1829-1843. 21 items (photocopies). Loan for duplication by John McIlroy, 1971. No. 2212.

Papers of the McIlroy family, early residents of Huntingdon County, Pennsylvania, including correspondence of John and Joseph McIlroy, newspaper clippings, birth register from the family Bible, and a list of volunteers for the "Home Guard."

546. **McKay, Joseph.** Papers, 1897-1905. Ca. 200 items. Gift of Miss Helen Boyers, 1961. No. 1476.

Correspondence, bills, receipts, and other business papers of a Sistersville oil developer and stockman pertaining to the development of the Sistersville oil fields, steamboat freighting on the Ohio River, and business activity in Sistersville.

547. **McKeever, Kenna Harwood,** *Compiler.* Typescripts, 1954-1957. 1 reel of microfilm (3 volumes). Originals in possession of Mrs. Kenna McKeever, 1961. No. 1403.

Genealogy and reminiscences of the Wardensville area including "History of Wardensville, West Virginia," "A Record of Paul McIvor and His Descendants [!] ," and "Dad's Younger Days, 1889-1955: A True Story of Life of the Past in the Mountains as Remembered and Told to His Family."

548. **McKown, Sarah Morgan.** Diaries, 1860-1899. 2 reels of microfilm (39 volumes). Originals owned by Mrs. W. E. Gordon, 1955. No. 718.

Yearly diaries of Sarah Morgan McKown of Berkeley County.

549. **McLane Family.** Letters, 1826-1841. 7 items. Gift of Simon B. Chandler, 1952. No. 476.

Letters of Charles and Joseph A. McLane, and J. M. Lazzell, from Philadelphia, Pennsylvania, and Morgantown, to Charles McLane, pioneer physician in Morgantown. Published in part in "The Three McLane Doctors of Morgantown," in *Bulletin of the History of Medicine,* May-June, 1951.

550. **McNeel, Isaac (b. 1830).** Papers, 1850-1908. 4 ft. Gift of Joseph W. McNeel, 1961. No. 1451.

Correspondence, legal and business papers, mercantile records and tax receipt books of Isaac McNeel, who operated a store at Edray and Mill Point, Pocahontas County, served as sheriff of the county, operated a gristmill, raised livestock, and was appointed provost marshal of the county in 1862 by the Confederate Army.

The collection also includes letters and school reports of McNeel's sons, Winters and Summers, while students at Washington and Lee and the Medical and Law Departments of the University of Virginia, 1893-1897. Other school material pertains to the Hillsboro Male and Female Academy and the Lewisburg Female Institute.

Subjects include mercantile and cattle trade with Baltimore and Richmond; business conditions in the 1850s and in Richmond during the Civil War; slave hiring; ginseng trade; agriculture; the American Party, 1855; Henry A. Wise; Virginia Secession Convention; effect of the Union blockade on Richmond commerce; speculation in whiskey, tobacco, and cattle during the Civil War; and postwar economic and political conditions in the Pocahontas County area.

551. **McNeely, Joseph F. (b. 1868).** Papers, 1933-1955. 9 items. Gift of Joseph F. McNeely, 1954-1956. Nos. 602, 614, 758, 784, 857.

Typescripts and mimeographed articles and essays compiled and written by McNeely. Included are articles on the cemetery of the Presbyterian Church in Morgantown; "McNeely Family Records, with Historical Sketches and Key to Family Lineage," with data on the family, 1675-1908, which settled in Greene County, Pennsylvania, and in West Virginia; "From the Writings of J. F. McNeely," a collection of speeches, letters, poems, and statements concerning social and economic problems; "Historic Account of the Oil and Gas Development in Marion County, West Virginia, with Special Mention of Mannington and Fairview Fields"; and "A Fascinating Journey Over U. S. Highway 250 from Moundsville to Fairmont, West Virginia," a survey of the local history of this section. Also a brief genealogical sketch of Michael Benedum and Sarah Lantz Benedum of Bridgeport and Pittsburgh, Pennsylvania.

552. **McNeill Family.** Papers, 1770-1929. 1 ft. Gifts of John, William, and D. Brown McNeill, ca. 1948. No. 134.

Papers, mainly of Daniel and Daniel R. McNeill, stockdealers and mill owners of Hardy County. The early correspondence relates to the purchase and sale of livestock and the driving of herds to markets in the east. There is correspondence from members of the family in the vicinity of Chillicothe, Ohio, relating farm and market conditions and commenting on travel from Hardy County to Ohio. There are also references to river traffic on the Scioto and Ohio rivers and to the quantity of merchandise being shipped to the New Orleans market. There are account statements for school fees, books, and general school expenses for several years in the period 1809-1822, and 1870; a herd pedigree book, 1851-1861; and poultry and cattle records and accounts, 1913-1929.

553. **McNeill Hotel.** Registers, 1867-1873. 2 reels of microfilm (2 volumes). Originals in possession of Mrs. A. C. McNeill and the McNeill Hotel, 1958. Nos. 1097, 1098.

Guest registers of an old Moorefield hotel.

554. **Mallison, Samuel T.** Papers, 1915-1964. Ca. 200 items. Gift of Sam T. Mallison, 1966. No. 1913.

Correspondence, speeches, reminiscences, and newspaper clippings of a West Virginia newspaperman, state auditor, 1927-1929, and businessman. Subjects include the West Virginia gubernatorial campaign of 1924, Rush D. Holt's decision to run for the U. S. Senate in 1934, oil wildcatting ventures of Michael Benedum and J. C. Trees, the economy, oil imports, depletion allowances on the production of oil and gas, and labor legislation.

Correspondents include Holmes Alexander, Robert C. Byrd, Phil Conley, John W. Davis, Ken Hechler, Rush D. Holt, Robert E. Maxwell, Jim Comstock, M. L. Benedum, Frank Lausche, William R. Laird, A. B. Koontz, William Proxmire, Jennings Randolph, James A. Farley, Michael A. Musmanno, Robert S. Kerr, and Douglas MacArthur.

555. **Mannington District Fair.** Papers, 1953. 24 items. Gift of Walker Thomas, 1953. No. 545.

A file of newspaper clippings, programs, and advertising posters relating to the 1953 fair.

556. **Mansberger, Elwood C.,** *Collector.* Papers, 1850-1909. 8 items (photocopies). Loan for duplication, 1968. No. 2023.

One Morgantown Bridge Company receipt, 1869; one Monongalia County tax receipt, 1850; one Wood County teacher certificate, 1867; three Monongalia County teacher certificates, 1866-1871; one grade report from Monongalia Academy, 1858; and one postcard view of the Morgantown wharf, ca. 1909.

557. **Marion County.** Obituaries, 1848-1860. 1 typescript, 21p. Gift of Roderick Wilson, 1956. No. 865.

Copies of Marion County death records, 1848-1860. Survivors are sometimes given, as well as how death occurred, where funeral was held, minister in charge, and text of sermon.

558. **Marion County.** School records, 1868-1881. 21 items. Received, 1953. No. 452.

Report of J. N. Prickett, secretary of the Houltown Sunday School, August 30, 1868; a monthly report of the Mount Harmony School, 1877; a term report of the Boothsville School, 1879; and registers from various schools, 1871-1881, showing pupils' names, attendance records, teachers' salaries, books used, and number of students studying various subjects.

559. **Marmion, Nicholas (d. 1883).** Family papers, 1798-1951. 5 ft. Acquired, 1958. No. 1071.

Personal, medical, and business papers, account books, and daily journals of a prominent Harpers Ferry physician. Subjects include the practice of a small town doctor, his related business interests, and the education and careers of his children, three of whom became medical doctors. Included are the papers of William V. Marmion (1840-1922), who studied eye surgery in Vienna and established a practice in Washington, D. C. There are letters from George Marmion, acting surgeon and secretary of the National Home for Disabled Volunteer Soldiers, and letters of Robert A. Marmion (1844-1907), who was a naval surgeon and the first president of the Naval Medical School in Washington, D. C.

Many of the letters, especially after 1883, are those of the Marmion heirs and are concerned with family, personal, and financial affairs. Some letters shed light on the condition of the gold market after the Civil War and family activities as prominent members of the Roman Catholic faith.

560. **Marriage Records, 1816-1867.** 14p. (photocopies). Loan for duplication by Mrs. Herman Bowers, 1971. No. 2191.

Copy of a pamphlet, "Record of Marriages, Performed by Rev. William Welch of Mineral County," from 1816 to 1867. Marriages are listed for Hampshire County, 1816-1850; Hardy County, 1816-1859; Mineral County, 1865-1866 (1866-1867?); and Allegany County, Maryland, 1816-1858. There are copies of newspaper clippings of the column "Ancient History," from the *Keyser Tribune*, 1913, which contain a list of marriages solemnized by Rev. William Welch in Hampshire, Hardy, and Mineral counties and in Allegany County, Maryland.

561. **Marshall, Jacob Williamson (b. 1830).** Papers, 1852-1899. 1 ft. Received, 1938. No. 54.

Papers of a livestock broker, farmer, and merchant of Mingo Flats, who was associated with John T. McGraw in the development of Marlinton and the purchase and sale of land, coal, and timber in Pocahontas County. There are some items of Civil War interest, while the bulk of the correspondence relates to the marketing of ginseng, beeswax, wool, venison, animal pelts, and farm machinery. There is significant correspondence relating to state politics and railroads.

Correspondents include J. M. Bennett, J. N. Camden, David Goff, John J. Jackson, McCormick Harvesting Machine Company, John T. McGraw, and The Pocahontas Development Company.

562. **Marshall, Vause W.** Papers, 1880-1948. 3 ft. Acquired, 1959. No. 1198.

Papers of a Williamsport rare book and manuscripts dealer include correspondence relating to the book trade, dealer book lists and catalogues, and correspondence on West Virginia and national politics, 1880-1946; the Garner for President Committee; the Rush D. Holt campaign of 1940; the National Jeffersonian Democrats; and the state Democratic Executive Committee. There is one folder of John T. McGraw papers.

Correspondents include Charles H. Ambler, Roy Bird Cook, W. E. B. DuBois, P. S. DuPont, Andrew Edmiston, Walter S. Hallanan, Robert G. Kelly, Theodore R. McKeldin, and Earl G. Swem.

563. **Marshall County**. Archives, 1831-1948. 66 ft. Gift of the Marshall County Court, 1963. No. 1672.

County and circuit clerks records. Records for the years 1835-1857 include bonds of ministers, tavern operators, ordinaries, ferries, and county officials; estate settlements; records pertaining to road, bridge, and public building; records of the overseer of the poor; school commissioners' and surveyors' appointments; and lists of county officials. Records for 1863-1874 include county supervisors records; records of the Fairmont and Wheeling Turnpike; and muster certificates and reenlistment and bounty lists for the First, Second, Sixth, Seventh, Tenth-Fifteenth, Seventeenth, and Eighteenth West Virginia Volunteer Infantry Regiments, the First, Third, Fifth, Sixth West Virginia Cavalry, the First Light Artillery Regiment, and the Forty-fifth Regiment, United States Colored Troops. Papers for 1867-1907 include justice of the peace records, United States Admiralty Court records, and road surveyors' statements.

564. **Martin, John D.** Papers, 1839-1851. 1 reel of microfilm (20 items). Acquired, 1961. No. 1531.

Letters from John Ruff, Lexington, Virginia, to his son-in-law, John D. Martin, a Methodist clergyman stationed in Lewistown, Pennsylvania, Salem, Lewisburg, Front Royal and Leesburg, Virginia, and Baltimore, Maryland. Also one letter from Martin to his wife, Susan, dated Lewisburg, Virginia, 1841. Subjects include Methodism and meetings in the Lexington-Covington area, slavery controversy within the Methodist Church and in particular the Baltimore Conference, and farming in Lexington, Virginia.

565. **Martinsburg and Berkeley County**. Papers, 1781-1953. 1 reel of microfilm and 3 photostats. Originals owned by the Martinsburg Public Library, 1958. No. 1053.

Newspaper clippings, manuscripts, pamphlets, typescripts, correspondence, and pictures relating to the history of Martinsburg and Berkeley

County. The photostats are copies of the Martinsburg *Ladies Visiter* I:5, 6, 7 (1846).

566. **Maryland-West Virginia Boundary Line Survey.** Records, 1894-1898, 1910-1911, 1921-1929. 1 reel of microfilm (6 volumes). Originals in possession of Floyd Stiles, 1959. No. 1277.

Note and survey books.

567. **Mason, Charles (ca. 1730-1787).** Journal, 1763-1768. 1 reel of microfilm (1 item). Original in the National Archives, 1958. No. 1030.

The journal covers the activities of Mason and Dixon from their arrival in Philadelphia, 1763, to their departure from New York for London, 1768.

568. **Mason, J. M.** Correspondence, 1918. 2 items (photocopies). Loan for duplication by Paul L. Morgan, 1964. No. 1795.

Two letters from J. M. Mason at the University of Virginia with reference to the management of the Virginia-West Virginia debt controversy, the nature of the Virginia claims, the history of the case, and recommendations for handling the matter for the best interest of West Virginia.

569. **Mason, John W. (1842-1917).** Papers, 1831-1928. 15 ft. Gift of John W. Mason, 1936, 1966. Nos. 37, 1888.

Correspondence, legal papers, photographs, and printed materials of a circuit court and state supreme court judge, member of the Virginia State Debt Commission, and commissioner of Internal Revenue. Subjects include the early development of the Republican Party in West Virginia, state political campaigns, 1870-1916, Monongalia Academy, industrial development, Internal Revenue Service, 1889-1893, the Virginia debt question, early banking development at Grafton, and the development of coal companies, particularly those around Fairmont.

Correspondents include George W. Atkinson, James G. Blaine, Arthur I. Boreman, A. W. Campbell, W. E. Chandler, William M. O. Dawson, A. G. Dayton, Marmaduke H. Dent, Stephen B. Elkins, D. D. Farnsworth, Nathan Goff, Jr., J. M. Hagans, Benjamin Harrison, H. D. Hatfield, J. J. Jacob, J. C. McGrew, William McKinley, J. M. Mason, F. H. Pierpont, Nathan B. Scott, W. E. Stevenson, G. C. Sturgiss, and A. B. White.

570. **Mason County.** Archives, 1772-1908. Ca. 76 ft. Gift of the Mason County Court, 1956, and various dates. Nos. 398, 663, 914.

Court case papers, 1772-1908, and record books, 1804-1903. A chronological index to the case papers is available in the manuscripts section. Part of the collection is unprocessed and unindexed.

571. **Mason County.** Documents, 1787-1806. 3 items. Gift of Mrs. F. A. and Miss Helen Couch, 1961. No. 1408.

Grant of a 3,248-acre tract near Point Pleasant to Michael Gratz and Charles Willing of Philadelphia, and deeds of this land to Robert Hare and Charles Hare.

572. **Mason-Dixon Survey.** Papers, 1970. 6 items (photocopies). Loan for duplication by Dr. Eldon B. Tucker, Sr., 1971. No. 2177.

Correspondence and papers concerning location of the termination of the survey in 1767, and an application for a historic marker on the site.

573. **Matheny, H. E.,** *Collector and Compiler.* Papers, 1828, 1861-1961. 87 items (typescripts and 1 reel of microfilm). Loan and gift of H. E. Matheny, 1960-1962. Nos. 1330, 1391, 1399, 1410, 1416, 1431, 1446, 1567.

Published and unpublished manuscripts, Civil War correspondence, and historical records and accounts collected, compiled, or written by an Akron, Ohio, bookman and antiquarian.

Manuscripts include "Some Notes of Camp Chase"; "The Saga of Red Neck Nellie and West Virginia's Wild Volcano" (oil town of Volcano); "The Common Soldier in the Civil War"; "The Lighter Side of the Civil War"; "A History of West Virginia's First Picture Post Cards"; "Parkersburg . . . and the Early Railroad Conventions"; "Some Incidents of the 1913 Flood"; "The Night They Rioted in Harrisville" (race riot in 1882); "Hunting the Wild Guinea. West Virginia's Most Elusive Game Bird"; "The 'Shetting Out' of John Morgan" (famous Ripley hanging in 1897); "The Life of Mad Ann Bailey, the Kanawha Valley Eccentric"; and "West Virginia's Rare Civil War Books."

Compilations and records include: "A Partial List of the Confederate Soldiers Who Lived in or near Charleston . . ."; "Muster Roll of Company G, 11th Virginia Cavalry, Rosser's Brigade, . . ."; "The Burning of Chambersburg, A Reminiscence of the Hunter Raid to Lynchburg, Virginia, and the Retreat down the South Branch Valley," by James Z. McChesney; "A Complete List of Post Offices in (West) Virginia in 1828"; and a typescript copy of a published letter from Thomas M. Harris to the editor of the New York *Sun,* August 4, 1901, defending his action as a member of the military commission that tried the Lincoln conspirators.

Civil War correspondence includes the letters of Ephraim W. Frost of Company J, 116th Regiment, Ohio Volunteer Infantry, who was stationed in the Eastern Panhandle on the line of the Baltimore and Ohio Railroad; Company C, Fourteenth Virginia Cavalry (Confederate), McCausland's Brigade; letters from William E. Kimble, from Camp Allegheny; and a letter from General Thomas M. Harris to General W. S. Rosecrans, December 5, 1861, pertaining to the Third West Virginia Infantry Regiment (Union) and guerrilla activities in Braxton, Gilmer, and Webster counties.

Subjects include federal forts and the secession crisis in Virginia; Battle of Rich Mountain; fighting in the vicinity of Winchester and Harpers Ferry, August, 1862; Battle of Cedar Mountain; camp life and picket duty in the Confederate Army; Battle of Droop Mountain; Battle of Mononcacy and Jubal Early's 1864 raid on Washington; fighting in the Shenandoah Valley, 1864; McNeill's Rangers, Imboden's Partisan Rangers, and Mosby's Rangers, Battle of Dublin; and the Albert G. Jenkins Brigade.

574. **Mathers, Max (1880-1958).** Tape recording, 1957. 3 items. Acquired, 1957. No. 937.

One tape and two typed transcripts of reminiscences on the history of Morgantown by one of its older residents, a descendant of Zackwell Morgan.

575. **Mathews, Henry Mason (1834-1884).** Letter, 1882. 1 item. Gift of William E. Stewart, 1963. No. 1718.

Letter from Governor Henry M. Mathews to John R. Donehoo pertaining to Mathew's candidacy for the U. S. Senate.

576. **Maxwell, G. Ralph,** *Collector.* Papers, 1849-1918. Ca. 100 items. Gift of G. Ralph Maxwell, 1951. No. 311.

Letters from Hu Maxwell written from Fresno, California, 1887, to Mrs. S. J. Maxwell at St. George, Tucker County, relating to mining, schools, size of and social conditions in towns, and Maxwell's intentions concerning his historical publications. Included is an account book of Captain James L. White, commander of a Confederate military unit at Laurel Hill.

577. **Maxwell, Lewis.** Papers, (1825-1861) 1903. 162 items. Gift of Frank J. Maxwell, 1957. No. 963.

Papers of Lewis Maxwell, an attorney at Weston. The main part of the papers are letters from clients, concerning land in West Virginia counties, 1840-1859. There are letters from J. H. Diss Debar, John S. Carlile,

Matthew Edmiston, J. M. Bennett, and Benjamin H. Latrobe regarding railroad legislation and construction, surfacing of the Weston-Clarksburg road, and land transactions.

578. **Maxwell Family.** Papers, ca. 1845-1950. 9 ft. Gifts of Mrs. Anna H., C. J., Claud, and Selby F. Maxwell, 1932-1952. Nos. 10, 132, 149, 181, 188, 194, 199, 205, 214, 216, 217, 219-228, 277, and 311.

Papers of Hu Maxwell (1860-1927), historian, editor, and author of several county histories of West Virginia, along with papers and records of other family members. There are manuscripts of fiction, verse, and local history written by Maxwell, as well as a number of his manuscripts and publications dealing with wood uses and forestry prepared while he was a member of the Forest Service of the United States Department of Agriculture. Maxwell kept a diary during the years 1901-1919 while residing in Morgantown, Chicago, Illinois, and Washington, D. C., which is very full for the period of World War I. This diary also contains notes on a diary of Rufus Maxwell (1855-1907), which is not in the collection. Other Rufus Maxwell items include an 1845 map of Weston and his correspondence. There is an unpublished autobiography of Abraham Bonnifield (1837-1885), of Randolph and Tucker counties; an account book of the Tyrone Forge, Monongalia County, 1807-1814; a few records of the Rector College Literary Society, Pruntytown, 1848-1849; St. George Academy records; and other materials on politics, the statehood movement, and the Civil War in West Virginia.

579. **Maysville, Kentucky.** Papers, 1858-1869. 3 items. Gift of Mrs. Charles B. Powell, 1957. No. 938.

Receipt for coal purchased from Ryan and Cooper by Mrs. Susan Beasley, 1858, Maysville, Kentucky; a bill of lading for goods shipped by Bischof and Loeb, Cincinnati, Ohio, to McDouble and Brother, Maysville, 1869; and a patriotic Civil War cover from Flemingsburg, Kentucky, June 24, [1861?].

580. **Mercer, Hugh.** Typescript, 1754-1825. 3p. Transfer, 1951. No. 235.

A narrative by Virginia N. Stribling giving an account of Mercer's life and of a 16,000-acre tract of land south of the Kanawha River which was given to Mercer by George Washington.

581. **Meredith, E. E.,** *Collector.* Papers, 1855-1951. 7 items. Gift of E. E. Meredith, 1951. No. 256.

Broadsides, 1855-1864, and other materials relating mainly to Marion County.

582. **Meredith, Edward E.** Papers, 1817-1954. 1 reel of microfilm and 22 items. Loan for duplication by Marion County Historical Society, 1965. No. 1814.

Clippings, letters, broadsides, and articles written or collected by E. E. Meredith, author of the newspaper column, "Do You Remember," which appeared in the Fairmont *Times-West Virginian.*

Topics include Marion County; Augusta County; farming account books ca. 1853, 1888; Barnsville; Barrackville covered bridge; banks and banking in Marion County, 1842-1892; blacksmith shops; buffalo; Marion County Historical Society; coal industry in Fairmont region; West Virginia Gold Mining and Milling Company certificate; Grafton and Greenbrier Railroad Company certificate; "Do You Remember"; stock of Weston and Fairmont Turnpike Company; schoolteaching, 1838, 1855; and tax receipts, 1817, 1819, 1824, 1850, and 1858.

Correspondents or persons mentioned include Charles H. Ambler, Edgar B. Sims, Lemuel Chenoweth, Eli Chenoweth, Paul M. Angle, J. M. Callahan, Ken McClain, William Haymond, Francis H. Pierpont, Ira E. Robinson, and Clem Shaver.

Copies of theatre programs, 1917-1919, and electoral tickets, 1860, 1864; a proclamation by George B. McClellan, commanding the Department of the Ohio, 1861; and an open letter, "Monongahela River Bridge Underwriting Syndicate Managers," concerning the construction of the million-dollar bridge in Fairmont.

583. **Mestrezat, Walter A.** Papers, 1862-1946. 1 reel of microfilm (3 folders). Originals in possession of Morgan D. Mestrezat-Sprigg, 1961. No. 1538.

Military papers and correspondence of the chief musician, First West Virginia Infantry and Thirtieth Regiment, United States Infantry Volunteers, 1898-1915; clippings of Mestrezat's letter from the Philippines in 1900; copies of letters written by Charles A. Mestrezat, Fourteenth Regiment, Pennsylvania Cavalry, 1862-1864, from various places in western Virginia, Richmond, and Belle Island where he died in a military prison, and papers relating to the history of the Two-hundred-first Infantry, West Virginia National Guard.

584. **Middleton, Henry O.** Correspondence, 1832-1867. 16 items. Gift of Mrs. Allene Reed Cutright, 1954. No. 626.

Letters to Middleton at Buckhannon and other places, regarding the purchase and sale of land in several West Virginia counties, with notes on court cases and comment on the fall of Richmond. Correspondents include Allen T. Caperton.

585. **Miller, Charles C.** Records, 1831-1847. 2 volumes. Gift of Vallie E. Tony, 1959. No. 1242.

Financial records of a Mason County farmer.

586. **Miller, Clay V.** Papers, 1867 (1928-1952). Ca. 200 items. Gift of Clay Miller, 1961. No. 1498.

Correspondence, clippings, and printed material collected by the historian of Andrews Methodist Episcopal Church, Grafton.

Subjects include Anna Jarvis and the Mother's Day movement and Andrews Church and Methodism in Taylor County. There are photographs of Ann M. Reeves Jarvis and her daughter, Anna.

Correspondents include Anna Jarvis and Okey L. Patteson.

587. **Miller, George W.** Papers, 1948-1971. 10 ft. Gift of George W. Miller, 1971. No. 2130.

Correspondence and financial records of a Gilmer County businessman, gas drilling contractor, schoolteacher, and elementary school principal who was involved also with coal, timber, real estate, and water-well businesses. The correspondence concerns Miller's business affairs; dealings with government agencies, such as the Federal Power Commission and the Small Business Administration; applications for teaching positions and to graduate schools; tax problems; campaign for a seat on the school board; and dealings with West Virginia politicians. The financial material includes cancelled check files and a month by month accounting of the profits from gas wells. Other subjects include drilling costs and contracts; coal sales; Gilmer County schools and politics; business problems; land sales; road maintenance and construction; and the Consolidated Gas Company. Correspondents include Chauncey Browning, Jr., James Kee, Robert H. Mollohan, Arch Moore, and Hulett Smith.

588. **Miller, Mrs. Lewis H.,** *Collector.* Papers, 1782 (1894-1921) 1940. 47 items. Gift of Mrs. Lewis H. Miller, 1956. No. 885.

Land grant to Samuel Hanway, Monongalia County, for 1,000 acres, dated December 19, 1782, and a grant to James Arnold, Harrison County, for 1,059 acres dated December 20, 1785. There is a map of the Edmund Law Rogers land in Jackson County, 1896, clippings concerning the candidacy of Lewis H. Miller for the governorship in 1940, and other items.

589. **Miller, Sue Proctor,** *Collector.* Papers, 1780, 1830-1879. 1 reel of microfilm and 44 photostats. Originals in the possession of Mrs. Sue P. Miller, 1956. Nos. 866, 886.

Photostat of a map of George Washington and Albert Gallatin lands in present Jackson and Mason counties; photostats of letters, some written in French, relating to the Charles Lisez family, including letters, 1863-1865, of Charles Lisez, Jr., a prisoner of war at Fort Delaware, Maryland; microfilm of typescripts of Braxton County marriage bonds,

1836-1853; and biographical and genealogical notes on Michael (Malcolm) Coleman in Jackson County, William White, the Staats family, the Anderson family of Wood and Jackson counties, and a sketch of early Ravenswood by Eunice Proctor Perkins.

590. **Millspaugh, C. F.** Letters, 1912. 10 items (typescript copies). Gift of Earl L. Core, 1962. No. 1554.

Letters of the curator, Department of Botany, Field Museum of Natural History, Chicago, Illinois, and J. L. Sheldon of West Virginia University, concerning Millspaugh's book, *Living Flora of West Virginia* (1913).

591. **Minehart, Jacob.** Ledger, 1841-1845, 1863. 1 volume. Acquired, 1961. No. 1389.

Ledger of a glassblower who worked for various glass companies in Wheeling, containing a record of his work and notes concerning his working agreements.

592. **Miners' Treason Trials.** Papers, 1921-1923. 4 reels of microfilm and 60p. (copies). Originals in the possession of the circuit court of Jefferson County, 1957, and gift of Festus P. Summers, 1964. No. 979.

Case papers for the trials of coal miners and United Mine Workers leaders indicted for treason in connection with the Logan County strikes of August and September, 1921. There is also a copy of the Charles Town treason trial indictment, dated February 4, 1922, and a copy of a typescript article, "Treason Trials in the United States," from the *American Law Review* 26:912-914. Persons mentioned include Walter Allen, William Blizzard, C. Frank Keeney, Rev. J. E. Wilburn, John Wilburn, Fred Mooney, and William Petry.

593. **Miscellany.** Papers, 1774-1960. 1 ft. Acquired, 1956-1963. Nos. 848, 900, 946, 966, 1115, 1120, 1121, 1134, 1137, 1138, 1149, 1154, 1157, 1164, 1201, 1204, 1217, 1223, 1226, 1273, 1305, 1319, 1341, 1351, 1370, 1400, 1421, 1493, 1497, 1503, 1531, 1537, 1566, 1585, 1620, 1624, 1677, 1682, 1690, 1692, 1696.

A group of manuscript and printed items, including the execution docket and indexed tax book of Isaac Van Meter, sheriff of Hardy County, 1818-1820 (848); a letter from Josiah Fleagle to his brother Noah, Camp Hill, Harpers Ferry, 1863 (900); a Christmas menu from Hill's Central Hotel, Parkersburg, ca. 1879 (900); a campaign ribbon of the Democratic state convention, 1892 (900); a poem, "The Battle of Blenheim," by D. H. Conrad, Martinsburg, 1852 (946); a copy of the Virginia land office record of a land bounty allowance for George Rogers'

State Navy service, 1833 (946); a freight receipt for salt shipped to Harpers Ferry, 1861 (966); a certificate of membership in the Sixty-seventh Regiment, Virginia Light Infantry in Berkeley County, 1818 (966); and a [C. J. Faulkner?] manuscript concerning the hanging of Mary Surratt (966); records of the Collins-Murphy-Hoge family (1493); Bible records of the J. L. Fisher family (1400), and the family line of Edith Eleanor Day (1273); Civil War papers of David Holmes (1537); veteran's records of Hiram J. Rogers, Company H, 191 Pennsylvania Volunteer Infantry (1319); holograph leaf from a report issued by George B. McClellan on the skirmish at Hart's Farm during his western Virginia campaign of 1861 (1620); discharge papers of John H. Marple, Tenth Regiment, West Virginia Infantry (1120); records of Sanford St. Clair, Company G, First Regiment, West Virginia Cavalry (1149, 1201); letter from Jacob Waddle, First West Virginia Volunteer Infantry, 1864 (1585); a letter from a Union soldier written from a field hospital at Sandy Hook, Maryland (1566); a clipping on iron furnaces in Barbour County (1115); articles of incorporation of the Graham-Yeager Lumber Company (1691); a check plate from the Farmer Bank of (Annapolis) Maryland, ca. 1850 (1692); a Parkersburg plumber's account book, 1908 (1204); clippings of Wellsburg town ordinances, 1804-1841, pertaining to markets, streets, animals, slaughterhouses, and taxes (1696); a few papers of Theodora Douglass while a student at St. Hilda's Hall, Charles Town, 1931 (1223); an antebellum seal of the Berkeley County Circuit Court (1341); page proofs from John A. Caruso's *Appalachian Frontier* (1677); a plate from a cornerstone document box in the old federal building at Parkersburg giving the population, and names of the city officials in 1875 (1421); land deeds from Hampshire and Greenbrier counties (1154, 1497); Historic American Buildings Surveys for Harpers Ferry structures, 1959 (1503); a folder of philatelic material pertaining to the West Virginia Centennial, 1963 (1682); lyrics and score of *Song of the Counties* of the state (1134); United War Work Campaign certificates, 1918 (1217); facsimile copy of the "Virginia Declaration of Rights," 1776 (1226); an invoice of articles received at the General Hospital, Point Pleasant, ca. 1865 (1624); and a letter from Michael Late Benedum, 1948 (1351).

594. **Mockler, R. Emmett.** Papers, ca. 1954, 1956. 1 item and 1 reel of microfilm (1 volume). Gift and loan of R. Emmett Mockler, 1959, 1960. Nos. 1252, 1337.

Typescript, "A Short History of Mannington," and Clippings of Mockler's serial, "The Mannington Story," from the Fairmont *Times*. These histories deal with Indian warfare, early settlers, mercantile establishments, the Civil War, and the development of the oil and gas fields in the Mannington region.

595. **Moldenke, Harold N. (b. 1909).** Papers, 1922-1962. 1 ft. Gift of Harold N. Moldenke, 1962. No. 1574.

Correspondence of the director of the Trailside Nature and Science Center, Watchung, New Jersey, curator of the Herbarium, New York Botanical Garden, and editor and publisher of *Phytologia.*

596. **Monongah Mine Disaster.** Papers, (1907-1909) 1952. 11 items. Gift of Carter D. Jones, 1953. No. 524.

A scrapbook containing newspaper clippings on the explosion, the rescue operations, inquest, and mine law reforms. In addition there are photographs of disaster scenes; maps of the mine; printed and typescript reports and pamphlets on mining operations; a script of a television broadcast on the explosion; materials on mine disasters in Alabama, Pennsylvania, and Illinois; newspaper accounts of the agitation for the removal of Judge Alston G. Dayton, and data on the imprisonment of Miss Fannie Sellins, a labor organizer.

597. **Monongah Mine Relief Fund.** Records, 1907-1920, 1925. 7 ft. Gift of the Marion County Historical Society, 1964. No. 1733.

Records of the Monongah Mine Relief Committee include correspondence and individual case files for each miner and rescue worker who lost his life. The case files contain age and place of birth of each victim; dependents' names, ages, and places of residence; and amount of each relief payment. There is also a record of all contributions to the Relief Committee, financial transactions with banks in Fairmont and Monongah, and correspondence and agreement concerning the transfer of funds between the Monongah Relief Committee and the Disaster Relief Unit of the American Red Cross for the Barrackville Mine Disaster, 1925.

598. **Monongalia Academy.** Papers, 1853-1867, 1939. 15 items. Gift of Pauline Forman Cairns [1939?] and transfers, 1953, 1956. Nos. 68, 400, 401, 402, 403, 529.

Manuscripts, printed materials, and photostats relating to the Monongalia Academy, Morgantown, including grade reports and tuition receipts, 1853-1860; printed invitations to examinations, 1834; a bond relating to a fund-raising lottery, 1832; a deed to the West Virginia Agricultural College transferring the Academy and the Woodburn Seminary property, 1867; a historical sketch written by Susan Maxwell Moore, 1939; and a letter from Ada Haldeman Ford giving biographical information on Samuel Haldeman.

599. **Monongalia and Harrison Counties.** Surveys, 1784-1789, 1795-1796, 1816, 1834-1836, 1843, 1903. 1 reel of microfilm. Originals in the possession of George W. Cunningham, 1955. No. 699.

Two manuscript volumes containing surveyors' field notes for Harrison County, and copies of Monongalia County surveys, compiled by members of the Haymond family. These notes also contain information concerning acreage cleared, location and type of construction of the homes of some early residents of Harrison County; dates of patents and name of person to whom patent was issued; street courses and survey of the corporation of Clarksburg, 1835; and names of members of a survey party, wages paid, miscellaneous expenses, and camp locations. Included also is a pamphlet, *The Haymond Family*, by Henry Haymond (Clarksburg, 1903).

600. **Monongalia County.** Archives, 1774-1936. 198 ft. Gift of the Monongalia County Court, 1934-1935, 1951-1953. Nos. 26, 240, 487, 541.

Court case papers, wills, licenses, bonds, deeds, school reports, and other papers commonly recorded and filed in the county, 1774-1938. Included are settlement papers; bound record volumes, 1781-1936, of deeds, estrays, estates, the jail, naturalization, surveys, taxes, voter registration, and marriage and deed indexes; also account books for businesses and organizations, including construction firms, gristmills, retail merchandising, the humane society, medical practice, coal and lumber firms, and minute books of the Society of the Sons of Temperance.

601. **Monongalia County.** Clippings, ca. 1908-1914. Ca. 20 items. Gift of Richard E. Hamstead, 1956. No. 1042.

Newspaper clippings of obituaries and political affairs.

602. **Monongalia County.** Corporation records, 1920-1927. 11 items. No. 486.

Certificates of incorporation and other papers of the State Coal Company, Swastika Oil and Gas Company, Sanitary Garbage Can Company, and a map of the Gillmore Mine of the Pittsburgh-Fairmont Coal Mining Company, all in Monongalia County.

603. **Monongalia County.** Papers, 1783, 1800. 2 items. Transfer, 1953. No. 586.

A clothing account, Morgantown, 1800, and a land grant to Casper Everly, Monongalia County, 1783.

604. **Monongalia County.** Scrapbook, 1838-1951. 1 reel of microfilm. Original in the possession of Max Mathers, 1957. No. 1007.

A scrapbook compiled by E. L. Mathers and Max Mathers, dealing with Morgantown and Monongalia County. There are photographs and newspaper clippings concerning civic, military, and social organizations; taverns and hotels; churches and schools; marriages and deaths; historic houses, early buildings, business places, and river navigation; and biographical sketches.

605. **Monongalia County.** Typescript, 1957. 1 item. Gift of A. D. Mastrogiuseppe, Jr., 1966. No. 1926.

A study of the Granville (Mona) Volunteer Fire Department, July-August, 1957, with photographs of the equipment, personnel, and firefighting.

606. **Monongalia County Art Guild.** Records, 1938-1941. 1 ft. Gift of David L. Brown, 1961. No. 1488.

Correspondence, news clippings, minutes, financial reports, posters and exhibition materials, photographs, and publications.

607. **Monongalia County. Battelle District.** Records, 1878-1916. 1 ft. Gift of Raymond Tennant, 1956. No. 926.

Dockets, 1878-1887, 1899-1911, and cases, 1881-1916, of various justices.

608. **Monongalia County Bible Society.** Records, 1840-1850. 1 volume. Transfer, 1956. No. 830.

A minute book of the Monongalia County Bible Society. Names of contributors and members of the society are recorded by the secretary, Waitman T. Willey.

609. **Monongalia County.** Cemetery readings, ca. 1956, 1958. 1 reel of microfilm, 1 typescript. Originals owned by Virgil McIntire, 1956, and gift of Mrs. H. L. Martin, Sr., 1958. Nos. 924, 1121.

Microfilm of records copied by Mr. McIntire from tombstones in all known cemeteries in Monongalia County, relating to soldiers from the county. Includes names of servicemen in U. S. wars and all known Confederate soldiers. Also, reading from Michael's Cemetery, Stewarts Run, Grant District.

610. **Monongalia County. Clinton District.** Papers, 1796-1964. 5 items. Loan for duplication by Michael Cover, 1964. No. 1777.

"History of Ridgedale School District" by C. G. Howell which includes a story of the Jones Raid, April [1963]; a history of the Goshen Baptist Church, written in 1863, and a list of ministers of the church. There is a clipping from a Fairmont newspaper in which a 100-year-old story, "The Road to Morgantown," is reprinted.

611. **Monongalia County Council for Drug Information.** Papers, 1970. 1 folder. Gift of John Michael Kelly, 1970.

Pamphlets, circulars, telephone record cards reflecting the operation of the council.

612. **Monongalia County. Defense Council, Office of Civilian Defense.** Radio scripts, 1942-1943. 47 items. Gift of E. H. Vickers, ca. 1946. No. 108.

Mimeographed radio scripts used by the Defense Council in promoting the war effort in Monongalia County.

613. **Monongalia County. Federal Relief.** Records, 1933-1937. 2 ft. Gift of Mrs. James R. Moreland, 1956. No. 890.

Correspondence, reports, and other records of the Monongalia County Relief Administration, the Civil Works Administration, and the Federal Emergency Relief Administration, from the office of the Director of Women's Work, Mrs. James R. Moreland. There are also two volumes of daily reports of the Lynchburg Coal and Coke Company, January-November, 1938.

614. **Monongalia County History.** Typescripts, 1775-1950. 1 ft. Transfer, 1952. No. 467.

Bound typescripts of reminiscences and local history prepared by James R. Moreland, Morgantown, including "History of the Various Courts of the County of Monongalia . . . ," and "Morgantown, West Virginia, Its Practical Jokes and Jokers . . . With Some Sketches Pertaining to Its History and Development." Indexed.

615. **Monongalia County Hospital.** Records, (1921-1929) 1940. 3 items. Gift of the Women's Auxiliary of the Monongalia General Hospital, 1958. No. 1092.

The records, 1922-1929, include minutes, reports, orders, bylaws, and newspaper clippings. A loose-leaf notebook, 1921-1925, contains the minutes of the Women's Hospital Association and deals with the organization of the Monongalia County Hospital and the activities of the Association.

616. **Monongalia County.** Land and Legal Papers, ca. 1783-1859. Ca. 125 items. Gifts of Victor R. Hoffman and Mrs. L. M. Stout, 1955, and transfers, various dates. Nos. 243, 244, 404, 405, 499, 583, 585, 700, 701, 1644.

Deeds, warrants, surveys, and other papers relating mainly to Monongalia County lands and residents.

617. **Monongalia County Land Office.** Manuscript, n.d. 6p. Gift of C. J. Maxwell, 1952. No. 319.

A description of the land office operated in the home of John Evans near Morgantown late in the eighteenth century, written by Hu Maxwell.

618. **Monongalia County Militia.** Muster roll, February 20, 1818. 1 item. Gift of Sigel O. Gardner, 1945. No. 95.

Printed muster roll of Captain John Launce's Company of Monongalia County, 118th Regiment.

619. **Monongalia County. North American Hill and Jew Hill Communities.** Reports, 1934. 64 items. Gift of Mrs. Gideon S. Dodds, 1960. No. 1313.

Surveys by Mrs. Gideon S. Dodds of the economic and social conditions in two mining settlements near Maidsville. The surveys record the poverty, educational, and moral standards of these two settlements.

620. **Monongalia County. Revolutionary Soldiers.** Typescripts, ca. 1940-1959. 4 items. Gift of the Daughters of the American Revolution, Colonel John Evans Chapter, 1942, and transfer, 1959. Nos. 91, 406, 1212.

Typescripts of names, dates of birth and death, and name of wife, of Monongalia County Revolutionary soldiers. Several names for Ohio County are also included, as well as a binder of typed copies of Revolutionary War pension applications. Also typescript records, "Revolutionary Soldiers Buried in Monongalia County," and "Revolutionary Soldiers Who Applied for Pensions in Monongalia County, West Virginia."

621. **Monongalia County. World War I.** Records, 1917-1918. 8 items. Transfer, 1936. No. 44.

Copies of rules and regulations determining the order of drafting by local boards; index to serial numbers in master list; list of names in registration of June 5, 1917; list of registrants, September 12, 1918; names of persons inducted by the Monongalia County Board; and an alphabetical list of the class of 1918.

622. **Monongalia Historical Society.** Records, 1827 (1925-1956). 5 ft. Gift of Monongalia Historical Society, 1955, 1958, 1960. Nos. 407, 722, 1060, 1310.

Clippings and miscellaneous printed materials relating to Monongalia County history; genealogical compilations, prepared by Thomas Ray Dille, relating to Monongalia County families; business correspondence and membership list of the society, 1924-1927, 1930; correspondence and records of the West Virginia Historical Society, ca. 1925-1931; court records, family letters and other manuscripts, 1827-1910; and various Civil Works Administration forms and records, 1933-1935, for Monongalia County. Included also are photographs and several issues of Morgantown newspapers; a typescript entitled "Spots in Monongalia County School History, 1837-1847"; and letters to Dr. Eldon B. Tucker, Jr., president, on historical preservation, 1953-1956.

623. **Monroe County.** Archives, ca. 1772-1923. 67 ft. Gift of the Monroe County Court, 1946. No. 102.

Court case papers, wills, deeds, surveys and plats, ca. 1772-1879, along with bound volumes of court records, deeds, estrays, road and tax records, a free Negro register, and private account books, 1783-1923. The account books include records of a U. S. Army post hospital at Union, 1867-1869; oil well drilling, 1886-1890; Union and Fort Spring Stage Line, 1876-1877; newspapers, 1867-1903; taverns, 1815-1872; and Union Lyceum minutes, 1845-1847.

624. **Monroe County.** Typescript, 1933. 1 item, 10p. Gift of the University of Chicago Library, 1968. No. 2020.

Typed transcript of reminiscences and recollections by an old resident of Monroe County which were recorded in Greenville, on Indian Creek, by Billy Meridith Hardy in 1933.

625. **Monroe County. Roads.** Records, 1812-1862. 3 volumes. Gift of Mary P. Osborne. No. 415.

An account book of stockholders in the Mountain Lake and Salt Sulphur Springs Turnpike Company, 1857-1862; a survey book of the Salt

Sulphur Springs Road, 1812; and a survey book for Giles County, Virginia, 1821-1824.

626. **Montague, Margaret Prescott** (1878-1955). Papers, 1893 (1906-1944) 1955. 6 ft. Gift of Miss E. L. Ball and R. Cary Montague, 1958, 1959, 1960. Nos. 1110, 1152, 1169, 1348.

Correspondence, manuscripts, notes and notebooks, diaries, press clippings, photographs, and printed material of a West Virginia essayist, short-story writer, poet and novelist, who won the first O. Henry Memorial Prize in 1919 for her short story, "England to America."

The papers include correspondence from editors, publishers, agents and critics; readers' correspondence; family letters; manuscripts of short stories, essays, novels, and other prose writings; plays and poetry manuscripts; outlines, plots, and drafts; and diaries and notebooks primarily concerned with religious meditation, Christian mysticism, and Miss Montague's concept of human ennoblement through suffering.

Correspondents include Bernard Baruch, Russell Doubleday, Howard M. Gore, M. A. DeWolfe Howe, Vachel Lindsay, Christopher Morley, Philip Van Doren Stern, Joseph P. Tumulty, and Woodrow Wilson.

627. **Mooney, Fred.** Manuscripts, ca. 1935. 1 reel of microfilm and 1 ft. Originals in possession of Mrs. Fred Mooney, 1961, and acquisition, 1967, 1968. Nos. 1428, 1956.

Manuscript and typescript drafts of "The Life of Fred Mooney, by Himself," and "Shootin Straight," by J. F. Pennington, a Mooney pen-name. Mooney, one-time secretary-treasurer of United Mine Workers District 31, writes of his experiences in the West Virginia labor movement, in particular, the disturbances at Cabin Creek and Paint Creek, 1912-1913, the abortive Miners March of 1919, the Matewan massacre of the Baldwin Felts detectives, the Miners' Treason Trials in 1922, and a later dispute with John L. Lewis and the United Mine Workers that led to Mooney's resignation. The collection includes one folder of correspondence and a scrapbook of newspaper clippings collected by Mooney. The autobiography was edited and published in 1967 by J. W. Hess as *Struggle in the Coal Fields: the Autobiography of Fred Mooney*.

628. **Moore, Elizabeth I.** (1832-1930). Typescript, 1931. 1 item. Gift of Mrs. Friend E. Clark, 1960. No. 1357.

Eulogy of a nineteenth century educator, principal of the Woodburn Female Seminary, and founder of the Morgantown Female Seminary, written by Emma H. Clark.

629. **Moore, George Ellis.** Manuscript, 1963. Ca. 200p.
Gift of Festus P. Summers, 1971. Nos. 1764, 2203.

Manuscript of *Banner in the Hills* by George Ellis Moore, presenting the story of secession and the Civil War in western Virginia and tracing the steps by which West Virginia was created.

630. **Moore, Robert T.** Records, 1797-1826, 1909. 33 items. Acquired, 1957. No. 982.

A ledger, and receipts, notes, and account statements for the general merchandise retail business of Robert T. Moore, Wellsburg, 1797-1826. Also, several account statements for the wholesale and retail meat business of George M. West, Wellsburg, 1909.

631. **Moreland, James Rogers (1879-1955).** Papers, 1809-1955. 65 ft. Gifts of Mrs. James R. Moreland, 1956, 1960. Nos. 870, 1146.

Correspondence, business and legal papers, clippings, and typescripts of a Morgantown lawyer, financier, business leader, and member of the House of Delegates, pertaining to his civic, religious, and professional activities. The collection includes correspondence of the Alexander Smith family, 1809-1838; papers of Joseph Moreland, 1849-1912; legal papers of the Connellsville Basin Coke Company; a manuscript, "History of the Various Courts of Monongalia County"; speech on the United Mine Workers in West Virginia; plats, maps, and legal documents pertaining to the residential and industrial development of Morgantown and the coal and gas fields of the Monongalia County area; memorandum book, 1858-1865, and account book, 1849-1850, of John Rogers, Morgantown sawmill operator; and papers concerning Davis and Elkins College, and Morgantown local history. In addition there are records of the Morgantown Hotel Company; Union Investment Company, Bank of Masontown; the LaMar Coal Company; the Monongalia Farmer's Company of Virginia, 1815-1818; the Deckers Creek Sand Company; Morgantown building contractors, 1877-1901; and other letter books and records of firms with which Moreland was associated.

632. **Moreland, William A.,** *Collector.* Papers, 1794-1958. 37 items. Gift of William A. Moreland, 1967. No. 1973.

Papers of Alexander Smith and George W. Brown. The Smith papers are letters and receipts, 1794-1814, and include a letter from N. Suter commenting on a naval battle of the War of 1812, current prices, government, and business conditions and receipts for the payment for slaves. The Brown letters, 1870-1886, concern a gift to West Virginia University, marriage, and payment of land taxes. Correspondents or persons mentioned include Alexander Martin and John W. Mason. Receipts, 1881-1894, are for taxes paid by the Brown, Miller and Co. Also included are certificates of appointment and commissions, 1858-1921, for Virginia Militia, Quartermaster General and Adjutant General of the state of West Virginia, Collector of Internal Revenue, U. S. Army Officer's Reserve Corps, the National Guard, and a membership certificate for the Society of the Army of West Virginia.

633. **Morgan, Ephraim F.** (1869-1950). Papers, 1920-1938. 13 ft. Gifts of Mrs. E. F. Morgan, 1950, and Albert M. Morgan, 1963. Nos. 203, 1660.

Official correspondence, reports, maps, proclamations, speeches, and papers of the sixteenth governor of West Virginia. Also included are newspaper clippings concerning the governor's administration, the launching of the U.S.S. *West Virginia,* and the building of the present executive mansion.

634. **Morgan, Zackquill.** Pension certificate, September 10, 1834. 1 item. Gift of Clifford R. Myers, 1924. No. 229.

Pension certificate showing Zackquill Morgan, of Monongalia County, as having served as a private in the Army of the Revolution.

635. **Morgan, Zackquill II (d. 1814).** Court papers, 1803-1806. 29 photostats. Transfer, 1951. No. 464.

Papers in the suit of *Amelia Tansey* v. *Zackquill Morgan II* in Monongalia County.

636. **Morgan County.** Archives, ca. 1820-1950. 144 ft. Gift of the Morgan County Court, 1956. No. 919.

Court case papers, record books, and papers from various county offices.

637. **Morgan County.** Records, 1820-1854. 1 reel of microfilm (103 items). Originals in possession of Fred T. Newbraugh, 1959. No. 1219.

School commissioners' papers, 1821-1846, containing reports to the president and directors of the Literary Fund; treasurer's accounts and reports; reports of tuition paid for poor children; and a report on the formation of school districts. The collection also includes a loose-leaf binder of marriage lists and certificates of the officiating clergymen, 1820-1854.

638. **Morgan County. Circuit Superior Court.** Calendars, 1960-1962. 6 items. Gift of Fred T. Newbraugh, 1960, 1961, 1962. Nos. 1387, 1392, 1434, 1549.

Typescript calendars, compiled by Fred T. Newbraugh, of cases tried before the Morgan County Circuit Superior Court, 1820-1830, listing the litigants, dates, and action taken in each case.

639. **Morgan County. Postmasters.** Records, ca. 1826-1925. 9 items (photocopies). Originals in the National Archives, 1960. No. 1289.

Selected pages pertaining to Berkeley Springs and Morgan County from the records of the Post Office Department, records of appointment of postmasters.

640. **Morgantown.** Miscellaneous papers, 1857-1956. 12 items. Transfers, 1953-1964; gifts of Miss Blake Snider, 1950; Mrs. Lizzie K. Lough, 1954; Mrs. Friend E. Clark, 1960; Miss Patricia Delardas, 1963; and Daisie D. Reeves estate, 1968. Numbers listed below with subjects.

A broadside, 1857, and commencement program, 1884, from the Morgantown Female Seminary (177, 411); a lapel ribbon and badge issued for the centennial celebration in 1885 (565); program for the sixty-third anniversary of the Rebecca Degree, I. O. O. F., certificates of membership, and a note concerning the Pythian Sisters, 1913-1934 (2013); certificate of incorporation of the Morgantown Woman's Hospital Association, 1925 (1290); scrapbook, 1942-1943, concerning the Morgantown Ordnance Works (560); transcript from the chancery case of *Louis T. Krebs, Jr., et al.* v. *Morgantown Bridge and Improvement Company*, 1954 (1725); speech by A. A. Hall, "Morgantown as a Part of Monongalia County, West Virginia," 1956 (1636); specifications for construction of a new opera house and business block, submitted by Leon H. Lempert and Son, architects, Rochester, New York (580).

641. **Morgantown.** Typescript and photographs, n.d. 119 items. Acquired, 1964. No. 1734.

Typescript, "Morgantown, West Virginia: Changes Through the Years," by Dr. and Mrs. Gideon S. Dodds, with color slides of Morgantown and West Virginia University subjects.

642. **Morgantown Bridge Company.** Minutes, 1851-1881. 1 volume. Gift of James R. Moreland, 1951. No. 312.

Manuscript extracts of minutes, apparently copied from original minutes.

643. **Morgantown Defense Council.** Records, 1941. 29 items. Gift of A. M. Reese, 1958. No. 1043.
Mimeographed letters and minutes of the executive committee.

644. **Morgantown in World War I.** Draft board records, 1917-1918. 4 typescripts, 129p. Gift of W. C. Davies, 1950. No. 196.
Lists of registrants, with serial and order numbers; also casualty figures for the United States, West Virginia, and Monongalia County.

645. **Morgantown Meteorological Records, 1876-1881.** 1 ft. Transfer, 1955. No. 785.
Four bound manuscript volumes of weekly meteorological records kept by the U. S. Army Signal Corps station at Morgantown, 1876-1881.

646. **Morgantown Rotary Club.** Papers, 1918-1969. 9 ft. Gifts of Morgantown Rotary Club, 1960, 1961, 1963, and Frederic Carspecken, 1970. Nos. 1331, 1491, 1693, 2157.
Correspondence, minute books, attendance lists, financial statements, and clippings of the Morgantown Rotary Club from 1918 to 1969. Included are papers pertaining to the first World Affairs Institute, held in Morgantown in April, 1960.

647. **Morgantown Service League.** Records, 1935-1969. 2 ft. Gift of the Morgantown Service League, 1961, 1965, 1967. No. 1472.
Printed annual reports, newspaper clipping scrapbooks, and Service League Follies programs of a voluntary women's service organization dedicated to civic and social welfare.

648. **Morgantown Women's Home Defense Club.** Papers, 1915-1960. 1 ft. Gift of the Morgantown Women's Home Defense Club, 1968. No. 2065.
Minutes, financial records, and president's records of a Parent and Teachers Association which changed its name to Home Defense Club with the advent of World War I.

649. **Morris, Mrs. Louise,** *Collector.* Papers, 1859-1971. 1 ft. Gift and loan of Mr. and Mrs. James Morris, 1961, 1965, 1971. Nos. 1454, 1808, 2195.

The collection includes a notebook kept by J. H. Wherry, a student at Jefferson College, Pennsylvania, in 1859; a genealogy of the DeVault, Haun, Fast families of Marion and Monongalia counties, 1817-1957; an essay on immigration by George Whitham, ca. 1896; land surveys from deed books, 1827-1933, mostly in Monongalia County; and a scrapbook of pictures, early twentieth century, including West Virginia University and the area. There are two letters of William S. Coburn, Third Regiment, [West] Virginia Volunteer Infantry, June 7 and October 17, 1863; Civil War diary of James Williams, Company A, Sixth West Virginia Infantry, August 31, 1864-June 8, 1865; a letter on conditions around Fort Scott, Kansas, 1867; a letter from R. W. Blue, Sixth Regiment, United States Volunteers near Fort Kearny, 1866; and "A Visit to the Centennial Exhibition in Philadelphia, 1876" by W. T. W. Crow. Also, copies of Revolutionary War pension records for Joseph Parsons, Samuel Bonnifield, and David Minear.

The microfilm contains manuscripts concerning Greene County, Pennsylvania, Fairview Church and Halleck Church areas in Monongalia County; genealogies on the Hall, Bailey, Austin, Miller, Shuttlesworth, Lanham, Joliffe, Morris, Baker, LeVelle, Bunner, Keister-Jenkins, Chadwick, Lewellen, Helmick, Ryan, and McNemar families; roster of the First West Virginia Volunteer Infantry, Spanish-American War, which includes certain West Virginia Civil War companies and newspaper clippings, 1910-1940, including articles on P. J. Crogan, Solomon Day, the Hacker family, Hacker's family, Hacker Valley, Simon Kenton, Kern's Fort, the old Preston County Courthouse, Robinson's Run, and old water mills.

650. Morris, Robert. Grant, 1795. 1 item. No. 412.

Survey and chain of title to 320,000 acres of land in present Wyoming, McDowell, Raleigh, Boone, and Logan counties, which were patented to Robert Morris, March 4, 1795, by the Commonwealth of Virginia.

651. Morris, Thomas A. Records, 1861. 1 reel of microfilm (1 volume). Original in the possession of the Wells Memorial Library, Lafayette, Indiana, 1961. No. 1502.

Copies of general orders, circulars, and letters, issued and received by Brigadier General Morris of the First Brigade, Indiana Volunteers, from May through July, 1861.

Most of the orders and letters pertain to the military operations of the United States Volunteers in western Virginia under the command of General George B. McClellan during the months of June and July. Morris was at Grafton, Philippi, Laurel Hill, Corricks Ford, and Cheat Mountain.

Correspondents include General George B. McClellan and General Charles W. Hill.

652. **Morrison, O. J.** Corporation record, 1910-1918. 1 reel of microfilm (1 volume). Original in possession of C. H. Morrison, 1962. No. 1486.

Corporation record of the O. J. Morrison Department Store, Charleston.

653. **Morrison, Gross and Company.** Records, ca. 1917-1950. 21 ft. Gift of C. A. Gross, 1957. No. 994.

Office correspondence, financial records, and account books of Morrison, Gross and Company, Rowlesburg and Southern Railroad Company, Woodford Lumber Company, and Keystone Manufacturing Company, in Preston and Randolph counties.

654. **Morton, Oren F. (1857-1926).** Papers, 1875-1926. 3 ft. Acquired, 1959. No. 1191.

Correspondence, diaries, sketch books, published and unpublished manuscripts, literary notes, business records, and printed material of a schoolteacher, newspaper writer, county historian, novelist and essayist from Kingwood, whose fiction and nonfiction writings deal primarily with the Virginia-West Virginia Allegheny highlands. His best known works are *Winning or Losing* (1901); *Land of the Laurel* (1903); *Under the Cottonwoods* (1900); and histories of Preston, Pendleton, and Monroe counties. The collection also includes a manuscript temperance paper, "The Meridian Temperance Banner," 1880; and a list of marriage bonds for Monroe County, 1799-1846.

655. **Mountaineer Statue, Charleston.** Correspondence, 1946-1953. 6 items. Gift of John M. Hamric, 1953. No. 519.

Copies of correspondence of Governor Okey L. Patteson and John Hamric regarding the repair of the Mountaineer Statue on the Capitol grounds; and other papers and clippings on the statue and Eli and Ellis Hamrick.

656. **Moylan, John.** Papers, 1783-1787. 28 items. Transfer, No. 573.

Papers concerning John Moylan's lands in Monongalia County.

657. **Mugler, Henri Jean.** Diary and memoir, 1838-1899. 3 reels of microfilm (38 volumes). Originals in possession of Mrs. L. B. Cardot, 1960. No. 1335.

Diary and memoir of a Confederate soldier, railroad laborer, and shop owner from Grafton. The memoir begins with Mugler's birth in Alsace-

Lorraine in 1838, and covers his immigration to the United States; his enlistment in the United States Army in 1851; military duty in New York, Boston, Rhode Island, Texas, California, and the Washington Territory where he participated in the expedition against the Yakima Indians as a member of Company B, Third Regiment, United States Artillery, under Phil Sheridan; and his return to Orange County, Virginia, where following the passage of the Secession Ordinance he enlisted in the Thirteenth Virginia Infantry serving as chief musician. The memoir concludes with Mugler's military career during 1861-1862.

The diary covers the remainder of his military service imprisonment at Elmira, New York, in 1864. Following the war, Mugler returned to Washington, D. C., and eventually gained employment with the National Cemetery Corps, working at various Virginia battlefields. While in Virginia he served as a delegate to the Virginia Republican Convention of 1867. He worked at the National Cemetery at Grafton and for the Baltimore and Ohio Railroad, eventually becoming superintendent of painters on the Road Division in West Virginia. After 1874 he worked briefly as a self-employed painter, and then opened a paint and hardware store in Grafton which he managed until the end of his life.

Subjects include the Battle of Mine Run, the retreat from Antietam, the Battle of the Wilderness, prison life at Elmira, New York; reconstruction in Virginia; railroading and the railroad towns of Keyser, Oakland (Maryland), Parkersburg, Fairmont, and Wheeling; the strikes of 1877; interviews with Generals Ord and Sheridan; the Murphy Temperance Movement and W. C. T. U. activities; the Liberal Republican movement of 1872; the Greenback Party; the Chicago World's Fair of 1893; political figures such as John S. Carlile, John G. Carlisle, John T. McGraw, John W. Mason, Frank Hereford, John E. Kenna, John A. Logan, James G. Blaine, and "Sockless" Jerry Simpson.

658. **Muhleman, Julius G.** Business papers, 1870-1901. 5 items. Gift of James R. Hunkler, 1950. No. 180.

Miscellaneous business papers of a manufacturing firm in Buck Hill Bottom, Ohio.

659. **Mullen Family.** Papers, 1841, 1865-1932. Ca. 200 items. Acquired, 1961. No. 1465.

Correspondence, bills, receipts, and memoranda books of Gordon, Gordon, Jr., Jacob, George H., and Mrs. F. R. Mullen of Charleston.

Subjects include farming operations; the management of a small Kanawha County store; Barboursville College; and the State Free Silver Headquarters. The collection includes letterheads, business cards, and calendars of Charleston mercantile establishments, ca. 1877-1914; and some Ku Klux Klan papers, 1928, of Dr. A. G. Mullen of Galesburg, Illinois.

660. **Murray, J. Ogden.** Scrapbook, ca. 1901-1906, 1949. 1 reel of microfilm (1 volume). Original in possession of Mrs. A. C. Sien, Jr., 1960. No. 1320.

Scrapbook pertaining to Confederate personalities, battles, reminiscences, and activities of the United Confederate Veterans compiled by J. Ogden Murray, member of the "Immortal Six Hundred" and active participant in Confederate veterans' affairs. This collection also includes a series of newspaper articles by Edward H. Sims, ca. 1949, based on Murray's *The Immortal Six Hundred* (1905).

661. **Musgrave, Clarence L.** Papers, 1839-1937. 2 ft. Gift of Mrs. R. A. Lough, 1959. No. 1238.

The papers of C. L. Musgrave, Fairmont mortician and editor, include family correspondence, 1861-1936; photographs; account books of his father, Eli, and his grandfather Zebulon Musgrave; record books and correspondence pertaining to the operation of the Musgrave Funeral Home and the Fairmont *Republican*, ca. 1895-1898.

Other materials include a ledger of the John Carlin Camp, No. 8, Sons of Veterans, United States Army, 1887-1894; record book, Ladies Aid Society of the First Methodist Episcopal Church, Fairmont, 1901-1906; account book of the estate of William Shaver, 1860-1868; account book of the Marion County Republican Executive Committee, 1908-1910; membership and dues records of the Fairmont chapter of the Sons of the Revolution; and class notes from Fairmont State Normal School, 1895.

662. **Musgrave, S. Corder.** Papers. 5 items. Gift of S. C. Musgrave, 1957. No. 1013.

Two printed sheets of verse; an article concerning a visit by Musgrave to Mooresville in Monongalia County; and two clippings of S. C. Musgrave's newspaper column, "Musings of Musgrave."

663. **Musical Programs, 1912-1919.** 13 items. Gift of Barbara Drainer, 1970. No. 2138.

Musical programs, newspaper clippings, and unidentified items relating to events held in West Virginia. Included are programs of the Marcato Music Club, Clarksburg, the Grafton Lodge No. 308 of the B. P. O. E., St. Patrick's Day at St. Augustine's Church, Grafton, and for two concerts at W. V. U.

664. **Musicians Mutual Protective Union of the Ohio Valley.** Records, 1894-1917, 1922. 2 ft. Gift of R. C. Muhlemen, 1961. No. 1542.

Minute books, dues ledgers, cash books, and membership applications of the Wheeling Local 142, American Federation of Musicians.

665. **Myers, Karl D.** Diary, 1927. 1 item. Gift of Mrs. M. L. Vest, 1964. No. 1768.

Diary of Karl D. Myers of Hendricks, wno was Poet Laureate of West Virginia, 1927-1937.

666. **National Association of Social Workers. West Virginia Chapter.** Papers, 1956-1968. 2 ft. Transfer, 1969. No. 2098B.

Correspondence and papers, including minutes of meetings, lists of officers and members; financial reports, newsletters, pamphlets, and publications from national headquarters.

667. **Neale, William Presley Lewis.** Manuscript, n.d. 1 item. Transfer, 1960. No. 1374.

Sketch of a western Virginia pioneer who settled in the Mercer County area about 1816 concerning the vicissitudes of frontier farming. The sketch was written by one of the subject's children and has anecdotes about Neale's boyhood and his parents.

668. **Neely, Matthew Mansfield (1874-1958).** Scrapbooks, 1900-1954. 7 reels of microfilm (17 volumes). Originals in possession of Alfred Neely, 1960, 1961. Nos. 1353, 1384, 1414.

Newspaper clipping scrapbooks of senator, congressman, governor, and Democratic political boss, M. M. Neely, cover his career as a law student at West Virginia University, Marion County lawyer, mayor of Fairmont, congressman, 1913-1921, 1945-1947, United States senator, 1923-1929, 1931-1941, 1949-1958, and governor of West Virginia, 1941-1945.

669. **Neil Family.** Papers, 1837 (1915-1952). Ca. 200 items. Gift of Mrs. Florence Groves, 1955. No. 804.

A miscellaneous collection of family papers, mainly photographs, from Nicholas County.

670. **Nestor, Huett,** *Compiler.* Papers, 1921-1940, 1963. 85 items. Gift of Huett Nestor, 1966. No. 1885.

Archives of the Fairmont Labor Temple, 1921-1940, including certificate of incorporation, bylaws, financial records, minutes, and correspondence. There are also notes on the labor movement in Marion County, compiled by Huett Nestor, concerning local unions, membership and officers of local unions, and a list of "Prominent Members of the A.F.L.-C.I.O. from Marion County."

671. **New River Coal Company.** Archives, 1913-1951. 1 reel of microfilm. Loaned for photoduplication by New River Coal Company, 1964. No. 1767.

Correspondence, newspaper clippings, shipping records, tonnage reports, records of grades of coal produced, and newspaper clippings. There are scattered issues of the *New River Employees Magazine* and *Spotlight*.

672. **Newbraugh, Fred T.**, *Collector.* Papers, (1787-1893) 1949. 18 items (14 photocopies and typescripts). Gift of Fred T. Newbraugh, 1956; originals in possession of Fred T. Newbraugh, Mrs. Paul George, Miss Katherine M. Hunter, Mr. and Mrs. Orville J. Michael, Franklin Institute, and the Library of Congress, 1960, 1962. Nos. 916, 1283, 1368, 1562.

Material primarily pertaining to Berkeley Springs (Bath), includes a genealogical history of the Joseph Durham family; typescript copies of the Civil War diary of Robert Atkinson, Morgan County, kept while a political prisoner at First Delaware, 1862; extracts from the diary of Deborah Comly, a governess for the Charles Tutt family of Berkeley Springs, 1873; notes on the Hinckle-Duckwell-Shade families; correspondence concerning Yoe, Fox, Hollingsworth, and Steiner families, 1952-1953; copies of letters and memoranda of Laura Shade Michael; and extracts from Donn Piatt's *Sunday Meditations* (1893) pertaining to Berkeley Springs.

The photocopied material includes a letter from David Hunter Strother to Perley Poore, 1858; lottery ticket for a town lot in Bath, 1814; a Porte Crayon (David H. Strother) autograph; slave list from Berkeley County; letter from William Wirt to his daughter, 1823, commenting on Berkeley Springs; letter from Thomas Jefferson to a Mr. Rodney, 1808, concerning the assault of the gambler Thomas Bailey on Jefferson's secretary; and selections from the journal of James K. Polk, 1848, the journal of Joseph Vaughan, 1787, and "Uria Brown's Journal," *(Maryland Historical Magazine,* volumes 11-12) concerning visits to the springs at Bath.

673. **Newbraugh Family.** Records, 1760-1854. 3 items (photostats). Originals owned by Fred T. Newbraugh, 1954. No. 692.

Birth, marriage, and death records of the Newbraugh family, 1760-1854; a receipt, 1800; and a letter, 1802, concerning the estate of Abraham Darlington.

674. **Newcomb, William H. (b. 1870).** Papers, 1865-1931. 1 reel of microfilm (2 volumes). Originals in possession of W. H. Newcomb, 1960. No. 1282.

Papers of a Huntington dry goods merchant, W. H. Newcomb, include a domestic diary, 1865, kept by his mother, Emily Cox of Guyandotte, and a clipping scrapbook pertaining to the Newcomb family and the Anderson-Newcomb Department Store. The scrapbook contains obituary notices, society notes, local history items, and an autograph letter from Theodore Roosevelt to W. Barkla, dated October 20, 1900.

675. **Newlon-Camden Families.** Genealogy, 1909-1934. Ca. 200p. (copies). Gift of Festus P. Summers, 1965. No. 1802.

Letters and information tracing the Newlon family from 1720 and other families from the early seventeenth century. Notes on the Camden family include participation in the Civil War.

676. **Newman, Eugene William (1845-1923).** Letter, 1909. 1 item. Gift of Mrs. Walter Stuart, 1961. No. 1401.

Letter, dated Washington, April 14, 1909, from Newman, an essayist and newspaper editorial writer, pertaining to the publication and sale of his *Essays on Men, Things and Events* (1904), written under the pseudonym of Savayard.

677. **Nicholas County.** Papers, 1942-1945. Ca. 50 items. Gift of Miss Gladys Vaughan, 1949. No. 159.

Newspaper clippings of World War II military service records taken from *The Nicholas Chronicle*, Summersville; soldiers' letters; and two typescripts, "Outline for Writing the History of Local Civilian Defense Activities in West Virginia," and "Brief History of the Civilian Defense Organization of Nicholas County, West Virginia, as Compiled and Reported by O. C. Lewis, its Director."

678. **Northwestern Bank of Virginia at Parkersburg.** Minute book, 1855-1868. 1 reel of microfilm (1 volume). Original in possession of the Parkersburg National Bank, 1961. No. 1429.

In 1865 this institution was incorporated as a national bank and renamed the Parkersburg National Bank. (See No. 706.)

679. **Northwestern Turnpike Association.** Records, 1922-1926. 78 items. Gift of Forest Stemple, 1956. No. 856.

Minutes, organizational correspondence, and other papers.

680. **Noyes, Bradford (b. 1860).** Recollections, 1948. 46p. Loan for photoduplication by Mrs. John J. D. Preston, 1966. No. 1906.

Uncorrected typescript copy of recollections by a Charleston businessman concerning Charleston, Kanawha County, 1866-1948, and recollections related to Noyes by early settlers or their descendants, 1790-1865. Subjects include Indian attacks, turnpikes and taverns, the first telegraph system, natural gas illumination, Civil War manufacture of saltpeter, schools and economy in post-Civil War Charleston, salt and chemical industries, carrier pigeons, steamboats on the Kanawha River, coming of the railroad to Charleston.

Persons mentioned include M. F. Maury, Jr., J. P. Hale, and J. Q. Dickinson.

681. **Nuttall, Lawrence William (1857-1933).** Papers, 1946-1952, 1971. 13 items. Transfer, 1956, and gift of Earl L. Core, 1971. Nos. 889, 2174.

Correspondence between John Nuttall, San Diego, California, and Dr. Earl L. Core, West Virginia University, and others, relating to the life of Lawrence William Nuttall, a West Virginia botanist. There are two printed items relating to Nuttall and the opening of the coal fields on Keeney's Creek in Fayette County. There is also information on the estate of John Nuttall (1817-1897) concerning coal, timberlands, and railroad branches in Fayette and Nicholas counties owned by the John Nuttall estate.

682. **O'Brien, William Smith (1862-1948).** Papers, ca. 1830-1950. Ca. 200 items. Gift of Perry Emmett O'Brien, 1958. No. 1105.

Correspondence, business and legal papers, notebooks, speeches, historical essays, genealogical records, clippings, and printed material of a Buckhannon lawyer, state jurist, member of Congress (1927-1929), and West Virginia secretary of state (1933-1948).

The collection also includes papers of O'Brien's father, Emmett J., a member of the state's first Constitutional Convention; letters from O'Brien's brother, Lieutenant A. L. O'Brien, 1874-1887, a West Point graduate serving at forts Assinniboine, Belknap, and Spokane in the Montana Territory and Washington State; letters of Henry M. White, O'Brien's brother-in-law, and a lawyer with the Immigration Bureau and the Federal Trade Commission; a diary of a trip to Texas in 1907; and genealogical records of the Joseph Hall, William Norris, O'Brien, and Jacob Reger families.

Subjects include West Virginia Wildlife League; Methodism in Upshur County; an expedition in pursuit of Sitting Bull; the Rush Holt contested election of 1934; the McAdoo-Smith contest of 1924; the

Townsendites; presidential election of 1936; state politics; pioneer history of West Virginia; and the Vandalia Company.

683. **Ogden Family.** Papers, 1791-1946. 1 ft. Gift of H. Leland Ogden, 1965. No. 1844.

Documents, 1791-1887, concerning lands and business in Harrison and Monongalia counties; history of the Ogden, Talkington, Hawker, and other families, 1911-1946; correspondence, 1904-1907, concerning Marshall W. Ogden's law practice and business; and a list of candidates endorsed by the Ku Klux Klan in West Virginia in 1924. There is no correspondence of direct political interest.

684. **Ohio County.** Archives, 1772-1935. 242 ft. Gift of the Ohio County Court, 1935, 1959. Nos. 31, 1245.

Court case papers, 1776-1930; court and county record books; birth and death records, 1887-1888; and account and minute books of individuals, companies, and organizations, 1772-1935. The bound volumes include records of brand registrations, deeds, estrays, land entries, marriages, military service, surveys, and wills. The private account books relate to general merchandising, coal sales, dental practice, a debating society, distilling, carriage manufacturing, hotels, steamboat freighting, the Ohio County Centennial Association, Ohio Valley Glass Company, Wheeling Masonic Hall Association, West Virginia Exposition and Fair Association, and the settlement of the Ebenezer Zane trust. Alphabetical, chronological, and subject indexes to the suit papers are available.

685. **Ohio Historical Papers.** Papers, ca. 1776-1872. 3 reels of microfilm. Originals in possession of Marietta College Library, 1959. No. 1202.

Papers relating to the early development of Marietta and the Ohio Valley include the journal, 1784-1790, and correspondence, 1776-1824 (3 volumes), of a Revolutionary War officer and organizer of the Ohio Company, General Rufus Putnam; papers of and assembled by Samuel Prescott Hildreth entitled: "Early Events in the Valley of Ohio, 1787 to 1847" (2 volumes); letter from Nathan Goodale to Rufus Putnam, March 15, 1788; journal of Joseph Buell, 1785-1789; and a journal of John Mathews, 1786 (holograph copy).

686. **Ohio River.** Shipping accounts, 1883. 1 item. Acquired, 1971. No. 2207.

Accounts of a cargo vessel which operated on the Ohio River between Marietta, Ohio, and Ravenswood, covering the period October to December, 1883. There is a record of the stops made, the items transported, and the parties to whom deliveries were made.

687. **Ohio River Valley.** Articles, 1754-1758. Ca. 25 items. Transfer, n.d. No. 414.

Photostats and transcriptions of contemporary newspaper accounts of the British-French activity in the Ohio Valley, taken from the *South Carolina Gazette, Maryland Gazette, Pennsylvania Gazette,* and *Virginia Gazette.*

688. **Ohio River Valley.** Scrapbook, ca. 1868-1879. 170p. Acquired, 1954. No. 685.

A scrapbook of newspaper clippings, with manuscript notes, prepared by Wills DeHass. The clips, mainly from Pittsburgh and Cincinnati papers, deal with the Monongahela and Ohio and other Ohio Valley rivers, steamboats, bridges, canals, dams, and levees. Mention is made of the Pittsburgh and Connellsville Railroad, 1868.

689. **Ohio Valley Trades and Labor Assembly.** Records, 1888-1951. 2 ft. Gift of A. Zitsman, 1958. No. 1055.

Twelve minute books in the period 1888-1950. Other materials include secretarial correspondence, rolls and accounts, newspaper clippings, correspondence, financial reports, convention reports, and various constitutions.

690. **Oil and Gas Operations in West Virginia.** Chart, 1954. 1 item. Gift of R. C. Tucker, 1955. No. 703.

Manuscript chart showing statistics on oil and gas operations in West Virginia, reported October 23, 1954, by R. C. Tucker, assistant state geologist.

691. **Oil Wells.** Chart, ca. 1916. 1 item. No. 543.

Chart showing names of wells, owners, elevation above sea level and other technical data.

692. **Orderly Book and Diary.** February 26, 1778-April 2, 1778; January 24, 1849-February 25, 1849. 1 item. Gift of David T. Rees, 1939. No. 59.

Copy of an orderly book of the Continental Army, originating at Lancaster and Valley Forge, Pennsylvania. In the back of the volume is a copy of a travel diary, "Journal of a Voyage to California in Brig *A Emery,*" which sailed from Sandy Hook, New York, January 25, 1849.

693. **Ordner Family.** Papers, ca. 1956. 1 item. Gift of Miss Mary Ordner, 1967. No. 2006.

Copy of a Civil War diary of George W. Ordner, Company B, Fifth Regiment, West Virginia Cavalry, and genealogy of Ordner family.

694. **Orr, Edward N.,** *Collector.* **Papers, 1886, 1960s. 6 items. Gift of Edward N. Orr, 1969, 1971. Nos. 2111, 2179.**

One page from the attendance book of a school at Snow, January 11, 1886; a newspaper clipping describing the attendance records; genealogical notes on the Neale family in LaFayette, Missouri; and information on the Burch, Henshaw, and Neale families from *The Prairie Gleaner.*

695. **Orr, George W. Papers, 1829-1891. 35 items. Gift of Henry Orr, 1956. No. 905.**

Family papers and miscellaneous printed materials, mainly from Preston County.

696. **Orton, Clayton Robert. Papers, 1938-1955. Ca. 200 items. Gift of Paul H. Price, 1963. No. 1662.**

Office files of a former dean of the College of Agriculture, West Virginia University. Files include papers of the Resources Committee of the West Virginia State Planning Board, 1938-1945; Potomac River Basin, 1945; Soil Conservation Society, West Virginia Chapter, 1953-1955; West Virginia Forest Council; and the Watershed Development Conference of 1949.

697. **Osenton, Charles W. (b. 1865). Papers, ca. 1847-1920. 1 reel of microfilm. Originals in possession of the Margaret I. King Library, University of Kentucky, 1959. No. 1215.**

Correspondence, newspaper clippings, and other papers, of a state senate minority leader, 1899-1901, prominent Fayette County lawyer, and Democratic committeeman.

Subjects include Osenton's early life; his law training at Georgetown University; his election to the state senate as a "silver" Democrat; William Jennings Bryan's tour of West Virginia, 1908; the presidential election of 1908; Champ Clark's battle for the Democratic nomination, 1912.

The papers also include a collection of broadsides pertaining to West Virginia, Kentucky, and national politics, 1898-1920; and the business and legal papers, ca. 1847-1880, of Osenton's father-in-law, Arthur J. Lansdowne of Grayson, Kentucky.

Correspondents include John D. Alderson, William J. Bryan, William E. Chilton, and Champ Clark.

698. **Otey, Ernest Glenwood (1895-1966).** Papers, 1935-1965. 19 ft. Gift of Mrs. E. G. Otey, 1967. No. 1909.

Correspondence, financial records, speeches, reports, blueprints, and pamphlets of a Bluefield banker and businessman who was a treasurer of the Democratic Executive Committee and a member of the Board of Governors of West Virginia University. Subjects include numerous businesses in the Bluefield area, Bluefield State College, Concord College, Bank of Bramwell, Island Creek Coal Company, Norfolk and Western Railroad, Pocahontas Fuel Company, Smokeless Operator's Association, Virginia Railway, Winding Gulf Collieries, and West Virginia University.

Correspondents include W. W. Barron, Joe F. Burdett, Robert C. Byrd, Clyde L. Colson, Phil Conley, Ken Hechler, Cecil B. Highland, John Hoblitzell, Rush D. Holt, Elizabeth Kee, Robert P. McDonough, Clarence W. Meadows, Paul A. Miller, Arch A. Moore, Jr., Okey Patteson, Jennings Randolph, Raymond E. Salvati, John M. Slack, Hulett Smith, James M. Sprouse, Elvis J. Stahr, and Irvin Stewart.

699. **Page, William Nelson (1854-1932).** Papers, 1860 (1881-1890) 1924. 1 reel of microfilm. Originals in possession of the Alderman Library, University of Virginia, 1964. No. 1755.

Papers of William Nelson Page, civil and mining engineer, who was manager of the Hawk's Nest Coal Company, 1877-1880; built and operated the Victoria Blast Furnace, Goshen, Virginia, 1880-1885; organized and developed the Gauley Mountain Coal Company, 1889-1917; served in the West Virginia National Guard for twenty years; and was mayor of Ansted for ten years.

Subjects include the American Society of Civil Engineers, Deepwater Railway Company, Guy's Run Iron Land, Iron and Steel Works Association of Virginia, Loup Creek Colliery Company, Mt. Carbon Company Limited, Tidewater Railway Company, Virginian Railway, and the West Virginia Mining Association.

Correspondents include Abram S. Hewitt and G. W. Imboden.

700. **Painters Local Union, No. 91, Wheeling.** Records, 1886-1958. 2 ft. Gift of Local Union No. 91 of the Brotherhood of Painters, Decorators and Paperhangers of America, 1959. No. 1249.

Minute books, account books, and membership and dues records, 1886-1924; typescript minutes, 1941-1954; correspondence, 1886 (1943, 1950, 1952); and receipts, contracts, and pamphlets, 1886-1958.

701. **Palmer, John C.** Papers, ca. 1900. 2 volumes. No. 416.

A Wellsburg attorney's case book and a record book of farms in Cross Creek District, Brooke County.

702. **Paper Mills.** Letter, 1851. 1 item. Acquired, 1965. No. 1863.

Letter dated January 29, 1851, addressed to Messrs. Smith, Winchester and Co., Windham, Connecticut, from the Fulton Paper Mill near Wheeling, Virginia, asking for information on a paper drying machine.

703. **Pardee and Curtin Lumber Company.** Records, 1889-1938. 99 items. Gift of George Curtin, 1954. No. 611.

Fifty-six account books of the Pardee and Curtin Lumber Company for the Cherry Run Mill, Hominy Mill, Palmer Mill and Sutton Mill. From company offices located in Curtin, Sutton and Clarksburg, and logging operations in Nicholas, Braxton and Webster counties. Also, photographs of railroads, mills, logging, and coal mining operations.

704. **Parker, William.** Papers, 1845-1886. Ca. 70 items. Gift of John Parker, 1949. No. 156.

Letters, legal papers, and accounts of William Parker, Hampshire County. Included also are scattered papers of John P., Benjamin, and James Parker and Company. Letters originate from Virginia; Greene County, Illinois, 1859; and Pleasant Hill, Dallas County, Alabama, 1849. Subjects include doctors' fees; election of 1851 in Berkeley, Jefferson and Morgan counties, and Frederick County, Virginia; prices of farm produce; and observations of Virginians newly settled in Illinois and Alabama in the middle of the nineteenth century.

705. **Parkersburg.** Typescript, 1969. 1 item (photocopy). Loan for duplication by Paul S. Bibbee, 1969. No. 2092.

"Parkersburg in the Eighteenth Century," by Paul S. Bibbee. A typed research paper prepared for a history class at West Virginia University.

706. **Parkersburg National Bank.** Minute books, 1865-1874, 1913-1934. 1 reel of microfilm (2 volumes). Originals in possession of the Parkersburg National Bank, 1961. No. 1510.

Bank was formed in 1865 from the Northwestern Bank of Virginia, Parkersburg Branch. (See No. 678.)

707. **Parkersburg Town Council.** Journals, 1826-1862, 1869-1874. 1 reel of microfilm (4 volumes). Originals in possession of the City of Parkersburg, 1961. No. 1422.

Aside from routine municipal affairs these journals contain material on the development of internal improvements in the Parkersburg area: viz., the Wheeling-Parkersburg struggle for the western terminus of the Baltimore and Ohio Railroad, the development of the Northwestern Virginia Railroad, and the demands for various river improvements. There are also a few references to Civil War military activities and the development of the oil industry in the Wood County area. Mayors include C. S. Despard, John J. Jackson, and Peter G. Van Winkle.

708. **Parrish, Edward Evans (1791-1874).** Diary, (1843-1845) 1863. 1 typescript, 27p. Gift of L. D. Arnett, 1945. No. 93.

A typescript copy of a diary of a Monongalia County native who traveled with his family in a company of wagons to Oregon in 1843-1844. The entries begin at Hoskinsville, Morgan County, Ohio.

Published in the sixteenth *Annual Report* of the Oregon Pioneer Association, 1888.

709. **Parsons, Jesse.** Papers, 1793 (1885-1888) 1911. 17 items. Gift of Norval R. Parsons, 1955. No. 731.

Two manuscript volumes listing taxable persons and property in the district of Daniel C. Adams, Tucker County, 1857, 1858; land and other papers of Parsons, including a federal pardon, signed by President Grover Cleveland, June 6, 1885.

710. **Parsons, Job W.** Diaries, 1874-1894. 2 reels of microfilm (13 volumes). Originals in the possession of Dickson W. Parsons and W. E. Parsons, 1954. Nos. 566, 598, 637.

Films of pocket diaries of a farmer, lumberman, and stockman of Randolph County. There are daily entries centering on routine farm chores, weather conditions, prices, and wages.

711. **Patrons of Husbandry. (West Virginia) University Grange No. 372.** Records, 1898-1923. 1 ft. Transfer, 1961. No. 1438.

Minute books, 1898-1908, 1916-1923, membership and dues records, 1914-1921, procedural handbook, songbooks, and official paraphernalia.

712. **Patton, Jack R.,** *Collector.* Papers, 1852-1958. 1 reel of microfilm. Originals in possession of Jack R. Patton, 1958. No. 1127.

Papers pertaining to Tyler County and Sistersville include genealogical data on the Wells family; a stock certificate of the Sistersville and Salem Turnpike Company; newspaper clippings on local affairs; and a manuscript list of Civil War volunteers from Tyler County.

713. **Pease, Louise McNeill.** Typescript, 1939. 86p. Gift of Louise McNeill Pease, 1971. No. 2215.

Typescript of Louise McNeill's book of poems entitled *Gauley Mountain,* first published in 1939.

714. **Peirpoint, Jacob.** Papers, 1861-1868. 30 items. Gift of Miss Willa Brand. No. 144.

Letters written by Peirpoint, Nineteenth Indiana Regiment, to his father, John J. Peirpoint at Morgantown. The letters are from Muncie, Indiana, and military posts and camps in Washington, D. C., and Virginia, 1861-1862.

715. **Pemberton, Robert L. (b. 1860).** Papers, 1880 (1891-1944). 137 items. Gift of Miss Margerie Pemberton, 1951. No. 278.

Letters, mainly incoming correspondence, speeches, and printed materials of R. L. Pemberton, for many years editor of the St. Marys *Oracle.* Correspondents include A. I. Boreman, G. W. Atkinson, Robert A. Armstrong, Louis Bennett, John J. Cornwell, W. E. Glasscock, H. C. Greer, P. I. Reed, Louis Johnson, and Homer A. Holt. The correspondence concerns politics and Pemberton's activities with newspaper associations in West Virginia. Included are religious pamphlets, newspapers, and a typescript, "Origin of the Wetzel Democrat," by D. L. Long.

716. **Pemberton, William.** Diary, ca. 1840. 1 volume. Acquired, 1970. No. 2161.

Diary of William Pemberton, containing religious devotions and expressions, "composed by himself and for his own comfort."

717. **Pendleton County.** Assessment book, 1797. 1 volume. Gift of Samuel V. Woods, 1899. No. 676.

List of names of taxpayers and taxable property.

718. **Pendleton County.** Court records, 1789-1889. 1 ft. Gift of Harlan M. Calhoun, 1936. No. 38.

Case papers and marriage bonds.

719. **Peterson Family.** Papers, 1858-1913. 1 reel of microfilm and 15p. (photocopies). Loan for duplication by Herbert Upton Peterson, 1968. No. 2028.

Correspondence, speeches, essays, financial notes, certificates, an account book, a class attendance book for 1860, and a term paper prepared for a Glenville College history class entitled, "The Aaron D. Peterson Family." The correspondence contains letters written by David T. Peterson to family and friends while serving with Federal forces in the Civil War. Subjects include schools, politics, farming, Civil War camps, units, troop movements, and battles at Droop Mountain, Moorefield, and Winchester, Virginia.

720. **Pharmacy.** Formulary book, ca. 1865-1894. 1 volume. Transfer, 1963. No. 1649.

Formulary or recipe book of G. H. Caperton, a Fire Creek, Fayette County, pharmacist.

721. **Phillips, Marcia Louise Sumner.** Journal, 1861-1863. 1 item (photocopy). Loan for duplication by Mrs. Beatrice Giffin, 1965. No. 1846.

A manuscript journal of Marcia L. S. (Mrs. Sylvester B.) Phillips of French Creek and Buckhannon, containing commentary on local and family affairs, and Civil War military activities in the western Virginia and Virginia areas. S. B. Phillips was Captain of Company E, Third Virginia Volunteer Infantry Regiment. Other subjects include local and family affairs, churches, travel, elections, holiday celebrations, and the 1863 statehood convention in Parkersburg. There are descriptions of and quoted conversations with officers of both the Union and Confederate armies. Military units mentioned or commented on are the Third Virginia Volunteer Infantry; One hundred thirty-third Virginia Military; Eighteenth Virginia Cavalry; Tenth Virginia Infantry; Second Virginia Infantry; the Ringgold Cavalry; and the Imboden Rangers. Military camps commented on are Flatwoods, Elkwater, and Baldwin.

722. **Physicians' Accounts,** 1895-1906. Ca. 200 items. Gift of Harry Jackson, 1956. No. 833.

Pocket memo books listing patients, fees, etc., account book, miscellaneous printed matter, and photographs, kept by W. J. Cox and A. M. Jackson, physicians at Knob Fork and Porter Falls, Wetzel County.

723. **Pierce, Carleton C., Jr.,** *Collector.* Papers, 1865-1958. 12 items. Gift of Carleton C. Pierce, Jr., 1952, 1958. Nos. 510, 1148.

Typescript, "Documentary History of the 150th West Virginia National Guard, 1656-1932"; a letter from Alston G. Dayton to John R. Pierce of Rowlesburg, 1897, relating to patronage and Dayton's political standards; and a photograph of the Captain Sampson Snyder family. Also, a statement of Ignatius Rudiger in account with N. Hardman, 1865-1867; a George Hardman letter July 7, 1869; six witness claim certificates for attendance at the circuit court of Preston County; and a photocopy of a survey and plat of Cuppett, Spurgin, Worall, Greathouse, Morris, and Worley lands in Preston County.

724. **Pierce, Carleton Custer (1877-1958).** Papers, ca. 1840-1955. 2 ft. Gift of Mrs. Carleton C. Pierce, Jr., 1963. No. 1674.

Military records, business papers, and correspondence of a brigadier general, Kingwood attorney, state legislator, secretary of the West Virginia Horticultural Society, state adjutant general, and state Selective Service director. Other papers include a letter book, West Virginia National Guard, 1903-1907; state Selective Service memoranda, 1940-1947; and a "Historical Record of Selective Service in West Virginia." Other subjects include the Morgantown and Kingwood Railroad, Pierce's coal mining, public utilities, oil, timber, gas, fruit growing, and other business activities.

Correspondents include William G. Conley, William M. O. Dawson, Davis Elkins, William E. Glasscock, Walter S. Hallanan, Lewis B. Hershey, Homer A. Holt, Harley M. Kilgore, J. Howard McGrath, Edward Martin, Clarence W. Meadows, E. F. Morgan, Matthew M. Neely, Okey L. Patteson, Chapman Revercomb, and Howard Sutherland.

This collection also includes the business and legal papers, ca. 1840-1890, of James H. Carroll, Kingwood attorney and editor of the *Preston County Herald*. Subjects include the presidential elections of 1856 and 1884 in West Virginia. Other papers relate to Kingwood and area mercantile firms, and the operation of the *Preston County Herald*. There is a record of the Democratic Congressional Executive Committee of Preston County, 1882-1884; daybook of the *Preston County Journal*, 1891-1894; and a circulation record of Preston County newspapers, 1889-1897.

Correspondents include Gideon D. Camden and Henry G. Davis.

725. **Pierpoint-Avery Community.** Typescript, 1940. 1 volume. Transfer, 1960. No. 1371.

"History of the Pierpoint-Avery Community," compiled by John C. Bayles, is a genealogical and local history study of a Monongalia County settlement on the Cheat River.

726. **Pierpont, Francis Harrison (1814-1899).** Letters, 1861-1864. 1 reel of microfilm. Originals in the Lincoln Papers, Library of Congress, 1958. No. 1034.

Letters to Abraham Lincoln from the Reorganized Government of Virginia.

727. **Pierpont, Francis Harrison (1814-1899).** Papers, 1830-1934. 8 ft. Transfers, and gifts of Anna Pierpont Siviter, Frances Pierpont Pryor, John Pierpont Helmick, E. E. Meredith, and Charles H. Ambler, 1932, 1952, 1953. Nos. 9, 113, 418, 419, 420, 497, 559.

Manuscripts, typescripts, printed materials, and photocopies consisting of correspondence, speeches, official messages, articles prepared for newspaper publication, diplomas, college essays, scrapbooks, and pamphlets. There are materials relating to Pierpont's education; his career as governor of the Restored Government of Virginia at Wheeling, Alexandria, and Richmond; the West Virginia statehood movement; politics; and Pierpont's later work in the Methodist Protestant Church. Included also are family correspondence and personal papers; correspondence and notes of Charles H. Ambler; and a typescript draft with holograph notes of Anna Pierpont Siviter's *Recollections of War and Peace, 1861-1868* (New York, 1938).

Among the correspondents are Gordon Battelle, Arthur I. Boreman, B. F. Butler, G. D. Camden, Simon Cameron, Archibald W. Campbell, John S. Carlile, Schuyler Colfax, Jacob D. Cox, Spencer Dayton, Nathan Goff, Thomas M. Harris, Abraham Lincoln, J. A. J. Lightburn, George B. McClellan, J. C. Rathbone, Whitelaw Reid, W. S. Rosecrans, J. M. Schofield, William H. Seward, Edwin M. Stanton, William E. Stevenson, David Hunter Strother, Peter G. Van Winkle, Benjamin R. Wade, James O. Watson, and Waitman T. Willey.

728. **Pierpont, John, and Francis H.** Papers, 1787, 1841, 1842. 3 items. Gift of Mrs. Frances Pierpont Pryor, 1953. No. 526.

Photostat negative of a land grant to John Pierpont for four hundred acres in Harrison County, 1787; and Francis H. Pierpont's licenses to practice law in Mississippi and Virginia.

729. **Pinick, Jacob.** Papers, 1853-1865. Ca. 200 items. Gift of Thomas Pinnock, 1941. No. 79.

Papers include letters written by Jacob Pinick, first sergeant of Company A, Thirty-second Regiment, Ohio Volunteer Infantry, to John and William McLaughlin in Ohio. The letters detail the service of Pinick's company in western Virginia, Virginia, Mississippi, Georgia, Alabama, Tennessee, North Carolina, and South Carolina. There are many detailed accounts of battles and marches, and expressions of political sentiments of soldiers. Also included is a record book of Company A containing rolls and service records, and notes on the history of the company for July 12, 1861, to July 27, 1865, when it was mustered out, and also several letters from members of the Pinick family in western Virginia, Wisconsin, and Ohio, 1853-1859.

730. **Pittman, Charles Edward.** Recordings, 1959-1960. 10 reels of tape and 6 typescripts. Gift of Charles Edward Pittman, 1962. No. 1598.

Taped interviews by Pittman, a minister, with individuals from the Pendleton County hamlets of Onego and Mouth of Seneca and surrounding areas. The subjects come from various social strata and comment on the history, culture, and mores of essentially isolated mountain communities.

731. **Poling, J. E., Mercantile Company.** Records, 1897-1927. 7 ft. Gift of W. A. O'Dell, 1956. No. 823.

Account books and loose business papers of a large general store in Hendricks.

732. **Polsley, John J.** Papers, (1862-1865) 1879. 1 reel of microfilm. Originals in possession of the University of Akron Library, 1962. No. 1601.

Correspondence and miscellaneous papers of a lieutenant colonel in the Eighth West Virginia Volunteer Infantry and later the Seventh West Virginia Regiment.

The letters, most of which are addressed to Polsley's wife, pertain to military activities in central West Virginia, 1862-1863, and the Shenandoah Valley of Virginia. These letters comment on the West Virginia statehood movement, camp life, guerrilla warfare, Polsley's confinement in Libby Prison, General John Imboden's raid, 1863, and the West Virginia capital question.

733. **Polsley, Julia C.** Scrapbook, 1879. 1 reel of microfilm. Original in possession of Roy E. Blessing, 1961. No. 1509.

Scrapbook of Julia C. Polsley, "Sunny Side," Point Pleasant, containing clippings on the career and death of her father, Daniel W. Polsley, editor of the Wellsburg *Transcript*, lieutenant governor of the Reorganized Government of Virginia, judge of the Seventh Judicial District, and member of the Fortieth Congress.

734. **Porter, George McCandless (1835-1864).** Papers, 1849-1864. 47 items. Gift of Dr. Stanton C. Crawford, 1965. No. 1821.

Letters written by a lawyer and businessman near Shanghai in Berkeley County to his sister Mary, who was residing in their father's home at New Cumberland, Virginia. There are letters from Wellsburg Academy, 1849-1850; Washington College, Washington, Pennsylvania, 1851-1855; four letters from Cuba, 1857; four letters from New Orleans, 1857; and two letters from Richmond, 1858-1860. A diary includes entries from January 1 to March 20, 1864. Porter had business relations with firms in Pittsburgh concerning brickmaking, coal lands, and shipping. Much of the diary concerns his wife's illness and his own poor health and there are a few minor references to Civil War developments and Porter's Union sentiments. Muster records of the Panhandle Greys, a state militia unit, 1861-1863, organized and captained by George McCandless Porter, are included.

735. **Porter, James.** Papers, 1870-1912. 30 ft. Gift of James Porter and Mrs. James Porter, Jr., 1933. No. 20.

Business and records and correspondence of the Relief Tow Boat Company, 1880-1900; the West Virginia Firebrick Company, 1878-1894; the Globe Firebrick Works, 1889-1902; the Claymont Brick Works, 1899-1902; McMahan, Porter and Company; and other business enterprises of James Porter, New Cumberland, Hancock County.

736. **Post, Melville Davisson (1871-1930).** Papers, 1897-1930. 1 ft. Gifts of Frank M. Atterholt, 1954, 1955, and Adrian H. Goldstone, 1958, 1962. Nos. 693, 723, 1143, 1635.

Correspondence and manuscripts of a novelist and short-story writer, noted for his writing in the detective story genre. Correspondence is with his publishers, Edward J. Close and W. G. Chapman, relating to the serial rights of *The Corrector of Destinies,* and with Louis E. Schrader, a Wheeling court reporter who edited and typed Post's manuscripts. There are manuscripts of short stories, World War I poster texts, essays, and other articles, some of which were published between 1920 and 1929 in popular magazines.

737. **Post Family.** Papers, 1842-1926. 7 ft. Gift of Mrs. Florence Hutchinson Ritchie, 1953. No. 538.

Business records of farms and general stores, and personal correspondence of various members of the Post, Davisson, and Coplin families. Included are manuscripts, and newspaper and magazine clippings, of Melville Davisson Post's stories.

738. **Postal Records, 1843-1888, 1921.** 32 items (1 photocopy). Gift of Jane Dille, 1951, Charles Carpenter,

1966, and loan for photoduplication by Thomas W. Dixon, 1968. Nos. 288, 1901, 2066.

Quarterly receipts for payments due to the U. S. from the postmaster at French Creek, Upshur County, 1843-1852; register of money orders drawn on the Morgantown Post Office, September, 1867, to October, 1888; a cashbook of the Morgantown postmaster, January, 1876, to May, 1879; and a book published for use by railway mail service clerks, 1921.

739. **Power, F. Ray (b. 1898).** Papers, 1925-1966. 9 ft. Gift of F. Ray Power, 1970. No. 2128.

Correspondence and speeches of F. Ray Power, Director of the West Virginia Division of Vocational Rehabilitation from 1945 to 1966. Some of the speeches were made in 1925, when Power was principal of Woodrow Wilson Junior High School in Charleston. There are six boxes of clippings covering the period from 1951-1966, and several pamphlets and government reports dealing with vocational rehabilitation and the problems of the disabled.

740. **Preble, Jack W.** Papers, 1872-1956. 1 volume. 1 folder and 1 reel of microfilm. Gift and loan of Jack W. Preble, 1960. Nos. 1315, 1680.

Correspondence, clippings, a series of newspaper articles on hunting and fishing published in the Steubenville *Herald Star*, 1939-1943, and the original manuscript of Preble's *Land of Canaan, Plain Tales from the Mountains of West Virginia*, 1960. Subjects include Tucker County local history; Maryland folk music festival at Mountain Lake; David H. Strother Memorial; and spelunking and snake hunting in West Virginia.
Correspondents include Felix G. Robinson and Jennings Randolph.

741. **Presbury Family.** Genealogy, ca. 1650-1950. 9 items (photocopies). Originals owned by Kenneth Walter Cameron, 1950. Nos. 200, 210.

Tables and charts tracing the Presbury family from Captain John Hall, d. ca. 1660, through the families of Bayless, Browne, Colgate, Hall, Kaminsky, Little, Lytle, and Parry.

742. **Presgraves, James S.,** *Collector.* Papers, 1825-1933. 38 items. Acquired, 1970. Nos. 2164, 2169.

Letters, tax statements, commissioners' reports and schedule of estate settlements, and an account statement. There are receipts and licenses for the Cabell family in Greenbrier County. Four Civil War letters give Confederate soldiers' accounts of the Battle of Carnifex Ferry, and a soldier's opinion on the effect of war on the soldiers, science and civilization.

743. **Presidential Primary, 1960.** Documents, 1960. 2 items (photocopies). Loan for duplication through Festus P. Summers, 1964. No. 1715.

Certificates of announcement of candidacy for the nomination for the office of President of the United States on the Democratic ticket, February 3, and February 6, 1960, by Hubert H. Humphrey and John F. Kennedy.

744. **Preston, David R.** Diary, 1828-1829. 139p. (photocopy). Loan for duplication by Mrs. John J. D. Preston, 1970. No. 2133.

Manuscript diary of David R. Preston, Presbyterian minister and missionary assigned to Pensacola, Florida, and St. Charles, Missouri, 1828-1829, containing information on the number of missionaries and regularly assigned ministers of the Presbyterian, Methodist, and Episcopal churches in the areas, the number of church services held, attendance and interest of the congregations, organization of Bible classes and Sunday schools. Preston also preached to Negro congregations and comments on their attendance and attitude. There is comment on the Roman Catholic Church, its activities, recommended means to combat the Catholic influence on the people, their social and business life. Preston also held services on the Escambia River area of Alabama.

Names of people living in the areas are given as well as descriptions of the land and business enterprises, and opinions concerning future settlement and economic development. The names of U. S. Navy ships in the Pensacola harbor are mentioned with comments on the officers, condition of the ships, and discipline maintained. Conditions and cost of travel by stage and boat are commented on with accounts of Preston's journeys from Philadelphia to Pensacola, and from Pensacola to St. Charles.

745. **Preston, Mrs. John J. D.,** *Collector.* Papers, 1783-1932, 1952. 5 ft. Gift of Mrs. John J. D. Preston, 1967, 1969, 1970. Nos. 1934, 2081, 2132.

Correspondence of the Preston, Davis, Rand, and Arnold families, ca. 1817-1924. Included are letters of John W. Davis, sermons of David R. Preston, pamphlets dealing with the important political and religious issues of the period, and copies of speeches delivered by John W. Davis, Waitman T. Willey, and other congressmen on national political issues. There are also newspapers and newspaper clippings related to the political career of John W. Davis and some Davis family photographs.

746. **Preston County.** Miscellaneous papers, 1836-1966. Ca. 95 items. Gifts of C. L. Nieman, 1954, C. William Myers, 1956, Victor R. Hoffman, 1957, C. C. Pierce,

Jr., 1957, Mrs. Mary L. Lewis, 1967, and Mrs. Archie R. Jennings, 1969. Nos. 607, 892, 950, 996, 1939, 2110.

Notes, maps, and clippings on the history and geology of Preston County, ca. 1769-1875, compiled by S. Scott Garner; a land grant, August 31, 1836, and a manuscript workbook of mathematical exercises, 1839-1840; papers relating to politics and the Democratic Party, 1842-1871; roster of Company E, Fifteenth Regiment, West Virginia Volunteers, 1863; papers relating to electric power lines in Bruceton and an early map of Coopers Rock State Forest, 1900-1930; and a reading for Freeland Cemetery, August, 1966.

747. **Preston County.** Newsletters, 1944-1945. 1 reel of microfilm (79 articles). Gift of Mrs. Mary Blaney, 1969. No. 2093.

Issues of "A Letter From Home," published in Valley District, Preston County, from February 12, 1944, to October 1, 1945. The local newsletters were sent to members of the armed forces from the area during World War II.

748. **Preston County.** Papers, 1775-1918. 3 ft. Gift of Ward Thomas, 1957. No. 956.

Papers from the Leroy Bucklew Museum in the Preston County Courthouse. The collection includes early papers relating to land, court cases, mills and furnaces, post offices, inns, mineral development, Morgantown and Kingwood Railroad Company, roads, the Virginia-Maryland boundary, and estate settlements. There are photographs of Preston County and Kingwood interest, and maps of Kingwood, Bruceton Mills, Rowlesburg, and Manheim, and of Berkeley Springs, Morgan County.

749. **Preston County.** Papers, 1788 (1802-1916) 1943. Ca. 200 items. Gift of Floyd Spiggle, 1955. No. 728.

Account books, and legal, business and personal papers of some early settlers at Aurora, Preston County. There are records of a tannery, blacksmith shop, a general merchandise store, and a sawmill, as well as deeds and subscription lists for the Lutheran and German Reformed churches. Included in the personal papers are wills, deeds, plats, school exercise books and other items.

750. **Preston County.** Papers, 1826-1927. 1 ft. Gift of John E. Jenkins, 1955. No. 791.

Papers centering on Preston County, including deeds, receipts, agreements, letters, typescripts, and manuscript volumes. There are a few Civil War letters of Ephraim Otto, Company H, Seventh Cavalry, Missouri Volunteers, to his brother, Herbert Otto, Morgan's Glade, Preston

County; also papers relating to George Rodeheaver, William H. Bishoff, the Otto family, and John E. Jenkins. There is a typescript, "Crab Orchard-Centenary Community History," describing the settlement of the area along the Terra Alta and Brandonville Pike near the Wesley Chapel Church.

The volumes include Pleasant District school registers and term report forms (1907-1927), and a board of education minute book, 1906-1924; a general store daybook, 1849-1870; and quarterly conference records of the Brandonville and Oakland, Maryland, district of the Methodist Church, 1885-1889, 1914-1919.

751. **Price, Calvin W.** Recording and 2 transcripts, 1956. Acquired, 1956. No. 875.

Tape recording, with two typed transcripts, of an interview with Dr. Calvin W. Price, March 12, 1956, in Marlinton. Subjects covered include Price family history, Pocahontas County local history, lumbering, wildlife and conservation, agriculture, and education.

752. **Price, Norman Randolph.** Tape recording, ca. 1900-1956. 1 tape and 2 typescripts, 1956. Acquired, 1956. No. 874.

Tape recording and typescripts of an interview with Norman R. Price, a Marlinton physician. Subjects covered include medical practice in Pocahontas County, 1900-1950; Price family genealogy; schoolteachers; the English colony, and the introduction of soccer in Pocahontas County.

753. **Price, William (1803-1881).** Papers, 1787 (1805-1885) 1912. 1 ft. Gifts of Brown Price, 1934, and Mrs. A. Brown Price, 1965. Nos. 28, 1809.

Papers of a Monongalia County resident, member of the Wheeling Convention, and state legislator, 1869-1873, include correspondence, diaries, notebooks, legal documents, pictures, and continental currency. The correspondence, 1858-1912, concerns farming, the cattle business, and observations on the Civil War. Land papers also relate to Greene County, Pennsylvania. There is a diary and memo book of William Price, 1861-1863, containing only two references to his membership in the Wheeling Convention, June 20, 1861; an account book, 1885-1890; and a journal maintained by Price during two business trips to Philadelphia in June and July, 1865.

There are also letters from Monongalia County citizens commenting on legislative enactments. Correspondents include R. L. Berkshire and Alexander Martin.

754. **Price Family.** Papers, 1813 (1900-1945). 11 ft. Gift of Norman Randolph Price, 1954. No. 682.

Family papers, periodicals, newspapers, clippings, maps, and other materials of the Price family in Marlinton. Most of the papers are those of Andrew Price, a Marlinton attorney, including records of the law firm of Price, Osenton and McPeak. Other materials, ca. 1901-1949, concern J. W. Price, a Marlinton physician. There are muster rolls of Company C, Sixty-second Virginia Infantry, C. S. A., from Pendleton County; and manuscripts of essays, verse, and historical articles written by Andrew Price.

755. **Price Family.** Papers, 1830-1945. 62 items. Gift of Joseph W. Summers, 1952. No. 492.

Business and personal papers of Edward Price (1818-1907), William Edward Price (1856-1938), and other members of the Price family in Monongalia County. Included are birth and death records and newspaper clippings on the Price, McCue, and Lazzelle families, 1830-1945; and other papers centering on Morgantown and Monongalia County.

756. **Price-McBee Families.** Papers, 1825-1896. Ca. 30 items. Gift of T. Fleming Price, 1934. No. 27.

Letters to Thomas McBee and members of the McBee family in Monongalia County, from relatives in the Baird, Corns, England, and Noel families of Sharpsburg and Pittsburgh, Pennsylvania, 1859-1896. There are also several letters to Thomas and Elizabeth Price of Clinton Furnace, Monongalia County, 1873-1896; and subscription lists for the building of the "Union" meeting and schoolhouse, 1830, and for a school to be taught by William Price on the J. Barnes place, Monongalia County, 1825.

757. **Price-Morgan Family.** Manuscript, ca. 1962. 1 item. Gift of Mr. and Mrs. K. B. Lohr, 1962. No. 1607.

Genealogical records of the Hugh Morgan and Peter P. Price families.

758. **"Progress, West Virginia."** Records, 1954. 9 items. Gift of Station WCHS, Charleston. No. 658.

Phonograph recordings of talks made by eighteen political, educational, business, and labor leaders associated with West Virginia in the program series "Progress, West Virginia," sponsored by Station WCHS, Charleston.

759. **Purinton, Daniel B.** (1850-1933). Letter, October 21, 1901. 1 item. Gift of Bruce C. Harding, 1966. No. 1872-2.

Letter from the President of West Virginia University to President W. O. Thompson, Ohio State University, concerning athletic policy.

760. **Purinton Family.** Papers, 1873-1934. 11 ft. Gift of Harry A. Pettigrew and John A. Purinton, 1967. No. 1964.

Correspondence, notes, lectures, books, manuscripts, newspaper clippings, financial records and photographs of a president of West Virginia University, 1901-1911, and his sons Edward E., a writer, and John A., a lawyer.

Subjects include Alderson-Broaddus College; Phi Beta Kappa; a trip to Jerusalem, 1904; Baptist Church; West Virginia gubernatorial election, 1908; Sunday school; Moro Missions; Philippine Islands; Western Electric; Swift and Company; Peabody Coal Company; and health culture.

Correspondents include I. C. White, W. W. Trent, Waitman Barbe, Albert Bushnell Hart, and Thomas E. Hodges.

761. **Raleigh County.** Archives, 1850-1916. 10 reels of microfilm (14 volumes). Originals in possession of Raleigh County Court, 1959. No. 1262.

Trial docket; order, oath, bond, minute and land books; and court of quarterly sessions, overseers of the poor, marriage, and supervisors records.

762. **Ralston, Richard H., Sr.,** *Collector.* Papers, 1825-1934. 36 items. Loan for photoduplication, 1971. No. 2205.

Correspondence of William A. Harrison, a Clarksburg lawyer, assistant federal district attorney, member of the Virginia Assembly, and judge of the Supreme Court of Appeals of West Virginia; most letters are from members of the family to Mrs. Anna M. Robertson Harrison. Subjects include construction of the Chesapeake and Ohio Canal; Civil War loyalty oaths, Camp Chase, land purchases, and road building.

There are also grade school attendance certificates and notes concerning the Lunatic Asylum West of the Allegheny Mountains and Weston State Hospital, 1860, 1866-1867.

763. **Ramsay, Robert L. (1877-1956).** Papers, 1932-1952. 7 volumes. Gift of Mrs. Robert L. Ramsay, 1957. No. 969.

Bound volumes of speeches, bills, and correspondence, 1941-1952, of Robert L. Ramsay while a member of the U. S. House of Representatives from the first congressional district of West Virginia.

764. **Randolph Academy.** Papers, 1803-1851. 4 items. Gift of the estate of Harvey Harmer, 1961. Nos. 503, 1592.

Minute book of an early Clarksburg academy. There is also a typed copy of the minutes of the board of trustees. Loose papers include a letter from Alexander Martin and pertain to Northwestern Virginia Academy, the name of the school after 1842.

765. **Randolph County.** Assessor's list, January 7, 1900. 1 item (photocopies). Loan for photoduplication, Mrs. O. D. Linder, 1971. No. 2196.

Assessor's List of Qualified Voters in Election Precinct No. 4, Leadsville Magisterial District, Randolph County. The list shows name, age, occupation, location and duration of residence, and place of birth.

766. **Randolph County.** Papers, 1858, 1861. 2 items. Gift of Mrs. Angela Boserman, 1951. No. 261.

Letter of Patrick Durkin to David Goff, March 17, 1858; and a photostat copy of the account of Cyrus Kittle, school commissioner of district number 12, with W. H. Mills, for teaching indigent children in Randolph County, February 23, 1861.

767. **Randolph County.** Surveys, 1850-1909, 1933-1943. 1 ft. Gift of Mrs. Lewis Vest, 1956. No. 901.

Field notes of Nicholas and Charles M. Marstiller of surveys made in Randolph County.

768. **Ranwood Lumber Company.** Photographs, 1920s. 46 items. Gift of Mrs. Ralph Jones, 1968. No. 2039.

Pictures and postcards showing lumbering activities in Randolph and Webster counties.

769. **Rathbone Family.** Family papers, ca. 1851-1958. 1 reel of microfilm (1 volume and 2 folders). Originals in possession of Mrs. Nina Paden Powell, 1960. No. 1324.

Genealogical records and clippings pertaining to the Paden and Rathbone families. Clippings concern Parkersburg local history and the development of Burning Springs and other oil fields in the Wood County area.

770. **Ray, Thomas P.** Diary, 1829-1852. 1 typescript. Gift of Thomas Ray Dille, 1932. No. 798.

Copy of a diary of a Morgantown resident, with references to early merchants and public officials; the building of schools, churches, and business buildings; volume of river traffic; and roads and mail routes opened.

771. **Rector, C. R.,** *Compiler.* Typescript. 1 item (19p.). Transfer, n.d. No. 424.

A typescript, "Westward Down the Ohio," relating highlights of Ohio River history, ca. 1750-1880, in West Virginia.

772. **Rector, Enoch (1804-1898).** Papers, 1824-1853, 1916, 1966. 27 items. Gift of Mrs. Laura Rector Hedrick, 1966. No. 1902.

Correspondence of Enoch Rector, a Baptist minister in the state of Ohio and in Wood and Wirt counties, West Virginia. Subjects include land sales, Western Virginia Education Society, Rector College, family affairs, and Rev. Joshua Bradley's work.

There are pamphlets and typescripts on Mt. Zion Baptist Church in Wood County.

773. **Rector-Hiett-Hall Families.** Records, ca. 1802-1962. Ca. 50 items. Gift of Mrs. Irving Gavett, 1957, and Mrs. Cora Hall Gavett, 1963. Nos. 945, 1637.

Bible record, land papers, typescripts, and family photographs of three related family lines. Typescripts include "Enoch Rector, his Forefathers and Descendants," by Thomas Rector, and "The (Reynear) Hall Family," by D. B. Hall. There is also a short historical sketch of the First Baptist Church of Parkersburg and the family record from James Hiett's Bible.

774. **Red Sulphur Hotel.** Register, July 8-October 30, 1907. 1 item. Gift of Mrs. L. M. Campbell, 1952. No. 480.

Pages from a guest register when the hotel was under the proprietorship of Hunter & Company.

775. **Reed, Bessie Jane.** Papers, 1918-1924. 25 items. Gift of Mary A. Hervey, 1965. No. 1845.

Correspondence, poems, and clippings of a secondary and normal school librarian in Fairmont and West Liberty. Subjects include the West Virginia Library Association. There is one letter each from Mary Meek Atkeson and Waitman Barbe.

776. **Reese, Albert M.** (1872-1965). Papers, 1873-1954. Ca. 200 items. Gifts of A. M. Reese, 1957, 1958, and Earl L. Core, 1965. Nos. 929, 1058, 1852.

Correspondence, lecture and speech notes, and memorabilia of a professor of zoology at West Virginia University. Subjects include evolution. There is also correspondence of General John R. Kenly concerning his Civil War service and his book on the Mexican War.

777. **Reger, David B.** Records, 1931-1957. 2 reels of microfilm (36 volumes). Gift of Mrs. David B. Reger, 1959. No. 1155.

Office files of a Morgantown consulting geologist include monthly time sheets and record of jobs, 1934-1957; payroll books, 1939-1947; records of the production of natural gas by utilities in Ohio, 1931-1936; a volume pertaining to the Carl Reger estate; and an index to Reger's notes.

778. **Rehm, Sebastian.** Papers, ca. 1869-1890. 2 items. Gift of A. K. McClung, 1956. No. 902.

An indexed physician's account book, 1869-1887, for a practice in Mason County, West Virginia, and Pomeroy, Ohio; and a folder of loose invoices for household accounts, building supplies, groceries, harness and leather goods, and clothes.

779. **Rendell, Kenneth W.,** *Collector.* Correspondence, 1909-1910. 3 items. Gift of Kenneth Rendell, 1963. No. 1690.

Letters from United States Senator Nathan B. Scott and Representative Joseph H. Gaines concerning the Telepost Bill, H.R. 19402, and the Republican presidential campaign of 1904.

780. **Reneau, Isaac Tipton** (1805-1885). Papers, 1833-1900. Ca. 30 items and 1 reel of microfilm. Originals in possession of Oren Reneau, 1961. No. 1433.

Correspondence, discourses, and sermon notes of a physician, schoolteacher, bookseller, and traveling evangelist for the Kentucky Christian Missionary Society from Albany, Clinton County, Kentucky. There is a folder of financial papers of Reneau's brother-in-law, Elijah Stover.

Subjects include a dispute with the Sons of Temperance, accounts of Reneau's travels, the support of the Missionary Society, and troubles at the College of the Bible and the Christian Church in Lexington, Kentucky. Several letters are written to Reneau's children and there are numerous statements from several publishers, book concerns, and other

creditors pressing Reneau for money. The discourses include the manuscript drafts of Reneau's *A Discourse . . . on the Claims of the Baptist Churches to Descent from John the Baptist* (1859).
Correspondents include Alexander Campbell.

781. **Reynolds, Francis Marion (1843-1931).** Papers, 1845-1931. 13 ft. Gift of E. Bunker Reynolds, 1937. No. 50.

Business papers of a Keyser attorney who was judge of the Sixteenth judicial circuit, 1904-1920; member of the West Virginia Legislature, 1895-1896 and 1901-1904; and a member of many educational, commercial, and financial boards in Mineral County. Correspondents include John J. Cornwell, H. G. Davis, A. G. Dayton, S. B. Elkins, and Cecil B. Highland.

782. **Reynolds, Powell Benton (1841-1914).** Correspondence, 1861-1885. 12 items. Gift of Mrs. John A. Gibson, 1959. Nos. 390, 1195.

Correspondence of a Confederate soldier in the Fifth Kentucky Infantry and Company K, Fiftieth Virginia Infantry, and university professor. Subjects include Reynolds' argument for the right of secession, military life in the Army of Northern Virginia; and Reynolds' election to the Chair of English at West Virginia University.
Correspondents include William P. Willey.

783. **Reynolds, William.** Diary, May-July 6, 1841. 1 typescript. Gift of Mrs. Harriet L. French, 1936. No. 48.

Typed extracts from a diary of a tour of the eastern states by a resident of Meadville, Pennsylvania, with descriptions of travel through Greenbrier, Fayette, Kanawha, and Cabell counties.

784. **Richardson, Robert (1806-1876).** Typescript, ca. 1930. 1 reel of microfilm. Original in possession of the Bosworth Memorial Library, College of The Bible (Lexington, Kentucky), 1959. No. 1247.

Biography by Cloyd Goodnight of Robert Richardson, a Disciples of Christ minister, educator, writer, physician, agriculturalist, and member of the Bethany College faculty. The manuscript contains long extracts from Richardson's correspondence and daybook.

785. **Rigg Family.** Papers, ca. 1900-1968. 22 items. Gift of Robert S. Rigg, 1967-1971. No. 1979.

Papers and pictures relating to the James Rigg family, including genealogical charts, a photograph of the Kanawha Falls Hotel, and typescript copies of letters dated 1845, 1852, 1853, and 1854 written in Moniteau County, Missouri, and at Kanawha Falls.

786. **Ripley.** Typescript, ca. 1940. 1 reel of microfilm. Original in possession of Miss Anita Harpole, 1962. No. 1616.

Brief sketch of the founding of the town of Ripley, its early history and settlers; cemetery readings of the Old Ripley Cemetery copied by the Historic Records Survey, 1940; and a copy of the deed from John Swan, Jr., to Jacob Starcher for the land on which Ripley was settled.

787. **Roberts, Walter M.,** *Collector.* Papers, 1881. 2 items. Gift of Walter M. Roberts, 1955. No. 775.

A report to the president and directors of the Little Kanawha Navigation Company for the year ending February 1, 1881, and a photograph of Francis A. Guthrie (1840-1904), circuit judge of Mason, Putnam, and Kanawha counties.

788. **Robinson, Ira Ellsworth (1869-1951).** Papers, 1818-1951. 42 ft. Gift of Mr. and Mrs. Ira E. Robinson, 1949, 1951, 1957. Nos. 155, 294, 965.

Business, personal, and family papers of an attorney in Grafton and Clarksburg, 1891-1951, who was in the state legislature in 1902-1904, judge of the State Supreme Court of Appeals, 1907-1915, Republican candidate for governor, 1916, and a member of the Federal Radio Commission, 1929-1932. There is material on the development of coal properties and mining in the Cheat River valley, the Revolutionary War, the Civil War. Family papers include letters and memorabilia of the Sinsel and Robinson families, ca. 1818-1951, and business records of William Robinson, shoemaker and leather goods dealer in Taylor County, 1861-1896.

Correspondents include Calvin Coolidge, William M. O. Dawson, Stephen B. Elkins, Davis Elkins, Albert B. Fall, and Herbert Hoover.

789. **Rogers, Benjamin F.** Papers, 1847-1914. 10 items. Gift of Mrs. Effie Swiger, 1956. No. 814.

Business and legal papers of Benjamin F. Rogers of Harrison County.

790. **Rogers, John (1786-1864).** Papers, 1777-1857. 3 ft. Acquired, 1931, 1952, and gift of Brad Laidley, 1961. Nos. 5, 504, 1397.

Business and personal papers of John Rogers, merchant, land agent, and owner of grist, carding, fulling, and sawmills in Monongalia County. Rogers served as a director of the Morgantown and Fishing Creek Turnpike; director for Virginia of the Morgantown Bridge Company; and he was associated with many committees responsible for the construction of Morgantown schools and public buildings. Correspondence includes letters from individuals and firms in Ohio, Maryland, Mississippi, Pennsylvania, and Virginia. Correspondents include Captain R. L. Baker at the Pittsburgh, Pennsylvania, United States Arsenal.

791. **Rosecrans, William Starke (1818-1898).** Correspondence, 1841-1879. 49 items (1 reel of microfilm). Originals in the Library of the University of California at Los Angeles, 1967. No. 1943.

Correspondence of a Civil War general who had business interests in the Cannel Coal Company, Coal River Navigation Company, James River and Kanawha Company, and the Western Oil Company. Subjects include coal, oil, iron and steel; improvements on the Kanawha, Coal, and Ohio rivers; English investments in the Cannel Coal Company and the Winifrede Mining & Manufacturing Company; and timber prices. Civil War correspondence includes letters from Francis H. Pierpont and General Jacob D. Cox. There are letters from Rosecrans to his wife while commander of Union forces in western Virginia; persons mentioned include Generals John B. Floyd, R. C. Schenck, Jacob D. Cox, George Crook, George B. McClellan, Braxton Bragg, and U. S. Grant. There is postwar political comment on ex-Confederate officers in government positions and U. S. Grant's terms as president.

792. **Ross, M. H.,** *Collector.* Papers, 1931-1957. 6 ft. Gift of M. H. Ross and acquisition, 1967. Nos. 1936, 1937.

Papers and materials collected by a labor organizer and union employee include correspondence, reports, handbills, pamphlets, newspapers, posters, political and labor buttons. There are court reports involving labor cases for the period 1940-1956. Subjects include the Subversive Activities Control Board, integration in the labor movement, labor during World War II, communism in the labor movement, union constitutions, and agreements between industry and unions.

Also included are papers, 1935-1947, of the Fairmont General Hospital Graduate Nurses' Alumni Association, including correspondence, bonds, tax returns, bank records and account books.

793. **Rowan, Andrew Summers (1857-1943).** Papers and memorabilia, ca. 1940-1960. 18 items. Gift of Miss Agnes Kast and transfer, 1964. No. 1780.

Burial flag, cord, pictures, and correspondence, 1963-1964, concerning disposition of these items. There is a resume of Rowan's life after 1922 and information on his military service, which included a mission in Cuba prior to the Spanish-American War which was glorified in Elbert Hubbard's "A Message to Garcia."

794. **Rowan, Richard B.,** *Collector.* Papers, 1894-1950. Ca. 200 items. Gift of Mrs. Richard B. Rowan, 1957. No. 973.

A collection of envelopes with unusual postmarks; a file of ca. 3000 cards of names of all known West Virginia post offices; and scrapbooks of clippings concerning the Civil War, the formation of West Virginia counties, biographies written by Ella May Turner, and West Virginia authors.

795. **Rowe, Edgar B.** Papers, 1950-1957. 2 ft. Gift of Al Rowe, 1961. No. 1482.

Correspondence, decisions, and briefs of the umpire for the Northern West Virginia Coal Association, Big Sandy-Elkhorn Coal Operators' Association, Western Pennsylvania Coal Operators' Association, and United Mine Workers of America.

796. **Rudd, R. S. (b. 1846).** Records, 1839-1912. 2 reels of microfilm (4 volumes). Originals in possession of Marco Rudd, 1959. No. 1162.

Diaries, accounts, and statistical records of a schoolteacher from Montgomery and Campbell counties, Virginia, and Monroe County, West Virginia. These records list the schools in which Rudd taught, the homes where he boarded, and his friends and acquaintances. The records also cover his employment with the Virginia and Tennessee Railroad at Central Depot, Virginia, and with the Chesapeake and Ohio Railroad at Allegheny Station.

Volume III is a guest register of the White Sulphur Springs Hotel (The Greenbrier), 1860-1861, 1867-1868, and contains entries for James Buchanan, Winfield Scott, Robert E. Lee, and other nineteenth century notables.

797. **Ruffner, Henry (1790-1861) and William Henry (1824-1908).** Papers, 1829-1913. 1 reel of microfilm (310 items). Originals held by the Historical Foundation of the Presbyterian and Reformed Churches, Montreat, North Carolina, 1967. No. 1942.

Correspondence, pamphlets, and manuscripts of a minister, educator, missionary, and author. Pamphlets include Henry Ruffner's antislavery pamphlet, 1847, and his Union speech, 1856. Subjects of the manuscripts and correspondence include family history; travel; Kanawha Salt Works; schools in Virginia and Kanawha County; Lane Seminary Library; Presbyterian Church; slavery, coal, gas, iron, and timber; Johns Hopkins, Washington and Lee, Harvard, Hobart, Cornell, and Hampden-Sydney colleges; Greenbrier County; Alabama; election of

1904; University of Virginia; Kanawha Valley floods; Venezuela; American Colonization Society; and Philippine Islands.

Persons mentioned or commented on include Philip Doddridge, John Letcher, Hugh Mercer, and Nelson A. Miles. Correspondents include Charles H. Ambler, John Eaton, John P. Hale, H. R. Helper, W. S. Laidley, David L. Ruffner, John W. Wayland, and William L. Wilson.

798. **Ruffner-Donnally and Company.** Records, 1833-1885. 10 volumes. Gifts of Willard Oakes and F. P. Summers, 1939, 1941. Nos. 69, 70.

Account books, 1833-1885; statements of receipts and disposition of salt by the Cincinnati agency of Ruffner-Donnally, 1851-1852; and letter books, 1853-1868.

799. **Ruffner Family.** Papers, (1813-1841) 1866. 21 items. Gift of C. G. Krebs, 1964. No. 1744.

Letters and copies of eight letters, 1813-1841; pages 5-10 from Kanawha Salines general merchandise account book, March 6-9, 1827; three manuscript volumes by Henry Ruffner—"Notes on a Tour to the West" and "An Expedition to the North," 1815, and "An Account of Amounts Paid to Rev. Nath'l W. Calhoon," 1826-1834; and "Subscription for Church, 1836-1842," by David Ruffner. There is also a printed brief involving Ruffner-Donnally estates, 1875, and information on the Shackelford family.

800. **Salt Manufacturing.** Typescript, 1960. 1 item. Gift of James M. Crump, 1960. No. 1356.

Unpublished manuscript, "Salt Manufacturing in Mason County, West Virginia," by James M. Crump.

801. **Salt Sulphur Springs.** Records, 1819-1932. 94 volumes. Gifts of E. A. Barnes and Payne Brown, 1943, 1952, deposit by A. A. Barnes, 1960. Nos. 85, 512, 1377.

Financial records, letter books, guest registers, and other materials relating to the various business enterprises of the Salt Sulphur Springs Company, including a general store, hotel, stage line, telegraph company, and farm in Monroe County. Among the other volumes is a letter book of the Oriental Powder Mills, Charleston; daybooks of the E. D. Ballard general store; Mill Creek school records; and guest register of the Salt Sulphur Springs Hotel, 1894-1904.

802. **Sammons, Forest Charles.** Papers, ca. 1939-1940. 4 items. Gift of Mrs. Forest Charles Sammons, 1961. No. 1522.

Manuscript writings of Sammons, a Huntington contractor and founder of the West Virginia Anti-Communist League.

803. **Sanders, John C.**, *Collector.* Papers, ca. 1816-1900. 1 ft. Gift of John C. Sanders. Nos. 64, 138, 153.

Typescripts, clippings, photographs, and account books. Records of marriages performed by the Reverend William Welch, Mineral County, 1816-1867; Civil War typescripts, including "Capture of Generals Kelly and Crook," by Capt. Jesse C. McNeill, and "Capture of a Railroad Train," by John T. Peerce. There are photographs and scrapbooks of South Branch valley history, and account books for grain, carding, and other activities in Morgantown.

804. **Schaeffer, Lewis.** Diaries, 1862-1863, 1865. 1 reel of microfilm (3 volumes). Originals in possession of Raymond B. McClain, 1961. No. 1540.

Civil War diaries of Lewis Schaeffer, Company A, Sixty-eighth Regiment, Pennsylvania Volunteers (Scott Legion of Philadelphia). Schaeffer was at Fredericksburg, Chancellorsville, and Gettysburg. In 1865 he was at Point City, Virginia, and Hart's Island, New York, where he was in charge of Confederate prisoners.

805. **Schools.** Miscellaneous papers, 1818-1968. 77 items (9 photocopies). Transfers, 1954-1963; gifts of R. H. Ferguson, 1953, Price W. Williams, 1956, 1957, K. T. Rexrode, 1958, Arthur V. G. Upton, 1959, Earl L. Core, 1960, Patsy Hazlet Dague, 1966, and Charles F. Lasure, 1967, 1968; and loan by George A. Shingleton, 1964. Nos. 518, 694, 842, 921, 999, 1044, 1218, 1237, 1311, 1355, 1369, 1726, 1864, 1891, 1947, 2101.

Records of Mason County schools, 1818-1849; arrangement of pupils and assigned lessons in Harpers Ferry Seminary, April 28, 1819; typescript resume of Monongalia County School Commissioners annual report, 1819-1829; minutes of the Board of Education for Clay Township, Monongalia County, for July 1, 1864; typescript copy of minutes of the Robinson Township School Board, Mason County, 1864-1875; records of Cove Township Board of Education, Barbour County, 1865-1868; statistics on West Virginia schools, 1865-1892; report form for teachers in Barbour County, 1881; minute book of Sand Hill District Board of Education, Marshall County, 1884-1920; letter concerning a school conducted by Albert Modisett near the mining town of Berryburg, 1895; program for the Raleigh County Teachers' Institute at Beckley, 1913; report forms; photograph of West Virginia University summer school students, 1916; a letter from the State Supervisor of

Rural Schools, June 23, 1917; "Uniform examination" questions issued by the Department of Free Schools, 1917, 1919; examination schedule and question forms for teachers certificates, 1924-1925; a typescript "History of Harrison County Schools (1787-1956)"; and letters, circulars, and regulations from the Wetzel County Superintendent of Schools, 1966-1968.

806. **Schools. Berkeley County Board of Education.** Records, 1866-1935. 3 reels of microfilm (17 volumes). Originals in possession of the Berkeley County School System, 1961. No. 1404.

Records of the Arden District, 1916-1930; Gerrardstown District, 1877-1925; Hedgesville District, 1866-1927; Martinsburg District, 1908-1918; Mill Creek District, 1921-1935; and the county superintendent, 1893-1911.

807. **Schools. Desegregation.** Newspaper and magazine clippings, 1954-1960. 13 ft. Gift of Harry H. Jones, 1963. No. 1648.

Clippings on desegregation of schools, compiled by Harry H. Jones, give a day-by-day coverage of the school integration controversy and the fight for Negro civil rights from 1954 to 1960.

808. **Schools. Hardy County Board of Education.** Records, 1866-1933. 2 reels of microfilm (6 volumes). Originals in possession of the Hardy County Board of Education, 1961. No. 1405.

Record books of the Capon District, 1911-1921; Lost River District, 1880-1907; Moorefield District, 1866-1925; the South Fork District, 1873-1926; and the County Financial Secretary's Record Book, 1919-1933.

809. **Schools. Harrison County.** Minutes, 1866-1878. 1 reel of microfilm (2 volumes). Originals in possession of Arthur V. G. Upton, 1960. No. 1354.

Minute books of the school commissioner for the Clarksburg Independent School District.

810. **Schools. Harrison County.** Papers, 1835 (1879-1915). 1 reel of microfilm (6 volumes) and 3 items (photostat copies). Originals in possession of the Harrison County Board of Education, 1961. No. 1390.

Minutes of the Board of Education, Clarksburg District, 1879-1915; a typescript copy of a teaching contract, Buffaloe Creek, 1835; and a note concerning the school fund for Harrison County, 1863-1865.

811. **Schools. Monongalia County Board of Education.** Minute books, 1864-1961. 7 reels of microfilm (41 volumes). Originals in possession of the Monongalia County Board of Education, 1963. No. 1665.

Minute books of Battelle, Cass, Clay, Clinton, Grant, Morgan, Union, and Morgantown districts, 1864-1933, and the Monongalia County Unit, 1933-1961.

812. **Schools. Monongalia County Board of Education.** Typescript, 1955-1960. 10 volumes. Gift of the Monongalia County Board of Education, 1960. No. 1375.

"Monongalia County Schools and Local History, 1864-1960," compiled by Lynn Hastings, includes lists of various county and school officials, rosters of teachers and students, and organizational data of the school system.

813. **Schools. Monroe County.** Records, 1818-1902. 2 ft. Gift of A. W. Boon, 1948. No. 123.

A printed circular relating to the allocation of revenues of the Literary Fund under the Act of Assembly of February 21, 1818; manuscript financial reports, receipts, orders for tuition and teachers' salaries, attendance and progress reports, lists of books and supplies, reports on the number of schools in operation, and other papers.

814. **Schools. Morgantown.** Miscellany, 1889-1931. 26 items. Gift of Daisie Fleming Reeves, 1967. No. 1984.

School records of Daisie Fleming, including grade reports, commencement programs, pictures, and Parent-Teachers Association materials. Most pertains to Morgantown High School.

815. **Schools. Pendleton County Board of Education.** Records, 1894-1933. 1 reel of microfilm (9 volumes). Originals in possession of the Pendleton County Board of Education, 1962. No. 1560.

Records of the Circle, Franklin, Will Run, Sugar Grove, and Union school districts.

816. **Schools. Preston County Board of Education.** Records, 1878-1933. 3 reels of microfilm (16 volumes).

Originals in possession of the Preston County Board of Education, 1960. No. 1296.

Register, School No. 6, 1878-1879; records of the Preston County School Book Board, 1897-1907; Record of Proceedings of the Board of Education, Kingwood District, 1908-1913; and Board of Education Minutes for the Kingwood, Lyon, Pleasant, Portland, Reno, and Valley districts, 1899-1933.

817. **Schools. Secondary.** Social Studies Survey, 1960. 1 reel of microfilm. Transfer, 1960. No. 1326.

Correspondence from West Virginia college teachers, questionnaires from West Virginia University students, and checklists of social studies offerings in state high schools. This material was compiled by Mary Ann Feldmeier for a study on West Virginia high schools (unpublished M. A. thesis, West Virginia University, 1960).

818. **Scott, Thomas (1772-1856).** Papers, 1700-1856. Ca. 40 items (photocopies). Loan for reproduction by Boyd B. Stutler, 1968. No. 2052.

Manuscripts and typescripts of a traveling minister of the Methodist Episcopal Church who became a lawyer and a judge. Manuscripts cover Captain Michael Cresap, Chief Logan, western massacres during the Revolutionary War, customs and privations of the western settlers, the Kentucky frontier, Methodism in the west, old preachers and historical recollections.

819. **Scott Lumber Company.** Ledger, 1911-1929. 1 reel of microfilm. Original in possession of N. C. Hamm, 1958. No. 1096.

Ledger containing financial statements and reports of the company's operations in Morgantown and Follansbee, and records of a subsidiary, the Cecil Lumber and Hardware Company of Elm Grove.

820. **Scott-Palmer Family.** Papers, 1829-1917. 3 ft. Acquired, 1961. Nos. 1423, 1458.

Correspondence, journals, clipping scrapbooks, military records, genealogical records, biographical notes, and printed material of the Theodore Scott and Jewett Palmer families.

The papers, 1829-1876, of Theodore Scott, a schoolmaster at Portsmouth and Marietta, Ohio, and Williamstown, West Virginia, include his diaries, correspondence and letter book, and school reports and registers. The papers of Scott's daughter, Saida Scott Palmer, consist of correspondence, school papers, clippings, and a register of her music school pupils, 1862-1883. The papers of Saida's husband, Jewett Palmer, a Union officer and later mayor of Marietta, include the military and veterans records of Company B, Eighteenth Ohio Volunteer Infantry, and Company G, Thirty-sixth Ohio Volunteer Infantry; Civil War letters and diaries; the journal of Captain Wallace S. Stanley (36th OVI), 1861-1864; and a copy book of outgoing letters from Palmer as District Deputy Collector of the Internal Revenue office at Marietta.

Subjects include the Marietta Universalist Society; (Marietta) Western Liberal Institute; temperance; schools and pedagogical methods; New York merchants and the secession crisis; civil service reform; Grand Army of the Republic veterans affairs; Republican politics in Washington County (Ohio); and family activities.

There is information on Civil War military activity of the Eighteenth and Thirty-sixth Ohio Volunteer Infantry at Summersville, Lewisburg, Meadow Bluff, and Kanawha Valley, (West) Virginia; at Nashville and Carthage, Tennessee (1861); in the Shenandoah, at Second Manassas, and Antietam (1862); at Chickamauga, Chattanooga, and Missionary Ridge (1863); at Camp Crook, Charleston, along the line of the Virginia Central Railroad, the Shenandoah Valley and Martinsburg (1864).

Correspondents include Nathan Goff, Rutherford B. Hayes, and William McKinley.

821. **Scotts Run, Monongalia County.** Reports, 1925-1938. 3 typescripts. Transfer, 1952. No. 516.

Reports of surveys made of coal properties, development of mining, and labor and social conditions in Scotts Run; also materials on studies of West Virginia retail trade and the development of University-business contacts.

822. **Seckar, Alvena V. (1916-   ).** Papers, 1940-1968. 3 ft. Gift of Miss Seckar, 1953, 1954, 1956, 1967, 1968. Nos. 556, 589, 903, 2002.

Correspondence, 1954-1968, typescripts, class notes, course outlines, clippings, pamphlets, and photographs of an artist and author. Subjects include Islamic, Arabic, and Near Eastern art and the work of Paul Hogarth. There are manuscripts of juvenile books written and illustrated by Miss Seckar, including *Zuska of the Burning Hills, Trapped in the Old Mine,* and *Mischko.*

823. **Seely, Simeon Franklin.** Letter, 1859. 1 item. Acquired, 1961. No. 1457.

Letter of October 17, 1859, written by a merchant from Beverly, Ohio, who, on the night of the 16th arrived at Harpers Ferry as John Brown was taking possession of the armory. The letter describes the raid during the time the train was held up.

824. **Seibert Family.** Papers, 1813-1918. Ca. 45 items. Acquired, 1965. No. 1857.

Papers of the Seibert family located in the Martinsburg area.

825. **Shahan, James B.** Letter, 1861. Transfer, 1961. No. 1444.

Letter of September 12, 1861, by Dr. E. Mead, concerning the cutting, burning, and marketing of pine timber in the Grafton area.

826. **Sharps, A. B.** Papers, 1875-1876, 1968. 4 items. Gift of A. B. Sharps, 1955, 1968. Nos. 737, 2041.

A student's notebook on geometry from West Virginia College, Flemington, Taylor County, 1876; an announcement from Glenville Normal School, December, 1875; one item of correspondence, dated June 23, 1876; and a notebook of typescripts on the Samuel Barr family.

827. **Shaw, John C.** (1865-   ). 1 tape recording, 1956. No. 876.

Interview, with typescript, sketching John C. Shaw's education, career, and homelife in Barbour and Upshur counties.

828. **Shaw, Sidney F.** Papers, 1865-1908. 28 items. Gift of Miss Alice E. Shaw, 1957. No. 944.

Papers mainly relating to Shaw's efforts to secure a Civil War pension, also include certificates of stock for the Chicago, Parkersburg and Norfolk Railway Company, 1885-1888.

829. **Shelby Family.** Papers, 1850-1860, 1962. 6 items. Gift of Mrs. Minerva Shelby, 1962. No. 1558.

Papers of a Greene County, Pennsylvania, family, include three letters from Waitman T. Willey pertaining to legal matters, and a letter from the Washington National Monument Office to Richard L. Bugh, acknowledging a donation from the citizens of Pittsburgh.

830. **Sheldon, John Lewis** (1865-1947). Papers, 1905-1951. 1 ft. Gift of Damon C. Shelton, 1966. No. 1895.

Correspondence consisting mainly of family news and business. There is comment on prohibition, President Woodrow Wilson's reelection, World War I speculation, the Food Administration under Herbert Hoover, and the influenza outbreak of 1919-1920.

831. **Sheltering Arms Hospital.** Records, 1902-1940. 17 volumes and 1 folder. Gift of Roy Bird Cook, 1961. No. 1527.

Minute book, 1906-1923; medical case records, 1902-1922; and miscellaneous papers of a hospital founded at Hansford in 1886 by the Protestant Episcopal Church, Diocese of West Virginia. The hospital, designed to serve the medical and surgical needs of miners and railroad workers and their families, closed in 1923.

832. **Sherwood, Lawrence,** *Collector.* Diaries, 1853-1854, 1861-1870. 1 reel of microfilm. Originals lent by Lawrence Sherwood, 1956. No. 826.

Pocket diaries of William M. Randolph of Moorefield, 1853-1854, and Lettie Smith of Grant and Tucker counties, 1864-1870.

833. **Shingleton, Samuel W.,** *Collector.* Records, 1848-1863. 1 reel of microfilm (2 volumes). Originals in possession of Samuel W. Shingleton, 1959. No. 1158.

Ledger, 1849-1851, of Samuel D. Thorn, a purveyor of groceries, grain, and whiskey from Thorntown, Monongalia County; and a Sunday school minute book, Mt. Morris Methodist Episcopal Church, Barbour County, 1848-1863.

834. **Shott, Hugh Ike (1866-1953).** Papers, 1848-1954. 35 ft. Gift of Hugh Ike Shott, Jr., and Jim H. Shott, 1956, and Ned Shott, 1962, 1964. Nos. 908, 1583, 1783.

Personal and business papers and memorabilia of a newspaper publisher, founder and owner of radio station WHIS in Bluefield, and Republican congressman. Subjects include politics, 1915-1944; prohibition, 1905-1932; newspaper publishing, 1930-1942; and home front activities during World War II. There are also campaign and convention buttons.

835. **Signature Collection.** Letters, 1843-1907. 1 folder. Transfers. No. 435.

A miscellaneous group of autographed, signed, letters transferred from various collections or acquired as single items. Writers of letters include Andrew Carnegie, 1908; William H. Taft, 1908; Varina Jefferson Davis, Jr., 1906; J. H. Diss Debar, 1859; Benjamin Harrison, 1887-1889; James M. Todd, 1843; John Tyler, 1860; and Cole Younger, 1898.

836. **Silver, Gray** (1870-1935). Papers, 1903-1935. 10 ft. Gift of Mrs. Gray Silver, 1949, 1950. Nos. 164, 212.

Personal and business papers of the Martinsburg agriculturalist and banker who was a representative of the American Farm Bureau Federation in Washington and a member of the West Virginia Senate, 1907-1913. Much of the material relates to fruit growing and marketing and other business activities of Silver, as well as Democratic politics.

837. **Simpson, F. A.** Records, 1909-1942. 3 ft. Gift of Mrs. J. A. Viquesney, 1954. No. 647.

Records of F. A. Simpson, a justice of the peace in Barbour County. Also included, dating between 1914-1942, are a few papers and speeches of J. A. Viquesney, West Virginia Game and Fish Warden, 1909-1916, and justice of the peace; 1930 election campaign material relating to Henry D. Hatfield, James Ellwood Jones, and Carl B. Harvey; and references to politics, game laws, cost of medical service, and prohibition.

838. **Simpson Chapel and Community.** Typescript, 1961. 1 item (mimeograph copy). Gift of Hartzell G. Strader, 1961. No. 1496.

"A History of Simpson Chapel and Community," written and prepared by Hartzel G. Strader for the Rexroad Family reunion and Simpson Chapel homecoming group, gives the religious background and family histories of a Lewis County settlement.

839. **Sistersville. City Council.** Minutes, 1846-1955. 4 reels of microfilm (11 volumes). Originals in possession of the city of Sistersville, 1961. No. 1479.

840. **Slaughter's Creek Coal & Land Company.** Papers, 1905-1948. Ca. 200 items. Gift of Miss Donnie Krebs, 1962. No. 1789.

Deeds, contracts, maps, and engineering reports concerning coal lands owned by the company in the Cabin Creek District. Other companies involved are Pure Oil Company, Winifrede Collieries Company, Mott Core Drilling Company, Wet Branch Mining Company, Chelyan Coal & Land Company, Standard Ore and Alloys Corporation, and Charleston Interurban Railroad Company.

841. **Slaves and Slavery.** Papers, 1797-1829. 11 items. Acquired, 1968, 1969. Nos. 2059, 2078.

Documents from Berkeley and Jefferson counties and Frederick County, Maryland, relating to transportation of slaves, manumission, free-papers, suits for freedom, appraisals. There is also a bill of sale for land in Jefferson County, 1815.

842. **Sloan Brothers.** Papers, 1757 (1827-1839). 1 ft. (photocopies). Gift of Clyde Bonar, 1961. No. 1489.

Deeds and farm account books of John, James, Thomas, Richard, and George Sloan, farmers and stockbreeders from Burlington, Mineral County. One volume is an inventory of the debts due to the estate of Edward Taylor, deceased partner of Alfred Taylor in the operation of a tannery, 1835-1839.

843. **Smith, Agnes (1906-   ).** Papers, 1959-1966. Ca. 200 items. Gift of Agnes Smith, 1964, 1966. Nos. 1774, 1877.

Typescript of *An Edge of the Forest,* a children's book published in 1959; a draft of a script prepared from the book by BBC; letters concerning use of the book; six short stories by Agnes Smith; a typescript, "On Reading."

844. **Smith, Clarence Edwin (1885-1959).** Papers, 1787-1957. 22 ft. and 1 reel of microfilm (1 volume). Gift of C. E. Smith, 1951, 1957, and loan of Mrs. Carter D. Jones and Mrs. Herschel Rose, 1962. Nos. 258, 468, 990, 1604, 1606.

Correspondence, business and legal records, account books, news releases, clippings, and family papers and photographs of a U.`S. marshal (1916-1922); editor of the Fairmont *Times* (1925-1959) and Wheeling *Register* (1933-1935); Democratic politician; member of the National Bituminous Coal Commission (1935-1939); and businessman.

Subjects include Smith's student days at Virginia Military Institute; West Virginia National Guard; Monongah Mine Relief Committee; Associated Press; Association Against the Prohibition Amendment; Eighteenth Amendment; presidential elections and national and state politics, 1916-1956; John W. Davis; Alfred E. Smith; post-World War I radicalism and reaction; Ku Klux Klan; United Mine Workers; National Miners' Union; labor conflict, 1920s; U. S. Railway Administration; New Deal agencies; and Mountain Lake Park, Maryland.

Correspondents include Van A. Bittner, William E. Chilton, William G. Conley, John J. Cornwell, John W. Davis, Eugene V. Debs, James A. Farley, William Green, Averell Harriman, Homer A. Holt, Rush Dew Holt, Hugh S. Johnson, Louis Johnson, Harley M. Kilgore, H. G. Kump, John L. Lewis, William A. MacCorkle, J. Howard McGrath, Clarence W. Meadows, M. M. Neely, Okey L. Patteson, Jennings Randolph, Franklin D. Roosevelt, Adlai E. Stevenson, Harry S Truman, Clarence W. Watson, and James O. Watson.

There are also papers of Clarence L. Smith (1850-1905), editor of the Fairmont *Index* (1889) and founder of the Fairmont *Times* (1900), which include a domestic diary of his wife, 1876-1910; minute book of the Fleming Association, 1890-1894; papers of Clarence Edwin Smith, Jr., 1940-1941; papers of Thomas Barns (1750-1836), and his sons, John S. and James F.; Marion County millers and manufacturers, 1795-1908. There are also papers of Waitman T. Willey and a taped interview with C. E. Smith, 1956. Correspondents include John L. Lewis, George B. McClellan, Matthew M. Neely, Francis H. Pierpont, John J. Cornwell, Franklin D. Roosevelt, and Harry S Truman.

There are also papers, 1917-1950, of Smith's brother, Earl H. (1880-1941), co-founder and editor of the Fairmont *Times* (1900-1925), state legislator, officer in the National Guard, and state commander of the American Legion. Subjects include World War I; Woodrow Wilson; American Legion; and state and national politics, 1918-1940. Correspondents include John J. Cornwell, John W. Davis, Sam T. Mallison, M. M. Neely, Jennings Randolph, and Howard Sutherland.

The collection also includes papers, 1908-1940, of Herschel H. Rose, Smith's son-in-law, Fairmont attorney, Democratic politician, and circuit court judge. Correspondents include M. M. Neely.

Financial records include account books, 1826-1893, of Thomas Barns, John S. Barns and Company, Barns, Fleming and Company (1857), James R. Fleming, woolen and flour milling, shoe manufacturing, and general merchandise operations in Marion County; account book of Mary Fleming Smith, 1888-1912; Fairmont Newspaper Publishing Company, 1919-1949; Fairmont Broadcasting Company, 1932, 1947-1949; and Jackson Coal Company, 1917-1924.

845.   **Smith, Donald E.,** *Collector.* Records, 1884-1956. 5 reels of microfilm. Loan from Donald E. Smith, 1967. No. 1944.

Correspondence, account books, and tax reports of the Liverpool Salt and Coal Company, American Calcium Chloride Works, Liverpool Salt Company, Jackson Coal and Mining Company, and Jackson Valley Bell Farm of Hartford. In addition, there are account books for the G. Y. Roots and Company of Cincinnati, Ohio.

846.   **Smith, George W.** Papers, 1818-1885. 1 ft. Gift of Margaret McIntosh Starcher. No. 427.

Business and family correspondence of George W. Smith of Jackson County, a merchant, justice of the peace, and agent for land in Jackson, Wirt, Putnam, and Roane counties.

Correspondence includes letters from Nehemiah Smith, a delegate to the Virginia Assembly, 1831-1842, and letters concerning the Gilmer, Ripley and Ohio Turnpike Company. There are a few items of correspondence from sons in school at Morgantown and at Washington,

Pennsylvania, 1858-1861, and from Confederate prisoners of war at Point Lookout, Maryland, Elmyra, New York, and other camps in Virginia and West Virginia. Correspondents include Gideon D. Camden.

847. **Smith, John.** Journal, 1786-1788, 1963. 2 items (typescripts). Gift of Judge Nickell Kramer, 1963. No. 1717.

Journal of John Smith, Methodist circuit rider, concerning his work on the Greenbrier Circuit, July 4, 1787, to July 8, 1788; work on the Redstone Circuit in western Pennsylvania and western Virginia, May 12, 1786-1787; the Holston Circuit, November 29-December 27, 1787; and the Greenbrier Circuit, July 4, 1787, to July 8, 1788. Smith preached on Calvinist doctrines of unconditional election, reprobation, and perseverance. There is a typescript, "Greenbrier Circuit—Its First Year; 1787-1788," by the Reverend Lawrence Sherwood, based on the Smith journal.

848. **Smith, W. W.** Papers, 1823-1875. 1 ft. Gift of James H. Smith, 1933. No. 19.

Papers and correspondence relating to retail merchandising in Uniontown, Pennsylvania, Clarksburg, and Bruceton Mills. Included is information on road construction; the Hazel Run Baptist Church in Preston County; agriculture; the Civil War; and social and academic life at West Virginia University, 1868-1870.

849. **Smith Family.** Papers, 1800-1942. 1 ft. Gift of Mrs. Mortimer Smith, 1956. No. 840.

Papers of the Mortimer Wilson Smith family, Clarksburg. There are letters of the Chapin family of Springfield, Massachusetts, and Clarksburg, 1800-1904. Subjects include descriptions of Clarksburg, schools, churches, and family affairs.

Later materials include three scrapbooks of the Mortimer W. Smith family covering family history, and typescripts of speeches made by Smith, 1936-1939, as chief engineer of the West Virginia State Road Commission, and director of the Motor Carrier Department, Public Service Commission of West Virginia.

850. **Smokeless Coal Industrial Exhibition.** Records, 1936. Ca. 20 items. Gift of Stanley Higgins and C. C. Ballard, 1936. No. 49.

Records of the exhibit held at Mt. Hope, August 27-29, 1936.

851. **Smokeless Fuel Company.** Papers, 1935-1957. 3 ft. Gift of Justus C. Beury, 1967. No. 1928.

Correspondence, reports, financial records, pamphlets, maps, pictures, clippings, and other papers of a southern West Virginia coal company. Subjects include operators' associations, wages, prices, mine inspection reports, sales, strip mining, and freight rates.

852. **Smokeless Operators Association.** Papers, 1886 (1925-1961). 5 reels of microfilm and 1 item. Loan for duplication by Smokeless Operators Association, 1962, 1965. Nos. 1564, 1830.

Production statistics and extracts from historical files of an association of operators in the Pocahontas coal field. There is a brief history of the coal industry in West Virginia, 1800-1951, and a typescript entitled "Princess Pocahontas."

853. **Snider, Joseph C. (1839-1864).** Diary, 1861-1864. 1 reel of microfilm (3 volumes) and 1 folder. Originals in possession of Mrs. Maude Ladell Fletcher, 1961. No. 1504.

Diary of a soldier in Company C, Thirty-first Virginia Infantry, Second Corps, Army of Northern Virginia. Subjects include the fighting at Laurel Hill, Cheat Mountain, Allegheny Mountain, the retreat from western Virginia, the war in the Shenandoah Valley early in 1862, the march to Gettysburg, the battles of the Wilderness, Spotsylvania Court House, Cold Harbor, and Early's 1864 raid into Maryland. Snider was killed at the Battle of Winchester, September 19, 1864.

854. **Snider, Martin.** Papers, 1834-1889. 200 items. Gift of Mrs. Leafy M. Hinkle, 1954. No. 681.

Business papers primarily concerning Gilmer County.

855. **Snider, Sampson.** Records, (1864-1866) 1905. 37 items. Gift of Mrs. Nettie Harman, 1955. No. 762.

Records relating to the organization of the Independent Company of Scouts for Randolph County in 1864 by Snider, and his postwar service in the West Virginia Militia. Included are letters and papers of A. I. Boreman.

856. **Snyder Family.** Papers, 1790-1937. Ca. 200 items. Gift of Victor Bliss Snyder, 1953. No. 490.

Personal and business correspondence of Harmon, Molly, John, and other members of the Snyder family; genealogical information on the Lantz and Snyder families; land grants, surveys and deeds for land in Barbour, Greenbrier, and Randolph counties; and poll and registration books, Randolph County. Included also is Harmon Snyder's daybook and diary, listing accounts for the years 1866-1896 and incidents of the Civil War.

857. **Sommerville, William (1756-1826).** Papers, 1712-1888. 1 ft. Acquired, 1964. No. 1750.

Correspondence, diary (1810-1812), and other papers of a Revolutionary veteran from Martinsburg who operated a general store and served as postmaster in Martinsburg (1802-1821). Subjects include smallpox vaccine, politics, postal business, elections, business affairs, genealogy, slaves and slavery, War of 1812, churches and the ministry, and Civil War service.

858. **Speers, Anita Buchanan.** Papers, ca. 1916-1957. 13 ft. Gift of Fred T. Newbraugh, 1960. No. 1338.

Correspondence, typescripts, notes, clippings, photographs, and printed material of a local historian and promoter of patriotic societies from Berkeley Springs. Many of the papers pertain to the local history of the Jefferson-Berkeley-Morgan county area. Subjects include the town of Bath (Berkeley Springs); James Rumsey; George Washington; Porte Crayon (David Hunter Strother); Washington Bicentennial; National Flag Day; D. A. R.; and American Indian Day.

859. **Spivak, John L.** Papers, 1888 (1929-1946) 1967. 1 ft. Acquired, 1967. No. 1962.

Correspondence, notes, manuscripts, photographs, and clippings relating to *Devil's Brigade,* the story of the Hatfield-McCoy feud.

860. **Stadlbauer, Frank,** *Collector.* Papers, 1919-1937. 1 reel of microfilm. Loan for duplication by Frank Stadlbauer, 1965. No. 1818.

Papers collected by a coal miner in Monongalia County, including pay envelopes and records, 1919-1937; certificates of appointment as a second class mine foreman and check weighman; official tally sheet for a United Mine Workers election; bylaws of the Mountaineer Craftsmen's Cooperative Association; production statistics for Rosedale Coal Company's Mine No. 2; and class notes and materials from the W. V. U. Mining Extension Course, 1928.

861. **Stahr, Elvis J., Jr. (1916-   ).** Recordings, 1958, 1960. 2 reels and typescript. Acquired, 1958, and gift of radio station WAJR, 1960. Nos. 1116, 1287.

Interviews with Elvis Stahr, president of West Virginia University, concerning his policy and plans for the university, and the decision to retain football coach Art Lewis on a probationary status.

862. **Steamboats.** Records, 1877-1939. 1 ft. and 3 volumes. Acquired, 1959, 1961, 1962, 1971, and transfers, n.d. Nos. 650, 844, 1253, 1406, 1409, 1417, 1548, 2207.

Bills of lading, receipts, accounts, and ledgers for steamboats operating on the Ohio, Kanawha, Mississippi, and Missouri rivers. Names of vessels include *C. W. Batchelor, Return, Abner O'Neal, C. W. Anderson, Sallie J. Cooper, Sonoma, Victor, Greenbrier, New State, Salt Valley, Welcome,* and *Emma Graham.* Names of places include Ravenswood; Parkersburg; Wheeling; Ironton; Huntington; Pomeroy; Marietta, Ohio; Pittsburgh, Pennsylvania; Cincinnati, Ohio.

863. **Stedman, Lyman (1827-1916).** Diary, 1880-1885. 1 reel of microfilm (1 volume). Loaned for duplication by Mrs. Eleanor S. Dawson, 1968. No. 2042.

Diary of a farmer and former member of the House of Delegates, 1877, from Brown's Island, Hancock County. Entries concern farm operation, Republican political activities on the district and county level, comments on state and national organization, floods on the Ohio River, steamboat and barge traffic, Hopedale School, Methodist Episcopal Church, railroad travel, circuses and fairs, taxes and land valuations, Memorial Day. Persons frequently mentioned include George W. Atkinson, A. W. Campbell, Nathan Goff, and Winfield Scott.

864. **Steele, Virginia,** *Collector.* Papers, 1900-1961. 4 items. Gift of Miss Virginia Steele, 1962. No. 1594.

Typescript copy of a letter from Mark Twain to a Mr. Day giving the writer's attitude toward religion in general and Mary Baker Eddy in particular; a record of Callaway, Keadle, and Ruddle family history (Monroe County); excerpts from a letter dealing with Steele family history; and a picture of Birdie May Windell, 1915.

865. **Stephenson Family.** Ca. 1802-1840. 3 items. Gift and loan for filming from Mrs. J. B. Sammel, 1957. No. 943.

Microfilm of a manuscript journal of Edward Stephenson, and typescript copies of letters and reminiscences of John, Edward, and James M. Stephenson, of Wood County, including a journey in Mexico in the 1850s; also two photographs of the Stephenson home, built in 1812 in Parkersburg.

866. **Stewart, D. Boston.** Papers, 1782 (1852-1916). Ca. 200 items. Gift of Mrs. E. E. Hamstead, 1952. No. 470.

Letters and papers of a Monongalia County member of the Forty-fourth Virginia Regiment, C. S. A. Included are letters to Stewart while a prisoner at Camp Chase, reflecting civilian opinion in the border region.

867. **Stewart Family.** Typescript, 1945. 10p. Gift of Miss Carrie E. Stewart, 1945. No. 98.

A sketch of the descendants of William Stewart (1727-1811) who settled in Monongalia County and built Stewarts Fort.

868. **Stickney, A. B.,** *Compiler.* Papers, 1838-1959. 2 ft. Gift of Charlotte B. Stickney, 1969. No. 2123.

Notes, letters, and family histories, dealing primarily with the descendants of John, Francis, and Larkin Pierpont.

869. **Storer College.** Records, 1865-1956. 70 ft. and 5 reels of microfilm (12 volumes, 1 file drawer, and 32 items). Gift of Storer College, 1958, 1961. Originals of copied material in possession of Mrs. John Newcomer and the National Park Service, 1959, 1961. Nos. 1131, 1168, 1322, 1471.

Office files, correspondence, faculty and student records, Veterans Administration records, financial records, clippings, photographs, scrapbooks, building blueprints, and campus plans of the state's first Negro institution of higher learning chartered at Harpers Ferry in 1867 by the New England Free Will Baptist Association. The collection also includes the guest register from the John Brown Fort-Museum.

Subjects include the attempts of the missionaries from the Free Will Baptist Association to establish schools and missions for the freedmen of the Shenandoah Valley area; the efforts of Henry J. McDonald, president of the college from 1899 to 1944, to put the school on a sound financial and academic basis; and general college operations and activities.

Correspondents include George H. Ball, J. M. Brewster, Silas Curtis, George T. Day, William Pitt Fessenden, Henry J. McDonald, and I. D. Stewart.

870. **Strausbaugh, Perry D.** (1886-1965). Papers, 1913-1964. 7 ft. Transfer, 1965, 1968. Nos. 1848, 1997.

Correspondence and manuscripts of the chairman of the Department of Botany (later Biology) at West Virginia University and author of a college biology textbook, *Elements of Biology.* Much of the correspondence concerns the writing, editing, and revising of the textbook in cooperation with B. R. Weimer and Earl L. Core. Other subjects include making of the film, *Wild Flowers of the Alleghanies*, and other motion pictures; Strausbaugh's tenure at Wooster College, 1920-1923; Earl L. Core's travel in South America as a researcher on quinine; and West Virginia University athletics and development.

Correspondents include Robert A. Armstrong, A. B. Brooks, Phil Conley, A. J. Dadisman, *Encyclopedia* America, Harley M. Kilgore, McGraw Hill Book Company, Matthew M. Neely, Jennings Randolph, Chapman Revercomb, W. P. Shortridge, George Smathers, Irvin Stewart, and Frank B. Trotter.

871.   **Strother, David Hunter.** Letter, 1882. 1 item (photocopy). Gift of Fred T. Newbraugh, 1962. No. 1595.

Letter to Joseph S. Duckwall pertaining to Strother's father's estate and the estate of Philip C. Pendleton.

872.   **Stuart, Jesse (1907-   ).** Recording, 1970. 1 item (cassette). Acquired, 1971. No. 2194.

Cassette from the series, "Contemporary American Poets Read Their Work."

873.   **Stuart, Walter.** Papers, 1910-1950. 189 items. Gift of Mrs. Walter Stuart, 1956, 1966. Nos. 910, 1884.

Correspondence received by Stuart as editor of the *West Union Record*, West Union, including letters from Alben W. Barkley, William Jennings Bryan, Pearl S. Buck, W. E. Chilton, John J. Cornwell, John W. Davis, James A. Farley, Douglas S. Freeman, Henry D. Hatfield, Homer A. Holt, Rush D. Holt, Louis Johnson, H. G. Kump, Allan Nevins, Franklin D. Roosevelt, and others. There are two scrapbooks of clippings covering the years 1924-1950.

874.   **Sturgiss, George Cookman (1842-1925).** Papers, 1838-1896, 1909-1910. Ca. 190 items. Gift of Mrs. Robert C. Price, 1963, 1966. Nos. 1671, 1899.

Correspondence and other papers of a Morgantown judge, railroad promoter, and U. S. congressman, and his mother, Lucinda (Miner) Sturgiss. There is also an engagement book used by Sturgiss and Charlotte Kent Sturgiss for 1907-1909. Subjects include the activities of Alfred Galletin Sturgiss, a Methodist Episcopal minister in northeastern Ohio and northwestern Pennsylvania, 1837-1845; Millerism; Henry Ward Beecher; P. T. Barnum; Duff's College; oil wells, 1859; Civil War; evangelism; Sturgiss' political troubles in his bid for renomination to Congress in 1910; and the unveiling of the Francis H. Pierpont statue in Statuary Hall, Washington.

875. **Summers, Festus P. (1895-1971).** Papers, 1843-1957. 5 ft. Gift of Festus P. Summers, 1959, 1964, 1968, 1969. Nos. 1210, 1760, 2035, 2068, 2072, 2079.

Correspondence, notes, manuscripts, photographs, and clippings of a historian and university professor. There are research notes and materials compiled on William L. Wilson from various libraries, manuscripts of Summers' books on Wilson and Johnson Newlon Camden, a scrapbook covering Monongalia County and other subjects, 1850-1897, and papers relating to West Virginia University.

Correspondents include D. B. Purinton, Charles McCamic, and Charles D. Washburn.

876. **Summers, Joseph W.** Papers, 1831 (1920-1956). 9 ft. Gift of the estate of Joseph W. Summers, 1956, 1957. Nos. 927, 984.

Correspondence, photographs, clippings, scrapbooks, maps, newspapers, and other materials of the family of Joseph W. Summers, Morgantown. Included are deeds for Summers land in Preston County, 1831-1903; genealogical notes compiled by Summers on the Barker, Buzzard, Harris, Hoffman (Huffman), Holland, Knapp, Swisher, and Tarleton lines of the Summers family in West Virginia; and nineteen scrapbooks of clippings of verse and political and historical events, ca. 1913-1956.

877. **Summers, Lewis (1778-1843) and George W. (1804-1868).** Papers, 1828-1890, 1901, 1935. Ca. 200 items. Gift and loan of Miss Lucy Quarrier, 1964. No. 1791.

Papers of Lewis Summers, a lawyer, businessman, member of the Virginia House of Delegates, 1817-1818, delegate to the Virginia Constitutional Convention, 1829-1830, and his brother George W., a lawyer in Charleston, a judge, a member of the House of Delegates, 1830-1832, 1834-1836, the U. S. House of Representatives, 1841-1845, a delegate to the Virginia Constitutional Convention of 1850, candidate for governor in 1851, member of the 1861 Peace Convention, and delegate to the Richmond Secession Convention, 1861.

Correspondence between the brothers is for the years 1828-1843. There are also business, legal, and family papers, speeches, and an autograph book of George W. while a student at the University of Virginia, 1854-1857. Correspondents include George Carlisle, James Craik, James M. Laidley, and Luke Willcox.

Persons mentioned or commented on include John Q. Adams, John C. Calhoun, Lewis Cass, Henry Clay, Thomas R. Dew, Andrew Donnally, Millard Fillmore, John Floyd, William H. Harrison, Andrew Jackson, the Ruffner family, Martin Van Buren, Daniel Webster, and Henry A. Wise.

878. Summers County. Archives, 1859-1949. 33 ft. Gift of the Summers County Court, 1954. Nos. 652, 655.

County court papers consisting mainly of marriage and financial administration records, including roads, schools, and poor funds. There are also estate administration and lunacy proceedings papers; tax books; school records; and an account book of the firm of Meador and Graham at Hinton.

879. Surveyor's Field Books. 1753, 1760-1765, 1848. 9 volumes. Transfer, 1951, 1953. No. 577.

Surveys of land in Preston County by I. A. Dalrymple and in several Virginia counties, including Frederick, Rockingham, and Shenandoah, part of which are now in West Virginia. Some of the latter surveys were made by Thomas Rutherford.

880. Sutton, John D. Diaries, 1792-1793, 1798. 2 items. Transfer. Nos. 430, 796.

Typescript copy of a diary concerning teaching and social life in the vicinity of Charleston and Dorchester, South Carolina, a journey by sea to Maryland, and travel by land to Alexandria, Virginia. Also an original diary, October-November, 1798, of a journey from New Market, Virginia, to the Elk River in western Virginia, by way of Strasburg, Staunton, Warm Springs, Lewisburg, and Charleston.

881. Sutton Brothers. Papers, 1897, 1899, 1921. 3 items. Gift of David D. Sutton, 1961. No. 1478.

Two letterheads of Sutton Brothers, contractors and oil producers, and an article on their development of gasoline.

882. Sweet Springs. Records, 1860-1927. 36 volumes. Gift of West Virginia Board of Control, 1952. No. 479.

Business records of the Sweet Springs Hotel, including journals, registers, departure books, inventories, and miscellaneous volumes.

883. Sydenstricker, O. P. Records, 1884-1886, 1888-1889, 1893-1894. 3 volumes. Gift of Emmet H. Crickenberger, 1957. No. 1005.

Three prescription books of O. P. Sydenstricker, a druggist in Lewisburg.

884. Tabler, Edward C. Typescript, 1955. Ca. 600p. Gift of Edward C. Tabler, 1956. No. 819.

Manuscript and page proofs of Edward C. Tabler's *The Far Interior; Chronicles of Pioneering in the Matabele and Mashonga Countries, 1847-1879* (Capetown, 1955).

885. **Talbott-Tolbert Family.** Papers, 1784-1914, 1931. 1 ft. Gift of Mrs. S. F. Talbott, 1957. No. 1026.

Mainly papers of Samuel T. Tolbert, a onetime constable of Lewis County and postmaster at Frenchton, who operated a general store and acted as agent and surveyor for out-of-state landowners. Included are the papers of Zadock Lanham, J. S. Wilson, and John L., Jacob, and W. C. Tolbert. There are surveys, legal papers, correspondence, and lottery certificates from Ohio and Delaware, and Democratic state and county election tickets.

Correspondents include Lewis Maxwell, J. M. Bennett, and F. H. Pierpont.

886. **Taverns.** Typescripts and pictures, ca. 1960. 1 notebook. Gift of Mrs. Innis C. Davis, 1964. No. 1793.

History and pictures of early taverns and inns along main roads in western Virginia between 1740 and the 1850s, written and compiled by Mrs. Innis C. Davis.

887. **Taylor, Gustavus Friend (1843-1915).** Scrapbook, 1862-1878. 1 volume. Gift of J. Holt Byrne, 1960. No. 1303.

Scrapbook of the editor of the Sutton *Mountaineer*, member of the Wheeling Convention, 1861, and the state legislature, 1867. Clippings consist of election returns for Braxton County and the nation; Taylor's editorials; letters to the editor; population statistics; and politics. A section of the volume consists of Taylor's record of visits to the county schools as County Superintendent of Free Schools, 1869, and a record of personal accounts.

888. **Taylor County.** Justice Docket, 1935-1937. 1 volume. Gift of William C. Lawson, 1962. No. 1575.

Civil docket of justices of the peace W. E. Rightmire and A. B. Knabenshue.

889. **Temple, Harry F.,** *Compiler.* 2 typescripts. Transfer, n.d. No. 431.

A typescript, "Women's Suffrage," written by Temple, and a copy of an 1801 apprenticeship indenture in Pendleton County.

890. **Tetrick, W. Guy,** *Compiler.* Records, ca. 1780-1950. 343 reels of microfilm. Originals in possession of Mrs. W. Guy Tetrick and Willis G. Tetrick, Jr., 1960. No. 1306.

Marriage, birth, and death records; wills; estate inventories and settlements from various West Virginia counties; Sons of the Revolution applications; Harrison County family records and obituaries, and obituary clippings for West Virginia.

891. **Thistle, Roy,** *Collector.* Papers, 1853-1934. Ca. 30 items (photocopies) and 1 reel of microfilm (1 volume). Originals in possession of Roy Thistle, 1961. No. 1443.

A scrapbook containing a brief history of Sistersville and the oil industry in Tyler and other counties and states; a stock certificate of the Sistersville & Salem Turnpike Company, 1853; bills of lading for Ohio and Muskingum River steamers, 1855-1934; and a list of steamboats operating on the Muskingum River, 1830-1890.

892. **Thompson, George Benjamin (1870-1957).** Tape recording, 1956. 2 items. Acquired, 1956. No. 877.

Recorded interview and transcript concerning genealogy, Tucker County history, and lumbering operations.

893. **Thompson, John and Robert.** Diaries, 1804-1811, 1862-1863. 2 volumes (photocopies). Loan for duplication by T. Leigh Thompson, 1966. No. 1881.

Diary and account book, 1804-1811, of John Thompson containing accounts of items bought and sold, money owed by and to Thompson, two journeys on the Mississippi River between Nashville, Natchez, and New Orleans in 1804 and 1805, and numerous remedies for diseases and medical complaints. There is a second diary by Robert C. Thompson, a Confederate soldier, from August, 1862, to February, 1863. Robert Thompson was a member of a Tennessee unit, was imprisoned at Camp Morton, was exchanged in September, 1862, and spent the remainder of the time covered by the diary with his reorganized company in Mississippi near Vicksburg.

Places mentioned include Camp Morton near Indianapolis, Indiana; Richmond, Virginia; Gallatin and Memphis, Tennessee; Cairo, Illinois; Columbus and Hickman, Kentucky; Vicksburg, Clinton, Jackson, Corinth, Holly Spring, Tippa Ford, and Oxford, Mississippi.

894. **Thorn, Macajah Anderson.** Letter, November 18, 1864. 1 item (photocopy). Loan for duplication by Gordon Thorn, 1971. No. 2210.

A letter written by Macajah Anderson Thorn, a Confederate soldier imprisoned at Camp Chase, Ohio, to his father, Gordon Cloyd Thorn.

895. **Tobacco Workers' Union.** Minutes, 1890-1905. 1 volume. Gift of Local 2, Tobacco Workers' Union of America, 1959. No. 1248.

Minute book of a Wheeling tobacco workers' local.

896. **Townsend, Thomas C.** Scrapbook, 1932. 1 reel of microfilm (1 volume). Originals in possession of Hillis Townsend, 1962. No. 1596.

Publicity file of T. C. Townsend covering his primary race for the Republican gubernatorial nomination and his subsequent race against the Democratic nominee, H. Guy Kump, in 1932. The scrapbook also contains some loose clippings pertaining to Townsend's support of the Dewey-Bricker presidential ticket in 1944.

897. **Trent, William W. (1878-1960).** Papers, 1896 (1933-1956). 6 ft. Gift of Mrs. Paul A. Burdette, 1960, 1961. Nos. 1381, 1448.

Correspondence, circular letters, clipping scrapbooks, news releases, and printed materials of the State Superintendent of Free Schools, 1933-1957. The collection includes Trent's college essays, reports of the Board of Public Works, and utility assessment hearings of the superintendent, 1933-1956.

898. **Tucker, Eldon, Jr.,** *Collector.* Papers, ca. 1833 (1953-1956). 2 ft. Gift of Eldon B. Tucker, Jr., 1958. No. 1061.

Newspaper clippings of obituaries, marriages, anniversaries, and historical items, 1953-1956, from various West Virginia towns; a manuscript and clipping notebook (ca. 1888-1947) primarily concerning Cumberland, Maryland, and an unidentified merchandise account book, 1833-1858.

899. **Tucker County.** Archives, 1853-1870. 2 ft. Gift of the Tucker County Court, 1939. No. 60.

Circuit and county court suit and other papers. Alphabetical, chronological, and subject indexes are available.

900. **Tucker County.** Records, 1909-1922. 51 items. Gift of Harrison Bennett, 1954. No. 675.

Records of the post office at Jenningston, 1909-1922, Frank G. Rice and John H. Babb, postmasters; and bound volumes of business records from Red Creek of the Elkins Lumber Company, J. C. Myers Lumber Company, and J. C. Myers Mercantile Company.

901. **Turner Family.** Papers, 1874-1906. Ca. 20 items. Gift of John W. Barger, 1957. No. 951.

Correspondence of members of the Turner family at Shinnston and Capon Bridge and issues of newspapers with Turner family and local history features.

902. **Tuttle, Virginia,** *Collector.* Papers, 1879-1913. 10 items. Gift of Mrs. Virginia Tuttle, 1965. No. 1865.

Manuscript record book of a Methodist Episcopal Sabbath School at Wolf Run, 1888-1893, 1898-1901, and Porter's Falls, 1894-1896; five books containing records of the Turkey Run Sunday School, 1898-1913; a price list book of the Latimer & Company, general mill suppliers, Philadelphia, 1884; an illustrated and descriptive book of James Lettel's improved "Double Turbine Water Wheel" for 1879-1880; and a Methodist Episcopal hymnal and a Methodist Discipline book, 1892.

903. **Twyman and Dickinson Families.** Papers, 1750-1911, 1822-1858. 37 items. Gift of John E. Stealey III, 1966. No. 1911.

Letters from the Twyman and Dickinson families concerning family matters and personalities in the salt industry. Other items include a specie circular, several summonses, and payment on demand notes. (RESTRICTED)

904. **Tygart Valley Homesteads.** Mimeograph, 1935. 1 item (photocopy). Original in possession of Mrs. Forest Bell, 1962. No. 1631.

Fact sheet entitled: "Facts about Tygart Valley Homestead, Elkins, West Virginia," a New Deal resettlement project of the Subsistence Homestead Division, Department of the Interior.

905. **Tyler, John (1790-1862).** Papers, 1739-1862, 1930s. Ca. 200 items. Gift of O. P. Chitwood, 1963. No. 1689.

Research notes and copies of the correspondence of John Tyler, collected by Oliver Perry Chitwood for his biography, *John Tyler, Cham-*

pion of the Old South (1939), from manuscripts in private collections and the New York Public Library, Huntington Library, and Duke University Library.

Correspondents include Duff Green.

906. **Tyler County.** Archives, ca. 1788-1933. 36 ft. Gift of the Tyler County Court, 1940. Nos. 433, 434.

Circuit and county court and other papers and dockets.

907. **Underwood Family.** Papers, ca. 1812-1861, 1964. 2 items (1 typescript copy). Gift of Edward N. Orr, 1965, and transfer, n.d. Nos. 436, 1807.

Charts showing the descendants of William Underwood (1780-1866) of Middlebourne, first sheriff of Tyler County, who include Cecil Highland Underwood (b. 1922), twenty-fifth governor of West Virginia; copies of scattered diary entries, ca. 1812-1861, by William Underwood, and his will.

908. **Union Carbide Corporation. Hawk's Nest Project.** Papers, 1873-1966. 7 ft. Gift of Homer A. Holt, 1966. No. 1916.

Correspondence, memoranda, drafts, briefs, exhibits, reports, and newspaper clippings on the Federal Power Commission's licensing of Union Carbide Corporation's Hawk's Nest and Glenn Ferris power dam projects. Subjects include FPC hearings, history of navigability of Kanawha River, efforts to dam the Kanawha River, the navigability of the New River, and the New-Kanawha Power Company.

Correspondents include H. G. Davis, Russell A. Alger, Homer A. Holt, Robert C. Byrd, and Jennings Randolph.

909. **United Association of Journeyman Plumbers.** Contract, 1916. 1 item. Gift of James Jordan, 1966. No. 1889.

Agreement between the Master Plumbers of Wheeling and vicinity, and Local Union No. 83, United Association of Journeymen Plumbers, Gas Fitters, and Steam Fitters of the United States and Canada, April 1, 1916.

910. **United Mine Workers of America.** Certificate, October 18, 1899. 1 item. Gift of Lawrence Downey, 1969. No. 2102.

Certificate of membership in Local No. 90 of the United Mine Workers at Watson.

911. **United Mine Workers of America.** Papers, 1969. Ca. 30 items. Gift of John Spears, 1970. No. 2126.

Material and campaign literature from the campaign of Elijah Wolford for the presidency of the union, 1969. Included is a letter from a campaign committee, the campaign platform, reprint of remarks by Congressman Ken Hechler in the United States House of Representatives, and a report on "Conspiracy in Coal" by T. N. Bethell.

912. **United States. Bureau of the Census.** Papers, 1830-1860, 1870-1880, 1890. 74 reels of microfilm. Originals in the National Archives, 1951, 1952, 1955, 1956. Nos. 263, 501, 756, 882.

Census population schedules for Virginia, 1830-1860, and for West Virginia, 1870-1880; and special schedules, 1890, enumerating Union veterans and widows of Union veterans of the Civil War.

913. **United States. Claim Agency.** Records, ca. 1862-1879, 1890. 2 ft. Acquired, 1961. No. 1456.

Records of a pension, bounty land, and bounty money agency in Orange, Massachusetts, operated by Damon E. Cheney, include the War of 1812 military service rosters of the Delaware, Ohio, Pennsylvania, Maryland, and Virginia militias; record of the Georgia and Florida militias in the Second Seminole War, 1835-1843; and an "Index to Militia in the Florida War; and the New York Militia, Northern Frontier Disturbance, 1837-8." Records are indexed. Other records include applications for bounty lands under the Act of March 3, 1855, and applications for invalid pensions under the Act of July 14, 1862.

914. **United States. District Court. District of Virginia.** Records, May 9, 1867-June 22, 1870. 1 reel of microfilm. Original in the Library of Congress, 1953. No. 1035.

Copyright records of the United States District Court of Virginia, May 9, 1867-June 22, 1870.

915. **United States. District Court. Western District of Virginia.** Records, 1843-1880. 2 volumes. Gift of Shirley Donnelly, 1952. No. 481.

Trial docket and minute book of the court in Charleston, 1843-1873; and an indexed fee book, 1843-1880.

916. **United States Leather Company.** Records, 1902-1906, 1940. 28 items. Gift of J. H. Schaefer, 1956. No. 864.

Legal papers of the United States Leather Company of Marlinton, including deeds for tannery sites in and around Marlinton, and tax receipts, letters, and property agreements.

917. **United States Ship** *West Virginia.* Papers, 1961-1963. Ca. 60 items. Gift of Alpha Phi Omega Service Fraternity, West Virginia University, 1967, and L. S. Hartley, 1968. Nos. 2005, 2026.

Letters, photographs, and newspaper clippings relating to the bringing of the mast of the World War II battleship, U.S.S. *West Virginia,* to the University campus; materials concerning the dedication of the bell of the World War I armored cruiser, U.S.S. *West Virginia,* including programs, invocations, newspaper clippings, an essay about the dedication, and a notebook containing correspondence, photographs, and the history of the ship.

918. **United States. Treasury Department.** Documents, 1816-1826. Ca. 30 items (photocopies). Originals in possession of Mrs. George P. Bohack, 1959. No. 1176.

Sight drafts on the Superintendent of Indian Trade by M. Irwin, United States factor, Green Bay, Wisconsin.

919. **Van Liere, E. J.,** *Collector.* Papers, 1836, 1865, 1901. 3 items. Gift of E. J. Van Liere, 1954. No. 620.

A prospectus of the *Richmond Medical Journal,* November 20, 1865; a fee bill of Dr. J. Schwinn, Wheeling, March 1, 1901, listing rates for various types of services; and a facsimile copy of the Philadelphia *Public Ledger,* March 26, 1836.

920. **Van Meter Family.** Papers, 1758 (1775-1889) 1926. Ca. 100 items. Transfer and gifts of Mrs. Hilda Van Metre, 1950, and Hampshire County Court, 1951. Nos. 189, 260, 569.

Business and personal papers of Isaac, Jacob, and James E. Van Meter in Hampshire and Hardy counties.

921. **Van Winkle, Peter Godwin (1808-1872).** Papers, 1827-1872. 1 ft. Gifts of Judge Lewis H. Tavenner, 1933; Julietta Camden, 1948; and Mrs. Ralph Wandling, 1949. Nos. 18, 136, 142.

Personal papers and clipping scrapbooks of a Parkersburg attorney who was a delegate to the Constitutional Convention of 1850-1851; a member of the Second Wheeling Convention, 1861; the Constitutional Convention of 1861-1862; a legislator from Wood County in 1863, and a participant in railroad and business enterprises in West Virginia.

The papers include a private journal, holographs of speeches and essays, and contributions to newspapers. Subjects include the West Virginia statehood movement, the Liberia Colonization Society, sale of railroad bonds, the Tyler administration, national currency, and politics. There are scrapbooks concerning the Northwestern Turnpike, politics, and the development of Parkersburg.

922. **Vandiver, J. W.** Records, 1877, 1907-1920. 12 items. Acquired, 1954. No. 688.

Business records of a dealer in agricultural implements at Burlington.

923. **Varnell, James N.** Papers, 1897-1935. Ca. 30 items. Gift of James N. Varnell, Jr., 1952. No. 478.

A scrapbook of clippings relating to the pastorate of the Reverend J. N. Varnell and other printed and pictorial items.

924. **Varner Family.** Papers, 1864-1940. 1 ft. Gift of B. R. Conrad, 1956. No. 891.

Letters written by various members of the Varner family in Gilmer County and Baltimore, Maryland, and a number of letters of S. W. Varner, a physician in Kingwood, relating to his medical practice.

925. **Virginia.** Records, 1623-1933. 733 reels of microfilm. Acquired from the Genealogical Society, Salt Lake City, Utah, 1959, 1960. Nos. 1240, 1246, 1257, 1293.

Deeds, wills and estate administration, marriages, and vital statistics; land office records, surveys, grants, warrants, and patents; tax lists, land and personal property; index to legislative petitions; Revolutionary War service and pension records; War of 1812 muster and payrolls; Confederate soldiers service records; Bible records, genealogical notes, family histories, Mott-Alston collection of colonial families, and church records. For a more detailed description, see index file to the Virginia Records filmed by the Genealogical Society.

926. **Virginia Debt Controversy.** Correspondence, 1888-1898. 7 items. Acquired, 1958. No. 1117.

Letters from Colonel R. P. Chew, R. B. Roosevelt, Jenkins Van Schaick, and George Pierce concerning Virginia deferred certificates and the attempt of the Council of Foreign Bondholders to force Virginia to redeem its tax coupons.

927. **Virginia Saline Bank.** Papers, 1814-1830, 1933. 4 items (photostat copies). Gift of H. E. Matheny, 1962. No. 1593.

Bank note; lottery ticket for the improvement of Clarksburg; title page of *Articles of Association of the Virginia Saline Bank* (Clarksburg, 1814); and a typescript copy of Boyd B. Stutler's article on the Virginia Saline Bank of Clarksburg, "Money is What You Make It," *West Virginia Review*, May, 1933.

928. **Virginia. University.** Papers, 1859-1860, 1866-1867. 1 notebook. Gift of Mrs. Montague Blundon, 1966. No. 1924.

Manuscript lecture notes for a course, "The National History of Greece," at the University of Virginia, November 4, 1859-March 2, 1860.

929. **Voegele, F. B.,** *Collector.* Papers, ca. 1877-1884, 1925-1940. Ca. 10 items. Gift of F. B. Voegele, 1958. Nos. 1088, 1102.

An autograph letter of Governor J. B. Jackson, 1884; an embossed state seal with the autograph signature of Governor Henry M. Mathews, ca. 1877-1881; a picture of Joseph H. Diss Debar; and articles dealing with the history of Virginia, West Virginia, and the Southern Seaboard. There are a few contemporary articles and obituary notices of West Virginians.

930. **Volcano.** Papers, 1857-1964. 1 reel of microfilm. Loan for duplication by Herman E. Matheny, 1965. No. 1800.

Material relating to Volcano, in Wood County, the center of a booming oil industry between 1865 and 1879. Wells were operated by the Stiles Oil Company, owned by William Cooper Stiles, Jr. The collection consists of articles, photographs, court proceedings, correspondence, and record books.

931. **Volga Community, Barbour County.** Manuscript, 1955. 47p. Acquired, 1955. No. 704.

Includes sketches of pioneer life, mentioning Jacob Reger, Joseph and Joel Martin, Sam Hughs, and others.

932. **Wade, Charles A. and Charles W.** Papers, ca. 1880-1940. 1 ft. Gift of W. W. Kelley, 1955. No. 765.

Correspondence and business papers of Charles A. Wade, a farmer in Burnsville, and of Charles W. Wade, a justice of the peace in Braxton County.

933. **Wade, George.** Pension certificate, September 5, 1834. Transfer, n.d. No. 439.

Certificate of Revolutionary service of a private from Monongalia County.

934. **Wallace, George Seldon (1871-1963).** Papers, 1898-1963. 9 ft. Gift of George S. Wallace, 1963. No. 1710.

Papers of a Huntington attorney, member of the West Virginia National Guard, 1909-1916, employee of the C. & O. Railway Company, president of the Union Bank and Trust Company of Huntington, president of the Ben Lomond Company, president of the Blackberry, Kentucky and West Virginia Coal and Coke Company, attorney for Central City, prosecuting attorney of Cabell County, 1905-1908, chairman of a county Democratic committee, a member of the state Democratic committee, and delegate to the National Convention, 1912.

Wallace served in the Spanish-American War and as judge advocate general in West Virginia during the coal strike in 1912-1913. During World War I he was a state draft executive, a major in the judge advocate general corps in Washington, and a lieutenant colonel in France. Subjects include the influenza epidemic of 1918, the depression of 1929-1932, state and national politics, and genealogy of the Wallace and allied families. The collection also includes three typescripts, "Runnymede Receipts," "Train Running for the Confederacy," and "Norborne Parish and St. George's Chapel," by Philip P. Gibson; Civil War data; an account of the taking of San Juan Hill in 1898; a military diary; a scrapbook of Cabell County court records; a speech against the League of Nations; and notes on a trip to Nice, ca. 1919.

Correspondents include John W. M. Appleton, Newton D. Baker, Henry Breckinridge, J. M. Callahan, W. G. Conley, Roy Bird Cook, John J. Cornwell, Innis C. Davis, John W. Davis, T. B. Davis, William E. Glasscock, Samuel Gompers, Wells Goodykoontz, Walter S. Hallanan, H. D. Hatfield, Thomas E. Hodges, H. G. Kump, W. A. MacCorkle, Ira E. Robinson, Howard Sutherland, W. W. Trent, C. W. Watson, and Woodrow Wilson.

935. **Wallace, Matthew.** Papers, 1860-1893. 128 items. Transfer, 1955. No. 781.

Papers of a physician of Mill Point, Pocahontas County, including accounts of a colleague, Dr. Larue. Also accounts of the carding firm of Barkley and Wallace, and the leather business of Wallace and McCarty.

936. **War of 1812.** Records, 1812-1814. 16 items. Transfer, 1955. No. 808.

Copies of regimental rosters and pension lists of Monongalia County militia in the Revolutionary War; and copies of regimental rosters of Virginia, Maryland, and Pennsylvania militias in the War of 1812.

937. **Ward, Evermont (1819-1882).** Typescript, 1947. 13p. Gift of Samuel Price, 1948. No. 127.

A copy of a speech on the life of Ward made by Col. George S. Wallace at a meeting of the Huntington Bar Association in 1947.

938. **Ward, Henry Dans.** Diary, 1843-1862. 1 reel of microfilm. Original owned by Charles Carpenter, 1958. No. 441.

A journal kept by Henry Dans Ward while rector of the St. John's and St. Luke's Episcopal churches in Charleston and Malden and as proprietor of a school in New York. From 1843 through 1857 there are notes on churches and social, economic, and political affairs in the Kanawha Valley. Accounts for school and household expenses in New York cover the years 1858-1862.

939. **Warder, Francis L.** Papers, 1934-1952. Ca. 100 items. Gift of Richard Bord, 1963. No. 1669.

Papers of a Grafton attorney, judge of the Ninth Judicial Circuit, and coal producer. Material includes papers of the Taylor County Democratic Executive Committee, 1934; Anna Jarvis' correspondence concerning her legal affairs in Taylor County; and records of coal production at the Warder mine, 1948-1952.

940. **Warder, William Wesley.** Papers, 1860-1863, 1869, 1939. 18 items (typescript copies). Transfer, 1962. No. 1633.

Correspondence and sketches of Warder and his wife, Evaline C. Farnsworth. The letters, written by Warder while a member of the First West Virginia Constitutional Convention, 1861-1863, pertain to the activities and proceedings of the convention.

941. **Ware, Anthony,** *Collector.* Papers, 1773-1886. 9 items. Gift of Mr. Ware, 1948. No. 125.

Invoices of ordnance stores at Mannington, 1862 and 1863; telegrams sent from or to Fairmont and Wheeling concerning troops and train movements in 1863; an 1810 letter from Albany, New York, requesting information about Daniel Loring of Belpre, Ohio; and newspaper facsimiles.

942. **Washington, George (1732-1799). Papers, 1750, 1773, 1774. 3 items (photocopies). Gift of Roy Bird Cook, 1959, and transfer, n.d. Nos. 442, 443, 1164.**

Photocopies of a survey for 400 acres made by Washington in 1750 in Frederick County; a survey for 587 acres on the Ohio River made by Thomas Lewis for Washington in 1773; and a statement of account from Washington to Colonel Stephen for Stephen's share of the cost of a survey by Washington.

943. **Washington and Ohio Railroad. Papers, 1871. 7 items. Transfer, 1961. No. 1536.**

Correspondence and legal papers concerning a $250,000 Mason County subscription to the railway company.

944. **Waterman, Joseph M. Typescripts, n.d. 2 volumes. Acquired, 1960. No. 1300.**

Manuscripts of *With Sword and Lancet: The Life of Brig. General Hugh Mercer—Patriot;* and an unpublished novel, "The Man from West Virginia," written by Joseph M. Waterman, a Parkersburg minister.

945. **Watson, Martha Dent (1837-1905). Diary, December 31, 1864-December 21, 1865. 1 item (photocopy). Loan for duplication by Mrs. Logan Carroll, 1965. No. 1798.**

Diary written in Fairmont by an unmarried daughter of Thomas Watson and Rebecca Haymond Watson. The youngest sister of James Otis Watson. Comments concern the Civil War, the Southern cause, Lincoln and his assassination, and the attitudes of Fairmont residents toward Southern sympathizers and returning Confederate soldiers.

946. **Watson Family. Papers, 1694 (1783-1953). 1 ft. and 1 reel of microfilm. Gift of James O. Watson, 1954; loan for duplication by Miss Lucy A. Sipe, 1967, and Marion County Historical Society, 1965. Nos. 601, 630, 1815, 1949.**

Correspondence, land papers, accounts, receipts, notes, wills, clippings, and other papers of a prominent Marion County family.

Subjects include business transactions in Harrison, Marion, Randolph, and Barbour counties; coal and iron mining; agriculture; schools; churches; social and economic conditions in Kentucky, Georgia, Louisiana, South Carolina, Missouri, Illinois, Iowa, California, Morgantown, Fairmont, and Wheeling; Ireland and European travel; westward migration, 1849; gold mining; slaves; genealogy of the Watson and Haymond families; strikes and labor meetings; conservation; politics; the Barrackville covered bridge; and the Beverly-Fairmont Turnpike.

Correspondents include Creed Haymond, Archbishop John Hughes, and Henry, James G., James O., Rebecca D., Thomas and Benjamin H. Watson. Other persons or firms mentioned include the Fairmont & Palatine Bridge Company; and W. C. Haymond.

947. **Webster County**. Archives, 1851-1951. 90 ft. and 12 reels of microfilm. Gift and loan of the County Court, 1955, 1959. Nos. 763, 1235.

Includes court cases, 1851-1949; marriage licenses, 1834-1930; county financial, and other records; articles of incorporation of boom and lumber companies; court order books (numbers 5-9), 1893-1910; and deed books (numbers 12-28), 1888-1910.

948. **Welshans, Harriet**. Sentiment book, 1845-1868. 1 volume. Acquired, 1963. No. 1699.

Sentiment book of a Shepherdstown girl.

949. **Welton Family**. Papers, 1770-1928. Ca. 200 items. Gift of A. A. Welton, 1955. No. 806.

Receipts and land records of two generations of the Weltons in Hampshire and Hardy counties, including papers of Job, Aaron, Archibald, and A. Archibald Welton. There is a Fairfax deed for eighty-four acres in Hampshire County in 1770, and a pocket diary of A. A. Welton for 1880-1881.

950. **West, Clarence**. Records, 1914-1918. 30 items. Gift of Barbara Drainer, 1970. No. 2162.

Bills and receipts of Clarence West, a grocery store operator in Grafton.

951. **West, Rufus A.**, *Collector*. Papers, 1774 (1830-1952). 4 ft. Gift of Mrs. C. F. Garrison, 1954, 1956. Nos. 576, 599, 821.

Manuscripts, printed and pictorial materials collected by Rufus A. West, a Morgantown antiquarian and faculty member of the College of Engineering, West Virginia University. In addition to personal papers relating to his teaching career, the Oak Grove Cemetery Association, and the Wesley Methodist Church in Morgantown, there are business records and papers, 1842-1875, of George M. Hagans in Morgantown; records of the Morgantown Female Academy, West Virginia Agricultural College, and West Virginia University; construction costs for the Kingwood and West Union Turnpike, 1855-1864; and papers dealing with real estate transactions in Illinois, Missouri, and West Virginia.

Many phases of nineteenth century West Virginia history are dealt with, although the papers are centered on Monongalia, Preston, and Taylor counties.

Names appearing in the correspondence and other papers include Thomas R. Dille, H. C. Greer, Hagans and Frum, Hagans and Spahr, Hagans, Lynch and Protzman, C. R. Huston, Elizabeth I. Moore, and Waitman T. Willey.

952. **West Virginia Agricultural College.** Document, February 7, 1867. 1 item (copy). Loan for duplication by Melvin Kahle, State Records Administrator, 1966. No. 1915.

Act from the handwritten journal of the legislature creating the West Virginia Agricultural College.

953. **West Virginia Association of Collegiate Registrars and Admissions Officers.** Records, 1953-1959. Ca. 200 items. Gift of Stanley Harris, 1962. No. 1621.

Minutes, annual reports, financial records, and other papers.

954. **West Virginia Association of Student Councils.** Minute book, 1934-1954. Gift of the Association, 1955. No. 749.

The association was formerly called the West Virginia Co-Government Association.

955. **West Virginia Centennial Commission.** Papers, 1956-1964. 2 ft. Gifts of J. Arthur Butcher, 1956, and Festus P. Summers, 1968. Nos. 909, 2050.

Correspondence, reports, financial records, and minutes of the West Virginia Centennial Commission from 1958 to 1964. The material consists primarily of correspondence and material collected by Festus P. Summers, a commission member. There are also letters of J. Arthur Butcher concerning appeals for preservation of historical materials.

956. **West Virginia Chamber of Commerce.** Papers, 1938-1968. 4 ft. Gift of the West Virginia Chamber of Commerce, 1969. No. 2074.

Correspondence, pamphlets, and newspaper clippings of chamber officers concerning business and economic subjects. Correspondents include Robert C. Byrd, Robert H. Mollohan, Cleveland M. Bailey, Arch A. Moore, and W. W. Barron.

957. **West Virginia College.** Diploma, 1873. 1 item. Gift of Madison V. Scott, 1962. No. 1568.

Diploma of John Benjamin Hardwicke granted by a Flemington, Taylor County, college sponsored by the Free Will Baptists of Ohio.

958. **West Virginia College and University Libraries.** Report, 1947. Mimeograph. Transfer, 1958. No. 1122.

"Statistics of West Virginia College and University Libraries, 1946-1947," compiled by W. P. Kellam, Librarian, West Virginia University.

959. **West Virginia. Commission on Constitutional Revision.** Records, 1957-1963. 3 ft. Gift of the West Virginia Commission on Constitutional Revision, 1964. No. 1743.

Correspondence, membership lists, drafts of revisions and new articles considered, procedures for the committee, reports to the governor, minutes of meetings, and press notices.

960. **West Virginia Commissioner of Agriculture.** Office files, 1934 (1945-1953). 9 ft. Gift of the West Virginia Department of Agriculture, 1961. No. 1499.

Office files and correspondence of James Blaine McLaughlin (1884-1955), commissioner of agriculture from 1933 to 1955.

Correspondents include Clinton Anderson, William Blizzard, Robert C. Byrd, John J. Cornwell, James A. Farley, Rush D. Holt, Harley M. Kilgore, Okey L. Patteson, Chapman Revercomb, and Harley O. Staggers.

961. **West Virginia. County Court Records.** Typescript, 1968. 16p. Gift of Edward M. Steel, Jr., 1968. No. 2031.

Research report, "Court Records of Ante-bellum Virginia as Sources for Historical Investigation," by Edward M. Steel with particular attention to the Brooke County Court records.

962. **West Virginia. Department of Mines.** Reports, 1916-1932. 113 reels of microfilm. Loan for duplication by the West Virginia Department of Mines and State Records Center, 1970. No. 2143.

Accident and inspection reports from the West Virginia Department of Mines, subdivided into fatal accidents, 1919-1932; nonfatal accidents, 1916-1932; minor accidents, 1919-1932; inspection reports, 1919-1927; sand mines and prosecutions, 1927-1932.

963. **West Virginia. Executive Department.** Journals, 1863-1904. 3 reels of microfilm (11 volumes). Originals in possession of West Virginia Board of Public Works, 1962. No. 1487.

Executive Journals, 1863-1890; Executive Minutes, 1863-1867, 1875; and Board of Public Works Records, 1863-1904.

964. **West Virginia. Executive Mansion.** Documents, 1893-1903. 19 items. Transfer, 1970. No. 2150.

Original documents, correspondence, leases, and deeds pertaining to the old executive mansion in Charleston.

965. **West Virginia Federation of Labor.** Papers, 1897-1959. 5 ft. Gift of the West Virginia Labor Federation, 1963. No. 1658.

Executive council minutes and proceedings, correspondence, and printed material of the state organization of the American Federation of Labor, founded in 1903. Papers include congressional correspondence, 1950-1957; correspondence of President E. A. Carter, 1949-1957; a few papers of H. M. Rogers, 1905-1959, and Frank W. Snyder, 1906-1911; records of the Parkersburg Central Trades and Labor Council, 1924-1942; and a typescript copy of the minutes of the Wheeling Typographical Union, No. 79, 1904-1907, 1921.

Correspondents include Cleveland M. Bailey, W. W. Barron, William M. Boyle, Jr., Paul M. Butler, Robert C. Byrd, John J. Cornwell, Marriner S. Eccles, William Green, Homer A. Holt, Rush D. Holt, Hubert H. Humphrey, Paul R. Hutchings, Elizabeth Kee, John Kee, Harley M. Kilgore, Herman Guy Kump, William C. Marland, George Meany, Robert H. Mollohan, Arch A. Moore, M. M. Neely, Okey L. Patteson, Jennings Randolph, Chapman Revercomb, Franklin D. Roosevelt, Jr., Joe L. Smith, Maurice J. Tobin, Cecil H. Underwood, and W. Willard Wirtz.

966. **West Virginia Folklore.** Papers, 1915-1926. 8 ft. Transfer, 1958. No. 883.

Correspondence and records of the West Virginia Folklore Society with clippings and songbooks collected by members, and manuscript and typescript copies of folktales and ballads collected by John Harrington Cox, some of which were used in his *Folk-songs of the South* (Cambridge, 1925).

967. **West Virginia. Governors' Papers, 1931-1964.** 31 ft. Transfer, State Records Center, 1967. No. 1977.

General correspondence and papers, 1931-1964, of Governors William G. Conley, Herman G. Kump, Homer A. Holt, Matthew M. Neely, Clarence W. Meadows, Okey L. Patteson, William C. Marland, Cecil H. Underwood, and William W. Barron. There is material on the "flower fund" for 1944. The correspondence of the Barron administration concerns mainly state employment applications. (RESTRICTED)

968. **West Virginia Heritage Bookshelf.** Typescripts, 1960. 2 items. Gift of Okey L. Patteson and E. G. Otey, 1960. No. 1370.

Remarks by Okey L. Patteson and E. G. Otey at the formal presentation of the West Virginia Heritage Bookshelf to the Mt. Hope High School and the Spanishburg High School.

969. **West Virginia Historic Records Survey, 1750-1939.** 96 ft. Gift of the West Virginia Historic Records Survey, 1936. No. 46.

Copies of records from each county in West Virginia. Included are registers of births, marriages, deaths, wills, estate settlements, and land records. Transcriptions of county and circuit court minute and order books are in the papers, as well as cemetery readings and registers; church record surveys; mimeographed calendars of the papers of West Virginia governors; and American Imprint Inventory slips of the holdings of several West Virginia libraries.

970. **West Virginia Historical Society.** Records, 1869-1881. 14 items. Transfer, 1953. Nos. 447, 575.

Correspondence and other materials, including notices of, and resolutions adopted at, the founders meeting at Morgantown, September 30, 1869.

971. **West Virginia History.** Papers, ca. 1748-1942. Ca. 200 items. Acquired, 1950. No. 183.

The manuscript items include commissions in the Third and Seventy-seventh Regiments of the Virginia Militia, 1821-1835, and letters of resignation, 1826-1834, a letter from Nathan Goff to Abijah Dolly concerning affairs at the state capitol, 1867; Hardy and Pendleton County deeds, 1826, 1829; and receipts for military supplies, 1864.

The typescripts and clippings relate mainly to Hampshire, Mineral, Randolph, Hardy, Grant, and Pendleton counties. There are biographical and genealogical extracts from family Bibles, obituaries, cemetery readings, and marriage records. Subjects of biographical sketches include John J. Cornwell, J. H. McNeill, and David H. Strother.

972. **West Virginia. Human Rights Commission.** Archives, 1961-1966. 3 ft. Gift of Thomas W. Gavett, chairman of the West Virginia Human Rights Commission, 1966. No. 1887.

Papers, 1961-1966, of Chairman Thomas W. Gavett of the West Virginia Human Rights Commission. Subjects include surveys of equal employment opportunities, newspaper clippings, material from the Kentucky Commission on Human Rights, correspondence regarding nondiscriminatory college applications for West Virginia institutions of higher learning, memoranda from the executive director to commission members, minutes of meetings, hearings, West Virginia Interracial Commission created by Governor M. M. Neely, West Virginia Advisory Commission to the U. S. Civil Rights Commission, statement to the West Virginia Board of Education from a committee of the West Virginia State NAACP on September 2, 1964, First Governors Conference on Human Rights in Charleston on December 16, 1965, special report on the New Year's Eve incident in Huntington on January 14, 1966, the special hearing at Lakin State Hospital on April 21, 1966, and the resignation of Howard McKinney.

Correspondents include Governor W. W. Barron, Rabbi Samuel Cooper, Paul Crabtree, Rev. C. Anderson Davis, Thomas W. Gavett, Ken Hechler, Senator Paul Kaufman, Paul A. Miller, Julius W. Singleton, and Governor H. C. Smith.

973. **West Virginia League of Municipalities.** Papers, 1935-1940, 1954-1968. 11 ft. and 1 reel of microfilm (2 mimeograph volumes). Originals in possession of the Bureau of Business Research, West Virginia University, 1959, and gift of West Virginia League of Municipalities, 1970. Nos. 1211, 2146.

Bulletins, reports, correspondence, and miscellaneous material. Subjects include state aid, the Tax Limitation Amendment, New Deal agencies, police education and training, and various municipal services and problems.

974. **West Virginia Library Association.** Records, 1914-1964. 4 ft. Gift of the West Virginia Library Association, 1955, 1964. Nos. 715, 721, 783, 786, 794, 832, 918, 931, 949, 980, 1012, 1090, 1124, 1151, 1153, 1442, 1530, 1643, 1709, 1778.

Correspondence, committee reports, treasurer's reports and records, executive board minutes, annual conference minutes, old constitutions and bylaws, membership records, financial records, and miscellaneous papers.

975. **West Virginia Library Commission.** Records, 1942-1963. 1 volume (photocopy), 1 reel of microfilm (2 volumes), and 7 items. Gift and loan of the West Virginia Library Commission, 1958, 1960, 1964. Nos. 1103, 1292, 1721.

Minutes, 1942-1958, of a state commission created in 1929 to promote minimum standards of public library service; a report of a library service survey of the Harrison, Randolph, and Upshur County library region, 1955-1956, by Kenneth E. Brown; and letters and reports.

976. **West Virginia-Maryland Boundary Line Survey.** Account, 1915. 1 item. Gift of Carleton C. Pierce, Jr., 1962. No. 1632.

State of West Virginia in account with Julius K. Monroe, engineer for the state in the case of *Maryland* v. *West Virginia*, Kingwood, May 18, 1915.

977. **West Virginia. Mining Investigation Commission.** Records, 1912-1913. 1 ft. Gift of R. G. Kelley, 1968. No. 2036.

Typescript copies of the proceedings of the West Virginia Mining Investigation Commission at Charleston in 1912 and the military commission at Pratt in 1913. The commissions were appointed by Governor William E. Glasscock to investigate conditions in the Cabin Creek and the Paint Creek coal fields. Included are military commission orders, newspaper excerpts from the Charleston *Labor Argus*, names of individuals appearing before both commissions, and extracts of speeches of persons involved, including five speeches of Mary "Mother" Jones.

978. **West Virginia Music Educators Association.** Minute books, 1925-1950. 3 volumes. Gift of Clifford Brown, 1962. No. 1599.

Prior to 1936 this association was the Music Section of the State Education Association.

979. **West Virginia Press Association.** Papers, August 23, 24, 1887. Ca. 20 items (copies). Gift of Francis P. Fisher, 1964. No. 1727.

Reproductions of clippings and photographs concerning the Seventeenth Annual Convention of the West Virginia Press Association held on August 23-24, 1887, at Berkeley Springs.

980. **West Virginia Pulp and Paper Company.** Papers, 1892-1939. 19 reels of microfilm. Loan for duplication by Kyle Neighbors, 1970. No. 2134.

Correspondence and business records while the company was operating near the present site of Cass. Subjects covered are the Blackwater Lumber Company, Condon-Lane Boom and Lumber Company, Chesapeake and Ohio Railroad, Greenbrier River, logging, lumber agents, Martin-Lane and Company, railroads, J. L. Rumbarger Lumber Company, R. M. Sutton Company, Stearns Manufacturing Company, Saint Lawrence Boom and Manufacturing Company, S. E. Slaymaker and Company, timberlands, West Spruce Lumber Company, and William Whitmer and Sons, Inc. Places mentioned include Greenbrier, Pocahontas, and Randolph counties; Green Bank, Horton, Cass, Piedmont, and Ronceverte; and Covington, Virginia.

Correspondents include Joseph K. Cass, T. B. Davis, H. G. Davis, S. B. Elkins, and P. I. Reed. (RESTRICTED)

981. **West Virginia Pulp and Paper Company.** Reports, 1920. 1 reel of microfilm. Originals lent by Roy B. Clarkson, 1958. No. 1051.

Two typescript reports on the company's timberlands in Pocahontas, Randolph and Webster counties, including two maps and four photographs on forestry and lumbering.

982. **West Virginia School of Banking.** Notebook, 1963. 1 item. Acquired, 1968. No. 2018.

Material from the West Virginia School of Banking held at Jackson's Mill, October 13-18, 1963.

983. **West Virginia. State Board of Centennial Managers.** Report, 1876. 1 item (photocopy). Original in possession of Mrs. Eva Margaret Carnes, 1963. No. 1640.

Report to the State Board of Centennial Managers by Matthew Fontaine Maury giving an account of the proceedings of the State Centennial Office from its inauguration in 1875 to October, 1876. The report is particularly concerned with the construction and operation of the West Virginia Exhibition Hall on the Centennial Grounds in Philadelphia.

984. **West Virginia State Board of Control.** Correspondence, 1909-1949. 102 ft. Transfer from State Records Center, 1967. No. 1976.

Correspondence of the West Virginia State Board of Control, which was responsible for all state correctional institutions, educational institutions, and hospitals from 1909 to 1949. Individuals serving on the three-man board at various times were John S. Lakin, J. W. Barnes, J. A. Chambers, J. S. Darst, Edgar B. Stewart, J. Z. Terrell, W. R. Thurmond, John B. White, and F. W. McCullough.

State institutions covered in the correspondence are the Bluefield State College; Berkley Springs Sanitarium; Berkley Springs Park; Concord State College; Colored Orphans Home; Colored Insane Asylum; Colored Old Folks Home; Denmar Sanitarium; Demonstration Packing Plant at Inwood; Droop Mountain Battlefield; Fairmont Emergency Hospital; Fairmont State College; Glenville State College; Gore Hospital; Industrial Home for Girls; Industrial Home for Colored Girls; Industrial School for Boys; Industrial Home for Colored Boys; Hopemont Sanitarium; Huntington State Hospital; Jackson's Mill 4-H Camp; Indian Mound Cemetery; Lakin State Hospital; Marshall College; McKendree Hospital; Medium Security Prison; Miner's Hospitals 1, 2, and 3; Pinecrest Sanitarium; New River State School; Potomac State College; Spencer State Hospital; Storer College; Reymann Memorial Farms; Andrew S. Rowan Memorial Home; Rutherford Sanitarium; School for the Deaf and Blind; School for the Colored Deaf and Blind; Shepherd College; Weston State Hospital; West Liberty State College; Welch Emergency Hospital; West Virginia Training School; West Virginia State College; West Virginia Tech; and West Virginia University.

Correspondents include Charles H. Ambler, R. A. Armstrong, Thurman Arnold, Cleveland M. Bailey, Charles Baker, J. J. Cornwell, Brooks Cottle, William M. O. Dawson, John W. Davis, W. E. Glasscock, Howard M. Gore, Denzil L. Gainer, C. Howard Hardesty, Henry D. Hatfield, Thomas E. Hodges, Homer A. Holt, Rush D. Holt, B. M. Laidley, E. F. Morgan, J. F. Marsh, C. W. Meadows, Robert H. Mollohan, Matthew M. Neely, Jennings Randolph, John D. Rockefeller II, A. M. Reese, D. B. Purinton, Frank B. Trotter, J. R. Turner, W. R. Thurmond, and I. C. White.

985. **West Virginia State Building Trades Council.** Archives, 1946-1957. 2 ft. Gift of the West Virginia State Building Trades Council, 1966. No. 1867.

Correspondence, resolutions, receipts, bills, invoices, and credentials, including material for conventions, 1946-1957, organizational campaign, 1948-1949, first annual legislative conference in West Virginia, 1957, and the fiftieth anniversary convention, 1957.

986. **West Virginia State Buildings.** Records, 1912 (1926-1931). 2 ft. Transfer, 1955. No. 711.

Blueprints, correspondence, contractors' accounts, photographs, and other papers for buildings at West Virginia University, Marshall College, Glenville State Normal School, West Liberty State Normal School, New River State School, and other institutions.

987. **West Virginia State Dental Society.** Records, 1900-1958. 1 ft. Gift of the West Virginia State Dental Society, 1950, 1952, 1954, 1958, 1959. Nos. 179, 500, 506, 563, 766, 1101, 1141, 1185.

Correspondence, official records, transactions, reports of examination, press clippings, *West Virginia Dental Journal,* and a typescript, "A History of Dentistry in West Virginia, 1907-1952," by William Patrick Turner, Jr. (unpublished M.A. thesis, West Virginia University, 1962).

988. **West Virginia State Industrial Union Council, CIO.** Archives, 1939-1951. 21 ft. Gift of the West Virginia Labor Federation, AFL-CIO, 1960, 1961. Nos. 1380, 1449.

Correspondence, legal papers, reports, and printed material of the state CIO organization founded in 1937.

Subjects include the trade unions and councils allied with the Industrial Union Council; IUC state conventions; the activities of the CIO Political Action Committee at the state and national levels; congressional and presidential elections, 1940-1950; state and national labor legislation, particularly the anti-poll tax bill, fair employment practices legislation, and the Taft-Hartley Act; organizing activities including the Steel Workers' Organizing Committee, and the CIO Southern Drive Committee; national defense and wartime agencies such as the War Production Board, War Labor Board, Wage Stabilization Board, Office of Price Administration, and the War Manpower Commission; New Deal projects including the Works Progress Administration, and the Red House Homestead project at Eleanor (Red House); labor mediation and arbitration; the National Labor Relations Board; West Virginia Co-operative Labor Legislative Council; Labor's Non-Partisan League; organizational disputes between the AFL and the CIO, particularly in the communications and chemical industries; Interracial Council; crippled children's work; and the National CIO Community Services Committee.

Correspondents include Cleveland Bailey, Van A. Bittner, Chester Bowles, James B. Carey, Jonathan Daniels, D. Boone Dawson, Andrew Edmiston, Raymond J. Funkhouser, Sidney H. Hillman, George W. Johnson, Louis Johnson, Elizabeth Kee, John Kee, Harley Kilgore, James M. Landis, David J. MacDonald, Clarence W. Meadows, Philip Murray, M. M. Neely, Okey L. Patteson, Jennings Randolph, Eleanor Roosevelt, Joe L. Smith, and Harley O. Staggers.

989. **West Virginia State Newspaper Council.** Records, 1924-1953. Ca. 200 items. Gift of the West Virginia Press Association, 1959. No. 1187.

Proceedings, minutes, and papers of the West Virginia State Newspaper Council from its formation in 1924. The collection also concerns the annual West Virginia Journalism Conference sponsored by the Council and the West Virginia University School of Journalism.

990. **West Virginia. State Treasurer.** Records, 1861-1867. 1 reel of microfilm. Original volumes in the State Treasurer's office, 1955. No. 761.

A ledger, 1861-1863, and a volume of receipts for certificates, 1861-1867, of the Reorganized Government of Virginia at Wheeling and the state of West Virginia.

991. **West Virginia Statehood.** Papers, 1861. 1 reel of microfilm. Originals in possession of the Library of Congress, 1961. No. 1435.

Selected correspondence from the Salmon P. Chase and Orlando M. Poe papers include two letters from John S. Carlile of Clarksburg requesting the removal of General William S. Rosecrans and more troops from the western Virginia theater; a letter from Governor Francis H. Pierpont concerning a loan of $200,000 for the Reorganized Government of Virginia; a letter from K. V. Whaley concerning the effectiveness of Northern arms shipped to the Ceredo area; and letters from Poe, an aide to McClellan, to his wife pertaining to the fighting in the Tygarts Valley and at Rich Mountain.

992. **West Virginia University.** Archives, 1867-1972. Ca. 430 ft. Transfers, 1936-1972.

Correspondence and records from the president's office; the office of the registrar; the comptroller's office; various schools, colleges, and departments; governing boards; official observances and commencements; news and information releases; faculty and student associations and organizations; special committees and councils; and miscellaneous material. (RESTRICTED)

993. **West Virginia Vital Statistics.** Records, ca. 1853-1862. 10 reels of microfilm. Gift of the Genealogical Society of Utah, 1957. No. 968.

Birth, death, and marriage records from fifty West Virginia counties, copied from originals in the Virginia State Library, Richmond.

994. **West Virginia Volunteer Infantry.** Records, 1898. 4 items. Gift of Mrs. Durward B. Brown, 1956. No. 861.

Rosters and clippings on Company M, First Regiment.

995. **Weston State Hospital.** Records, 1860-1893. 5 ft. and 1 reel of microfilm. Gifts of Charles Williams,

1970, and Richard H. Ralston, 1971. Nos. 2125, 2193.

Business records for the Weston State Hospital (formerly the Lunatic Asylum at Weston) for the mentally ill, concerning the purchase of supplies, listing of employees, and statistics on the operation of the facility.

996. **Wetzel County.** Archives, 1846-1872. 30 reels of microfilm. Gifts of the Wetzel County Court, 1940, and the Church of the Latter Day Saints. No. 455.

Court case papers and record books, 1846-1872. See Mormon microfilm index.

997. **Wetzel County. Cemetery Readings.** Records, 1959. 10 items. Gift of Mrs. C. F. Foster, 1959. No. 1261.

Tombstone readings from the Pursley Church, Beaver Run, and Old Wayman cemeteries located near Proctor, Wetzel County, and incidental data on the Peter Lehew family.

998. **Wheeling Convention, Second.** Document, 1861. 1 item (photostat copy). Original in the National Archives, 1961. No. 1453.

"A Declaration of the People of Virginia Represented in Convention at the City of Wheeling Thursday, June 13th, 1861," drafted as a protest against the action of the Secession Convention at Richmond and to demand the reorganization of the Commonwealth.

999. **Wheeling. Schools.** Papers, 1831. 2 photostats. Transfer, n.d. No. 195.

Petition of Ohio County physicians and others praying for the establishment of a medical school in western Virginia; and a memorial regarding the establishment of the school at Wheeling.

1000. **White, Albert Blakeslee (1856-1941).** Papers, 1888-1929. 20 ft. Gift of Mrs. William Wolfe, 1946, 1951. Nos. 110, 252, 300.

Business, political, and official correspondence of the eleventh governor, 1901-1905, of West Virginia. Owner and editor of the *State Journal*, Parkersburg, 1881-1899, White was associated with many banking and manufacturing enterprises, and was tax commissioner of West Virginia in 1907 and 1908, collector of internal revenues in 1889, 1897, and 1921, and a Republican member of the legislature in 1926.

Among the correspondents are G. W. Atkinson, Waitman T. Barbe, Calvin Coolidge, John J. Cornwell, H. G. Davis, Thomas B. Davis, W. M.

O. Dawson, Alston G. Dayton, Davis Elkins, Stephen B. Elkins, Guy D. Goff, Howard M. Gore, M. A. Hanna, Henry D. Hatfield, William McKinley, A. W. Mellon, E. F. Morgan, H. C. Ogden, N. B. Scott, Hugh I. Shott, Joseph P. Smith, George C. Sturgiss, and I. C. White.

1001. **White, Henry Solomon.** Papers, 1861-1865. Ca. 200p. (photocopies). Loan for duplication by the Clarksburg Public Library, 1964. No. 1732.

The manuscript diary of Henry Solomon White, a Corporal and Orderly Sergeant in Company N, Sixth Regiment, [West] Virginia Volunteer Infantry, covering the period of September 24, 1861 to September 26, 1864. Company N was organized at Camp White, in 1861 for a three-year tour of duty guarding the B. & O. and North Western railroads. The company was stationed at various times at Burton, Littleton, Barrackville, Fairmont, Clarksburg, Bridgeport, Grafton, and Webster. Squads of this company were detailed for special duty and scouting detail to Cornwallis, Ritchie County; Camp Burne; Camp Wilkinson; and in Monongalia, Marion, and Roane counties; and Fayette and Greene counties, Pennsylvania.

Company N was on duty in Fairmont during the Jones Raid in 1863. The diary records the activities of the company, comments on Confederate sympathies and activities of various citizens; the Ringgold Raiders; and Confederate scout, John Righter.

1002. **White, Israel C. (1847-1927).** Papers, 1867-1941. 30 ft. Gift of the estate of I. C. White, 1955, and transfer, 1955. Nos. 469, 710, 797.

Personal and business papers of a Morgantown geologist relating to his career as assistant geologist, Pennsylvania Geological Survey, 1876-1883; professor of geology at West Virginia University, 1877-1892; and state geologist of West Virginia, 1897-1927. There are some materials bearing on White's participation in geological congresses in St. Petersburg, Russia, 1897, and in Paris, France, 1900; and correspondence and notes, 1904-1906, concerning White's activities as chief of the Brazilian Coal Commission.

1003. **White, Kemble (1873-1965).** Papers, 1898-1965. 3 ft. Acquired, 1957, and gift of Mr. and Mrs. John S. Ewing, 1971. Nos. 940, 2209.

Papers of a lawyer, specialist in oil and gas law, representative for the West Virginia subsidiaries of Standard Oil (Hope Natural Gas, South Penn Oil, and Eureka Pipeline), veteran of the Spanish-American War, and onetime president of the West Virginia Bar Association.

Subjects include oil, gas, and coal lands; land titles and leases; Fairmont Coal and Coke Company; Twin Mountain Orchards; Monongahela

Valley Traction Company; Twin Mountain and Potomac Railroad; West Virginia political campaigns; and constitutional revision in West Virginia.

Correspondents include Luther Anderson, Carl G. Bachman, Fred Blue, John C. Bond, Linn Brannon, William E. Chilton, J. J. Cornwell, J. S. Darst, Wells Goodykoontz, Howard M. Gore, J. W. Harman, John H. Hatcher, Henry D. Hatfield, Frank C. Haymond, Rush D. Holt, Guy Kump, Howard B. Lee, M. M. Neely, Okey L. Patteson, William H. Sawyers, E. B. Stephenson, Robert Taft, and L. Judson Williams.

Additional items include newspaper clippings, White's West Virginia University student notebooks, correspondence and pamphlets dealing with Mrs. White's gardening activities, White's proposals for constitutional revisions, two diaries (ca. 1868), a Spanish-American War muster roll for Company M, Second West Virginia Volunteers, and a taped interview with Captain White in Clarksburg, covering family history and his career as an attorney.

1004. **White, Mary (1791-1878).** Typescript, 21p. Gift of Virginia White Breakiron, 1940. No. 75.

Autobiographical sketch of the life of Mary White, mother of I. C. White, centered in Monongalia County.

1005. **White Sulphur Springs Company.** Records, 1816-1914. 8 volumes. Deposited by White Sulphur Springs Company, 1963. No. 1656.

Records of the Old White Sulphur Springs Hotel (now the Greenbrier Hotel) include ledgers for 1816 and 1827, an account book, 1830-1831, and guest registers for 1896, 1898, 1910, 1911, and 1913-1914.

These records have entries for many prominent nineteenth century Americans including Henry Clay, Stephen Decatur, John Tyler, John Floyd, and General John Preston.

1006. **Whitmer, William and Sons, Inc.** Minute book, 1895-1924. 1 reel of microfilm (1 volume). Original in possession of Fred J. Overly, 1960. No. 1317.

Minute book of a West Virginia lumber corporation with mills and timberlands in the Tucker County area.

1007. **Wiley, Samuel T. (1850-1905).** Papers, 1872-1905. 1 ft. Gifts of Miss Sara Leosa Wiley, 1955, and Mrs. Earl Wiley as a memorial to Samuel T. Wiley, 1965, 1966. Nos. 735, 1842.

Letters, notebooks, scrapbooks, diaries, manuscripts, and memorabilia of a secondary schoolteacher in Fayette County, Pennsylvania, and

Preston County, and an author and local historian of Preston and Monongalia counties. The collection includes notes on history, orthography, new method arithmetic, two teachers report books of 1872-1885 and 1879-1880, teachers' certificates, membership certificates in the Masons and the International Order of Odd Fellows, a Wiley family genealogy, manuscripts on slavery, Odd Fellowship, public schools, after-dinner speeches, history of the United States, short stories, assorted sayings and aphorisms, notes for a history of Fayette County, Pennsylvania, a biographical sketch of Wiley and copies from his diaries and works, photographs of the Wiley family, and an autograph book and information on Monongahela College at Jefferson, Pennsylvania.

1008. **Wilkin, James R.,** *Collector.* Papers, 1828-1957. 9 ft. Acquired, 1957. No. 987.

Printed and manuscript miscellany relating to West Virginia state and local history, with emphasis on the Northern Panhandle. There are 110 folders of newspaper clippings, ca. 1880-1950; photographs and picture postcards; and a minute book of the 163rd Regiment, Virginia Militia, Hancock County, 1861-1865.

1009. **Willcox, Luke (1795-1854).** Diary, 1843-1854. 1 reel of microfilm (3 volumes). Loan for duplication by Mrs. Mattie S. Price, 1968. No. 2015.

Diary of Luke Willcox, a Kanawha County farmer, merchant, salt well and furnace owner and operator, written in memorandum form except for scattered entries giving more information on specific subjects. Subjects include weather observations, churches and ministers, farm operation information, travel, comment on salt well and furnace operation, slaves, names of personal and business correspondents, coal, and land purchases. Detailed lists of correspondents and subjects are available.

1010. **Willey, Waitman T. (1811-1900).** Papers, 1830-1900. 8 ft. Gift of Miss Lily Hagans, 1930, and Miss Judy Flenniken, 1960. Nos. 3, 1361.

Papers of one of the founders of West Virginia. Included are a two-volume diary and several thousand pieces of correspondence concerning political, social, and economic affairs for the period 1830-1900. Willey, a resident of Monongalia County, was a delegate to the Constitutional Convention of 1850, the Secession Convention of 1861, the First Wheeling Convention, and the Constitutional Convention of 1871. He was United States senator from the Restored Government of Virginia, 1861-1863, and senator from West Virginia, 1863-1871. There is much material on the temperance movement in Virginia, 1845-1860, the Civil War, and the statehood movement in West Virginia.

Correspondents include Gordon Battelle, Arthur I. Boreman, Gideon D. Camden, Archibald W. Campbell, John S. Carlile, John J. Davis,

Spencer Dayton, Nathan Goff, J. Marshall Hagans, Granville D. Hall, Alpheus F. Haymond, John J. Jackson, John L. Pendleton, Francis H. Pierpont, Edwin M. Stanton, George W. Summers, Peter G. Van Winkle, Alexander L. Wade, and James O. Watson.

1011. **Willey, William P.** 1 item. Transfer, 1955. No. 702.
Indexed bound clippings from a Bible, illustrating promises of the New Testament, compiled by Willey.

1012. **Williams, Charles R.,** *Collector.* Papers, 1834, 1851-1905. 33 items. Gift of Charles R. Williams, 1969. No. 2108.
Letter, 1851, from Harriet Burdett, Pruntytown, to Rebecca Coplin; an account book, 1859-1863, owner unidentified; steamboat bills of lading for the steamers *Kathryn* and *French* of the Little Kanawha Packet Line, 1899 and 1905; and an unissued stock certificate for the South West Production Company. Complete list of subjects, correspondents, and persons mentioned is available.

1013. **Willis, Dennis M.** Scrapbook, 1925-1929. 1 volume. Gift of Mrs. D. M. Willis, 1965. No. 1816.
Scrapbook of State Senator Dennis M. Willis, who represented Monongalia County from 1925-1929. The material covers state political and economic questions.

1014. **Willis, Captain Edward J.** Papers, 1863-1887. 22 items (photocopies). Gift of Mrs. William F. Hanks, 1967, originals in the National Archives. No. 1990.
Civil War records of Captain Edward J. Willis, co-commander of the Fifteenth Virginia Infantry Regiment of the Confederate States Army. Included are Willis' report of the battle of Sharpsburg, September 23, 1862, and his resignation, February 10, 1864.

1015. **Wilson, David L.** Papers, 1853-1899. 88 items. Gift of Mrs. H. D. Kuhn, 1955. No. 807.
Letters and business records of the mercantile establishment of David L. Wilson in Moorefield.

1016. **Wilson, Minter L. (d. 1968).** Papers, 1920-1944. 1 ft. Gift of Mrs. Sarah Eloise Wilson, 1968. No. 2064.
Eight volumes of copies and original speeches and legal opinions of Minter L. Wilson, lawyer and judge of the Seventeenth Judicial Circuit, Monongalia County, 1937-1945.

1017. **Wilson, Nathaniel V.** Correspondence, 1834-1850. 10 items. Gift of Mrs. C. C. Pierce, 1952. No. 509.

Letters to Wilson at Farmville, Virginia, and Charleston, West Virginia, from members of his family at the University of Virginia; Lewisburg, West Virginia; Philadelphia, Pennsylvania; and Clarksville, Virginia. Mention is made of family business affairs, the Ruffner-Donnally salt works at Charleston, purchase of slaves, and medical education in Philadelphia, Pennsylvania, in 1836 and 1844.

1018. **Wilson, William Lyne (1843-1900).** Papers, 1862-1900. 2 ft. and 13 reels of microfilm. Deposited by Festus P. Summers. Originals in possession of William L. Wilson II, Phillip P. Chase, Houghton Library, Library of Congress, Massachusetts Historical Society, and the Southern Historical Collection (University of North Carolina), 1963, 1964, 1970. No. 1694. (Restricted)

Correspondence, diaries, writings, newspaper clippings, and miscellaneous papers of Wilson, a private in the Twelfth Virginia Cavalry (Confederate), President of West Virginia University, 1882-1883, member of Congress, 1883-1895, Postmaster General, 1895-1897, author of the Wilson-Gorman Tariff, 1894, and President of Washington and Lee University, 1897-1900.

The collection includes portions of the diaries covering the years 1862-1863, 1865, 1868-1870, 1877-1891, 1896-1899. Most of the correspondence pertains to Wilson's career as Congressman and Postmaster General and his acceptance of the presidency of Washington and Lee University. Subjects include the tariff, the currency and bimetalism controversy, West Virginia state politics, the income tax, and foreign affairs. There is also a memorandum by Dr. Arthur L. Wilson, July 19, 1937, containing recollections of his father, "William Lyne Wilson."

Correspondents include Edward Atkinson, Waitman T. Barbe, William C. P. Breckenridge, James Bryce, Johnson N. Camden, John G. Carlisle, W. Bourke Cockran, John Warwick Daniel, William M. O. Dawson, W. E. Dodge, Charles W. Eliot, Charles J. Faulkner, Daniel Coit Gilman, Wade Hampton, Judson Harmon, Abram S. Hewitt, David B. Hill, Daniel S. Lamont, Samuel P. Langley, Fitzhugh Lee, Daniel Lucas, John Bassett Moore, Thomas Nelson Page, Walter Hines Page, Josiah Quincy, William E. Russell, Isidor Straus, Eli Thayer, William P. Thompson, William Vilas, Henry St. George Tucker, Andrew White, and Horace White.

In addition to the Wilson writings, the collection includes photocopied material collected by Wilson's biographer, Festus P. Summers. This material includes Wilson's writings and speeches from the *St. Louis Republic, New York Tribune, Harper's Weekly*, Baltimore *Sun*, and other newspapers and magazines; material pertaining to Wilson's presidency of West Virginia and Washington and Lee universities; photographs and political cartoons; and letters from the papers of Edward Atkinson, William C. P. Breckenridge, H. S. Carruth (Norcross Collection), Daniel S. Lamont, Manton Marble, William S. Russell, Carl Schurz, Isidor Straus, John Randolph Tucker and Henry Villard. Correspondents in these collections include Edward Atkinson, R. R. Bowker, C. R. and William C. P. Breckenridge, John G. Carlisle, Grover Cleveland, Worthington C. Ford, David B. Hill, James J. Hill, Collis P. Huntington, William A. MacCorkle, Charles Nordhoff, William E. Russell, Isidor Straus, Oscar Straus, and David A. Wells.

1019.   **Wilson and Stribling Families.** Papers, ca. 1781-1934. 1 ft. Gift of Mr. Otis Young, 1956. No. 880.

Correspondence, clippings, land papers, and other records of James Wilson, an attorney in Wood County, ca. 1800-1820; Robert M. Stribling and other members of this family in Mason County, 1821-ca. 1909; and James A. and Otis Young, ca. 1900-1934, in Mason County. A pocket diary of James Wilson gives information on his law practice in Kanawha, Monongalia, and Wood counties in 1804.

1020.   **Wilson-Lewis Family.** Papers, 1774, 1829-1942. Ca. 200 items (photocopies). Loan for duplication by Mrs. Frank Payne Lewis, Jr., 1970. No. 2135.

Papers relating to the Wilson, Lewis, and Ruffner families of Prince Edward County, Virginia, Kanawha County, [West] Virginia, St. Charles County, Missouri, and Fairfield County, Ohio. Correspondence between Nathaniel V. Wilson and Dr. Goodridge Wilson, concerning land purchases, preparation for the settlement of the family, care of livestock, employment of slaves, salt making and marketing, and the market price of salt. Other members of the family migrated to St. Charles County, Missouri, and to Fairfield County, Ohio, and land prices, suitable crops, settlement, and railroad building in Missouri comprise much of their correspondence. A third generation member of the family, Virgy Wilson Hall and her husband, John G. Hall, were missionaries in Matamoras, Mexico, and Colombia, South America, and her correspondence with her mother comments on living conditions, progress of the missionary work, revolution in Colombia, and health and living conditions of the residents of the Barranquilla area.

In addition there is a will of Col. Charles Lewis, a series of letters between two doctors concerning health problems and treatment of various illnesses, and two diaries by Mrs. Daniel Ruffner, 1846, and Elizabeth Ruffner Wilson, 1871-1872, commenting on family life and community activities in Fairfield County, Ohio, and Kanawha County, [West] Virginia.

1021. **Winding Gulf Coals, Inc.** Records, 1888-1950. 20 ft. Gift of Winding Gulf Coals, Inc., 1961. No. 1525.
Ledgers, journals, and cashbooks of the Goodwill Coal and Coke Company, the Greenbrier Coal and Coke Company, the Gulf Coal Company, the Louisville Coal and Coke Company, the Lynwin Coal Company, the Superior Pocahontas Coal Company, the Winding Gulf Coal and Coke Company, and the Winding Gulf Colliery Company. A few volumes pertain to the operation of company stores.

1022. **Winding Gulf Colliery Company.** Correspondence, 1911-1915. 1 ft. Gift of Winding Gulf Coals, Inc., 1966. No. 1897.
Correspondence between the managers of mines at Winding Gulf and Davy. Subjects include production levels of the various mines; demand for coal; availability of railroad cars and freight rates; New River and Pocahontas Operators Organization; financing mine development; operation difficulties and equipment failures; quality of Winding Gulf coal; problems with water in mines; employment of minors in mines; shortage of labor; working conditions of miners; German "socialists" at Mabscott; Mabscott mine strike; Bottom Creek mine explosion at Vivian; law suit; Justice Collins and the United Mine Workers; 1915 agreement made by New River and Winding Gulf operators with the United Mine Workers of America; and the good roads movement in Raleigh County, 1915.
Correspondents include Justus Collins, A. M. Herndon, George W. Stevens, J. A. Renahan, and George Wolfe.

1023. **Window Glass Workers' Unions.** Records, 1886-1920. 72 items. Gift of Miss Vera E. Jones, 1954. No. 683.
Union materials collected by William J. Jones of Morgantown, including bylaws, constitutions, convention proceedings, and letters.

1024. **Winifrede Mining and Manufacturing Company.** Documents, 1854. 3 items. Transfer, 1961. No. 1526.
Two writs of supersedeas and an opinion of counsel in the case of *Dickinson et als.* vs. *Winifrede Mining and Manufacturing Company*, a coal mining corporation chartered in 1850 and operating in Kanawha and adjoining counties.

1025. **Winter, John E.** Papers, 1906-1958. 3 ft. Gift of J. Lawrence Winter, 1959. No. 1230.
Office and academic papers of a former head of the Psychology Department, West Virginia University. The papers include his college notebooks, lecture notes, class outlines, speeches, reprints, and material

relating to his study of the cardio-pneumosphygmograph, and the psychology of faith healing, mesmerism, and spiritualism.

1026. **Wintz, William D.**, *Collector.* Papers, 1789-1960. 9 items. Gift of William D. Wintz, 1971. No. 2214.

A survey for a plot of land in Greenbrier County dated 1789, a map showing coal fields in the Kanawha Valley dated 1867, genealogies of the Chapman and McGlathlen families, and letters from M. M. Neely, Arthur Capper, and Walter F. George.

1027. **Withers and VanDevender.** Papers, 1899-1951. 5 ft. Acquired, 1969. No. 2109.

Correspondence, ledger books, account and cashbooks of the Parkersburg firm of Withers and VanDevender (later Wiant and VanDevender), specializing in timber cutting, but also dealing in real estate, coal, oil, and orange growing. Subjects include timber cutting methods, costs, timber shipping, floods, freezes, droughts, log jams, timberland locations, timber purchases and sales, salaries of timber workers, and fruit groves in Florida. Counties mentioned include: Boone, Braxton, Calhoun, Gilmer, Lewis, Marshall, Mercer, Nicholas, Ritchie, Roane, and Wirt. Firms and corporations mentioned include the Copen Creek Coal Company, Gilmer Fuel Company, MCCAA Coal Company, Marietta Chair Company, Nixolette Lumber Company, and the Parkersburg Mill Company.

1028. **Wood, Oscar.** Typescripts, 1960-1961. 3 volumes. Gift of Oscar Wood, 1960, 1961. Nos. 1350, 1481.

Verse composed by a retired Morgantown glassworker whose subject is the Monongalia County area, its scenery, life, labor, and culture.

1029. **Wood and Ritchie Counties.** Manuscript, ca. 1859-1879. 50p. Transfer, 1951. No. 271.

Manuscript of an address, "Oil Field of Wood and Ritchie," prepared for the West Virginia State Historical Society by Dr. W. H. Sharp, Volcano.

1030. **Wood County.** Archives, 1785-1935. 125 ft. Gift of the Circuit Clerk of Wood County, 1940. No. 458.

Records from the offices of the circuit clerk and county clerk.

1031. **Wood County.** Records, September 1-December 12, 1845. 1 item. Transfer, 1964. No. 1752.

Transcript of a trial in the circuit superior court of Wood County and appeal to the General Court of Virginia concerning citizens of Ohio who were arrested in Ohio by Virginia authorities while helping slaves escape from Virginia.

1032. **Woodbridge-Blennerhassett.** Papers, 1797-1818, 1935, n.d. 1 reel of microfilm. Typescript copies in possession of Mrs. Josephine Phillips (originals in possession of the Ohio Historical Society), 1961. No. 1459.

Correspondence and financial records of the firm of Dudley Woodbridge and Company of Marietta, Ohio, pertaining to Woodbridge's partnership with Harman Blennerhassett.

Subjects include early Ohio River trade, transportation, and markets; Blennerhassett's financial misfortunes; the Burr conspiracy; and family and social affairs. Included in the collection are extracts from the Silas Brown letters in the Library of Congress relating to the Burr Conspiracy; and an unpublished manuscript by Josephine Phillips, "The Blennerhassett-Woodbridge Partnership: An Experiment in Chain Store Operation, 1798-1806."

1033. **Woodbridge Mercantile Company.** Records, 1788-1870. 10 ft. Acquired, 1961. No. 1455.

Letter and account books, clipping scrapbooks, and miscellaneous family papers of a pioneer Ohio Valley general merchandise firm founded by Dudley Woodbridge, Sr., at Marietta, Ohio, and operating under various names for a period of more than sixty years. The collection also includes the account books of Daniel, Richard, and John Greene, 1808-1844; account books of F. B. Loomis, 1842-1844; a medicinal formulary book; the estate records of John Brody; records of a pension and bounty land claims agency operated by George M. Woodbridge, 1861-1864; and justice of the peace accounts, 1832-1863.

Subjects include the development of river markets, transportation, and the livestock industry in the early Ohio Valley; fur trade and commerce with England and Europe; the Marietta and Susquehanna Trading Company; Kanawha and Sciota salt works; Ohio Company lands; Woodbridge-Harman Blennerhassett partnership; ginseng trade; Wheeling Cotton Manufacturing Company; ropewalk and shipbuilding in Marietta; military land warrants; estate of George Morgan; career of William Woodbridge, United States senator and governor of Michigan; pioneer education; Meadville Seminary; Ohio University; Miami University; Marietta Collegiate Institute; Belpre, Ohio; American Catholic missions; early history of Marietta; the American Colonization Society; Washington County Colonization Society; churches; Washington County Tract Society; recruiting in Marietta during the Civil War; impact of the War of 1812 on westward migration and labor; and Woodbridge family affairs.

Letters are addressed to merchants in London, France, New York,

Philadelphia, Pittsburgh, Charleston (W. Va.), Lexington and Louisville (Kentucky), Cincinnati, St. Louis, New Orleans, Washington, Detroit, and Baltimore. Correspondents include Lewis Cass, Philip Doddridge, and Benjamin Reeder.

1034. **Woodburn Female Seminary, Morgantown.** History, ca. 1852-1870. 1 typescript. Transfer, n.d. No. 457.

"A Sketch of Woodburn Seminary," by Susan Maxwell Moore, written in 1939, tracing the school property through the Thomas P. Ray estate.

1035. **Woods, Samuel (1822-1897).** Family papers, 1824-1958. 1 ft. Gift of Mrs. Ruth Woods Dayton and transfer, 1958, 1961. Nos. 1111, 1445.

Correspondence, family historical and genealogical records, clippings, printed material, and sketches of Samuel Woods and his son, Samuel Van Horn Woods. The former was a Philippi lawyer, instructor at Monongalia Academy, member of the Richmond Secession Convention, Confederate captain in Stonewall Jackson's Corps, chairman of the Committee on the Bill of Rights and Elections in the Constitutional Convention of 1872, and a judge of the State Supreme Court of Appeals, 1881-1888. Samuel Van Horn (1856-1937), was a lawyer, Democratic politician, and president of the state senate, 1913.

Subjects include Meadville and Allegheny colleges; Monongalia Academy; secession crisis in northwestern Virginia; the Richmond Secession Convention, 1861; Civil War in Barbour County; camp life in the Army of Northern Virginia in the vicinity of Verdon, Richmond and Waynesboro, Virginia; secession sentiment in western Virginia; John Imboden; the Constitutional Convention of 1872; Francis H. Pierpont's business affairs; student life at West Virginia University, 1877; formation of West Virginia Wesleyan College; business, legal, political, and civic affairs of Samuel Van Horn Woods; and Woods family history and genealogy.

The collection also includes a few Dayton family papers pertaining to the A. G. Dayton-William L. Wilson contest for the United States Senate in 1894; letters, 1824-1830, from Daniel Nesson of Ireland to his brother (Samuel Woods' father-in-law) in New York state; and a manuscript map of Philippi, 1868.

1036. **Woods, Samuel Van Horn.** Letter, 1896. 1 item. Acquired, 1963. No. 1708.

Letter to Daniel B. Lucas, Charles Town, giving the value and assessment of Stephen B. Elkins' property in Randolph County and commenting on William J. Bryan's campaign.

1037. **Woodson, Mrs. Mary,** *Collector.* Papers, 1863-1906. 20 items (photocopies). Loan for duplication by Mrs. Mary Woodson, 1971. No. 2211.

Receipts for land, school, personal property, and road taxes in Kanawha and Putnam counties, 1863-1886 and 1898-1899; grade reports from the Wesleyan Female Institute, Staunton, Virginia, 1882, Putnam County schools, 1904-1906; a printed souvenir list of the students and teacher at the intermediate school, Poca; two manuscript poems concerning the medical profession, 1879-1880; and other items.

1038. **Woodyard, Richard L.** Papers, 1808-1872. 1 reel of microfilm (60 items). Originals in possession of Mrs. Eugene Ware, 1959. No. 1189.

Sermons, essays, lectures, correspondence, lists of the Murrayville (Jackson County) and Parkersburg Circuits, and miscellaneous papers of a Methodist preacher who served in Clarksburg and Sutton; Louisa, Kentucky; and along the Ohio River from Ashland, Kentucky, to Parkersburg.

1039. **Woofter, Carey,** *Compiler.* 1 ft. Gift of Carey Woofter, 1946. No. 112.

Ballads and folklore of West Virginia collected by Woofter. Included are music scores, written by Dr. Patrick Ward Gainer, for some of the ballads.

1040. **Worden, Riley.** Tape recording, 1958. 1 reel. Acquired, 1958. No. 1093.

Interview with the proprietor of Worden's Hotel and a longtime resident of Davis, West Virginia.

1041. **World War I.** Posters, 1914-1918. 31 items. Deposited by Miss Lucy A. Sipe, 1967. No. 1957.

French and American posters; American posters depict war-support efforts of such groups as the Salvation Army, YMCA, YWCA, and Catholic Workers of America.

1042. **World War I.** Scrapbook. 1 item. Transfer, 1957. No. 962.

Newspaper clippings concerning World War I. Also a list of postmasters at the Morgantown Post Office from 1795 to ca. 1912, and other local history.

1043. **World War II.** Clippings, 1932-1945. Ca. 200 items. Gift of O. D. Lambert, 1953. No. 554.

Newspaper clippings on World War II, education, government, and other subjects. Also a typed outline of the Kennerly family inheritance of Greenway Court from 1798 to 1919.

1044. **World War II.** Papers, 1945-1947. 3 items (copies). Gift of Julian G. Hearne, Jr. (originals in Library of Congress), 1947. No. 709.

Copies of papers of the U. S. Twenty-fourth Infantry Regiment, commanded by Col. Julian G. Hearne, Jr., relating to the surrender of Japanese garrisons in the Pacific Theater.

1045. **World War II.** Records, 1942-1945. 521 items. Gift of Harvey B. Bowman, 1951, 1970. No. 299.

Official orders, reports, pictures, newspapers, and miscellaneous materials reflecting the World War II career of Air Force Captain Harvey Bowman. Additional items include a Pacific Islands Yearbook, 1942; newspaper clippings of the Wadestown High School reforestation project; and other items.

1046. **World War II. War Loan Drives.** Records, 1942-1946. Ca. 200 items. Transfer, 1956. No. 234.

National and state correspondence and other records, including materials on the American Book Center for War Devastated Libraries, Inc.

1047. **World War II. West Virginia War History Commission.** Records, 1928-1946. 58 ft. Gifts of the War History Commission and the Office of Civilian Defense, 1946, and Festus P. Summers, 1963. Nos. 103, 109, 1705.

Correspondence, reports, photographs, posters, maps, clippings, and printed materials of state and county Civilian Defense offices; also War History Commission records, letters of servicemen, and a detailed card index to the Charleston *Daily Mail*, 1939-1946; and newsletters, clippings, forms, and speeches of Festus P. Summers, chairman of the West Virginia War Commission.

1048. **Worley, William Gordon (b. 1846).** Papers, 1853-1921. 1 ft. Gift of Carleton C. Pierce, Jr., 1962. No. 1547.

Correspondence, newspaper clippings, and financial papers of a lawyer and state senator from Kingwood, who was instrumental in the organization of the West Virginia Northern Railroad, and the Kingwood Coal and Coke Company.

Subjects include state politics, 1888-1895, Virginia Debt Question, the tariff debate, land development, coal mining and railroads.

Correspondents include J. M. Mason, W. E. Chilton, S. B. Elkins, and George C. Sturgiss.

1049. **Wright, John Stillman.** Genealogical records, 1917-1948. 7 items. Gift of Mrs. George H. Zinn, 1959. No. 1241.

Collection includes a typescript genealogical history of John Stillman Wright (1782-1849) and his ancestors and descendants compiled by Dana Wright and Agnes Snover in 1948; history of the Wright family who are descendants of Samuel Wright (1722-1789) of Lenox, Massachusetts, compiled by William Henry Wright and Gertrude Wright Ketcham; and D. A. R. application of Misses Iva K. and Corrine E. Cutright. The D. A. R. records pertain to the Robert Wiley, John and Benjamin Cutright, John McLaughlin, Jacob and John W. Westfall, John Anderson, and James and Thomas Hughes families.

1050. **Writers' Program.** Papers, 1930s. 53 ft. No. 454.

Manuscript and typescript materials compiled for use in projected publications, including a Fact Book, West Virginia Folklore, and the Negro in West Virginia. There are also maps, photographs, clippings, and correspondence concerning program activities in all counties, as well as the sources used in publishing *West Virginia: A Guide to the Mountain State* (New York, 1941, 1948).

1051. **Yoak, J. B. F., Jr.,** *Collector.* Papers, 19 items. Acquired, 1964, 1970. No. 1759.

Histories and recollections of churches, schools, and early settlers in Mercer, Wayne, Jackson, and Lewis counties, by W. M. King. Communities or areas covered include Athens, Wayne, Cow Run, Antioch, Cherry Grove, and Smith Run. There is also an article on Aracoma Lodge, No. 99, A.F. and A.M.

1052. **Young, Guy B.** Papers, 1880-1940. 2 ft. Gift of Guy B. Young, 1954. No. 661.

Personal papers of a Glenville attorney, dealing with his law practice, service in the Spanish-American War, and his education at Glenville State Normal School and West Virginia University College of Law.

1053. **Zane Family.** Genealogy, 1747-1899. 2 items. Gift of H. C. Headley, 1953. No. 531.

A genealogy of the Zane family in West Virginia, compiled by H. C. Headley; and a typescript, "Betty Zane," tracing her life and descendants, prepared by J. Roy Conway.

1054. **Zinn, Pearl Post,** *Compiler.* Family records, ca. 1960. 1 volume. Gift of Mrs. Pearl Post Zinn, 1961. No. 1440.

Record of the Rohrbough, Williams, Archibald, Hinkle, Joseph Graham, and related families. There are census reports, obituaries, newspaper clippings, marriage announcements, correspondence, and a portrait of Joseph Graham.

Index

Abner O'Neal, 862

Abraham Johnson and Descendants, 466

Academies, 81, 90, 183, 212, 316, 408, 493, 543, 550, 578, 593, 598, 764, 951, 1035. *See also* Schools; Seminaries

Accounts and account books, 1, 5, 14, 23, 25, 40, 43, 62, 63, 68, 69, 71, 72, 85, 89, 92, 99, 104, 126, 155, 175, 183, 195, 201, 203, 206, 212, 214, 222, 224, 234, 242, 246, 247, 249, 251, 273, 275, 277, 281, 311, **313**, 316, 327, 329, 343, 346, **347**, 352, 354, 355, 366, 369, **378**, 379, 400, 401, 419, 423, 435, 436, 450, 457, 463, 471, 483, 487, 491, 497, 512, 516, 538, 544, 552, 578, 582, 585, 591, 593, 600, 603, 623, 625, 631, 637, 653, 661, 664, 684, 700, 703, 704, 731, 735, 737, 738, 749, 750, 753, 778, 788, 796, 801, 803, 819, 833, 842, 844, 845, 862, 878, 882, 893, 898, 900, 925, 935, 938, 1005, 1012, 1015, 1021, 1027, 1033

Action for Appalachian Youth, 108

Actors, 62

Adams, Daniel C., 709

Adams, John Q., 877

Adams, Sherman, 413

Adams Express Co., 249

Ade, George, 416

"Adventure of Two Years in Webster Springs High School, 1915-1917," 522

Advertisements, 180, 275, 285, 307, 516

A Emery, 692

Africa, 884

Agassiz, Louis, 265

Agricultural College: Morgantown, 16

Agricultural Experiment Station. *See* West Virginia University

Agriculture, 3, 16, 99, 155, 156, 193, 195, 211, 214, 277, 280, 293, 314, 316, 387, 395, 400, 455, 464, 497, 513, 526, 534, 550, 585, 659, 667, 724, 784, 842, 844, 848, 863, 960, 1009; Blacksville, 496; Congo, 428; Co-ops, 192; Farm Bureau, 336; Farm records: 5, 421, 737, Marion County, 946, Monroe County, 801, Randolph County, 710; Farmers' papers: Burnsville, 932, Huttonsville, 203, Martinsburg, 836, Mingo Flats, 561, Hardy County, 43, Lewis County, 147; machinery, 346, 516, 561, 922; Pocahontas County, 751; produce prices, 704; statistics, 527; tenancy, 5

Ailes, Stephen, 413

Alabama, 302, 596, 704, 729, 744; United Mine Workers, 56

Alaska, 214

Albany, Ky., 780

Albany, N. Y., 312, 941

Albright, 459

Albright, Erbie E., 2

Alcorn, Meade, 413

Alderson, 249

Alderson, John D., 91, 221, 697

Alderson, Joseph, 453

Alderson-Broaddus College, 760

Alderson family, 319

Alderson Presbyterian Church and Masonic Hall, 249

Alexander, Harriette Boswell, 100

Alexander, Holmes Moss, 3, 554

Alexander family, 183

Bailey, Samuel, 23
Bailey, Thomas, 672
Bailey, Vida, 24
Bailey family, 319, 509, 649
Baker, B. J., 25
Baker, Charles, 984
Baker, Charles G., 26
Baker, George, 324
Baker, Henry, 27
Baker, Mary, 27
Baker, Newton D., 111, 486, 934
Baker, R. L., 790
Baker family, 326, 649
Baldwin, 721
Baldwin, Robert D., 28, 264
Baldwin-Felts Detective Agency, 175, 627
Ball, Arthur, 29
Ball, George H., 869
Ball family, 319, 324
Ballads and hymns, 117, 153, 290
Ballard, E. E., 801
Ballard, Evelyn, 325
Baltimore, Md., 102, 156, 292, 478, 550, 564, 1033; description, 222; livestock commission merchants, 447; locomotive works, 4; resident's papers, 280; surveying instruments manufacturing, 271; Varner family, 924
Baltimore and Ohio Railroad, 30, 98, 102, 146, 280, 292, 369, 573, 657, 707, 1001; circular of, 921; early history, 69; letters of an agent at Grafton (1858), 32; log book, 31; papers of counsel of, 38, 192, 202, 543; Taylor County, 31
Baltimore United Oil Co., 91
Bancroft, George, 280
Bandar Log Press, 416
Bane, Frank J., 324
Bane, James Alfred, 324
Bane family, 324
Bank of Bramwell, 698
Banking, 982
Banks, Nathaniel, 144
Banks and banking, 111, 183, 221, 249, 582, 593, 678, 698, 706, 927; Hampshire County, 356; Masontown, 631; Pittsburgh, Pa., 428; Virginia, 538; Wheeling, 431; Weston, 272
Bankers' papers, 836, 1000

Banner in the Hills, 629
Baptist Church, 114, 116, 117, 121, 122, 136, 425, 493, 760, 773, 925; Forks of Cheat, Monongalia County, 294; Grafton, 69; John Corbly, Greene County, Pa., 114; minister's papers, 516; Preston County, 848; schools, 772, 780, 869, 957
Barbe, Waitman T., 33, 511, 760, 775, 1000, 1018
Barbour, James, 47
Barbour County, 167, 324, 474, 593; birth and death records, 324; Board of Education, 805; boundary-Taylor County, 191; churches, 833; Civil War in, 1035; Civil War map, 146; commissioners' minutes, 191; deeds, 191, 420; early settlers, 931; families, 323; genealogical records, 319; gristmills, 34; history of Cove District, 35; iron furnaces, 34; justice of the peace records, 837; land papers, 191, 856; marriage bonds, 323; Nestor family, 324; resident's papers, 232, 234, 256, 421; resident's reminiscences, 827; schools, 805; surveyor's papers, 191
Barbour Democrat, Philippi, 34
Barboursville, 493
Barboursville College, 659
Barker, Morgan, 322
Barker family, 322, 876
Barkla, W., 674
Barkley, Alben W., 111, 480, 486, 873
Barkley and Wallace, 935
Barlow, A., 561
Barnes, J., 756
Barnes, J. W., 984
Barnes, James F., 844
Barnes family, 319
Barnet family, 319
Barns, Bernie Hodges (Mrs. John S.), 36
Barns, Fleming and Co., 844
Barns, James F., 844
Barns, James R., 844
Barns, John S., 36, 844
Barns, Sally, 114
Barns, Thomas, 844
Barns, Thomas Rufus, 36

Bethell, T. N., 911
"Betty Zane," 1053
Bevan papers, 185
Beveridge, Albert J., 330
Beverly, 143, 333, 649; Civil War in, 74, 143, 146, 333, 507; resident's papers, 333
Beverly, Ohio, 823
Beverly, W., 432
Beverly-Fairmont Turnpike, 946
Bibber, Paul S., 705
Bible, 515
Bible Class, 115
Bible Society, 875
Big Creek Development Co., 304
Big Moses Gas Well, 209
Big Sandy-Elkhorn Coal Operators Association, 795
Bimetalism, 1018
"Biographical History of Schools and Education in Doddridge County," 258
Biographical sketches, 493, 971
Birth control: Maryland, 3
Birth records, 115, 844, 890
Bischof & Loeb, Cincinnati, O., 579
Bishoff, William H., 750
Bishop, Charles Mortimer, 55
Bishop, John G., 141
Bittner, Van A., 56, 345, 419, 844, 988
Black, Hugo L., 419
Black, James, 134
Blackberry, Kentucky and West Virginia Coal and Coke Co., 934
Blacksmith's records, 749
Blacksville: general store and gristmill account, 1; Ku Klux Klan, 485; postmaster's papers, 496
Blackwater Lumber Co., 980
Blagg, Donald O., 231
Blaine, James G., 221, 268, 569, 657
Blair, Jacob B., 90, 96, 224
Blair, Montgomery, 96
Blake family, 319
Blakeslee, George H., 88
Bland, George W., 382
Blease, Cole L., 111
Blennerhassett, Harman, 57, 83, 1032
Blennerhassett, Margaret, 400
"Blennerhassett-Woodbridge Partnership: An Experiment in Chain Store Operation, 1798-1806," 1032

Blind and mentally ill, 417
Blizzard, William, 331, 387, 592, 960
Bloodletting in Appalachia, 505
Bloomingdale, 493
Blooming Valley, Pa., 246
Blue, Fred O., 232
Blue, John, 4
Blue, R. W., 649
Blue Creek, 484
Bluefield, 102, 698, 834, 852
Bluefield State College, 698, 984
Bluestone River, 24
B'nai B'rith, 480
Boardman, Daniel, 58
Boat companies, 735
Boats: construction, 359
Boggess, Caleb, 90
Boggs, Ira Brooks, 59
Bok, Edward W., 33
Bolton, Channing M., 60
Bonafield, Julia A., 61
Bonds, 488
Bonnett family, 319
Bonnifield, Abraham, 578
Book dealers: letters and papers, 562, 573
Books: Civil War, 184, 573
Boom companies. See Lumber industry
Boone County, 116, 170, 513, 650; census records, 493; court records, 493
"Boot Shaped Bend," 504
Borah, William E., 111, 345, 349
Borchert, C. A., Glass Co., 262
Boreman, Arthur I., 182, 184, 287, 569; letters, 47, 96, 333, 715, 727, 855, 1010; papers, 62
Boreman family, 321
Boreman and Bullock, 62
Boston, Mass., 657
Bosworth family, 234
Botany and botanists, 51, 189, 338, 371, 381, 385, 590, 595, 681
Botetourt County, Va., 442
Boughman family, 319
Boughner, James Vance, 63
Boundaries: Virginia-Maryland, 748; West Virginia-Maryland, 235
Bounties, 913, 925
Bounty agency, 1033
Bouslog family, 322
Bower family, 325
Bowker, R. R., 1018

248

Bowles, Chester, 988
Bowling family, 325
Bowman, Harvey B., 1045
Bowman family, 508
Boxing, 239
Boxley, George, 359
Boyers, Jacob Edgar, 64
Boyle, William M., Jr., 965
Braddock's Field, Pa., 65
Bradley, J. G., 417
Bradley, Rev. Joshua, 772
Brady, Carrie, 66
Brady, James W., 149
Brady, Rose, 66
Bragg, Braxton, 791
Brake family, 319
Branch Mountain, 366
Brand, Charles I., 286
Brand, Frank M., 67, 324
Brand, John M., 67
Brand, Willa, 67
Brand, William N., 67
Brand family, 67
Brandonville, 346
Brandonville and Terra Alta Telephone Co., 459
Brand registrations (cattle), 684
Brannan, Charles F., 480
Brannon, Henry, 243
Branson family, 366
Braxton County, 474, 573; birth records, 68; county archives, 68; county superintendent of free schools, 887; court records, 68; death records, 68; deeds, 68; election returns, 68; elections, 887; estate settlements, 68; justice of the peace records, 930; land records, 68; logging operations, 703; marriages, 68; newspapers, 68; population statistics, 887; tax records, 68; World War I soldiers, 68
Brazilian Coal Commission, 1002
Breakiron family, 324
Breckenridge, C. R., 1018
Breckenridge, William C. P., 1018
Breckinridge, Henry, 934
Brethren Church, 136
Brewster, J. M. 869
Brick companies, 355, 735
Brickmaking, 91, 97, 355, 734
Bricker, John W., 353, 387, 896
Bridgeport, 411, 551, 649, 1001
Bridges, Styles, 3

Bridges, 369; Barrackville, 582, 946; Eli and Lemuel Chenoweth, 333; Fairmont, 582; Morgantown, 195, 642, 790; Ohio Valley, 688; Valley River, 293; Wheeling, 280
"Brief History of Methodism in Kingwood and Vicinity from the Earliest Times to March, 1874," by W. C. Snodgrass, 123, 124
"Brief History of the Civilian Defense Organization of Nicholas County, West Virginia, as Compiled and Reported by O. C. Lewis, its Director," 677
Brights Mill, Alderson, 249
Brinkman, Charles, 69
Brinkman, George, 69
Brinkman, George W., 69
Brinsmade, Robert Bruce, 70
Brisbane, Arthur, 111
Bristol, Mrs. Franklin, 324
British Isles, 67, 94, 100
Broaddus Institute, Philippi, 420
Broadsides, 92, 456, 475, 697, 875, 951, 1041; Civil War, 96, 146; Grafton, 69; Marion County, 581; Martinsburg, 280; Monongalia County, 200; political, 844; Pruntytown, 69; W. Va. statehood movement, 921
Brody, John, 1033
Brooke, Charles Frederick Tucker, 73, 372
Brooke, Francis T., 73
Brooke, St. George Tucker, 73, 372
Brooke family, 73, 372
Brooke County, 97, 961; accounts and account books, 71; churches, 97; county archives, 71; court records, 71; deeds, 72; farm record books, 701; National Guard, 844; papers from, 41, 72, 194; schools, 97; settlers, 97
Brooklyn Navy Yard, 544
Brooks, A. B., 214, 870
Brooks, H. L., 387
Brooks, Van Wyck, 541
Brooks, William E., 74
Brown, David Dare, 75
Brown, George W., 532
Brown, John, 4, 76, 100, 146, 182, 226, 246, 359, 823, 869
Brown, Joseph, 486
Brown, Kenneth E., 975

Brown, Lloyd W., 163
Brown, Samuel Boardman, 77
Brown, Silas, 1032
Brown, Thomas, 73
Brown, Uria, 672
Brown, Wendell, family, 63
Brown, William G., 78
Brown family, 63, 73, 201
Browne family, 741
Browning, Chauncey, Jr., 587
Browning, Joseph W., 79
Browning, Orville H., 280
Brown's Island, 863
Bruceton, 746
Bruceton Mills, 748, 848
Bryan, William Jennings, 80, 188, 221, 697, 873, 1036
Bryants, Pa., 346
Bryce, James, 1018
Buchanan, James, 280, 796
Buck, Pearl S., 873
Buck, Solon J., 480
Buck Hill Bottom, O., 658
Buckhannon, 61, 213, 584, 682, 721
Buckhannon Creek, 160
Buckhannon Relief Oil and Gas Co., 268
Buell, Joseph, 685
Buffalo, 81
Buffalo Academy and Seminary, 81
Buffalo Creek, 42
Bugh, Richard L., 829
Building supplies, 421
Bukey, Peter, 333
Bull Run, Second Battle of, 414, 820
Bullock, John O., 62
Bunker, Edward C., 82
Bunker Hill: churches, 137
Bunner family, 649
Burch family, 694
Burdett, Harriet, 1012
Burdett, Joe F., 698
Burlington, 842, 922
"Burning of Chambersburg, A Reminiscence of the Hunter Raid to Lynchburg, Virginia, and the Retreat down the South Branch Valley," 573
Burning Springs, 155, 209, 769
Burns, Annie Walker, 324
Burnside family, 183
Burnsville, 932
Burr, Aaron, 83, 400, 535, 1032
Burr family, 319

Burris family, 326
Burrough, John, 198
Burrough family, 198
Burton, 1001
Bush family, 319, 321
Bushfield, Mrs. Louis S., 84
Butcher, J. Arthur, 955
Butcher family, 468
Butler, B. F., 727
Butler, Paul M., 965
Butterflies of North America, 265
Buzzard family, 433, 876
Byrd, Harry F., 413, 419, 480, 486
Byrd, Richard E., 486
Byrd, Robert C., 413, 554, 698, 908, 956, 960, 965
Byrnside, James M., 85

Cabell, David S. G., 507
Cabell County, 86, 493, 745, 934; account of travel in, 783; Civil War letters from, 74
Cabell family, 742
Cabin Creek, 317, 339, 345, 505, 627, 840, 977
Cabin Creek strike, 330
Cacapon River, 366
Caddis family, 322
Cairo, Egypt, 183
Cairo, Ill., 893
Calabrese, Nicolo, 87
Caldwell family, 183
Calhoon, Rev. Nath'l W., 799
Calhoun, John C., 280, 289, 877
Calhoun County, 29, 36
California, 48, 268, 497, 576, 657, 692, 946; politics, 480
Callahan, James Morton, 88, 299, 460, 582, 934
Callahan family, 88
Callaway family, 864
Calvert family, 468
Camden, 89
Camden, E. D., 182
Camden, Gideon D., 47, 90, 91, 333, 391, 724, 727, 846, 1010
Camden, John S., 92
Camden, Johnson Newlon, 47, 90, 91, 221, 268, 283, 350, 405, 543, 561, 875, 1018
Camden, Mary Belt Sprigg, 184
Camden, R. P., 47
Camden, T. B., 92

Camden, Wilson Lee, 90
Camden family, 184, 675
Camden Consolidated Oil Co., 91
Camels, 93
Camel transportation, 93, 214
"Camel Transportation in the United States," by A. J. Dadisman, 93
Cameron, Simon, 727
Campaigns and elections, 37 (1892), 44, 90, 159, 222 (1900), 224, 225 (1924), 227, 280, 287, 330, 353, 387, 413, 418, 480, 486, 498 (1930), 544, 562, 657, 682, 697, 704 (1851), 712, 724, 743, 779, 797, 834, 844, 857, 885, 887, 896, 988, 1018 (1888), 1035; Braxton County, 68; gubernatorial, 62, 837; Tyler County, 209
Campbell, A. W., 349, 569, 727, 863, 1010; papers, 96
Campbell, Alexander, 54, 90, 94, 780
Campbell, Andrew Nelson, 95
Campbell, Charles L., 97
Campbell, David, 495, 522
Campbell, Jacob M., 98
Campbell, James, 97, 99
Campbell, James L., 99
Campbell, James Wilson, 99
Campbell, William, 443
Campbell family, 97, 99
Campbell County, Va., 796
Camp Branch Run, 366
Camp Chase, Ohio, 513, 866
Camp Conrad, Ga., 148
Camp George H. Thomas, Ga., 148
Camp Hill, Harpers Ferry, 593
Camp Lee, Kanawha City, 148
Camp Poland, Tenn., 148
Camps: Allegheny, 573; Branch Run, 366; Carlile, 143; Chase, 513, 573, 762, 866, 894; Confederate, 183; Conrad, 148; Crook, 820; Hill, 593; Lee, 2, 148; Morton, 893; Poland, 148; Taylor, 2; Thomas, 148
Canaan Valley, 333
Canada, 214, 486
Canadian Reciprocity Agreement, 486
Canals, 280, 340, 688
Canepa, A. P. "Pat," 239
Canfield, Cass, 541
Canham, Erwin D., 413

Cannel Coal Co., 791
Caperton, Alice Beulah, 100
Caperton, Allen T., 584
Caperton, G. H., 720
Caperton, Isabel, 100
Caperton, John, 100
Caperton, William Gaston, 100
Caperton family, 100
Capital punishment, 417
Capon Bridge, 901
Capper, Arthur, 1026
Captives of Abb's Valley, 141
"Capture of Generals Kelly and Crook," 803
"Capture of a Railroad Train," 803
Carber family, 319
Carbide and Carbon Chemicals Corporation, 101
Carder Lowe & Co., 1
Carding accounts, 935
Cardio-pneumosphygmograph, 1025
"Ca-Re-Ma," 324
Carey, James B., 988
Carlile, John S., 47, 90, 91, 224, 292, 333, 349, 391, 415, 577, 657, 727, 991, 1010
Carlisle, George, 877
Carlisle, John G., 657, 1018
Carnegie, Andrew, 221, 268, 835
Carney family, 213
Carnifex Ferry, 742
Carpenter, Charles, 102
Carpenter family, 319, 322
Carpenters, 347
Carr family, 322
Carriage manufacturing, 684
Carroll, James H., 103, 347, 724
Carroll family, 319
Carruth, H. S., 1018
Carry On, Mr. Bowditch, 500
Carter, E. A., 965
Carter family, 324
Carthage, 820
Cartoons, 1018
Caruso, John A., 593
Caruthers, Isaac, 1
Cary, J. H. Oley, 183
Case, Clifford P., 413
Casey family, 364
Cass, 980
Cass, Joseph K., 980
Cass, Lewis, 877, 1033
Cassady, James S., 182

Chew, R. P., 926
Chicago, Ill., 578
Chicago Art Institute, 416
Chicago Exposition of 1933, 490
Chicago, Parkersburg and Norfolk Railroad, 90, 828
Chicago, Rock Island and Pacific Railroad, 155
Chicago World's Fair, 657
Chickamauga, 820
Chickamauga Park, Ga., 148
Chickens, 110
Children, 222, 285
Chillicothe, Ohio, 340, 552
Chilton, William E., 91, 111, 221, 262, 330, 350, 387, 697, 844, 873, 1048
Chilton, William E., Jr., 111
Chilton family, 111
China, 37, 369; Foochow, 61
Chipps family, 322, 326
Chitwood, Oliver Perry, 112, 146, 460, 905
Chladni plates, 176
Cholera, 44, 359
Chopin, Kate, 33
Chrislip family, 319
Chrisman, Lewis H., 113
Christ church, 137
Christian Church, 94, 114, 119, 398, 777, 784
Chronicles of Border Warfare, 182
Church services, 114
Churches, 24, 48, 365, 465, 487, 497, 586, 721, 744, 857, 946, 1009; Baptist, 114, 116, 117, 121, 122, 136, 425, 493, 772, 773, 780, 869, 925; Beaver Run, 997; Berkeley County, 193; Boone County, 116; Brandonville, 750; Brethren, 136; Brooke County, 97; Bunker Hill, 137; Catholic, 1033; Christ, 137; Church of Christ, 24; Clarksburg, 118, 224, 849; Congregational, 493; Connellsville, Pa., 119; Disciples of Christ, 94, 114, 119, 398, 777, 784; Doddridge County, 259; Episcopal, 137, 138, 925; Evangelical Lutheran, 136; Freewill Holiness, 114; German Reformed, 133, 136; Goshen Baptist, 610; Grant County, 133; Greenbrier County, 183; Hampshire County,

114, 356; Hancock County, 52; Harpers Ferry, 374; Harrison County, 369; histories, 140; Holiness, 114; Holly Creek, 116; Huntersville circuit, 127; Jefferson, Pa., 114; Jones Run Baptist, 122; Kanawha County, 513; Kanawha Valley, 359; Kingwood, 124; Lewisburg, 183; Lewis County, 838; Lowgap, 116; Lutheran, 197; Martinsburg, 137, 139 Methodist, 46, 90, 139, 195, 259, 369, 463, 493, 682, 761, 1038; Methodist Episcopal, 124, 127, 129, 183, 661, 833, 863, 874, 902; Methodist Episcopal South, 118, 130, 193; Methodist Protestant, 114, 115, 130; Monongalia County, 114, 131, 161, 189, 398, 756; Moorefield, 132; Morgantown, 115, 189, 951; North Mill Creek, 133; Oakland, Md., 750; Old Wayman, 997; Parish registers, 138; Parkersburg, 138; Pierpont, Francis H., and, 727; Pisgah, 161; Presbyterian, 79, 114, 132, 134, 183, 212, 224, 493; Preston County, 197, 346, 459; Protestant Episcopal, 831; Pursley, 997; records, 114, 117, 119, 121, 124, 127, 130, 132, 133, 137, 139, 183; records survey, 969; Romney, 134; St. Augustine's, 663; Somerset County, Pa., 136; Springfield, 134; Summers County, 117; Sunday schools, 161; Uniontown, Pa., 121; Upshur County, 682; West Liberty, 212; West Virginia Centennial, 140; Winchester, Virginia, Presbytery, 141. *See also* the various denominations
Churchill, Winston, 33
Cincinnati, Ohio, 10, 14, 107, 340, 367, 478, 510, 688, 798, 862, 1033
Circuit riders, 463, 847
Circumnavigator's Club, 39
Civil Aeronautics Administration, 480
Civil rights, 807
Civil War, 4, 11, 74, 96, 103, 118, 143, 144, 146, 147, 182, 210, 333, 349, 408, 480, 561, 578,

253

594, 675, 680, 742, 788, 803, 848, 857, 874, 941, 971, 1014

Allegheny Mountain, 853; amnesty oath, 262, 408; Antietam, 657, 820; John W. M. Appleton in, 11; Appomattox, 316; Army of the Potomac, 308; W. W. Averell in, 143; Henry Baker in, 27; Baltimore, 156; Baltimore and Ohio Railroad, 98, 202, 573; Nathaniel Banks in, 144; Barbour County, 1035; Bath County, Va., 316; battle flag, 147; Battle of Rich Mountain, 78; Battle of Shiloh, 224; Battle of the Wilderness, 657, 853; Battle of Vicksburg, 514; battles and military operations, 98, 142, 143, 144, 146, 182, 183, 333, 394, 467, 508, 534, 573, 651, 657, 660, 719, 729, 732, 820, 853; Belle Island, 583; Bermuda Hundred, Va., 15, 308; Beverly, 74, 143, 146; books about, 184, 573; bounty acknowledgement lists, 146; bounty claims, 55; bounty lists, 563; bounty receipts, 195; James W. Brady in, 149; Braxton County, 573; Edward C. Bunker in, 82; business conditions, 550; James M. Campbell in, 98

Camps: 11, 146, 513, 593, 714, 719, 846, 866; Allegheny, 573; Burne, 1001; Carlile, 143; Chase, 573, 762; Confederate, 183; Crook, 820; life in, 146, 308, 573, 732, 1035; Morton, 593; Pryor, 534; White, 1001; Wilkinson, 1001

Carthage, 820; Cedar Creek, 183; Cedar Mountain, 144, 414, 573; Ceredo, 991; Chambersburg, 573; Chancellorsville, Va., 74, 414, 804; Charleston, 146, 573, 820; Charles Town, 207; Chattanooga, Tenn., 74, 820; Cheat Mountain, 651, 853; Chickamauga, 820; circulars, 651; civilian attitudes, 866; civilian-military relations, 98; clippings about, 147, 372, 794; William S. Coburn in, 649; Cold Harbor, 853; commerce during, 146; the common soldier, 573

Confederate: camps, 183; companies, 493; currency, 207; sympathizers, 98; veterans, 211, 533

Joseph W. Cooper in, 187; Corricks Ford, 651; courts-martial, 62; courts of inquiry, 146; Covington, Va., 143; George Crook in, 143; customs certificate, 146; delinquent muster lists, 146; Department of West Virginia, 23; deserters, 98; diaries, journals, reminiscences, 19, 36, 69, 73, 74, 92, 98, 143, 146, 182, 184, 212, 302, 316, 409, 414, 467, 548, 649, 657, 672, 803, 804, 820, 853, 856, 893, 945, 1044; discharge papers, 146, 324; Droop Mountain, 719; Dublin, 573; Gen. Duffie in, 143

Jubal Early in, 142, 183, 573, 853; Eastern Panhandle, 98, eastern West Virginia, 538; John Echols in, 142, 183; Fayette County, 432; federal forts, 573; First Bull Run, 534; John B. Floyd in, 142; Fort Wagner, 11; Fort Warren, 11; forts, 11; fraternization, 308; Fredericksburg, 804; freighting, 155; William H. French in, 306; Ephraim W. Frost in, 573; Henry H. Fry in, 308; Alpheus Garrison in, 314; A. C. L. Gatewood in, 316; general orders, 651; Georgia, 183; Gettysburg, 414, 804, 853; Gilmer County, 573; Grafton, 69, 651; U. S. Grant, 183; Greenbrier Valley, 461; guerrillas, 98, 146, 182, 573, 732; Guyandotte Massacre, 493

Hampshire County Confederate veterans, 146; Hardy Blues, 183; Harpers Ferry, 144, 149, 573; Thomas M. Harris in, 573; Harrisonburg, Va., 15; Hart's Island, 804; Charles W. Hill in, 651; John E. Hoffman in, 414; David Holmes in, 593; hospital records, 307; David Hunter in, 143; Hunter raid, 573; John D. Imboden in, 98, 143, 732, 1035; Imboden's partisans, 573; "Immortal Six Hundred," 211; Indiana units, 182, 651, 714; Jacksonville, Fla.,

11; Stonewall Jackson in, 144; James River, 73; Jefferson Guards, 183; James W. Johnson in, 146; Jesse Johnston in, 467; William E. Jones in, 143, 316; Jones Raid, 529, 610, 1001 Kanawha Valley, 143, 820; John R. Kenly in, 776; Walter Kimble in, 573; Ladies Relief Hospital, Lynchburg, Va., 100; Laurel Hill, 651, 853; William H. Lawrence in, 146; Robert E. Lee in, 183; letterheads, 146; letters, 11, 27, 74, 98, 103, 142, 144, 146, 147, 152, 156, 184, 308, 399, 414, 430, 461, 499, 507, 514, 573, 583, 589, 593, 651, 714, 729, 732, 734, 742, 750, 782, 820, 894; Lewisburg, 183, 207, 820; J. A. J. Lightburn in, 516; the lighter side, 573; lists of soldiers, 925, Melville D. Long in, 156; looting, 143; W. W. Loring in, 142; F. C. Loveland in, 146; loyalty oaths, 762; Lynchburg, Va., 100, 143, 573

T. H. McBee in, 144; John McCausland in, 533, 573; James Z. McChesney in, 573; George B. McClellan in, 146, 593, 651; Albert F. McCown in, 146; Van D. McDaniel in, 146; Isaac McNeel in, 550; John H. McNeill in, 143; McNeill's Rangers, 364, 573; maps, 146, 147, 514; Marion County, 146; John H. Marple in, 593; Martinsburg, 144, 146, 820; Maryland, 593, 853; Mason County, 146; Massachusetts, 54th Massachusetts Volunteers, 11; Meadow Bluff, 820; medals, 150; Charles A. Mestrezat in, 583; military claims, 62; military records, 145, 146, 212; military units, 649; Mineral County, 803; Mine Run, 657; Missionary Ridge, 820; Missouri troops, 750; Monocacy, 573; Monroe County, 100; Morgantown, 414; Brig. Gen. Morris in, 651; Morris Island, S. C., 11; Mosby's guerrillas, 144; Mt. Jackson, 143; Henri Jean Mugler, 657; J. Ogden Murray in, 660; musicians, 657; muster fines and receipts, 293; muster rolls, 62, 147, 150, 573, 754; Nashville, 820; Negro soldiers, 11, 563; New Creek, 15, 27; northern arms, 991

Ohio: military units, 74, 144, 729; Ohio Volunteer Sharp Shooters, 146; 6th Cavalry, 146; 18th Infantry, 820; 36th Infantry, 820; 116th Volunteer Infantry, 573

Orders, 98, 146, 147, 507; ordnance and quartermaster returns, 98; Palatine, 146; Jewett Palmer in, 820; Panhandle Greys, 734; papers, 146; pass book, 146; passes, 293; patriotic cover, 579

Pennsylvania: military units: 14th Cavalry Regiment, 583; 15th Volunteer Cavalry, 302; 54th Volunteers, 98; 68th Regiment, 804; 191st Volunteer Infantry, 593; Scott Legion of Philadelphia, 804

Pension application, 828; Philippi, 651; photographs, 147, 518; picket duty, 573; Piedmont, 143; Pocahontas County, 550; poetry, 40, 147; Point City, 804; Point Lookout Prison, 156; Point Pleasant, 593; John L. Polsley in, 732; "Porte Crayon" in, 143; postwar Virginia, 100; Princeton, 146; prisons, 69, 156, 583, 657, 672, 732, 804, 893, 894; provost marshal at Grafton, 32; Rapidan River, 144; Frank Smith Reader in, 143; records, 149; recruiting in Marietta, 1033; reenlistment lists, 563; Alexander W. Reynolds in, 183; Powell Benton Reynolds in, 782; Richmond, 550, 583, 1035; Richmond Camp of Instruction, 100; Rich Mountain, 394, 991; Ringgold Raiders, 1001; Hiram J. Rogers in, 593; William S. Rosecrans in, 573, 791, 844, 991; rosters, 146, 804

Sandy Hook, Md., 593; Lewis Schaeffer in, 804; scouts, 144; secession crisis, 100, 573, 595; Second Bull Run, 414; Second Manassas, 820; service records, 925; Sharpsburg, 1014; Shenandoah Valley, 98, 143, 533, 573, 732, 820, 853; Shepherdstown, 187;

Gen. W. T. Sherman, 183; Franz Sigel in, 143, 144; sketches, Peninsula Campaign, 308; B. M. Skinner in, 511; C. W. D. Smitley in, 144; Joseph C. Snider in, 853; social and economic life, 100; songs, 36; South Branch Valley, 142; South Carolina, 308; Spotsylvania Court House, 853; Wallace S. Stanley in, 820; Staunton, Va., 143, 316; subsistence accounts, 62; Milton Stewart in, 146; substitute hiring, 146; Summersville, 820; Sweet Springs, 143; telegrams, 98, 146, 147; Tennessee, 183; test oath, 62; B. F. Thomas in, 146; Tucker County, 144; Tygarts Valley, 991; Union, Monroe County, 207; Union blockade, 550; Union veterans, 912; United States Signal Corps, 302; United States Volunteers, 293, 651; Verdon, 1035; veterans, 316; veterans' organizations, 183; Vicksburg, Miss., 183; Virginia, 15, 143, 145, 573

Virginia: military units: Bryan's Battery, 183; Albert G. Jenkins Brigade, 573; Laurel Brigade, 316; McCausland's Brigade, 573; Rosser's Brigade, 573; 1st Cavalry, 183, 312; 3rd Cavalry, Co. C, 414; 10th Cavalry, Co. G, 150; 11th Cavalry, 316, 573; 12th Cavalry, 1018; 13th Cavalry, 721; 14th Cavalry, 573; 19th Cavalry, Co. C, 187; 36th Battery, Virginia Cavalry, 183; Rosser Cavalry Division, 316; Stonewall Jackson corps, 1035; 2nd Infantry, 183, 721; 3rd Infantry, 721; 8th Infantry, 732; 10th Infantry, 721; 13th Infantry, 146, 183, 657; 14th Infantry, 27; 15th Infantry, 782; 25th Infantry, 394; 31st Infantry, 183, 184, 853; 113th Infantry, 721; Greenbrier Light Infantry Grays, 183; 13th Regiment, Virginia Militia, 834; 147th Regiment, Virginia Militia, 146; 45th Regiment, 142; 60th Regiment, Co. F., 146

Virginia and Tennessee Railroad, 143; Virginia Central Railroad, 820; Virginia Military Institute, 143; Jacob Waddle in, 593; Washington, 573; Waynesboro, 1035; Webster County, 573; West Virginia, 145, 150, 184, 459

West Virginia: military units: 1st Light Artillery Regiment, 563; 1st Cavalry, 563; 2nd Cavalry, 144, 467; 3rd Cavalry, 146, 563; 5th Cavalry, 143, 563, 693; 6th Cavalry, 146, 563; 9th Cavalry, 143; 1st Infantry, 143, 563, 593; 2nd Infantry, 499, 563; 3rd Infantry, 146, 573, 649; 6th Infantry, 563, 649; 7th Infantry, 103, 563, 732; 8th Infantry, 147, 732; 9th Infantry, 511; 10th Infantry, 1, 36, 593; 10th-15th Infantry, 563; 11th Infantry, 15, 19, 147; 12th Infantry, 146, 212; 13th Infantry, 147; 14th Infantry, 27; 15th Infantry, 146; 17th Infantry, Co. E, 314, 563; 18th Infantry, 563; Berkeley County Company, 183; Independent Company of Scouts for Randolph County, 855; Lambert's Independent Company of Scouts for Tucker County, 282; 18th Militia, 146, 183; Putnam County Volunteer Infantry, 183; 31st Regiment (Confederate), 150; 45th Regiment, U. S. Colored Troops, 563; 163rd Regiment, 1008; Ringgold Raiders, 143; Volunteers from Tyler County, 712

Western Virginia, 316; Wheeling, 430, 941; Henry Solomon White in, 1001; White Sulphur Springs, 143; James Williams in, 649; Simon Williams in, 146; Edward J. Willis in, 1014; William Lyne Wilson in, 1018; Winchester, 573, 853; Samuel Woods in, 1035. *See also* Confederate States of America

Civilian defense, 677, 1047
Cladonica, 338
Clark, A. B., 1
Clark, Boyers Morgan, 151
Clark, Champ, 697
Clark, Emma H., 628
Clark, Frank Wells, 154
Clark, Friend E., 67, 152, 154, 460
Clark, Gen. George Rogers, 160

Clark, J. M., 484
Clark, Joseph S., 3
Clark, Mary Vinson, 153
Clark, Robert, 264
Clark, William v. U. S., 531
Clark family, 151, 154, 326
Clark & Leap Co., 1
Clarke, Belle, 14
Clarke, J. P., 14
Clarke, James C., 155
Clarke, John P., 155
Clarke, William, Sr., 151
Clarke family, 14, 151, 155
Clarksburg, 118, 146, 224, 366, 389,
762, 764, 848, 927, 991, 1001,
1038; churches, 79; description of
early life in, 107, 849; Fifty Year
Club, 369; history, 369; lawyers'
papers and reminiscences, 38,
369, 788; obituaries, 213; plat of
(1835), 599; Presbyterian Church,
120; residents' papers and remi-
niscences, 107, 380, 390, 1003;
schools, 79; Mortimer W. Smith
family in, 849
Clarksburg and Philippi Turnpike,
224
Clarksburg *Conservative,* 333
Clarksburg Public Library, 156
Clarksburg Women's Club, 490
Clarkson, Roy B., 157
Clarkson manuscripts in the Library
of Congress, 268
Clarksville, Va., 1017
Clay, Cassius M., 96
Clay, Henry, 1005
Clay County, 484, 513; archives,
158; deed books, 158; order
books, 158
Claymont Brick Works, 735
Claypoole family, 322
Claysville Borough, 159
Claysville Town Council, 159
Clayton family, 322
Cleaver, Benjamin, 160
Cleaver, William, 160
Cleaver family, 160
Clemens, Samuel, 864
Clendenin family, 183
Cleveland, Grover, 91, 268, 709,
1018
Clifton, 359
Clinton, Miss., 893
Clinton County, Ky., 780

Clinton Furnace, Monongalia County, 530, 756
Clip, Jefferson County, 519
Close, Edward J., 736
Cloth prices, 234
Cloverdale, Va., 442
Coal, 317, 734
Coal and Coke Railway, 102, 221
Coalburg, 265, 317
Coalburgh-Kanawha Mining Co., 266
Coal mining, 1, 10, 14, 56, 62, 87,
90, 91, 111, 162, 163, 164, 165,
166, 167, 169, 174, 175, 221,
235, 262, 265, 268, 304, 339,
345, 387, 421, 455, 484, 493,
513, 528, 587, 596, 602, 613,
631, 684, 703, 724, 795, 797,
840, 844, 845, 850, 852, 860,
939, 962; accidents, 181, 419,
597; Cheat River Valley, 788;
companies, 174, 175, 216, 268,
313, 318, 423, 671, 699, 791,
851, 1021, 1024, 1027, 1048;
company stores, 423, 1021; explosions, 181, 419; Fayette County, 681; fires, 181; hospitals, 831;
Kanawha County, 216, 266, 471,
1024; Marion County, 284, 946;
marketing conditions, 175; mine
guards, 175, 627; mine safety,
175; miners, 167, 597, 860; Monongahela Valley, 283; Monongalia County, 600, 631, 821;
Nicholas County, 168; Preston
County, 55, 168; price fixing,
175; profits, salaries, and taxes,
175; safety, 181; settlements,
619; stories about, for children,
822; strikes, 62, 169, 170, 175,
223, 228, 330, 418, 484, 505,
592, 627, 946, 977; wages, 175
Coal mining and resources, 102, 505,
569, 1009, 1022, 1026
Coal River, 360
Coal River and Kanawha Mining and
Manufacturing Co., 471
Coal River Navigation Co., 791
Coalsburgh, 265
Cobun. *See* Coburn
Coburn, James, 198
Coburn, William S., 649
Coburn (Cobun) family, 198, 324
Coburn's Fort, 389
Cochran, Nathaniel, 508

Cochran, W. Bourke, 1018
Cochran, William, 171
Cockrell, Monroe F., 172
Coke, 270, 421, 631
Cold Harbor, 853
Cole, E. Luther, 146
Cole, Harry Outen, 173
Cole family, 378
Colebank, George, 264
Colebank family, 326
Coleman, Mrs. Charles, 73
Coleman, Michael (Malcolm), 589
Colfax, Schuyler, 96, 727
Colgate Coal Co., 174
Colgate family, 741
College of the Bible and the Christian Church, 780
Colleges and universities, 55, 73, 90, 212, 263, 313, 316, 340, 369, 430, 462, 493, 507, 544, 550, 578, 631, 659, 661, 697, 780, 784, 817, 826, 844, 869, 925, 951, 957, 958, 986, 999, 1007, 1018, 1033, 1035, 1052. *See also* individual college and university names
Collins, A. L., 475
Collins, Jairus, 175
Collins, James C., 146
Collins, Justus, 175, 1022
Collins family, 593
Collison, Dorothy Clutter, 290
Colombia, South America, 513, 1020
"Colonial Ancestors of Edward Jackson . . . ," 324
Colonial families, 925
Colonial Timber and Coal Corporation, 484
Colonization, 1033
Colorado Territory, 155
Colored Insane Asylum, 984
Colored Old Folks Home, 984
Colored Orphans Home, 984
Colson, Clyde L., 698
Columbian Literary Society, 244
Columbia University, 310
Columbus, Ga., 148
Columbus, Ky., 893
Columbus, Ohio, 22, 146, 340, 428
Colwell, Robert C., 176
Comly, Deborah, 672
Commerce, 550, 1033
Committee on Political Education (COPE), 384

Communications: labor disputes, 988
Communism, 56, 387, 792, 802
Community Services Committee, C.I.O., 988
"A Complete List of Post Offices in West Virginia in 1828," 573
Compromise of 1850, 90
Comstock, Jim, 554
Conaway, Virginia H., 437
Conaway family, 324
Concord College, 698, 984
Condon-Lane Boom & Lumber Co., 525, 980
Confederate States Army, 394, 533; activity in Fairmont-Morgantown area, 144; Greenbrier County, 92; Laurel Hill, 576; muster rolls, 95; officers, 4, 74, 147, 1014; removal of graves from Rich Mountain Battlefield, 78; soldiers: 894, diaries, letters and papers, 95, 143, 782, 846, 866, 893; graves in Monongalia County, 609; troops and military organizations, Virginia: 4th Infantry, 152, 5th Infantry, 782, 11th Cavalry, 215, 19th Cavalry, 182, 36th Infantry, 146, 44th Regiment, 866, 62nd Infantry, 754, guerrillas in Tucker County, 144, Kanawha Riflemen, 182, Jacob W. Marshall's Guerrilla Band, 182, Thurmond's Company of Partisan Rangers, 147, Wise Legion, 461; veterans' organizations, 95, 146, 660. *See also* Civil War
Confederate States of America, 47, 146, 182, 207, 320; bond, 488
Conger, A. L., 268
Congo, 428
Congregational Church, 493
Congress of Industrial Organization (C.I.O.), 419, 670, 988; Organizing Committee, 56; Political Action Committee, 56
Conley, Phil, 179, 554, 698, 870
Conley, William G., 111, 330, 387, 419, 724, 844, 934, 967
Conn, Ellsworth, 324
Conn, George, 324
Conn, Hezekiah, 324
Conn, Jacob, 324
Conn, Lloyd H., 324
Conn family, 324
Connell, John, 71

Pennsylvania," by Raymond M. Bell, 46

Daugherty family, 322

Daughters of the American Revolution, 219, 220, 325

Daughters of the American Revolution, Morgantown Chapter, 501, 620, 858, 1049

Davidson family, 230, 319

Davis, 1040

Davis, Albert, 229

Davis, Annie Dent, 466

Davis, C. Anderson, 972

Davis, Edgar Johnson, 466

Davis, Henry Gassaway, 55, 90, 91, 184, 221, 222, 234, 268, 283, 287, 330, 405, 494, 543, 724, 781, 908, 980, 1000

Davis, Innis C. *See* Davis, Mrs. Thomas B.

Davis, Isaac, 229

Davis, Jefferson, 93

Davis, John, 224

Davis, John J., 224, 324, 451, 486, 745, 1010

Davis, Mrs. John J., 156

Davis, John W., 50, 62, 111, 153, 224, 225, 226, 353, 369, 418, 434, 486, 492, 554, 745, 844, 873, 934, 984

Davis, Julia McDonald, 224, 226

Davis, Rezin C., 224

Davis, Richard Harding, 33

Davis, Silas R., 229

Davis, Thomas B., 222, 934, 980, 1000

Davis, Mrs. Thomas B. (Innis C.), 223, 886, 934

Davis, Varina Jefferson, 835

Davis, William P., 227

Davis family, 225, 229, 319, 322, 324, 468, 745

Davis and Elkins College, 631

Davis Child Shelter, 221, 222

Davis Coal and Coke Co., 228, 268

Davis-Cox family, 152

Davison, A. H., 230

Davison family, 230

Davisson, E. M., 584

Davisson family, 230, 737

Davy, 1022

Dawson, D. Boone, 988

Dawson, William M. O., 231, 330, 349, 511, 569, 724, 788, 984, 1000, 1018

Dawson Station, Pa., 1

Day, Edith Eleanor, 593

Day, George T., 869

Day, Solomon, 649

Day family, 593

Dayton, Alston G., 90, 106, 178, 195, 221, 232, 283, 543, 569, 596, 723, 781, 1000, 1035

Dayton, Arthur S., 233

Dayton, Mrs. Arthur S., 234

Dayton, Ruth Woods, 234

Dayton, Spencer, 47, 90, 221, 232, 234, 287, 333, 727, 1010

Dayton, Ohio, 392

Deakins family, 235

Dean family, 326

Death records, 115, 844, 890

Debar, J. H. Diss, 47, 62, 90, 236, 258, 333, 510, 577, 835, 929

Debating society records, 684

deBrahm, John Gerald William, 237

Debs, Eugene V., 844

Decatur, Stephen, 1005

Deckers Creek Sand Co., 631

"A Declaration of the People of Virginia Represented in Convention at the City of Wheeling, Thursday, June 13th, 1861," 998

Deeds. *See* Land: deeds, grants, and papers

Deep Bottom, Va., 143

Deep Hollow Coal Co., 266

Deepwater Railway Co., 95, 699

DeHass, Wills, 4, 688

DeHaven family, 468

Delaware, 885, 913

Demain, E. R., 238

Demain, Henry, 238

Demain, R. H., 238

Demain family, 238

Dement, George, 198

Dement family, 198

Democratic National Committee, 482, 543

Democratic National Convention: 1876, 90; 1928, 112

Democratic Party, 91, 111, 221, 225, 262, 350, 405, 443, 447, 476, 482, 486, 513, 542, 543, 562, 593, 697, 698, 724, 746, 836, 844, 896, 939, 1035

261

Dempsey, Jack, 239
Denmar Sanitarium, 984
Dennis, Thomas H., 183
Dent, Herbert Warder, 240
Dent, John, 241
Dent, Marmaduke, 242
Dent, Marmaduke H., 243, 569
Dent, William M., 244
Dent family, 240, 322
Dentists and dentistry, 215, 684, 987
Department stores, 652, 674
Depew, Chauncey, 268
Depression, 111, 473, 934
Dering, F. A., 738
"Descendants of James Arnett of Monongalia County," by L. D. Arnett, 324
Descriptive List of Manuscript Collections of the State Historical Society of Wisconsin, 254
Desegregation, 792, 807
DeSellem, A. G., 428
Des Moines, Iowa, 230
Despard, C. S., 707
Detectives, 627
Detroit, Mich., 1033
DeVault family, 649
Devil's Brigade, 857
Devore, John, 198
Devore family, 198
Dew, Thomas R., 877
Dew family, 324
Dewey, Thomas E., 353, 387, 896
Diaries and journals, 14, 19, 36, 45, 50, 67, 69, 77, 92, 94, 143, 146, 155, 156, 182, 184, 193, 195, 198, 209, 212, 214, 256, 266, 301, 312, 316, 340, 366, 372, 388, 400, 414, 427, 458, 463, 464, 467, 478, 487, 497, 513, 537, 548, 567, 578, 626, 649, 654, 665, 672, 674, 682, 685, 708, 721, 734, 744, 753, 770, 783, 796, 804, 820, 832, 844, 847, 853, 856, 857, 880, 893, 907, 938, 945, 949, 1007, 1009, 1010, 1018, 1019
"Diary Extracts, Capt. James S. Cassady, 1866," 182
Diaz, Porfirio, 221
Dickinson, J. Q., 680
Dickinson, J. Q. & Co., 245
Dickinson family, 513, 903

Dickinson et al. v. Winifrede Mining and Manufacturing Co., 1024
Dickinson Salt Works, 245
Dickson, James, 246
Dickson, William, 246
Dickson Brothers, 246
Dille, Thomas R., 247, 622, 951
Dille family, 247
Dils family, 468
Dimmitt, John, 248
Dimmitt family, 248
Dirksen, Everett M., 387, 413, 480
Disarmament, 490
Disciples of Christ, 94, 114, 119, 398, 777, 784
A Discourse . . . on the Claims of the Baptist Churches to Descent from John the Baptist, 777
Dispanet family, 368
Displaced persons, 480
Distilling, 684
District of Columbia. *See* Washington, D. C.
Dixie, 522
Dixon, Jeremiah, 567
Dixon, Thomas W., 249
"A Documentary Case Study of Education in West Virginia, 1910-1960 . . . ," 263
"Documentary History of the 150th West Virginia National Guard," 723
Dodd, Thomas J., 3
Doddridge, John, 250
Doddridge, Philip, 250, 797, 1033
Doddridge family, 250
Doddridge County, 261, 381, 522; churches, 258; education, 258; history, 258; reminiscences, 258
Dodds, Gideon, 131, 641
Dodds, Mrs. Gideon, 131, 619, 641
Dodge, W. E., 1018
Dolliver, J. P., 347
Dolly, Abijah, 971
Donham, Ralph, 166
Donnally, Andrew, 877
Donnally family, 319
Donnally and Steele Kanawha Salt Works, 251
Dorchester, S. C., 880
Doubleday, Russell, 626
Douglass, Theodora, 593
Douglass family, 319

Doyle family, 324
"Do You Remember," 582
Dragoo family, 322
Drake, Leah Bodine, 253
Drake, William Clinton, 324
Draper, John W., 458
Draper, Lyman C., 254, 280
Droop Mountain, 573
Droop Mountain Battlefield, 984
Droving, 552
Drug abuse, 611
Drugs and druggists, 313, 512, 883.
 See also Physicians
Drummond family, 322
Dry Fork Lumber Co., 525
Dublin, 573
DuBois, Oscar, 331
DuBois, W. E. B., 562
DuBois family, 324
Duckwall, Joseph S., 248, 871
Duckwall family, 672
Duddington, E. E., 387
Dudley Woodbridge and Co., 1032
Duels, 400
Duff, Patrick, 146
Duffie, Gen., 143
Duff's College, 874
Dulles, John Foster, 299
Duluth, Minn., 36
Dunbar High School, 12
Duncan, John Steele, 146
Dunmore's War, 160
Dunn, Thomas L., 255
Dunn family, 255, 324
Dunnington, George A., 146
DuPont, P. S., 805
Durham, Joseph, 672
Durham family, 672
Durkin, Patrick, 766
Durrett, Braxton B., 256
Durrett family, 256
Durry family, 256
Dworshak, Henry, 413
Dyer, Roger, 257
Dyer, William, 257
Dyer, Zebulon, 257
Dyer family, 257, 319, 324

Eagan family, 319
Earl, J. A., 258
Earl of Dartmouth, 237
Early, Jubal, 142, 183, 184, 573, 853

"Early Days of Mining in Marion County," by Helen M. Fleming, 284
"Early Events in the Valley of Ohio, 1787 to 1837," 685
Eastern Panhandle, 466, 470
Easton, John B., 419
Easton-Avery Community, 115, 259
Easton-Avery Farm Woman's Club, 259
Eastwood family, 319
Eaton, John, 797
Eby, Cecil D., Jr., 260
Eccles, Marriner S., 965
Echols, John, 142
E Clampus Vitus, 261
Economic Development Agency, 413
Economics, 214, 340
Eddy, Mary Baker, 864
Edgar, Thomas, 100
Edge of the Forest, 843
Edison, Charles, 111
Editors: letters and papers, 33, 96, 111, 183, 188, 192, 217, 231, 262, 311, 330, 349, 531, 543, 661, 715, 724, 844, 873, 887, 1000
Edmiston, Andrew, 111, 214, 262, 419, 562, 988
Edmiston, Matthew, 47, 577
Edray, 550
Education, 4, 28, 33, 67, 73, 79, 81, 90, 113, 169, 183, 234, 264, 281, 419, 459, 493, 751, 752, 784, 796, 805, 820, 869, 1033; Arkansas, 224; Berkeley County, 806; desegregation, 807; Fairmont, 840; Hardy County, 808; Harpers Ferry, 805; Harrison County, 805, 809, 810; Marshall County, 805; Mason County, 805; Mississippi, 224; Monongalia County, 805, 811, 812; Morgan County, 637; music, 978; Pendleton County, 815; Preston County, 816; secondary schools, 817; West Virginia, 263, 897, 1035. *See also* Schools
Edwards, William, 266
Edwards, William Henry, 265, 266, 415
Edwards, William Seymour, 330
Edwards, William W., 266

263

Edwards family, 266, 321
Egypt, 37, 39, 183
Egypt, W. Va., 352
Eighteenth Amendment, 844
"18th and 19th Century . . . History . . . Virginia, (West) Virginia, and Kentucky Families," 361
"18th and 19th Century People . . . ," by Hazel Groves Hansrote, 361
Eight-hour day, 345
Eisenhower, Dwight D., 3, 267, 353, 413
Eleanor: Homestead project, 988
Elections. See Campaigns and elections
Electric power, 36, 746
Electronics, 176
Elements of Biology, 870
Eliot, Charles W., 1018
Elizabeth, Pa., 39
Elk Creek Oil and Gas Co., 421
Elkins, 187; homesteads, 904
Elkins, Davis, 330, 724, 788, 1000
Elkins, Stephen B., 90, 91, 221, 222, 268, 283, 330, 377, 430, 451, 569, 781, 788, 980, 1000, 1036, 1048
Elkins Lumber Co., 900
Elk River, 880
Elkwater, 721
Ellender, Allen J., 413
Ellis, Hubert S., 387
Elm Grove: lumber industry, 819
Elmira, N. Y., 657, 846
Emigration, 1033; West Virginia, 211
Emma Graham (steamboat), 862
Encyclopedia Americana, 870
Engineers' papers, 39, 173, 458, 484
England, 429, 491, 492, 1033
England family, 756
"England to America," 626
Engle family, 323
"Engle Family of Barbour County, West Virginia," 323
English, 687, 752
English investors, 791
"Enoch Rector, His Fore-fathers and Descendants," 773
Ensminger family, 433
Entomologists, 424
Entomology, 265
Envelopes, 794
Episcopal Church, 137, 138, 744, 925, 938

Equality Oil Co., 269
Erskine and Caruthers, 1
Escambia River, 744
Eschman family, 474
Essays on Men, Things and Events, 676
Estate settlements, 62, 193, 224, 313, 314, 391, 475, 497, 534, 552, 561, 563, 600, 661, 748, 777, 842, 871, 890, 925, 969, 1033
Estray records, 600, 623, 684
Etna-Connellsville Coke Co., 270
Eureka Pipeline Co., 1003
Europe, 67, 100, 180, 312, 513
Evangelical Lutheran Church, 136
Evangelists, 286, 874, 875
Evans, D. T., 345
Evans, David, 247
Evans, James, 32
Evans, John, 235, 247, 617
Evans, Thomas R., 844
Evans family, 324, 326
Evansville, 366
Evarts, William, 280
Evarts manuscripts in the Library of Congress, 268
"Events in the History of Cove District, Barbour County, West Virginia," by John C. Shaw, 35
Everett, Edward, 96
Everly, Casper, 603
Everly, Henry, 324
Everly, John Lafayette, 324
Everly, Joseph, 324
Everly, Peter, 324
Everly family, 324
"Evolution of a Midwestern Octogenarian," 88
Ewin, William, 55, 271
Ewing family, 322
Exchange Bank of Virginia, Weston Branch, 47, 272
Executive Mansion, 964

Fabius, Hardy County, 43
Fact book, 1050
"Facts about Tygart Valley Homestead, Elkins, West Virginia," 904
Fairbank family, 319
Fair Deal, 387
Fairfax, Elizabeth, 275

Goose Creek Oil Co., Wheeling, 431
Gore, Howard M., 336, 425, 468,
626, 984, 1000
Gore, John C., 592
Gore family, 425, 433
Gore Hospital, 984
Gorman, Arthur P., 91, 221
Goshen Baptist Church, 114
Gothard family, 187
Goudy, William M., 143
Gough family, 468
Gould, Henry Wadsworth, 324
Gould family, 324
Gower, Karl K., ed., 135
G. P. Putnam's Sons, 217
Grafton, 146, 293, 586, 651, 657,
939, 950, 1001; B. & O. agent at,
32; Baptist Church in, 69; broad-
sides, 69; Civil War, 69, 507; gen-
eral store records, 69; lawyer's
papers, 788; map of McGraw and
Yates addition, 240; Memorial
Day celebrations, 69; National
Cemetery, 69; photographs of,
69; residents' papers, 69, 543;
Rotary Club, 69
Grafton and Greenbrier Railroad, 55,
543
Graham, Joseph, 1054
Graham family, 1054
Graham-Yeager Lumber Co., 593
Grain, 552
Grand Army of the Republic (G. A.
R.), 820; Morgantown Post No. 5,
27; West Liberty Post, 78, 212
Grange and grangers, 14, 16, 155,
249, 324, 711
Grange Cooperative Association, 249
Grant, Howard B., 323
Grant, Ulysses S., 74, 146, 183, 268,
791
"Grant and Lee," by William D.
Ford, 146
Grant County, 21, 296, 487, 832,
971; churches, 133; justice dock-
et, 337
Grant District, Monongalia County,
609
Grant Township, 337
Granville, 242, 605
"Grasses of West Virginia," 51
Gratz, Michael, 571
Graves Creek, 400
Gray, Fred W., 338

Grayson, Ky., 697
Great Britain, 234
Greater Huntington Hospital Associ-
ation, 492
Great Falls and Old Dominion Rail-
road, 268
Greathouse family, 723
Great Kanawha Coal, Oil & Metal-
lurgic Co., 339
Great Warrior Trail, 440
Greece, 39, 180
Greeley, Horace, 96
Green, Duff, 905
Green, Theodore F., 480
Green, Thomas, 340
Green, William, 56, 111, 330, 419,
844, 965
Green family, 425
Green and Laing, 309
Greenback Party, 657
Green Bank, 980
Green Bay, Wis., 918
Greenbrier (steamboat), 862
Greenbrier Baptist Association, 117
Greenbrier, Cheat and Elk Railroad
Co., 102
Greenbrier Coal and Coke Co., 1021
Greenbrier County, 1, 92, 183, 249,
324, 341, 593, 742, 783, 797,
856, 980, 1026; biography, 183;
churches, 183; court records, 456
Greenbrier Hotel, 1005
Greenbrier Independent, 183
Greenbrier Male Academy, 316
Greenbrier Valley, 461
Greenbrier Valley Industrial Exposi-
tion Association, 341
Green County, Ill., 704
Greene, Daniel, 1033
Greene, John, 1033
Greene, Richard, 1033
Greene County, Pa., 468, 551, 649,
753, 829, 844, 1001
Greenville, 346, 624
Greenville Mining and Manufacturing
Co., 346
Greenway Court, 1043
Greer, H. C., 715, 951
Gregg family, 324
Gregory, Mahala Chapman Mace, 342
Griffin family, 324
Griffith, Romulus R., 324
Griffith, William, 324
Griffithsville, 304

Hangtown, Calif., 48
Hanna, M. A., 268, 1000
Hanna family, 324
Hansford, 831
Hansford, Felix G., 359
Hansford family, 359
Hanson, Thomas, 360
Hansrote, Hazel Groves, 361
Hanway, Samuel, 362, 588
Hardesty, C. Howard, 984
Hardin family, 468
Harding, Warren G., 353
Hardman, George, 723
Hardman, N., 723
Hardman, Sam W., 363
Hardman family, 319
Hardware stores, 309, 657, 819
Hardwicke, John Benjamin, 957
Hardwood sales, 285
Hardy, Billy Meridith, 624
Hardy County, 364, 365, 366, 367, 368, 435, 487, 560, 949, 971; agriculture, 43; Board of Education, 487, 808; county court minute book, 365; deeds, 495, 971; history, 367; justice of the peace, 43; Moorefield, 367; newspapers, 367; post office records, 43; residents' papers, 43, 552, 920; tax book, 593
Hare, Charles, 571
Hare, Robert, 571
Harkness, C. W., 91
Harkness, E. S., 91
Harkness, N. W., 91
Harman, George, 21
Harman, Joseph, 1
Harmer, Harvey W., 369, 387
Harmer family, 369
Harmison, Charles, 370
Harmon, Judson, 1018
Harmony circuit, 537
Harned, Joseph E., 371
Harness, 512
Harness family, 364
Harold, James, 73
Harold, Nan Brooke, 73, 372
Harper, Charles P., 373
Harper, Henry, 323
Harpers Ferry, 144, 149, 280, 375, 526, 573, 593, 823, 869; John Brown, 76; Camp Hill, 593; Civil War, 143, 593; history, 374; physician's papers, 559

Harpers Ferry Seminary, 375, 805
Harper's Weekly, 260, 1018
Harriman, W. Averell, 480, 844
Harris, Thomas M., 376, 573, 727
Harris family, 876
Harrison, Benjamin, 221, 235, 268, 377, 569, 835
Harrison, Jordan, 378
Harrison, Samuel, 379
Harrison, Thomas W., 380
Harrison, William A., 762
Harrison, William H., 877
Harrison family, 322, 378
Harrisonburg, Va., 340
Harrison County, 102, 122, 167, 324, 384, 389, 425, 474, 490, 683, 745, 762, 789; birth, death, and marriage records, 844; Board of Education, 810; Gideon Camden, 90; cattle raising, 107; churches, 369; construction of early residences, 599; family records, 890; genealogy, 319; history, 369; land papers, 156, 182, 235, 280, 320, 333, 382, 390, 522, 588, 599, 728; lawyer's case book, 17; library service, 975; Methodism, 369; National Guard, 844; newspaper clippings, 213, 381; obituaries, 890; school commissioner, 809; schools, 805; tax book, 383
Harrison County, Mo., 370
Harrison County Labor Federation, 384
Harrison manuscripts in the Library of Congress, 268
Harrisville, 36, 573
Harrisville circuit, 125
Hart, Albert Bushnell, 106, 760
Hart family, 319
Hartford, 504
Hartford Convention, 146
Hartford Fire Insurance Co., 309
Hartzell, B. F., 385
Harvard University, 62, 106, 154, 544, 797
Harvey, C. W. and Co., 410
Harvey, Carl B., 837
Hassler, Edgar Wakefield, 501
Hastings, Lynn, 812
Hatcher family, 319
Hatcher-McGinnis law firm, 542
Hatfield, Coleman, 386, 505

271

Hill, Sanford, 410
Hill, William H., 14
Hill family, 326
Hillman, Sidney H., 988
Hillsboro Male and Female Academy, 550
Hill's Central Hotel, Parkersburg, 593
Hinckle family, 672
Hiner family, 319, 320
Hinkle family, 1054
Hinton, 211, 878
Hinton dam, 484
Hinzeman family, 319
Hirst, Daniel, 412
Historians' letters and papers, 4, 39, 88, 106, 112, 247, 310, 349, 1007
"Historic Account of the Oil and Gas Development in Marion County, West Virginia, with Special Mention of Mannington and Fairview Fields," by Joseph F. McNeely, 551
"Historical Notes on Ice's Ferry," by John L. Johnston, 437
"Historical Record of Selective Service in West Virginia," 724
Historical Research Project, 400
Historical societies, 131, 369, 622, 970, 1029
"Historical Survey of the Churches of Monongalia County, West Virginia," by Mrs. Gideon S. Dodds, 131
"Historic American Buildings Surveys for Harpers Ferry," 593
"History and Genealogy of the Conns, 1736-1961," 324
History of American Schoolbooks, 102
"History of Big and Little Skin Creek Community (Vandalia), Lewis County, West Virginia," 363
"History of Dentistry in West Virginia, 1907-1952," 987
History of Grant and Hardy Counties, West Virginia, by E. L. Judy, 470
"History of Harrison County Schools (1787-1956)," 805
"History of Methodism in West Union and Doddridge County," 258
"History of Simpson Chapel and Community," 838

"History of the Forks of Cheat Baptist Church," by Millie Hunter, 294
"History of the George Foster Family," 299
"History of the History Department" (West Virginia University), 88
"History of the Pierpoint-Avery Community," 725
"History of the Various Courts of the County of Monongalia," by James R. Moreland, 614, 631
"History of Wardensville, West Virginia," 547
"History of West Virginia's First Picture Post Cards," 573
"History of West Virginia University," 88
Hite, Joist, 494
Hite family, 364, 474
Hoar, George F., 280
Hoblitzell, John D., Jr., 413, 698
Hockhocking Valley Railroad, 921
Hodges, Bernie, 36
Hodges, Charles E., 28, 262, 476
Hodges, Thomas E., 760, 934, 984
Hodges family, 201
Hoffman, John E., 414
Hoffman, John H., 414
Hoffman, John Stringer, 415
Hoffman (Huffman) family, 876
Hogarth, Paul, 822
Hoge family, 593
Hogg, Gory, 476
Hoke, Catherine White, 211
Hoke family, 211
Holiday's Cove, 97, 201
Holiness Church, 114
Holland, Spessard L., 455
Holland family, 876
Hollingsworth, Levi, 430
Hollingsworth family, 672
Holly Creek, 116
Holly River, 522
Holly River and Addison Railroad, 68
Holly Spring, Miss., 893
Holme, Frank, 416
Holmes, David, 593
Holmes, Oliver W., 33
Holstein Lumber Co., 525
Holston circuit, 463
Holt, Andrew E., 419

Hunting, 389, 740
"Hunting the Wild Guinea. West Virginia's Most Elusive Game Bird," 573
Huntingdon County, Pa., 545
Huntington, 180, 239, 492, 493, 674, 802, 972
Huntington, C. P., 91, 1018
Huntington Bar Association, 937
Huntington Memorial Hospital, 387
Huntington State Hospital, 434, 984
Hurst family, 319
Huston, C. R., 951
Huston and Demain, Contractors, 238, 631
Huston Engraving Co., 33
Hutchings, Paul R., 965
Hutter, Gottleib and Sons, 435
Hutton family, 319
Huttonsville, 203
Huttonsville Academy, 408
Hyden, Arthur M., 387
Hyman, Samuel, 198
Hyman family, 198, 326

Ice, W. T., Jr., 436
Ice family, 437
Ice company, 421
Ice's Ferry, 437
Ickes, Harold L., 262, 419, 486
Iden, Gay, 438
Iglehart family, 468
Illinois, 155, 156, 596, 659, 704, 946, 951
Imboden, G. W., 699
Imboden, John D., 90, 98, 143, 184, 573, 732, 1035; partisans, 573
Imboden Rangers, 721
Immigration, 82, 90, 236, 396, 415, 480, 493, 510, 649, 657, 682
The Immortal Six Hundred, 660
"The Impact of a Half Century of Professional Education," 264
Independence, 1
"Index to Militia in the Florida War; and the New York Militia, Northern Frontier Disturbance, 1837-8," 913
India, 369, 544
Indiana, 88, 322, 535, 651, 844
Indianapolis, Ind., 893
Indian captivities, 508

Indian Creek, Monroe County, 624
Indian Mound Cemetery, 984
Indians, 24, 48, 160, 280, 389, 400, 437, 439, 440, 493, 508, 511, 594, 657, 680, 682, 858, 918
Indian trails, 440
Industrial Home for Colored Boys, 984
Industrial Home for Colored Girls, 984
Industrial Home for Girls, 984
Industrial School for Boys, 984
Industrial Union Council, West Virginia, 988
Industries, 53, 391
Industry, 91
Influenza, 830, 934
Ingalls, James Monroe, 441
Inghram, Thomas, 324
Ingram, John, 324
"In Memory of Jessie Hickman Jamison," by Helen M. Fleming, 284
"In Memory of John Marshall Jacobs, a Good Churchman," by Helen M. Fleming, 284
Inns, 748, 886
Inskeep, William, 357
Insurance, 309, 356, 455
International Order of Odd Fellows, 640
Interracial Council, 988
Interstate Bridge Co., 532
Interstate Commerce Commission, 175
"Introduction to American Expansion Policy," 88
Inwood, Demonstration Packing Plant at, 984
Iowa, 155, 195, 230, 946
Ireland, 73, 94, 946, 1035
Iron, 97, 699, 791
Iron and Steel Works Association of Virginia, 699
Iron furnaces and iron industry, 34, 174, 274, 346, 442, 513, 535, 578, 593, 616, 723, 748, 946; Iron Valley and Pennsylvania Railroad, 55
Iron Valley and Morgantown Railroad, 543
Irons, J. C., 443
Ironton, Huntington, Pomeroy, Par-

Keeney, C. Frank, 592
Keeney's Creek, 681
Kefauver, Estes, 480
Keister family, 324
Keister-Jenkins families, 649
Kellam, W. P., 233, 958
Keller family, 321
Kelley, Benjamin F., 215, 803
Kelley family, 324, 326
Kellogg, Horace, 144
Kellogg, Joseph M., 474
Kelly, Edwin P., 475
Kelly, Henry R., 475
Kelly, Robert G., 419, 476, 562
Kelly, W. R., 475
Kelly, William, 151
Kelly family, 151
Kemper, J. L., 280
Kendall, Norman F., 477
Kenesaw Mountain, 302
Kenly, John R., 776
Kenna, John E., 90, 91, 184, 221, 405, 657
Kenna, John N., 111
Kennedy, Anna, 224
Kennedy, John F., 3, 743
Kennedy, John Pendleton, 280, 478
Kennedy, Philip Pendleton, 185
Kennedy, Robert F., 3
Kennerly family, 1043
Kenova, 493
Kent, Frank R., 3
Kenton, Simon, 649
Kentucky, 107, 324, 340, 360, 361, 513, 531, 697, 745, 818, 946, 1033, 1038; circuit court, 531; coal, 111; United Mine Workers, 56
Kentucky Christian Missionary Society, 780
Kentucky Commission on Human Rights, 972
Kentucky Gazette, 531
Kerens, R. C., 268
Kern's Fort, 649
Kerr, Robert S., 554
Kesecker family, 433
Kessler-Hatfield Hospital, 492
Kessler-Hatfield Hospital and Training School, 387
Kester family, 319
Ketcham, Gertrude Wright, 1049
Keyes, Bertha Holt, 421
Keyes, W. G., 421

Keyes family, 421
Keyes Lumber Co., 421
Keys, C. M., 5
Keys, H., 5
Keyser, 309, 479, 657, 781
Keyser Tribune, 560
Keystone Manufacturing Co., 653
Khedive, Army of the, 183
Kilgore, Harley M., 262, 387, 480, 724, 844, 870, 960, 965, 988
Kim's Run, 366
Kimball, Charles H., 387
Kimball, William E., 573
Kincaid family, 325
Kincheloe family, 468
King, H. M., 324
King, W. M., 1051
King family, 468
Kingwood, 347, 481, 544, 654, 724, 976, 1048; William G. Brown in, 78; churches, 124; map, 748; Methodist Church, 55, 123, 347; Methodist ministers, 123; photographs, 748; physician's papers, 924; residents' papers, 275, 346; survey of road to Morgantown, 273
Kingwood and West Union Turnpike, 951
Kingwood Coal and Coke Co., 1048
Kinsey's Run Brethren Church, 368
Kittle, Cyrus, 766
Kittle, Jacob, 151
Kittle family, 151
Knabenshue, A. B., 888
Knapp family, 876
Knight family, 319
Knights of Labor: traveling card, 834
Knob Fork, 329, 722
Knott, J. Proctor, 280
Knoxville, Tenn., 148
Koon family, 186
Koontz, Arthur B., 262, 482, 554
Korea, 369
Kortrecht family, 474
Kraft, J. C., 1
Kramer, S. E. B., 483
Krebs, Charles E., 484
Krebs, et al. v. Morgantown Bridge and Improvement Co., 640
Krock, Arthur, 353
Kuchel, Thomas H., 413
Ku Klux Klan, 227, 331, 485, 659, 683, 844

Kump, H. G., 111, 418, 419, 476, 486, 844, 873, 896, 934, 965, 967
Kurtz family, 321
Kurz family, 321
Kuykendall, George Benson, 487
Kuykendall, James William, 364, 487
Kuykendall, Mrs. Joe P., 488
Kuykendall family, 364, 487

Labor, 56, 167, 169, 216, 300, 334, 345, 384, 387, 418, 419, 480, 596, 627, 664, 670, 689, 700, 792, 795, 821, 834, 844, 852, 895, 946, 965, 988, 1023, 1033
Labor Argus, 977
Labor's Daily, 480
Labrador, 214
Ladies Aid Societies, 661
Ladies of the Maccabees: Progressive Hive No. 8 (Morgantown), 489
Ladies Visiter, Martinsburg, 565
Ladwig, Mrs. Otto Worthington, 490
LaFollette, Robert M., Jr., 111, 419
Laidley, 877
Laidley, B. M., 984
Laidley, James M., 510
Laidley, W. S., 797
Laidley family, 319
Laird, William R., 554
Laishley, Peter T., 240, 491
Laishley, Richard, 491
Laishley family, 491
Lakin, James S., 330, 492
Lakin, John S., 984
Lakin State Hospital, 972, 984
LaMar Coal Co., 631
Lambert, Frederick B., 493
Lambert, Oscar Doane, 268, 494
Lambert family, 187, 518
Lamon, Adrian W., 193
Lamont, Daniel S., 221, 1018
Lancaster, 355
Lancaster, Ohio, 921
Land, 55, 90, 235, 236, 249, 262, 333, 340, 455, 495, 580, 762, 840, 844, 1009, 1020; bounty, 913; bounty claims, 1033; deeds, grants, and papers, 18, 24, 40, 52, 68, 72, 78, 102, 158, 160, 191, 196, 235, 268, 281, 282, 283, 286, 296, 333, 344, 357, 359, 364, 370, 390, 391, 399, 420, 430, 470, 472, 487, 488, 495, 522, 526, 532, 535, 536, 538, 543, 571, 577, 584, 588, 593, 600, 603, 616, 623, 656, 684, 709, 728, 746, 748, 749, 753, 773, 786, 844, 846, 856, 876, 885, 925, 947, 949, 951, 969, 971, 1019; development, 1048; Harrison County, 382, 683; Marshall County, 563; Monongalia County, 683; plats and surveys, 18, 62, 78, 86, 182, 191, 194, 235, 280, 362, 366, 432, 481, 487, 495, 522, 538, 599, 600, 616, 623, 631, 650, 684, 723, 749, 767, 856, 879, 925, 942, 946, 1026; sales and ejectments, 44, 58, 333; speculation, 82, 91, 271, 570; titles, 382; warrants, 156, 495, 616, 925, 1033
Landis, James M., 988
Land of Canaan, Plain Tales from the Mountains of West Virginia, 740
Land of the Laurel, 654
Landon, Alfred M., 353
Lane Seminary Library, 797
Lang, John, 156
Langer, William, 417
Langley, Samuel P., 1018
Languages, 430
Lanham, Zadock, 885
Lanham family, 509, 649
Lanier, Clifford, 33
Lansdowne, Arthur J., 697
Lantz, 78
Lantz, R. S., 496
Lantz, William, 496
Lantz family, 856
Larew, John M., 497
Larew, Peter, 497
Larew family, 497
Larue, Dr., 935
"Later History of Moorefield and Hardy County," 367
Latham, George R., 499
Latham, Jean Lee, 500
Latimer and Co., 902
Latrobe, Benjamin H., 577
Launce, John, 618
Laurel Brigade, 316
Laurel Hill, Civil War battle of, 576, 651, 853
Laurel Lick circuit, 537
Lausche, Frank, 554
Lawrence, Kans., 474
Lawrence, William H., 146

Lawrence County, Ohio, 493
Lawrence-Townley family, 217
Lawson family, 319
Lawton, Sarah A., 507
Lawyers: letters and papers, 17, 38, 47, 49, 62, 82, 90, 95, 103, 111, 154, 192, 200, 202, 224, 225, 226, 232, 234, 247, 280, 283, 287, 296, 311, 333, 334, 335, 369, 391, 405, 415, 436, 445, 451, 486, 531, 532, 542, 543, 577, 631, 682, 683, 697, 701, 724, 734, 745, 754, 762, 781, 788, 844, 877, 921, 934, 939, 1003, 1019, 1035, 1048, 1052
Layman, Mildred Hassler, 501
Lazell, J. M., 549
Lazell, Thomas, 196
Lazelle family, 755
Leach, Julian G., 9
Leacock, Stephen, 33
League of Nations, 353
Lear, Tobias, 502
Leather, 498, 788, 916, 935
Leckey, Howard L., 503
Lecompton, Kans. Ter., 313
Lederer, Anna, 504
Ledgers. See Accounts and account books
Lee, Fitzhugh, 1018
Lee, Henry, 391, 535
Lee, Howard B., 505
Lee, Richard Henry, 506
Lee, Robert E., 74, 146, 183, 507, 796
Lee, William L., 505
Lee family, 319
Leeper, Thomas M., 508
Leeper family, 508
Leffel, James, 216
Lehew, Peter, 997
Lehew family, 997
Lemke, William, 419
Lempert, Leon H. and Son, 640
Lenox, Mass., 1049
Leonard, Flora Farnsworth, 349
Leonian, Nell Lanham, 509
Lesson books, 99, 195, 497, 623
Letcher, John, 90, 143, 152, 184, 797
Lettel, James, 902
"A Letter from Home," 747
Levassor, Eugene, 510
Levees, 688

LeVelle family, 649
Lewellen family, 649
Lewis, Art, 861
Lewis, C. C., 844
Lewis, Charles, 1020
Lewis, Charles C., Jr., 513
Lewis, Charles C., Sr., 513
Lewis, John D., 513
Lewis, John L., 56, 387, 419, 480, 627, 844
Lewis, O. C., 677
Lewis, Thomas, 942
Lewis, Virgil A., 330, 454, 543
Lewis family, 468, 513, 1020
Lewis and Hedge, 72
Lewisburg, 69, 142, 207, 456, 467, 564, 820, 880, 883, 1017; churches, 183; Civil War in, 183
Lewisburg Female Institute, 180, 183, 550
Lewisburg Landmarks, by Ruth Woods Dayton, 234
Lewisburg Seminary, 183
Lewis County, 184, 474, 838, 885, 1051; agricultural practices, 1853, 147; birth, death, and marriage records, 844; county archives, 512; county court records, 512; folklore, 291; genealogy, 319; land papers, 58, 495, 885; lawyer's papers, 17; New Englanders in, 58; pioneers, 363; residents' papers, 23, 516; subscription school, 305; Vandalia, 363
Lexington, Ky., 44, 340, 531, 780, 1033
Lexington, Va., 224, 564
Libby Prison, 732
Liberia Colonization Society, 921
Libraries, 102, 156, 374, 478, 775, 969, 958, 974, 975, 1046
Lichens, 338
"Life of Fred Mooney, by Himself," 627
"Life of Henry Floyd," by Robert L. Floyd, 4
"Life of Joseph H. Diss Debar," 258
"Life of Mad Ann Bailey, the Kanawha Valley Eccentric," 573
Lightburn, Benjamin, 516
Lightburn, Benjamin F. M. V., 516
Lightburn, John C. L., 516
Lightburn, Joseph A. J., 184, 514, 516, 727

Lightburn, Joseph B., 515
Lightburn family, 184, 319, 516
"Lighter Side of the Civil War," 573
Lilly, A. A., 517
Lilly, Edmund, 44
Lilly, Robert, 24
Lilly, Thomas, 24
Lilly, William Sellergrit, 24
Lilly Reunion, 517
Lincoln, Abraham, 268, 302, 480, 514, 573, 727, 726, 945
Lincoln family, 319, 361
Lincoln County, 510; census records, 493; court records, 493; oil industry, 304
Lincoln-Douglas debates, 224
Lindsay, Nicholas Vachel, 33, 626
Lindsay, Rella, 518
Lindsay, Vachel, 33, 626
Lindsey family, 322
Liquor, 1, 392
Lisez, Charles, 510
Lisez, Charles, Jr., 589
Lisez family, 589
Liston, Abraham, 746
Litchfield County, Conn., 234, 430
Literary societies, 146, 211, 244, 300, 430, 578
Little family, 741
"Little Hatch Bill," 418
Little Kanawha Navigation Co., 787
Little Kanawha Packet Line, 1012
Little Kanawha River, 155, 400, 527
Little Kanawha Syndicate, 268
Little Ridge, 366
Littleton, 1001
Little Warrior Trail, 440
Lively, Charles, 262
Liverpool Salt and Coal Co., 845
Livestock. See Cattle and livestock
Living Flora of West Virginia, by C. F. Millspaugh, 590
Livingston, Adam, 519
"Livingston's Conversion, History of Adam Livingston, . . . Jefferson County, Virginia," 519
Local history, 372, 578
Locomotive works, 4
Lodge, Henry Cabot, 413
Logan, 520
Logan (Mingo Chief), 818
Logan, John A., 657
Logan family, 468
Logan County, 170, 345, 493; cen-

sus, 1850, 521; coal strikes, 592; George Rogers Clark Floyd, 4; resident's papers, 288; Robert Morris land, 650
London, England, 567, 1033
London Naval Conference, 111
Long, D. L., 715
Long, Huey P., 419
Loomis, F. B., 1033
Loomis, Mahlon, 523
Looting, 143
Lorentz family, 319
Loring, Daniel, 941
Loring, W. W., 142, 183
Lossing, Benson J., 144
Lost City, 368
Lost River, 366, 511
Lot Bowen Mining Co., 224
Lott, John W., 844
Lotteries, 285, 598, 672, 885, 927
Loudin family, 319
Loudoun County, Va., 412
Lough, Elza T., 144
Lough, Glenn D., 42
Lough, Sarah Jane, 144
Louisa, Ky., 1038
Louisiana, 946
Louisiana Territory, 24
Louisville, Ky., 224, 340, 359, 478, 1033
Louisville Coal and Coke Co., 1021
Loup Creek Colliery Co., 699
Love, 493
Love family, 324
Loveland, F. C., 146
Lowell, Amy, 33
Lowgap, 116
Lowther, William, 524
Lowther family, 319, 324
"Lowther Family of West Virginia," 324
Lucas, Daniel B., 221, 224, 1018, 1036
Luce, Henry R., 353
Lucerne, 328
Ludlow, Colo., 56
Ludwig, William, 74
Lumber industry, 75, 90, 91, 157, 175, 195, 221, 235, 268, 315, 464, 513, 525, 587, 593, 681, 724, 751, 768, 797, 819, 825, 892, 1006, 1027; companies, 55, 281, 421, 447, 522, 600, 653,

McKeldin, Theodore R., 353, 562
McKemy family, 187
McKendree Hospital, 984
McKinley, William, 184, 569, 820, 1000
McKinney, Howard W., 972
McKinney, W. M., 182
McKown, Sarah Morgan, 548
McLane, Charles, 549
McLane, Joseph A., 549
McLane family, 319
McLaughlin, J. B., 960
McLaughlin, John, 729, 1049
McLaughlin, William, 729
McLaughlin family, 1049
McMahan, Porter, and Co., 735
McMaster, J. B., 310
McMechan family, 364
McMurtrie, William, 280
McNeel, Isaac, 550
McNeel, Summers, 550
McNeel, Winters, 550
McNeely, Hugh, 63
McNeely, Joseph F., 551
McNeely, Joseph Franklin, 551
"McNeely Family Records, with Historical Sketches and Key to Family Lineage," by Joseph F. McNeely, 551
McNeill, J. H., 971
McNeill, Jesse C., "Capture of Generals Kelly and Crook," 803
McNeill, John H., 143
McNeill, Louise, 713
McNeill family, 364
McNeill Hotel, 553
McNeill Rangers, 98, 143, 364, 573
McNemar family, 649
McNutt, Paul V., 418
McQuilkin family, 468
McWhorter, Minnie, 319
McWhorter family, 319
Madison, James, 495
Magistral Exploration Co. of Mexico, 268
Mahan family, 319
Maidsville, 494, 619
Mail routes, 333
Makowicz family, 319
Malden, 245, 938
Mallison, Sam T., 419, 554, 844
"The Man from West Virginia," 944
Manheim, 748
Mann, Isaac T., 175, 330

Mann family, 319
Mannington, 551, 555, 941
Mannington: gas industry, 594; history of, 594; oil industry, 594
Mannington District: history, 477
"The Mannington Story," 594
Mannington *Times,* 1
Manufacturers & Farmers Bank, Wheeling, 431
Maps, 175, 184, 268, 510, 876, 981, 1047, 1050; Baltimore and Ohio Railroad, 32; Barbour County, 146; Berkeley Springs, 748; Bruceton Mills, 748; Civil War, 146, 147, 182; east Florida, 237; Grafton, 240; Jackson County, 588; Kanawha River, 359; Kingwood, 481, 748; Manheim, 748; Mining, 163, 228; Monongalia County, 362; Morgantown, 631; Philippi, 1035; Preston County, 362, 746; Northern Neck, 494; Randolph County, 146; Rowlesburg, 748; Weston, 578
Marble, Manton, 1018
Marcato Music Club, 663
Marchand family, 322
Marietta, Ohio, 400, 685, 686, 820, 862, 1032, 1033
Marietta and Susquehanna Trading Co., 1033
Marietta Chair Co., 1027
Marietta College, 462
Marietta Collegiate Institute, 1033
Marietta Universalist Society, 820
Marion County, 167, 355, 389, 508, 582, 668, 844, 1001; broadsides, 581; civil war in, 146, 508; coal mining in, 284, 946; families, 477; flood in, 508; history, 477; history scrapbooks, 284; labor organizations, 670; land and school records, 36, 558; ministers in, 557; National Guard, 844; newspapers from, 1; oil and gas development in, 551; Republican Executive Committee, 661; residents' papers, 283, 284, 324, 508, 946; tax receipts, 171; teacher's register, 508; vital statistics, 508, 557
Marion County Historical Society, 582
Marketing, 836

283

Markets, 1032
Marland, William C., 353, 387, 965, 967
Marlinton, 561, 751, 754, 916
Marmion, George, 559
Marmion, Nicholas, 526, 559
Marmion, Robert A., 559
Marmion, William V., 559
Marple, John H., 593
Marple family, 319, 324
Marriage announcements, 1054
Marriage bonds, 323
"Marriage Bonds of Barbour County, Virginia, 1843," 323
Marriage records, 115, 183, 319, 320, 391, 491, 560, 684, 718, 803, 844, 890, 898, 947
Marsh, C. O., 34
Marsh, J. F., 984
Marshall, Jacob W., 182, 561
Marshall, John W., 193
Marshall, Vause, 416, 562
Marshall family, 364
Marshall Academy & College, 493
Marshall College, 984, 986
Marshall County, 229, 303, 902; archives, bonds, bridge records, case papers, Civil War bounty lists, court records, estate settlements, jail records, land, overseer of the poor, road records, school commissioners, surveyors, United States Admiralty Court, voter registration, 563
Marstiller, Charles M., 767
Marstiller, Nicholas, 767
Martha, 493
Martin, Alexander, 90, 179, 280, 369, 632, 753, 764
Martin, Clarence L., 480
Martin, Edward, 3, 413, 724
Martin, James H., 306
Martin, Joel, 931
Martin, John D., 564
Martin, Joseph, 166, 931
Martin, Joseph W., Jr., 387
Martin family, 322, 325
Martin Coal Co., 102
Martin Iron Works, 723
Martinsburg, 143, 144, 146, 280, 324, 478, 565, 820, 836, 857; churches, 137, 139
Martinsburg, Ohio, 190
Martinsburg Ladies Visiter, 565

Marvin, Langdon P., 480
Maryland, 235, 347, 361, 371, 470, 657, 740, 748, 790, 841, 844, 853, 880, 913, 936; birth control, 3; Methodist Church, 90; Methodist Episcopal Church, 129; stock raising, 3
Maryland Gazette, 687
Maryland Historical Magazine, 672
Maryland v. West Virginia, 976
Maryland-West Virginia: boundary line survey, 566, 976
Mason, Charles, 567
Mason, Frank, 3
Mason, James M., 90, 280, 452, 568, 569, 1048
Mason, James M., 2nd, 91, 221
Mason, John W., 224, 430, 455, 569, 632, 657
Mason family, 17, 324
Mason City, 423
Mason County, 324, 423, 585, 943; census records, 493; circuit judge's photograph, 787; Civil War, 146; coal industry, 304; county archives, 570; court records, 493; deeds and grants, 495, 571; early history, 204; map of Albert Gallatin lands in, 589; map of Washington lands in, 589; oil industry, 304; physician's papers, 778; resident's papers, 1019; Robinson Township School Board, 805; salt industry, 800; school records, 805
Mason-Dixon line, 369, 567, 572
Masons, 511, 684, 1051
Masontown, 631
Massachusetts, 913, 1049; Civil War, 11
Masters family, 324
Matamoros, Mexico, 1020
Matewan, 505
Matewan massacre, 627
Mathematics, 746
Matheny, H. E., 573
Mathers, E. L., 604
Mathers, Max, 574, 604
Mathews, Brander, 33
Mathews, Charles R., 211
Mathews, Henry M., 90, 280, 391, 575, 929
Mathews, Jacob W., 211
Mathews, John, 685

284

Mathews family, 319, 325
Matlick, Jacob G., 69
Matthews, Henry M., 333
Matthews family, 183
Maury, J. M., 359
Maury, M. F., Jr., 680
Maury, Matthew Fontaine, 500, 983
Maxwell, Edwin, 47
Maxwell, G. Ralph, 576
Maxwell, Hu, 498, 511, 576, 578, 617
Maxwell, Lewis, 577, 885
Maxwell, Robert E., 554
Maxwell, Rufus, 144, 578
Maxwell, Mrs. S. J., 576
Maxwell family, 319, 578
May, Samuel, 406
Mayse, Joseph, 425
Mayse family, 425
Maysville, Ky., 579
MCCAA Coal Co., 1027
Mead, Dr. E., 825
Meador, Jesiah, 24
Meador and Graham, Hinton, 878
Meadow Bluff, 820
Meadows, Clarence W., 111, 262, 387, 419, 698, 724, 844, 967, 984, 988
Meadville, Pa., 783
Meadville College, 1035
Meadville Collegiate Institute, 90
Meadville Seminary, 1033
Meany, George, 965
Mearns, David C., 480
Mechanics, 293
Medicine, 512, 600, 752, 883, 1037; formulary book, 720, 1033; home remedies, 291, 327, 420; medical education, 999, 1017; medical societies, 62, 307, 381; physicians' fees, 92, 704, 837, 919; practice of, 419. See also Physicians
Medill, Joseph, 96
Medium Security Prison, 984
Melbourne, Australia, 499
Mellon, A. W., 1000
Melrose, Va., 244
Melrose family, 468
Memorial Day, 863
Memphis, Tenn., 893
Mencken, H. L., 3, 419
Menear, David, 235
Menear, Philip, 235
Menefee family, 322

Mercer, Charles F., 280
Mercer, Hugh, 580, 797, 944
Mercer Academy, 493
Mercer County, 24, 44, 306, 534, 538, 667, 1051
Merchants. See General stores and merchandising
Meredith, E. E., 581, 582
"Meridian Temperance Banner," 654
Meriweather, Nicholas, 324
Mesmerism, 1025
"A Message to Garcia," 793
Mestrezat, Walter A., 583
Meteorological records, 645
Methodist Church, 90, 139, 259, 463, 493, 542, 544, 564, 744, 847, 1038; Baltimore Conference, 195; Bath, Va., circuit, 20; Berkeley, Va., circuit, 20; Brandonville, and Oakland, Md., district, 750; circuit riders, 15; discipline book, 902; in eastern Pennsylvania, 20; Harrison County, 369; Harrisville circuit, 125; journal of circuit rider of, 20; Kingwood, 123, 347; Morgantown, 951; Northwestern Virginia Academy, 761; Upshur County, 682; West Virginia, 369; West Virginia Conference, 195, 764; West Union circuit, 125; in western Virginia, 20
Methodist Episcopal Church, 55, 124, 586, 661, 818, 833, 863, 874; Baltimore Conference, 127; Brandonville circuit, 346; Greenbrier circuit, 114; Headsville, Mineral County, 114; Huntersville circuit, 127; Kingwood, 55; Morgantown, 128; Oakland Conference, 129; Redstone circuit, 114; Winchester, Va., district, 126
Methodist Episcopal Church South: Baltimore Conference, 193; Western Virginia Conference, 130
Methodist Protestant Church, 537, 727; Western Virginia Conference, 114, 130
Methodist Protestant Sentinel, Fairmont, 36
Mexican War, 103, 247, 776
Mexico, 209, 268, 865
Miami University, 1033
Michael, Laura Shade, 672
Michael's Cemetery, 609

285

Michigan, 351, 1033
Microwave theory, 176
Middlebourne, 537, 907
Middleton, Henry O., 584
Middleway, 519
Midland Railroad, 68
Migration, 946
Miles, Nelson A., 797
Military Order of the Royal Legion
    of the United States, 11
Military Service records, Ohio County, 684
Militia, 497, 936
Mill Creek, 403, 801
Miller, Mrs. Alexander McVeigh, 511
Miller, Amherst, 803
Miller, Charles C., 585
Miller, Clay V., 586
Miller, George W., 587
Miller, Jack, 413
Miller, Lewis H., 588
Miller, McVeigh, 249
Miller, Paul A., 698, 972, 992
Miller family, 324, 326, 649
Mill Point, 463, 550, 935
Mills, D. O., 268
Mills, Ogden, 268
Mills, W. H., 766
Mills and milling, 1, 34, 155, 203,
    246, 249, 343, 356, 359, 369,
    421, 512, 649, 748, 844, 1006;
    fulling, 346; linseed oil, 346
Millspaugh, C. F., 590
Milroy District, 337
Milton, 493
Milwaukee, Wis., 334
Mine doors, 162
Minehart, Jacob, 591
Mine posts, 421
Mineral County, 560, 971; agriculture, 842; in Civil War, 803; marriage records, 803; National
    Guard, 844; resident's papers, 781
Miner's Hospitals, 984
Mine Run, 657
Mingo County, 170
Mingo Flats, 561
Mining, 155, 224, 962; gold, 946. See
    also Coal mining
Ministers: bonds, 563; letters and papers, 20, 114, 120, 283, 313, 351,
    463, 491, 516, 537, 564, 744,
    780, 784, 818, 847, 923, 938,
    1038

Minnehaha: Methodist Episcopal
    Church, 127
Minnesota, University of, 113
Minor, Amanda, 324
Minor, Thomas, 324
Minor family, 324
"Miscellaneous Notes of Interest in
    Preston County," by Charles W.
    Hawley, 324
Misko, by Alvena Seckar, 822
Missionaries, 61, 120, 369, 428, 513,
    544, 780, 869, 1020; Methodist
    Episcopal Church, South, 130
Missionary Ridge, 820
Missions, 1033
Mississippi, 107, 224, 729, 790, 893
Mississippi River, 862, 893
Missouri, 211, 268, 359, 513, 946,
    951; frontier life, 313
Missouri River, 862
Mitchell, John, 56
Mitchell family, 326, 474
Mitra, S. K., 176
Mockler, R. Emmett, 594
Moffett, George B., 463
Moldenke, Harold N., 595
Mollohan, Robert H., 587, 956, 965,
    984
Money. See Currency
"Money Is What You Make It," 927
Moniteau County, Mo., 785
Monocacy, 573
Monongah, 87, 508, 596
Monongahela and Ohio Packet Co.,
    438
Monongahela College, Jefferson, Pa.,
    1007
Monongahela Gas and Coal Co., 313
Monongahela Railroad Co., 102
Monongahela River, 160, 285, 464,
    688
Monongahela River Railroad, 91
Monongahela Valley, 283, 389
Monongahela Valley Railroad, 195
Monongahela Valley Traction Co.,
    1003
Monongah Mine Relief Committee,
    597, 844
Monongalia Academy, 244, 247, 556,
    598, 1035
Monongalia County, 1, 48, 167, 195,
    196, 273, 314, 324, 402, 464,
    505, 510, 602, 605, 609, 610,
    611, 616, 683, 745, 833, 860,

286

875, 1001, 1004, 1007, 1013, 1016; Arnett family, 324; birth, death, and marriage records, 247, 491, 600, 601, 844; Board of Education, 811, 812; boundary, 362; business records, 602, 631; cemeteries, 247, 321, 609; churches, 114, 131, 161, 189, 398, 491, 756; Civil War, 144; civilian defense records, 612; Civil Works Administration, 613, 622; coal fields, 631; coal industry records, 600; county court, 640; court records, 600, 622; courts, 631; early residents in, 867; early history, 437; estate settlements, 274, 600; Federal Relief Administration, 613; frontier forts in, 219; gas fields, 631; genealogical records, 220, 326, 470, 622; history, 27, 39, 63, 189, 190, 220, 326, 614, 622, 640, 725, 812, 875; hospital records, 615; humane society records, 600; iron industry, 535, 578, 616; justice of the peace records, 607; land deeds, grants, and papers, 36, 40, 78, 235, 247, 286, 391, 495, 535, 588, 600, 603, 616, 617, 631, 844; land plats and surveys, 40, 362, 495, 549, 600, 616, 631; law practice in, 1019; livestock in, 616; maps, 362; militia, 618; mining settlements, 619; poetry about, 1028; prosecuting attorney, 82; relief administration records, 613; residents' papers, 255, 389, 491, 622, 656, 753, 755, 756, 790, 951, 1010; Revolutionary soldiers, 241, 326, 620, 634, 936; Revolutionary War, 198; roads, 616; schools, 2, 36, 600, 622, 756, 805, 811, 812; scrapbooks, 284, 604; Scott family in, 324; Seventeenth Judicial Circuit, 26; slaves in, 274; soldiers' tombstones, 247; tax lists, 274, 616; wills, 40, 247; World War I records, 621
Monongalia County Art Guild, 606
Monongalia County Historical Society, 131, 214, 622
"Monongalia County Schools and Local History, 1864-1960," 812

Monongalia Farmer's Company of Virginia, 631
Monongalia Iron Works, 535
Monongalian, 179
Monongalian Literary Society, 244
Monroe, James, 495
Monroe, Julius K., 976
Monroe family, 468
Monroe County, 1, 95, 324, 497, 623, 624, 625, 654, 796, 801, 864; Civil War, 100; marriage bonds, 654; roads, 625
Montague, Margaret Prescott, 33, 626
Montana: labor, 56; territory, 682
Montgomery, 382
Montgomery County, Md., 235
Montgomery County, Va., 24, 616, 796
Montgomery family, 212
Mooney, Fred, 469, 592, 627
Moore, Alvin Edward, 367
Moore, Arch A., Jr., 413, 587, 698, 956, 965
Moore, Berkeley W., 152
Moore, Elizabeth I., 67, 628, 951
Moore, George Ellis, 629
Moore, J. R., 247
Moore, Mrs. J. R., 640
Moore, John Bassett, 106, 1018
Moore, Robert T., 630
Moore, Samuel Preston, 324
Moore, Susan Maxwell, 598, 1034
Moore family, 319, 324, 326, 364, 378
Moorefield, 364, 366, 367, 435, 553, 719, 832, 1015; churches, 132
Moorefield and North Branch Turnpike Co., 538
Mooresville, Monongalia County, 662
Moreland, James R., 476, 614, 631
Moreland, Mrs. James R., 613
Moreland, Joseph, 631
Moreland, William A., 532
Morgan, Ephraim F., 331, 369, 633, 724, 984, 1000
Morgan, Hugh, 757
Morgan, J. P., 268
Morgan, James, 151
Morgan, John, 573
Morgan, Nancy Ann, 324
Morgan, Zacquill, 535, 634
Morgan, Zackquill II, 635
Morgan family, 63, 102, 151, 319, 757

Mosby, John, 184, 280; guerrillas, 144, 573
Mother's Day, 455, 586
Mott Core Drilling Co., 840
Mound Builders, 400
Moundsville, 844
Moundsville-Fairmont, history of area between, 551
"Mountain Ballads and Hymns," 153
Mountain Cove, 432
Mountaineer, 887
Mountaineer Craftsmen's Cooperative Association, 860
Mountain Lake, Md., 740
Mountain Lake and Salt Sulphur Springs Turnpike Co., 625
Mountain Lake Park, Md., 844
Mt. Carbon Company Limited, 699
Mount Carmel, Monongalia County, 235
Mount de Chantal Academy, 90, 543
Mt. Harmony Literary Society, 146
Mt. Hope, 850, 968
Mt. Jackson, 143
Mt. Morris, Pa., 63
Mount Pleasant, Ohio, 378
Mt. Zion Baptist Church, Wood County, 772
Mouth of Seneca, 974
Mowing machine, 346
Moylan, John, 656
Muddy Creek, 343
Mugler, Henri Jean, 657
Muhleman, Julius B., 658
Mules, 552
Mullen, A. G., 659
Mullen, Mrs. F. R., 659
Mullen, George H., 659
Mullen, Gordon, 659
Mullen, Gordon, Jr., 659
Mullen, Jacob, 659
Mullen family, 659
Mullinville, Kans., 66
Muncie, Ind., 714
Mundt, Karl, 413
Municipalities, 973
Murders and hangings, 493, 573
Murphy family, 593
Murphy Temperance Movement, 657
Murray, J. Ogden, 660
Murray, Philip, 56, 988
Murrayville Circuit, 1038
Musgrave, Clarence L., 661
Musgrave, Eli, 313, 661

Musgrave, Elizabeth, 67
Musgrave, S. Corder, 662
Musgrave, Samuel, 67
Musgrave, Zebulon, 313, 661
Musgrave family, 67, 313, 326
Musgrave Funeral Home, 661
Music and musicians, 583, 657, 663, 664, 740, 978
Musicians Mutual Protective Union of the Ohio Valley, 664
"Musings of Musgrave," by S. Corder Musgrave, 662
Muskets, 790
Muskingum River, 891
Musmanno, Michael A., 554
"Muster Roll of Company G, 11th Virginia Cavalry, Rosser's Brigade . . . ," 573
Mutual Assurance Society, 406
Mutual Building Co., 69
Myers, Clifford, 150
Myers, Karl D., 665

"Names of Pioneer Settlers Prior to 1860," 363
"Narrative of My Life: for My Family," by Francis T. Brooke, 73
Nash, Ogden, 3
Nashville, Tenn., 820, 893
Natchez, Miss., 893
National Association of Social Workers, 666
National Bituminous Coal Commission, 419, 844
National Cemetery Corp., 657
National Defense Program, 480
National Education Association, 2
"National History of Greece," 928
National Home for Disabled Volunteer Soldiers, 559
National Labor Relations Board, 419, 988
National League of People's McAdoo Clubs, 56
National Miners' Union, 844
National Petroleum Council, 353
National Recovery Act, 387
National Recovery Administration, 175, 419
National Road, 430
National Science Foundation, 480
National Youth Administration, 400

Norris, George W., 111
Norris, William, 393, 682
Norris family, 319, 682
North American Hill, 619
North Carolina, 302, 316, 324, 729; colonial families, 925
Northcott, R. S., 349
Northeast Mississippi Oil Co., 532
Northern Neck of Virginia, 494
Northern Panhandle, 1008
Northern West Virginia Coal Association, 795
North Mill Creek: churches, 133
Northwestern Bank of Virginia: Parkersburg branch, 706; minute book, 678
North Western Railroad, 1001
Northwestern Turnpike, 55, 293, 679, 921
Northwestern University, 544
Northwestern Virginia Academy, 764
Northwestern Virginia Railroad, 90, 510, 707
Noyes, Bradford, 680
Nullification controversy, 280
"No. 6 History, Mannington District, Marion County, West Virginia," 477
Nurses and nursing, 792
Nuttall, John, 681
Nuttall, Lawrence William, 681
Nutter family, 319
Nutter Fort: Methodist Church, 369
Nye, Gerald P., 419

Oakland, Md., 346, 347, 371, 657, 750
Obituaries, 425, 493, 674, 890, 898, 1010, 1054
O'Brien, A. L., 682
O'Brien, Emmett J., 682
O'Brien, William Smith, 682
O'Brien family, 682
Office of Price Administration (O.P.A.), 988
Ogden, H. C., 111, 387, 1000
Ogden, H. N., 393
Ogden, Marshall W., 683
Odgen families, 683
Oglebay, Earl W., 543
O. Henry Memorial Prize, 626
Ohio, 84, 322, 340, 495, 497, 504, 513, 535, 729, 772, 777, 790, 820, 874, 885, 913, 1031; Civil War, 146, 573, 820; historical papers, 685
Ohio County: archives, 684; birth and death records, 684; brand registrations (cattle), 684; court records, 684; land papers, 391, 430, 684; physicians, 999; resident's papers, 229; Revolutionary soldiers from, 620
Ohio County Centennial Association, 684
Ohio River, 62, 285, 360, 546, 552, 686, 688, 771, 862, 863, 891, 942, 1032, 1038
Ohio River Railroad, 91, 862
Ohio River Transportation Co., 862
Ohio State University, 759
Ohio University, 1033
Ohio Valley, 389, 493, 685, 1033; early settlement, 400; families, 468; history, 504
Ohio Valley Glass Co., 684
Ohio Valley Improvement Association, 413
Ohio Valley Trades and Labor Assembly, 689
Ohio Wool Growers Association, 155
Ohley, William A., 543
Oil, 90, 155, 175, 484, 510, 546; companies, 211, 268, 269, 304, 353, 421, 791, 862, 881; fields, 99; industry, 14, 62, 91, 315, 431, 493, 513, 554, 573, 594, 623, 707, 724, 769, 891, 930, 1029; wells, 97, 209, 623, 690, 691, 874
"Oil Field of Wood and Ritchie Counties," by W. H. Sharp, 1029
Okes, Lonnie L., Jr., 324
Okes family, 324
Oklahoma: United Mine Workers, 56
Oklahoma State University, 263
"Old Families of Barbour County," 323
"The Old Furnace," by C. O. Marsh, 34
Old Lewisburg Academy, 183
Old School Baptist Church, 116
Old South Illustrated, 260
Old Sweet Springs Co., 513

Parks, 844
Parrish, Edward Evans, 708
Parry family, 741
Parsons, Jesse, 709
Parsons, Job W., 710
Parsons, Thomas, 235
Parsons, William, 250
Parsons family, 364
Parsons Pulp and Paper Co., 525
"Partial List of the Confederate Soldiers Who Lived in or Near Charleston," 573
Patrons of Husbandry, 14, 16, 155, 249, 324, 711
Patterson, Andrew Johnson, 361
Patterson family, 361
Patteson, Okey L., 387, 586, 655, 698, 724, 844, 960, 965, 967, 968, 988
Patton family, 187
Paw Paw, 498
Payne, Daniel G., 102
Peabody, S. H., 265
Peabody Coal Co., 760
Peabody Institute Library, 478
Peadro family, 468
Peale, Rembrandt, 56
Pearies family, 474
Peck, John E., Sr., 1051
Peck family, 324
Pedlar Run, 314
Peek, George N., 419
Peerce, John T., 803
Peirpoint, F. P., 855
Peirpont, Francis H., Jr., 36
Peirpoint, Francis P., 62
Peirpoint, Jacob, 714
Peirpoint, John J., 714
Peirpoint. *See also* Pierpoint; Pierpont
Pemberton, R. L., 715
Pence & Clawson, N. Y., 21
Pence Spring Oil and Gas Co., 211
Pendleton, J. H., 47
Pendleton, John L., 1010
Pendleton, John S., 280
Pendleton, Philip, 871
Pendleton County, 287, 654, 730; apprenticeship, 889; assessment book, 717; Board of Education, 815; Civil War map, 146; Confederate infantry from, 754; court records, 718; land, 495, 538, 971;

marriage bonds, 718; resident's papers, 538; schools, 815
Pennell family, 325
Pennington, J. F., 627
Pennsylvania, 1, 20, 84, 90, 120, 246, 280, 322, 324, 474, 501, 513, 596, 631, 753, 790, 804, 829, 844, 853, 874, 913, 936; Civil War military units, 98, 583, 593, 804; Methodist Episcopal Church, 129; Senate, 155; United Mine Workers, 56
Pennsylvania Gazette, 687
Pennsylvania Geological Survey, 1002
Pennsylvania Wool Growers Association, 155
Pennybacker family, 468
Pensacola, Fla., 744
Pensions, 63, 219, 241, 272, 516, 620, 634, 828, 913, 925, 936, 1033
People's Party, 37
Pepper, Claude, 419
Pepper family, 509
Perkins, George W., 330
Perkins, Milo, 418
Perry, Bliss, 33
Peter, Martin Luther, 18
Petersburg, 1, 25, 296, 470
Petersburg, Pa., 346
Peterson, Aaron D., 719
Peterson, David T., 719
Peterson, W. H., 363
Peterson family, 319, 474, 719
Peterstown, 85, 249
Pethtel family, 326
Petroleum. *See* Oil
Petry, William, 592
Pharmacists, 720
Pharr, Dion C., 507
Phelps family, 468
Phi Beta Kappa, 760
Philadelphia, 33, 455, 478, 525, 549, 567, 649, 744, 753, 804, 919, 983, 1017, 1033
Philadelphia International Land Association, 415
Philately, 593
Philippi, 232, 234, 338, 420, 436, 651, 1035; early history of, 311; newspapers, 311
Philippine Islands, 369, 381, 583, 760, 797

293

Phillips, H. C., 1
Phillips, J. J., 78
Phillips, Josephine, 1032
Phillips, Marcia Louise Sumner, 721
Phillips, Sylvester B., 721
Phillips family, 319
Phoenix Insurance Company of Hartford, 309
Photographs, 40, 41, 63, 69, 74, 110, 131, 146, 147, 182, 228, 268, 284, 286, 351, 384, 419, 430, 438, 458, 480, 482, 494, 505, 513, 518, 539, 541, 569, 619, 622, 627, 669, 703, 722, 745, 748, 803, 805, 844, 865, 876, 923, 930, 981, 986, 1008, 1047, 1050
Physicians: letters and papers, 63, 92, 242, 307, 356, 387, 463, 483, 491, 492, 526, 549, 559, 722, 754, 778, 784, 919, 924, 935, 999. *See also* Medicine
Phytologia, 595
Piatt, Donn, 672
Piedmont, 143, 215, 980
Piedmont Grocery Co., 401
Pierce, Carleton Custer, 724
Pierce, Carleton C., Jr., 723
Pierce, George, 926
Pierce, John R., 723
Pierpoint, John, 324, 402, 728
Pierpoint Community, 725
Pierpont, Francis H., 47, 62, 65, 90, 96, 184, 224, 283, 292, 391, 514, 569, 582, 726, 727, 728, 791, 844, 868, 874, 885, 991, 1010, 1035
Pierpont, John, 868
Pierpont, Larkin, 868
Pierpont family, 324, 868
Pierpont. *See also* Peirpoint
Pigeons, 680
Pikes Peak, 518
Pinchot, Gifford, 330
Pindall family, 322, 326, 844
Pinecrest Sanitarium, 984
Pinick, Jacob, 729
Pinick family, 729
Pisgah Church, Monongalia County, 161
Pittman, Charles Edward, 730
Pittsburgh, Pa., 428, 447, 464, 478, 551, 688, 734, 756, 790, 829, 862, 929, 1033

Pittsburgh and Connellsville Railroad, 688
Pittsburgh as Viewed from Down River, 201
Pittsburgh coal, 196
Pittsburgh-Fairmont Coal Mining Co., 602
Pittsylvania County, Va., 439
Place names, 794
Placerville, Calif., 48
Plantations, 400
Plant pathology, 9
Platte River, 155
Plays and play companies, 62, 623
Pleasant Hill, Ala., 704
Pleasant Hill, Ky., 340
Pleasants County, 99
Plumbers, 593
Plymouth Oil Co., 353
Poage family, 141
Poca, 1037
Pocahontas coal field, 175, 318, 852
Pocahontas County, 187, 316, 456, 550, 561, 852, 980; agriculture, 751; deed, 495; economic and political conditions, 550; education, 751, 752; English colony in, 752; history, 751; land grant, 495; lumbering, 751; medical practice, 752; proposed railroad to, 333; timberland, 871; wildlife, 751
Pocahontas Development Co., 561
Pocahontas Fuel Co., 698
Pocahontas Operators Association, 852
Poe, Orlando M., 991
Poets and poetry, 33, 147, 185, 253, 350, 578, 626, 665, 713, 872, 1028
Poffenbarger, George, 324
Poffenbarger, M. S., 324
Poffenbarger family, 324
Poff family, 319
Point City, Va., 804
Point Lookout, Md., 846
Point Lookout Prison, 156
Point Pleasant, 160, 359, 571, 593, 723
Polack Cigar Factory, 345
Police, 973
Poling, J. E., 731
Poling, J. E. and Co., 401
Politics and government, 37, 47, 55, 62, 80, 90, 92, 96, 100, 103, 111,

112, 113, 175, 221, 224, 231, 232, 236, 262, 280, 287, 311, 317, 330, 333, 336, 340, 350, 353, 359, 387, 391, 405, 413, 417, 418, 419, 447, 476, 480, 482, 486, 492, 494, 496, 531, 543, 544, 554, 562, 578, 588, 657, 668, 682, 697, 715, 723, 724, 727, 745, 753, 820, 834, 837, 844, 857, 863, 874, 876, 877, 887, 896, 921, 934, 939, 988, 1000, 1013, 1018, 1035, 1048; Gilmer County, 587; Marion County, 946; Monongalia County, 200, 468, 601; Preston County, 746
Polk, James K., 672
Poll tax, 988
Polsley, Daniel, 733
Polsley, John J., 732
Polsley, Julia C., 733
Pomeroy, Ohio, 504, 778
Pond Creek Coal Co., 304
Poore, Perley, 672
Pope, Alfred, T., 54
"Porte Crayon," 143, 261, 672, 858, 871. *See* Strother, David Hunter
Porte Crayon; The Life of David Hunter Strother, 260
Porter, George McCandless, 734
Porter, James, 735
Porter Falls, 722, 902
Porterfield, George A., 507
Port Homer, Ohio, 428
Portsmouth, 820
Post, Melville Davisson, 33, 90, 511, 736, 737
Post family, 737
Postal cards, 573, 1008
Postal clerk, 475
Postmarks, 794
Post offices and postal records, 104, 313, 314, 328, 496, 573, 639, 794, 857, 900; Brandonville, 346; Brooke County, 97; Fabius, 43; Hancock County, 97; Jenningston, 900; Morgantown, 738, 1042; Preston County, 103, 748; Upshur County, 738
Potomac River, 432, 696
Potomac State College, 984
Poultry, 552
Powderly, T. V., 469

Powder mills, 801
Powhatan Point, Ohio, 397
Prairie Gleaner, 694
Prather-Tannehill family, 324
Pratt, 977
Preble, Jack W., 740
"Precarious Ground," by Leah Bodine Drake, 253
Presbury family, 741
Presbyterian Church, 79, 114, 132, 134, 183, 212, 224, 440, 493, 744, 797; Clarksburg, 158, 159, 438, 439; Fairmont, 440, 566; Winchester, Va., 635
Presgraves, James S., 742
"Presidents of West Virginia University," 88
Pressman, Leo, 418
Preston, David R., 744, 745
Preston, Gov. James P., 24
Preston, John, 289, 1005
Preston, John J. D., 225
Preston, Mrs. John J. D., 745
Preston, William, 289
Preston, William P., 292
Preston family, 745
Preston County, 78, 129, 167, 174, 197, 264, 343, 347, 654, 724, 746, 747, 750, 951, 1007; Board of Education, 816; boundary-Monongalia County, 362; Bucklew Museum collection, 748; business records, 653; census, 1830, 275; churches, 55, 346, 459, 848; Civil War, 1007; coal, 55, 168; courthouse, 649; court records, 273; Democratic Party, 746; education, 459; estate settlements, 748; fulling mill, 346; furnaces, 748; genealogies, 459; general store in, 750; history, 324, 746; inns, 748; iron industry, 346, 723; land deeds, grants, and papers, 18, 55, 78, 235, 240, 271, 746, 748, 876; land plats and surveys, 362, 723, 879; lawyer's papers, 111; linseed oil mill, 194; maps, 362; National Guard, 844; photographs, 748; politics, 746; post offices, 103, 748; residents' papers, 55, 103, 273, 346, 695, 749, 750; roads, 346, 748; schools, 346, 750, 816
Preston County Herald, 724

Salt, 471, 472, 593, 1020; industry, 245, 251, 359, 472, 493, 513, 797, 798, 799, 800, 845, 903, 1009, 1017, 1033; mining, 423
"Salt Case," 472
"Salt Manufacturing in Mason County, West Virginia," 800
Saltonstall, Leverett, 3, 413
Saltpeter, 680
Salt Rock, 493
Salt Sulphur Springs, 1, 478
Salt Sulphur Springs Co., 801
Salt Sulphur Springs Hotel, 801
Salt Sulphur Springs Road, 625
Salt Valley (steamboat), 862
Salvati, Raymond E., 698
Salvation Army, 1041
Samuels, Henry J., 64
Sand company records, 631
Sand Fork, 147
San Diego, Calif., 681
Sandy Hook, N. Y., 692
"Sanford and His Almanacs," 410
San Francisco, Calif., 48, 261
Sanitary Garbage Can Co., 602
Sanko, 537
Sanoma, 188
Santa Clara, Calif., 48
Sapling Lick Ridge, 366
Saratoga, N. Y., 312
Saturday Club, 280
Savage family, 325
Savayard, 676
Sawmills, 1, 75, 343, 359, 471, 631, 749
Schaeffer, Lewis, 804
Schaub (Shobe) family, 324
Schenck, R. C., 791
Schmedtgen, William, 416
Schofield, J. M., 727
Scholl family, 474
School books, 102
School for the Colored Deaf and Blind, 984
School for the Deaf and Blind, 984
School of Illustration, 416
Schools, 42, 66, 183, 263, 313, 316, 412, 416, 493, 513, 550, 582, 593, 680, 694, 719, 797, 805, 820, 946, 999; Barbour County, 805; Berkeley County Board of Education, 806; Braxton County, 887; Brooke County, 97; California, 497; China, 61; Clarksburg, 79, 849; County unit system, 28; desegregation, 807; Doddridge County, 258, 522; Gilmer County, 587; Grant County, 21; Hancock County, 97; Hardy County, 552, 808; Harpers Ferry, 374, 805; Harrison County, 805, 809, 810; Huttonsville, 408; Lewis County, 305; Marion County, 558; Marshall County, 805; Mason County, 805; Melrose, Va., 244; Mill Creek, 801; Monongalia County, 600, 622, 756, 805, 811, 812; Monroe County, 813; Morgan County, 637; Morgantown, 2, 244, 247, 814, 951; New York, 2, 938; Pendleton County, 815; Preston County, 346, 749, 750, 816; Putnam County, 1037; Randolph County, 766; St. George, 578; secondary schools, 817; Shepherdstown, 90; Summers County, 878; Superintendent of Schools, 28; taxation, 28; Thomas-Hill Education Bill, 28; Webster Springs, 522; West Liberty, 212; West Virginia, 897; West Virginia Superintendent of, 511; Wheeling, 543; Wirt County, 36. See also Academies, Education, Seminaries
Schrader, Louis E., 736
Schurz, Carl, 1018
Schwinn, J., 919
Science, 480
Scioto River, 552
"Scotia, The Glenn-Sanders House, or History of the Glenn Family," 332
Scotland, 180
Scott, Alexander, 322
Scott, J., 72
Scott, John, 347
Scott, John A., 134
Scott, Nathan B., 330, 569, 1000
Scott, Theodore, 820
Scott, Thomas, 818
Scott, Winfield, 507, 796, 863
Scott family, 322, 326, 820, 844
Scott Lumber Co., 819
Scotts Run, 821
Scrabble Creek Holiness Church, 114

305

Verdon, Va., 1035
Veterans, 417, 480
Vicksburg, Miss., 514, 893
Victor (steamboat), 862
Victoria Blast Furnace, 699
Vienna, 559
Vilas, William, 1018
Villard, Henry, 1018
Vincent, George A., 454
Vinson, Carl, 111
Vint family, 320
Viquesney, J. A., 837
Virginia, 268, 280, 302, 312, 313, 322, 324, 361, 379, 470, 474, 495, 500, 513, 550, 573, 657, 745, 790, 796, 804, 853, 913, 929, 991, 1010; agriculture, 156; auditor's papers, 47; boundary-Maryland, 748; Chesapeake and Ohio Railroad, 60; Civil War, 15, 73, 100, 142, 714, 729, 732; colonial families, 925; constitutional conventions, 234, 877, 921, 1010; debt controversy, 47, 62, 90, 91, 350, 387, 452, 568, 569, 926, 1048; deeds, 925; estate administration, 925; genealogies, 465; General Assembly, 47, 333, 846, members' letters and papers, 280, 877, petition to, 481; history, 361; iron furnaces, 442; land offices, 495, 925

Legislative petitions, 925; letters from, 1859, 704; lieutenant governors, clipping scrapbooks, 733; literary fund, 813; marriages, 925; Methodist Church, 90; militia, 64, 160, 280, 300, 459, 593, 936, 971, 1008; Northern Neck, 494; population schedules, 1830-1860, 912; Presbyterian Church in, 141; reconstruction in, 62; reform convention, 90; reorganized government, 224, 727, 733, 991; Revolutionary War in, 45; secession, 550, 877, 998; settlers from in Illinois and Alabama, ca. 1850, 704; surveyor's field book, 616; tax lists, 925; University of, 452, 550, 797, 877, 928, 1017; vital statistics, 925; wills, 925
Virginia and Tennessee Railroad, 142, 143, 796

Virginia Central Railroad, 109, 820
Virginia Debt Commission, 350, 569
"Virginia Declaration of Rights," 593
Virginia Gazette, 687
Virginia Illustrated, 260
Virginia Light Infantry, 67th Regiment, 1818, 593
Virginia Military Institute, 143, 316, 844
Virginian Railway, 175, 698, 699
Virginia Saline Bank, 927
Virginia State Agricultural Society, 280
Virginia State Library, 993
Virginia v. *West Virginia,* 486
Virginia-West Virginia Debt Controversy, 387. *See also* Virginia, debt controversy
A Virginia Yankee in the Civil War, 260
"A Visit to the Centennial Exhibition in Philadelphia, 1876," 649
Vital statistics, 925, 969, 993
Voegele, F. B., 929
Volcano, 573, 930, 1029
Volga, Barbour County, 931
Voorhees, Daniel W., 221, 405
Voting restrictions, 287

Waddle, Jacob, 593
Wade, Alexander L., 494, 1010
Wade, Benjamin F., 727
Wade, Charles A., 932
Wade, Charles W., 932
Wade, George, 933
Wade, T. S., 118
Wadestown, 315, 1045
Wages, 164, 209, 301
Wage Stabilization Board, 988
Waggoner family, 319
Wagle family, 324
Walker family, 324
Wallace, Anna McNeel, 463
Wallace, George S., 169, 934, 937
Wallace, Matthew, 463, 935
Wallace and McCarty, 935
Wallen family, 324
Walsh, John J., 387
Walsh, Thomas J., 111, 221
Walter, George F., 1026
Ward, Evermont, 937
Ward, Henry Dans, 938
Ward, William Hayes, 217

Ward family, 319
Ward-Bishop Addition to Bluefield, 102
Wardensville, 547
Warder, Francis L., 939
Warder, Henry, 102
Warder, William Wesley, 940
Warder family, 468
Ware, Anthony, 941
War Emergency Committee, 9
War Labor Board, 988
Warman, William, 275
Warman family, 275
War Manpower Commission, 988
Warm Springs, N. C., 316
Warm Springs, Va., 340, 880
Warner, Charles Dudley, 33
War of 1812, 103, 247, 532, 857, 936, 1033; military rosters, 913; muster roll, 925; payrolls, 196, 925
War Production Board, 988
Warrants, 406
Warren, Earl, 353
"War Times in Mountain Cove, Letters of Nancy Hunt to Refugee Friends in York State, 1862-1865," 432
Warwick, Jacob, 234
Warwick family, 234
Washburn family, 324
Washing machine, 346
Washington, George, 184, 490, 580, 589, 858, 942
Washington, S. W., 5
Washington family, 319, 326
Washington, D. C., 11, 400, 467, 559, 573, 578, 657, 714, 1033; slavery controversy, 100
Washington, Pa., 846
Washington, state of, 682
Washington and Lee University, 226, 550, 797, 1018
Washington and Ohio Railroad, 287, 333, 943
Washington Bicentennial, 858
Washington College, Pa., 734
Washington College, Va., 507
Washington County, Ohio, 820, 1033
Washington County, Pa., 46, 537
Washington County Colonization Society, 1033
Washington County Tract Society, 1033

Washington National Monument Office, 829
"Washington Special," 311
Washington Temperance Society, 359
Washington Territory, 657
Watchung, N. J., 595
Water, fluoridation, 515
Waterman, Joseph M., 944
Waters, John N., 1
Waters family, 326, 468
Watson, Clarence W., 91, 486, 844, 934
Watson, James E., 111
Watson, James G., 18
Watson, James O., 283, 727, 844, 945, 1010
Watson, Martha Dent, 945
Watson, Rebecca Haymond, 945
Watson, Thomas, 18, 945
Watson, Thomas G., 90
Watson family, 321, 324, 946
Wayland, John W., 797
Wayne, 1051
Wayne County, 105, 493, 1051
Waynesboro, Va., 1035
Waynesburg, Pa., 503
Weather data, 381, 1009
Weaver, Joseph, 324
Weaver, Nota K., 53
Weaver family, 324
Weaving, 300
Weber Run, 48
Webster, 31, 1001
Webster, Daniel, 877
Webster County, 358, 573, 703, 768, 947, 981; archives, 947; court order books, 947; deed books, 947
Webster Hardwood Lumber Co., 522
Webster Springs, 522
Webster Springs High School, 263
Weeks, Sinclair, 353
Weimer, B. R., 870
Weimer family, 319
Weirton Steel Employees' Security League, 418
Welch, Rev. William, 560, 803
Welch Emergency Hospital, 984
Welcome (steamboat), 862
Welfare, medical, 387
Wells, David A., 1018
Wells family, 324, 712
Wellsburg, 72, 97, 450, 593, 630, 701
Wellsburg Academy, 734

plan, 486; flags of, 480; Forest Council, 696; Free Silver headquarters, 659; game and fish warden, 837; garden clubs, 1003; Good Roads Association, 844; Governors' letters and papers, 967. *See also* under governors' names

Grange, 711; Health Department, 433; High School Principals Association, 28; Historian and Archivist, 511; Historic Records Survey, 969; history, 184, 212, 284, 322, 361, 511; immigration, 90, 236, 510; industrial development, 232; Jamestown Exposition Exhibit, 454; Legislature: 234, 417; members' papers, 47, 55, 62, 82, 90, 95, 221, 271, 283, 287, 288, 311, 333, 335, 350, 369, 419, 451, 532, 539, 542, 631, 724, 753, 781, 788, 836, 844, 863, 887, 921, 1000, 1013, 1035, 1048. *See also* legislators' names

Literature, 303; local history, 88, 929, 1008; lumbering, 75; medical societies and associations, 62, 307, 381; militia, 459, 855; mountain tales, 211; National Guard, 11, 480, 583, 699, 723, 844, 934; New Deal agencies, 973; northern counties, residents' occupations, 63; patronage, 111; penitentiary, 350; pioneer history, 682; police education and training, 973; Public Service Commission, 336, 849; Reconstruction, 90, 224; sawmills, 75; secondary schools, 817, 897; Secretary of State, 417, 434, 682; Selective Service, 724; semicentennial, 222; settlers, 465, 493; Soil Conservation Society, 696

State aid, 973; State Board of Centennial Managers, 989; State buildings, 986; State Capitol, 971; State Fair, 290; State finances, 373; State Geologist, 1002; statehood movement, 4, 224, 349, 391, 430, 499, 511, 578, 726, 727, 732, 921, 990, 991, 1010; State Planning Board, 696; State Road Commission, 849; state seal, 147, 929; State Treasurer, 990; Superintendent of Free Schools,

897; Superintendent of Schools, 28, 511; Supreme Court of Appeals, 240, 415, 762; Tax Commissioner, 726; Tax Limitation Amendment, 973; Utility Assessment Hearing, 897; Watershed Development Conference, 696; wild game birds, 573

West Virginia Advisory Commission to the U. S. Civil Rights Commission, 972

West Virginia Agricultural College, 598, 951, 952. *See also* West Virginia University

West Virginia and Pittsburgh Railroad, 91, 102

West Virginia Association of Collegiate Registrars and Admissions Officers, 953

West Virginia Association of Student Councils, 954

West Virginia Asylum for the Incurables, 434

West Virginia Bar Association, 418, 532, 1003

West Virginia Building Trades Council, 985

West Virginia Central and Pittsburgh Railway, 221, 268

West Virginia Christian Endeavor Society, 447

West Virginia Co-Government Association, 954

West Virginia College, Flemington, 826

West Virginia Commission on Constitutional Revision, 959

West Virginia Cooperative Labor Legislative Council, 988

West Virginia Dental Journal, 987

West Virginia Exposition and Fair Association, 684

West Virginia Farm News, 59

West Virginia Federation of Labor, 965

West Virginia Firebrick Co., 735

West Virginia Folklore Society, 966

West Virginia Foundation for Crippled Children, 433

West Virginia Gold Mining and Milling Co., 582

West Virginia: A Guide to the Mountain State, 418, 1050

archives, 1030; court records, 1030, 1031; early settlement, 400; genealogies, 589; land papers and surveys, 182; law practice, 1804, 1014; letters to a resident of, 57; newspaper clippings about, 29; oil development in, 99, 707, 769, 1029; petitions from, 57; residents' papers, 1019; U. S. Department of Agriculture Station at, 424

Woodbridge, Dudley, Sr., 1033
Woodbridge, George M., 1033
Woodbridge, William, 1033
Woodbridge family, 1032, 1033
Woodbridge Mercantile Co., 1033
Woodburn Female Seminary, 67, 224, 247, 598, 628, 1034
Woodell, Elizabeth, 187
Woodell, Joseph, 187
Woodell, Nancy Agnes, 187
Woodell family, 187
Woodford family, 319
Woodford Lumber Co., 653
Woodridge, Theodore, 92
Woods, Isabella, 234
Woods, Samuel, 1035
Woods, Samuel Van Horn, 1035, 1036
Woods family, 1035
Woodson, Mrs. Mary, 1037
Wood uses, 578
Woodworth, Robert B., 141
Woodyard, Richard L., 1038
Woodyard family, 468
Woodzell, James, 297
Woofter, Carey, 1039
Wool, 315, 561
Woolen mills, 844
Woolsey family, 324
Wooster College, 870
Worall family, 723
Worden, Riley, 1040
Workers Communist Party, 56
Workmen's Compensation, 175
Works Progress Administration, 111, 419, 988
World Court, 111, 490
World's Fair, 657
"World Walker Families," by Annie Walker Burns, 324
World War I, 2, 50, 262, 311, 336, 494, 513, 542, 593, 844, 1041; Braxton County, 68; diary, 578;

Food Administration, 830; Monongalia County, 219, 621, 644; newspaper clippings, 1042; poster texts, 736; soldiers' letters, 334, 381; speculation, 830; West Virginia University in, 468
World War II, 2, 5, 225, 262, 318, 475, 480, 494, 747, 792, 834, 1045; American Book Center for War Devastated Libraries, Inc., 1046; Monongalia County, 219, 612; Morgantown Defense Council, 643; Morgantown Ordnance Works, 640; newspaper clippings, 1043; Nicholas County, 653; Pacific Theater, 1044; soldiers' letters, 532, 677, 1047; War Loan Drives, 1046; West Virginia Bar Association, 532; West Virginia War History Commission, 1047
Worley, William Gordon, 1048
Worley family, 723
Worthington, 171, 508
Wotring, 18
Wright, Dana, 1049
Wright, John Stillman, 1049
Wright, Samuel, 1049
Wright, William Henry, 1049
Wright family, 1049
Writers' Program, West Virginia, 1050
W. W. Smith & Co., 447
Wyandotte, Mich., 351
Wyoming County, 650
Wytheville, Va., 467

Yakima Indians, 657
Yale University, 50, 73
Yawkey, William H., 304
Yawkey and Freeman Company, Ltd., 304
Yawkey and Freeman Drilling Co., 304
"Yellow-dog" contract, 175
"Yellow-dog" mines, 331
Yoak, J. B. F., 1051
Yocum family, 364
Yoe family, 672
York County, Va., 378
Young, Guy B., 1052
Young, Loyal, 120
Young, Robert, 58
Young family, 321, 325

316